Democracy Road

Doris "Granny D" Haddock

1

ISBN: 978-1-7345867-0-1

DORIS "GRANNY D" HADDOCK

"The big money lobbyists put money out in the troughs each morning on K Street, and then the great oinking starts up on Capitol Hill. Soon, members of Congress are all nudging each other at the troughs. It's enough to make you a vegetarian."

"If I have any single message for you it is that it is never too late to get in shape. It is never too late to do a great thing. It is never too late to go in search of your deepest values and your wildest dreams of brotherhood. Everything still awaits you."

Oil portrait by Karin Wells of Peterborough, New Hampshire; Copyright the artist

Contents

Appreciation

"Granny D, you exceed any small, modest contributions those of us who have labored in the vineyards of reform have made to this Earth."

— Sen. John McCain

"Doris Haddock is a true patriot, and our nation has been blessed by her remarkable life."

—Jimmy Carter

"The problem with Granny D is that she makes the rest of us look like such schlumps."

—Molly Ivins

"John McCain and Bill Bradley were looking over her shoulder, reading her speeches and watching how she succeeded in making campaign finance reform an emotional and patriotic issue with many Americans. When presidential candidate Al Gore finally signed-on to campaign finance reform, his speech cited McCain, Bradley and Doris Haddock."

— Bill Moyers

Foreword by Elizabeth "Libby" Haddock

I knew Doris for 52 years—for 50 as my mother-in-law. She was the best mother-in-law that any young wife could have wished for.

In October of 1960 I married her only son Jim. It was the fall of his junior year at Springfield College. We lived in a third-floor walkup apartment that cost $48.00 a month.

Doris knew that we had no money to speak of, so she took it upon herself to make my clothes. She always let me pick out the material and the pattern—why, she even made my winter coat!

One of the first things that I noticed about Doris was her inordinate amount of energy. She and her husband would get up at 5:30. She would make a quick breakfast, then off to work they would go. She had a good job in the city of Manchester, New Hampshire. I believe that she was the best-paid woman in the city at the time. She worked for Bee Bee Shoe Company. Their motto was: "We make a cheap copy of the very best." She was the secretary for the head of the company and soon became the person who analyzed the labor and material for a proposed new shoe, to see if it could bring a profit.

When she came home at the end of her work day, she would make a nice supper, after which would set to work, sewing. She would be making my clothes or a new best dress for her own daughter or one of her three granddaughters.

When she wasn't sewing she was knitting. She would knit sweaters, hats, scarves and mittens for whoever needed them.

To accompany her abundant energy, she had the ability to focus those efforts in a way that I had not witnessed before—with the exception of her son, Jim. My Father always said of Jim that he could accomplish in one day what it would take ten men to do in a week.

Doris was a Democrat and a true activist. I watched her as she took on cause after cause. The first one was in 1959-60, when she worked to stop the Atomic Energy Commission from blasting an artificial harbor in the Alaska coast with a hydrogen bomb. The village of Point Hope was located there and was the home of the oldest indigenous Eskimo people in Alaska. Scientists on the project estimated that strontium-90 would spread out and cover the tundra for a great distance—the Caribou eat the tundra grass and the Eskimos eat the Caribou. They all would have been wiped out. Doris and her husband battled with this for two years and they won, stopping the H-bomb and saving the village. The people of the village became their lifelong friends.

She took on a more local battle when the state wanted to move highway 101, which runs through our town and around our beautiful Dublin Lake. The state planned to move the road, sending it through the historic and picturesque town of Harrisville, paving over hundreds of acres and carving up the landscape, making life evermore dangerous for our wildlife. This fight made her unpopular with many very influential individuals in our tiny town. This was interesting for me to observe; she really did not like being perceived as a pariah, but she was willing to become one to accomplish her goal and preserve our community.

In her late eighties she became aware of the fact that many of our elections are now bought and paid for by special interests. This led her to develop a scheme to get the attention of the general public. She decided to walk across the country from California to Washington D.C., stopping along the way to give speeches in many towns and cities. She did so, walking ten miles a day for over a year, arriving in Washington at age 90.

She lived for another ten years, mostly fighting for campaign finance reform. She gave speeches at many high schools and colleges; She spoke at rallies for campaign finance reform. She traveled thousands of miles to get people registered to vote. At the age of 94 she agreed to run for the U.S. Senate in New Hampshire. She managed to get a third of the vote without taking any special interest donations from political action committees or the wealthy.

She was a force to behold. People who knew her have not forgotten her. Twice a year, a New Hampshire organization that cites Doris as its founder, The Coalition for Open Democracy, hosts a walk across New Hampshire or beyond in her memory. They do it to remind people (including visiting presidential candidates) of our evermore-desperate need for campaign finance reform.

Both Doris and my husband, Jim, moved the world joyfully in their lives of caring activism.

I hope you will imagine her as you read these speeches: her fist in the air but love all around her.

About Doris Haddock

By her own reckoning, Doris Haddock, 1910-2010, was the usual sort of New Englander: a bit flinty, persevering, practical to a fault, hardly special. She wrote thank you notes almost continuously.

On New Year's Day, 1999, 24 days before her 90th birthday, she began her walk from California to Washington, D.C. to promote political reform—specifically campaign finance reform (the attempt to get big, special-interest dollars out of politics).

She hitchhiked around New Hampshire and camped on the ground as a warm-up to her 3,200-mile walk, which, despite her arthritis, emphysema and a bad back, was accomplished by walking ten miles a day. Near the end of the trek, facing the worst snowstorm in 40 years, she cross-country skied the last 184 miles into Washington.

She took a few hitchhiking detours along the way in order to make speeches off the trail or to arm-twist members of Congress and presidential candidates.

She made hundreds of speeches, many of them extemporaneous to small groups in tiny city halls and living rooms; she often drew a diagram to show the flow of money from corporations and wealthy donors to politicians, and the resulting flow of tax breaks, environmental loopholes and other public benefits to the donors in repayment—a repayment costing taxpayers $10 for every dollar donated. The innate corruption of the system is better known now than when she began her one-woman education of America.

Many of her speeches are lost to history. Those surviving are collected here for the first time.

Her words have changed many lives. Her "Seven-Layer Cake" speech has been copied and folded into the personal papers of many people. Her "Center of the World" speech keeps many activists going despite all discouragement. Her "To Reorganize the Democratic Party" speech is still the roadmap—if less traveled—to long-term progressive victory.

Did she accomplish extraordinary things in her life? Yes, but she would remind you that everyone, without exception, has done extraordinary things, if you care to ask them about it—

including everyone in her wooded neighborhood of southern New Hampshire. You could not go for a walk or a drive through those woods with Doris or her son, Jim, without hearing mythic stories about the remarkable people living in every clearing. There is no finer way to become impressed with America—and the world—than to travel with someone who knows all the people and their stories.

She became interested in campaign finance reform in the mid-1990s, mainly through her New Hampshire women's book club and study group—the Tuesday Morning Academy, as they called themselves. It became clear to them that American democracy was being rapidly undermined by the quid pro quo of large political donations from corporations and billionaires. Oligarchy was rapidly displacing America's governance of, by, and for the people—or at least eroding that aspirational dream.

The old machinery of representative democracy may be awkward, but it still produces our equality and our freedom and remains the only machinery that can. The vote and voice of the poorest citizen must be made equal to that of the richest in order for all to be truly equal and free. Legislative and executive acts and court decisions can change many things, but not that simple truth. We have not achieved that equality, but we have achieved at least a deeply rooted dream of equality to guide and measure our progress.

Imagine the view from a long, low flight over our military cemeteries: The hundreds of thousands of lives cut short, plus all those who died or sacrificed years in other ways or suffered brutality to preserve and advance our freedoms, are buried there and around the world, row upon row, to remind us that this is not a trivial matter. It is a sacrificial effort on a grand scale that we honor when we Americans put out our flags on the Fourth. From the Edmund Pettus Bridge to Normandy's beaches, the struggle has not been and never will be easy or finished. But the virtues of human nature are as durable as its vices, so good people who would be free, and who care about justice and freedom for others, carry on.

That was the exact attitude that Doris held and gave voice to. Upset by the wholesale corruption in American politics, Doris and her friends followed the advice Gandhi gave to reformers intent on righting injustices: First, make sure of your facts. That was done: their study group members had been relentless in their research. The second step is to courteously ask for action by those with the power to correct the situation. Doris and the members of the study group spent several years, often in the cold and rain, gathering petition signatures to send to their representatives and senators in Congress. Those stacks of petitions and letters and phone slips were met with silence, inaction, and sometimes with active rudeness. When Doris seemed particularly frustrated by the situation, Bonnie Riley, the leader of the study group, asked her what she was going to do about it. That is one of the best questions you can ask a person of principle in a time of trouble.

Gandhi's third step is to bring the injustice to the attention of the wider community so that the conscience of full society can be engaged.

The fourth step is to make enough of a personal sacrifice to demonstrate the moral bankruptcy of the other side's position and to demonstrate the seriousness of the issue—as Gandhi did in his Salt March and as the Selma marchers did in proceeding across the bridge with Martin Luther King, Jr.

When Doris noticed an old man hiking along a highway with his pack, she suddenly stitched Gandhi's three and four together. (Gandhi's fifth step, by the way, is to be gracious in victory, as victory is the usual result, given enough sacrifice— gracious because we should love even our political enemies, whom we shall surely encounter again and perhaps as friends.)

On January 1, 1999, soon to be age 89, Granny D—as she was called by her grandchildren and soon by millions of others— boarded a plane to California, where she began a 3,200-mile walk to Washington. She did so in order to demonstrate her concern for the issue and, as she hoped, to drum-up popular support for a campaign finance reform bill. She did achieve that—it passed Congress and was signed into law. According to the bill's two Republican and two Democrat sponsors, it would not have happened without her sacrificial show of concern, which engaged the conscience of a nation.

> "I was still something of a desperado in those first months of the walk—roaming over the dry and blank space remaining at the end of a life. Or was it the lull between acts? Who can ever know at such times? There is an urge to just walk into the desert, away from the road and be done with it. There is also an urge to have some ice cream with chocolate sauce. Life is what we patch together between those competing desires." —from her first memoir

She walked for fourteen months, speaking to people individually and in town audiences along the way. She hiked across deserts and climbed the Appalachian Range in blizzard conditions. Over 2,200 supporters gathered to walk the last miles with her to the Capitol Building, including a dozen or more Members of Congress and live crews from Good Morning America, the Today show, and television crews from Japan, Germany and the UK.

The marchers—with reform hero Jim Hightower leading chants with his megaphone—made a big noise down K Street's lobbyist row and then swarmed the Capitol grounds. Though a permit for only 100 people had been allowed, she arrived with several thousand. The Capitol Police threw up their hands and let them pass onto the grounds. Her remarks on the Capitol steps, with Members of Congress all around her, are considered an American classic and have been taught in university rhetoric courses.

It took two more years after her walk to gain Congressional passage of the reform bill, during which time she engaged in a four-day, 24-hour walking fast around the Capitol Building in the snow, rallies in many states, and demonstrations in the Capitol Rotunda that twice landed her in jail. She conducted her own filibuster in the U.S. Capitol office of a corrupt congressman, reading from his list of compromising corporate contributions until she was removed. Through it all, she generated a flood of calls and messages to Congress.

When the bill did pass Congress (though it was later undermined by the Supreme Court's Citizens United decision), the sponsors, including Senators McCain and Feingold, and Representatives Shays and Meehan, credited Doris Haddock from the floors if the Senate and House with raising public awareness of the crisis in a way that finally allowed the bill to pass.

It passed the House late at night. The sponsors then walked out of the building into the dark with Doris, who had watched from the gallery as they voted and as Mr. Gephardt and others looked up to her and saluted.

Since her walk, campaign finance reform, though it has taken a serious but hardly permanent hit from the Supreme Court, has remained high on the list of changes demanded by democracy advocates of all parties. Her words are often quoted in that work, and many states have enacted reforms as a result of her visits and encouragement. Presidential candidates, especially when visiting New Hampshire, cite her as the embodiment of American democratic reform.

Doris was born on January 24, 1910 in Laconia, New Hampshire. She attended Emerson College for three years before being ejected for the offense of getting married. She was, however, awarded an honorary degree from the college in 2000, and to standing cheers.

She raised her family during the Great Depression, working in a shoe factory in Manchester. She and her husband retired to Dublin, New Hampshire, in 1972, where she was active in community affairs and was a leader in stopping a proposed interstate highway from carving up famed Mount Monadnock.

She nursed her husband through ten years of Alzheimer's disease. After his death in 1998, and then after the death of her closest woman friend, Elizabeth Foster, of Dundee, she picked herself up and started planning her walk for campaign reform.

She wrote two memoirs, one published by Random House and the other published posthumously by Dartmouth's consortium of university publishers.

In 2010, Doris Haddock died in her son and daughter-in-law's forest home at age 100. A week before her death she was still walking five miles a day and writing thank you notes to compatriots and letters of demand to politicians.

She left as her legacy to us the essential democratic gift of civic encouragement. "Democracy is not something we have, it's something we do," is a Frances Moore Lappé quote she loved.

In the years since her passing, how many times have we activists wondered what she would be thinking, what she would be saying, what she would doing, if she were here with us in these challenging times.

She would be of good spirit, for she looked at impossible political situations with deep humility and a sense of joy. To think that a big problem is too big to fix, too big for one person to even influence, is a certainty of opinion she did not allow herself, especially as the verdict of hopelessness is usually but an excuse to stay indoors, watching the world go by and shouting at the television news from your comfy chair. But to gather with friends to represent love in the world—and its products: justice, kindness and responsibility—is a great joy, regardless of the odds. In fact, the steeper the odds, the greater the joy, as we touch our deepest purpose in living when we confront the gravest dangers to our values.

She lived her life in that way.

An Eskimo village in Alaska was facing extinction in the late 1950s and early 60s, because the American government planned to use hydrogen bombs as an experimental way to make a new harbor. How are you going to fight forces that big and strong? Isn't it beyond the ability of one person, or even a few, to stop? Doris and a few others did stop those H-bombs. It was one of the planet's first big, successful environmental campaigns.

She was a young woman then. Move your view forward to the year 2000, when Doris was nearing the completion of her long walk across the U.S. She was in Cumberland, Maryland, when the worst snowstorm in forty years hit the whole region, from Cumberland to Washington. The roads were impossible for walking. But she noticed a wide, snowy path that opened in the woods outside Cumberland, and she asked, with a wry smile, "What's that?" It was the historic towpath that runs next to the C&O Canal, a route first surveyed by a young George Washington as an early route through the Appalachians, and now preserved as a national historic park.

"How long is it?" she asked a park ranger, who had just chained off the entrance because the snow was dangerously deep—too deep for hikers.

"Well, ma'am," he said, "it runs for 184 and one-half miles from here all the way into Georgetown, in DC," he said.

"I'll need my cross-country skis," she said.

The park ranger and his supervisor agreed to take their lunch break and look the other way, should someone slip under the chain. After all, the woman was not to be denied on her birthday. Her skis were in the support van.

So we must let the myth of her accomplishments suffer a correction: She did not walk all the way from California to Washington; she skied 184 and one-half miles of it.

She didn't fix democracy, but only because democracy is never fixed; it is always just propped up—fought for again, died for again—because the politics of fear and the politics of love are always pushing against each other in this world, as Doris reminded us.

In fact, just after the disastrous Citizens United decision by the Supreme Court, which happened shortly before she died, she told us, in her last delivered remarks, to please see it as an opportunity to create much better government reforms, now that we had the advantage of a clean slate.

Keeping our spirits up is important for another reason: If we ever lose the fight to save our democracy and our livable planet, it will have happened because people lost hope and could no longer see a good ending—and so they stopped trying.

So here is where Doris offers good advice: We must surely tell hard truths to get people engaged, but simply pounding away with a continuous stream of bad news adds to the mass anxiety and despair that makes our road steeper. We must temper our

Jeremiah work with forever shining a light on the yet-possible good future—as Jeremiah also did. When you inform people that promising things can yet be done for the climate, many suddenly stop denying the reality of climate change. Denial is, in fact, a protective shield, and its stubborn prevalence is merely a measure of how deeply worried people are for their children's futures—so worried that they often embrace the villainous denial messages pushed by dark forces.

So we must be agents of good news when we are able, just as Doris kept reminding us of the representative democracy we can surely restore and improve if we make a few more calls, write a few more letters, and walk—or ski—a few more miles.

It all adds up. She showed us that, one step at a time, one letter at a time, one meeting with a leader at a time, she was able to stop an H-bomb and get an impossible bill through Congress, though her only office was that of concerned citizen—a powerful office, as she showed us.

And we must have faith in this power of ours, just as she did, so we might see what history has in store for us in this time of danger and courage.

West of the Pecos

The first speeches Doris Haddock gave on her long walk were fully extemporaneous, often accompanied by her hand-drawn chart showing the flow of campaign dollars from companies and the rich to politicians, and then the resulting flow of beneficial tax policies and laws favoring those elite donors, leaving Main Street America and its families and individuals outside the loop and holding the bag for paying taxes that, more and more, bought precious little representation.

While that circle of corruption is now widely known and understood, it was not so when she began her walk. The idea of campaign finance reform was an issue known about and cared about mostly "inside the beltway" by reform organizations and, of course, by the practitioners of pay-to-play governance.

A volunteer or two always accompanied her on her long walk. They drove a donated support van where she could rest at midday or overnight, though she normally slept and ate in the homes of people she met along the road. The van was nevertheless useful in that it carried water, her clothes and some food so that she did not have to carry a pack. The volunteer—often from her circle of New Hampshire friends—would drive ten miles ahead and knock on doors (if any homes were in the area), asking if Doris might spend the night after her day's walk. She was turned down not once. It was not only an expression of the generosity of people, but it also resulted in an ever-growing club of Ms. Haddock's supporters, who called their members of Congress to support the bill. Some traveled to Washington to be with her when she finally arrived.

The friend driving the van or walking with her would also drive or hitchhike ahead to let towns know that Doris was approaching. Sometimes those communities quickly improvised a small ceremony. She had extraordinary luck in that regard. For example, in her last California steps, crossing out of the sweltering Mojave Desert at the river town of Parker, Arizona, it just happened that there was a Marine Band in town for the Parker Days parade. The band met her on the river bridge, played Happy Birthday (it was her eighty-ninth), and escorted her down the main street at the head of the parade. That sort of thing occurred so often that it came to be expected. "When you are doing the right thing with your life, these things happen," she explained to amazed volunteers. "The doors just open, and the right people you need appear like magic," she would explain. It is a phenomenon many fully committed reformers experience. The people of the little town of Salome, Arizona, on a few hours' notice, organized a makeshift parade for her, led by the town's fire truck, with half the town's kids aboard. After that arrival, she was hosted at a little reception of cookies and lemonade and was asked why she was walking across America at her age. As she later recalled:

"I simply reminded them that many people died or gave up their sons and daughters for our freedoms, and that we mustn't give it away now to the corruption that has become the normal business of Washington. It was my mention of the wartime sacrifices that made my remarks hit home. That part of the message has always been easy for me, as those laying in rows upon rows in our national cemeteries are the people who come to mind when I think of our duty to preserve our freedoms—and we are not free if we do not have control of our representatives."— From a draft of her first memoir.

Some of the magic on the road was the work of environmentalist and labor rights leader Ken Hechler, a retired member of Congress and former Secretary of State of West Virginia, who provided the support van and walked with her, off and on, for 500 of her 3,200 miles.

John Anthony, the young communications director of Common Cause in Washington, D.C., worked other kinds of magic for her. For example, the satellite truck of Good Morning America also met her at that birthday bridge, and the New York Times (Frank Bruni) would be walking with her in the deserts out of El Paso. By the time she reached Washington, John had arranged hundreds of local and national stories, and Members of Congress were talking about her—their comments, in fact, had motivated Frank Bruni to go see if she was for real. He returned with the news that she was very real, indeed, and so Congress had better brace itself or clean up its act.

Matt Keller, whose regular job was working the halls of Congress for Common Cause to get campaign reform bills crafted and passed, came to walk with her often. For Matt, Doris single-handedly destroyed the biggest obstacle he faced in Congress: the argument that Americans didn't care about the issue. He used her story constantly on the Hill, bringing more sponsors into the twin reform bills (McCain-Feingold in the Senate and Shays-Meehan in the House). Claudia Malloy and others from Common Cause and other organizations also walked with her and advocated for the reform in Washington.

Before any others (except her son, Jim), there was Doug Vance, a young Californian, thin as young Lincoln, who heard about her walk and hiked beside her through all of California and most of Arizona, just to keep her safe and advise her on energy foods that could keep her going. He massaged-out the severe cramps from her arthritic feet and calves after each day's ten miles, until—after 400 miles—she was in shape for the long grind ahead.

Nick Palumbo, of Minneapolis, who asked around about what might best help his country, was told about campaign finance reform. That led him to Granny D. He made a call. He showed up and would be her guide though more than half the long road to Washington. During the stormy hike up the Appalachians, for example, he drove the support van a few feet behind her, so that the two headlight beams would show in the blizzard and she could stay between them and not get lost. He was usually on the phone with John Anthony or others, arranging the next press interview or town arrival.

Nobody was paid a dime, of course—doing this all on the side of other careers. When the old van began seriously overheating and falling apart, Doris sent a note to Common Cause to ask for a set of tires, at least. They turned her down, but Ken Hechler, upset about that, bought her another old van, and the little enterprise kept going, living room meeting at a time, radio and television interview at a time, ten more miles and ten the next day.

Doris's son, Jim Haddock, a remarkable and historic national reformer in his own right, was the guardian angel of the whole enterprise. He would be the one to call in chips, get old neighbors to walk with her, and spring for another tank of gas and another and another on his (and wife Libby's) credit cards.

Dennis Burke, an Arizona political reformer who pushed through the public financing of election campaigns and constitutional gerrymandering reform in his state, and was the national originator of the "I Voted" stickers in the 1980s to encourage participation, was the other guide and organizer, especially in terms of getting information to her for the next speaking opportunity ahead. (Ken Hechler, who had researched and written whistle-stop campaign speeches for Harry Truman early in his life, impressed upon Doris and Dennis the necessity of knowing as much as possible about each coming town and region, and especially about how government corruption affected them.) Dennis also walked with her to interview her, as she asked him to help her with a book or two to keep the issue alive after her walk.

Most of her preserved speeches are those made to the larger groups where she did not feel extemporaneous remarks were appropriate or respectful of the occasion. In the end, her audiences ranged from suburban neighbors to the homeless, and from cowboys at chow time to cheering convention halls and national television audiences.

"By the time we got to Tombstone, it was just Matt [Keller] and myself. We walked along the covered wooden sidewalks of the old town, past the real OK Corral, and found the mayor, who was genuinely delighted to meet me, even without network news in tow. He gave me a key to the city and a nice certificate, and showed us around. Later, we tried to buy an ice cream cone at the Bird Cage Theater, but our money was no good anywhere in town. So we took our free ice cream and sat on a bench on the sidewalk. A beautiful dark-haired, dark-eyed, woman, the owner of the Silver Nugget Saloon... She took us out that night to her Silver Nugget for a drink, then to a nearby steakhouse for a grand, Western dinner, and finally to Big Nose Kate's for a nightcap. Well, that's why they put rails along the sidewalks in Western towns like that—not just for the horses. At Big Nose Kate's, (she) commanded the guitar-strumming cowboy to serenade me, which he did. A few rounds later, she had a tug-of-war with a cowboy poet over the microphone, both of them frothing with wonderful verse. And they had to hear from me. Well, everybody in Big Nose Kate's knows everything about Campaign Finance Reform now. You just go check and see if I didn't make them experts, if they remember anything at all."—From her first memoir.

As of Texas, more effort was made to write and preserve her speeches, now in your hands. She sometimes diverged from her prepared speeches; this collection is based on her prepared texts. Changes to this collection will be made as more audio and video recordings are compared to the texts.

The Long X Ranch at Evening, May 7, 1999:

Before the ranch dinner bell, a dozen ranch hands sat on the rails of a darkening corral to listen to why she was walking through their immense ranch:

Thank you, Mary Jo, and many thanks to all of you for literally showing me the ropes today. I watched as foreman Rick taught his young son, Clay, to tame a wild horse an hour ago. We all watched the sun go down and the Texas stars come out. The great McDonald Observatory, I am told, is just down the road, and you can see why they put it here—you've got all the stars, and you've got your mesquite smoke and sparks moving up there in the Milky Way tonight, and thank you for the guitar tunes. I will always remember this place and its long history.

In such places we know that the work of men and women on Earth is sometimes still a matter of muscle, cunning and courage. It is not all computers and automation, at least not yet. But your sons and daughters, and their sons and daughters, will have a hard road unless our world has leaders who care first for the human scale of life, and for the joys and freedoms of the human scale.

Many of the little towns I have walked through are now but ghosts. The stores are boarded up—including many stores in Van Horn, just up the road—because interstate highways have passed them over or because small ranches and farms are losing out to factory farming, or because people travel to the cities now to do their buying in huge stores owned by a few faraway people we'll never see or know, or because people do their buying on their computers.

What is missing from that, of course, is the capture of your own dollars back into your own communities, and what also is missing is the wealth of middle class jobs that are the solid ground under democracy. All the hardware store owners and all the bookstore owners are dissolved now into a couple of super-rich people who live thousands of miles away and seem to care nothing for any community or for the Earth itself. Their sense of entitlement has grown beyond any sanity, and they now think the Earth itself, all its creatures, and the futures of all of us are proper things for them to burn so that they might have a new yacht ten feet longer than last year's model.

I don't know how that gets unwound, but it is surely time for the rise of new creative leaders to take us forward in a more responsible fashion. I am walking for that. Perhaps we the people need to buy with our tax dollars a third-ownership of any overlarge company, so that we again share in the wealth of our own labor and commerce. Or perhaps companies that destroy the middle class are not proper corporations for licensing at all. In any case, something creative has to be done if Clay and your other children are to enjoy freedom and prosperity on a healthy Earth.

Well, I hear the bell, and you all must be hungry. I thank you for this star-lit evening of remembrance—remembrance of the hard work so many people do, day in, day out, well into the evenings with labor they love, surrounded by good friends and family. I don't know if I'll make it all the way to Washington, or even to Pecos, but I thank you for the encouragement you have all given me, some of you even trying to tuck a few of your very hard-earned dollars into my pack, which I must always give back, as others need your generosity and all I need is your good wishes and your good citizenship.

As to my mission, I don't imagine that one old woman walking can solve problems that have been so long in the making, but I'm not discouraged, and none of you should be discouraged for me, for yourselves or for your children, because democracy is a long road and the people—the source of all real political power—always win. And I'm glad to be on that road. Thank you.

A Texas Town Hall

Ms. Haddock's remarks at the Toyah Town Hall, Toyah, Texas, May 11, 1999 — it is representative of the many small speeches on her 3,200-mile walk:

Thank you very much. Friends, how would you feel if you were involved in a lawsuit and you found out that the other side was making big financial contributions to the judge, just before the ruling?

How would you feel if you were a baseball player in the World Series, and you found out that the other team was making big financial contributions to the umpires?

How would you feel if you were a citizen in a free democracy and you found out that the person who was elected to represent your interests was receiving huge financial contributions from people outside your district whose interests were completely opposed to yours and those of your community?

Is there a fundamental difference between these three situations? I don't think there is. That is why the U.S. Supreme Court, on several occasions, agreed that reasonable limits on campaign contributions, if they help eliminate corruption or the damaging appearance of public corruption, are legal and proper.

Now, would it matter if the contributions to the judge were not made directly, but were instead made to the judge's family foundation and passed back to the judge?

Would it matter if the contributions to the umpire were instead made to the umpire's union, and then passed in a curveball to the umpire?

Would it matter if the political contributions were made to the elected official's party, and then passed back to the official?

Well, in politics those are called unregulated, or soft money contributions, and they tend to be in very high amounts, quite beyond the reasonable limits imposed on donations made directly to candidates. Even a child can see that this back door approach is wrong and unfair. And there is no reason, so long as contribution limits are legal, why such deceptive practices should be allowed under the law.

That is the clear logic of it, and here are the feelings we carry to this issue in our hearts. Many of us have lived long enough to see great sacrifices made by a great many people to preserve our freedoms as a nation of equal citizens. People who try with their wealth to steal our representatives from us are attempting to steal our freedom. For this we have gone to war and have sacrificed the lives of our children. Do they think we will

permit it now for some reason? We will not.

Maintaining our freedom is constant work, and it is our business here today. Some will stand in our way, but they stand against our history as an equal and free people, and they stand against the tide of this reform. We should not shrink from our duty, which is to call them out in public for the damage they are doing to our system of government, and to remove them from office in favor of representatives who will help us assure equal representation and equal standing as citizens, regardless of our various economic positions.

It is, in fact, a great favor we do for all public officials. For, just as any honest judge wants the freedom to make wise and fair decisions, and just as no umpire would want to provide less than a proper and fair game, so our public servants need —and sometimes desire—the freedom to serve us wisely, without unfair pressures from the obsessively self-interested rich.

We speak against soft money. For those who are still confused by the term, let me be clear: we speak against corruption, unfair advantage, and we speak against those greedy interests who would steal away or government, our freedoms, and our equality.

We fight for the position of the individual, for ourselves, for our friends, family and neighbors, and we fight so that those who gave their lives to the defense of our equality and freedom may not have done so in vain.

Thank you. (*She then created a chart to show how special-interest campaign donations flow to become tax loopholes and other taxpayer-funded corruptions.*)

The Center of the World

Friday evening, May 14, 1999 at the Rodeo Arena in Pecos, Texas: Ms. Haddock was a guest speaker at an all-night walk around the arena to raise funds for cancer research. She had already walked through California, Arizona, New Mexico and Texas west of the Pecos.

Thank you. I am honored to be here in Pecos. I began my walk to Washington D.C. from Los Angeles some 1,200 miles ago, and all of those miles have been walked in a place described by earlier generations of Americans as the land west of the Pecos. On Sunday, I will wade across the Pecos and enter the other half of creation. But tonight I am here at the center of the world and am proud to meet all of you who live here.

I thank you for having me here on such a beautiful evening. Life is a beautiful experience, and here we all are together, alive at this moment, breathing the same cool air. The issue that brings everyone here tonight is a terrible disease, of course, and we Americans fight it because we naturally rise to the fight against any evil that threatens those we love.

Deep inside, we can be joyful to remember that nobody really dies in this great drama of the soul we live in eternally. Some of us move on faster than others, and we so deeply miss those who have left this stage before us. Tonight we see that there is something we can do with that loneliness and pain.

When my husband died several years ago, and when my best friend, Elizabeth, died last year, I looked at my life and my lifelong beliefs and said to myself, what shall I do now? What can I do to honor the memory of the people I have loved? How can I turn my pain into something beautiful in the world? Something beautiful? Let me tell you that great art and great writing often is the tricking of suffering into beauty. Life is full of suffering; what we must do when we have more than we can bear is to transform it into beauty through a medium of exchange such as art, or handiwork, or a written story or poem, or good parenting, or good friendship, or the creation of good work in the community, or the pursuit of some work we may find unfinished among our lifelong interests and concerns—some in the attic too long. So I asked myself, what work can I do that may be done as a memorial to those I miss? What can I do to amaze them as they watch lovingly from the other side?

And so, if you are here because you are remembering someone lost, you are turning that loss into the art of this special evening we are sharing together. And if you are here to pursue your own battle with a dangerous disease, or to give emotional support to someone you love who is doing that or who has lost someone, then you are a part of that creative transformation of pain into beauty. What is more beautiful than people warmly sharing an evening together in the glow of candles? What is more emotionally healing?

The issue that I decided to do something about as a memorial to the people I loved and still love is political reform of our elections. It is, of course, a fool's errand. It is just an old woman walking across the land, wearing my late friend Elizabeth's gardening hat, until it recently fell to tatters, talking to whomever will listen about the kind of political reforms most people don't believe can really happen.

Also, there are two things I would like you to understand about impossible missions. One is the fact that, sometimes, all you can do is put your body in front of a problem and stand there as a witness to it. That is part of healing because it is not denial of the problem, and our individual conscious mind is part of the larger conscious mind of society. What you think and how you think does affect the world, and your actions do matter.

Never be discouraged from being an activist because people might tell you that you'll not succeed. You have already succeeded if you're out there representing truth or justice or compassion or fairness or love. You already have your victory because you have changed the world; you have changed the status quo by you; you have changed the chemistry of things and changes will spread from you, will be easier to happen again in others because of you, because, believe it or not, you are the center of the world.

There is a second thing you need to know about impossible causes, which is that there are no impossible causes on this Earth, if they are good causes. We can do nearly anything together, and we really do remarkable things. We will cure cancer most certainly because people like you walk through the night to make it so. We have nearly eradicated polio worldwide; we have actually cured smallpox; we are curing many diseases— impossible dreams but a short time ago.

My dream of political reform will come true. I may live to

see it from this side of life, or I will smile to see it from the other side. But it will happen. It will happen because people love this country and this democracy, and because they have given their sons and daughters and the best years of their own lives to defend it. They will not let it be destroyed before their eyes by these obscene floods of special-interest money that come into our elections from big business and the very rich. I know we will end that outrage and we will be able to run our communities and our nation to look after the interests of the common people, for that is what a democracy is all about.

I wish all of you good health. I wish you the courage to live out your emotions and your beliefs in your daily lives, as you are doing tonight. I admire you all tremendously, and I will always remember this evening at the great center of our beautiful world.

Margaret Chase Smith Award

On Sunday, June 27, 1999, in St. Louis, by an earlier unanimous resolution, the National Association of Secretaries of State presented Ms. Haddock with their Margaret Chase Smith American Democracy Award. Previous winners: Margaret Chase Smith, Jim and Sarah Brady, Rosa Parks, Eunice Shriver.

Thank you very much. I am honored to be here, and honored to have come here in the company of the Secretary of State of West Virginia.

Since I am now on the home ground of Harry Truman, it is fitting to remember that Mr. Hechler was a speechwriter for that president, long before he was a member of the U.S. House and then West Virginia's Secretary of State, as he is today...

I would like to keep on the subject of President Truman for a moment longer. He is quoted to have said—and if Ken didn't write this for him he should have—"No government is ever perfect. One of the chief virtues of a democracy, however, is that its defects are always visible, and under democratic processes can be pointed out and corrected."

Ken and I are on the road to point out—to make more visible by our effort—a current truth about our democracy: that our government has become coin operated, driven more by campaign money than by ideas or beliefs or by the needs or voices of our people. That has to stop. But you are practical people and you are quite sure that it cannot be stopped, that it simply is the way it is. We all do quickly adapt to our current conditions. We tend to give the status quo more than its due. We soon think that things have always been this way and always shall be. Young people—and you all are terribly young—are particularly prone to this error, as you have no personal memory to inform you of the fact that this is quite new.

That is why, every now and then, you may need an 84 year-old man and an 89-year old woman to come along and say, well, you are very bright and charming young people, but no, this is not the way it has always been. This is a recent aberration, and it must be corrected. It has nothing to do with the long-term idea of America, or long-term history of America. The long-term history of America is that we move toward greater freedom for more and more of our people. This present erosion of our freedom—for that is what the supremacy of rich peoples' money over individual expression surely is—may constitute but a temporary glitch in our forward movement, and it will not stand long in our way.

While money has always influenced our politics, the idea of big business money so thoroughly controlling our democracy is new. Business corporations, let me remind you, are something we allow to be chartered in our states for business purposes that serve a public need, not for the purpose of getting in the way of our self-government.

Business corporations have been interfering mostly since 1978, when an ill-advised Supreme Court decision mistook corporations for people in granting their right to political speech. Corporations, however, are not people. The decision to allow their political activity needs to be reversed while we still have a chance of reclaiming the idea of government of the people. The resources of corporations, including the time they take to solicit employee contributions, must not be allowed into our campaigns because they overwhelm the process.

We must also begin to get a public benefit in return from corporations who profit from the use of public airwaves and citywide cable contracts. Mass media is now the speakers' platform in the town square, so we must regain free or more affordable use of it for our candidates, especially if our candidates and public officials are to be freed of the time-eating, ethics-devouring money chase.

As Secretaries of State, there is much that you are doing, and much more that you can do, to make democracy healthier in your own communities. People need good information in order to be good citizens. Certainly, with the availability of the Internet, you have a magnificent new tool to make democracy visible. If the chairman of a powerful legislative committee in your state receives thousands of dollars from industries he or she regulates—and from the executives and spouses of those industries—is that fact easy for the public to see at a glance on your Internet site? Many disclosure sites are so complex that one might think that obfuscation is their intent. Make the process as clear as glass, and the normal values and manners of society will have their reforming effect. For it is bad manners to take money from the very companies you regulate, whether or not it is illegal.

So, be the person who turns on that light, opens that window, makes the sausage machine visible in every glorious detail. You have the information or can get it. The public needs it. I'm glad to see that you have a workshop on this very subject at 10:15 tomorrow morning.

If you will make radical openness your issue, you will have the people behind you. You must make a decision these days to either have the people behind you, or to have easy money behind you. The more honorable path is always the more difficult, but it is ultimately the more successful...

I thank you for the honor of this occasion. I hope I haven't scolded too strongly, but you are the one group in America most entrusted with the fair operation of daily democracy.

Last year, leaders in Congress said, after they defeated the McCain-Feingold bill, that the people back home don't really care about campaign finance reform. I commenced to do what I could to show that at least I care. And here I am now, in the "show me" state, showing not only that I care, but also giving witness to the fact that everyone I have met along the way cares deeply, too. It is a great journey. You cannot imagine how people feel about this country and how moving the experience has been. I know you all care about our democracy, too. Aren't we lucky to have each other in such a country as this? Let's be tough and relentless in our defense of the idea that it is a government of the people, where big money should not, shall not, be allowed to shout down our individual voices.

Since I opened my remarks with Mr. Truman, let me end with a Republican. Here are words to remember from Theodore Roosevelt, who spoke them in Kansas in 1910, the year of my birth:

"Our government, national and state, must be freed from the sinister influence or control of special interests. Exactly as the special interests of cotton and slavery threatened our political integrity before the Civil War, so now the great special business interests too often control and corrupt the men and methods of government for their own profit. We must drive the special interests out of politics. That is one of our tasks today... The citizens of the United States must effectively control the mighty commercial forces, which they have themselves called into being. There can be no effective control of corporations while their political activity remains. To put an end to it will be neither a short nor an easy task, but it can be done." Unquote Mr. Roosevelt.

If I were a consultant for the Republican Party, I would say, if you want to win elections in the coming era, get back to Teddy. That is where the people are.

Let us end the American Century and begin a new one with the high-minded optimism that shone from Theodore's great grin 89 years ago. Let us make the democracy that so many have died for forever worthy of their sacrifices. Good luck to us. We are all on the road to reform.

The Road So Far

In Texas, Ms. Haddock's trek was the subject of regular coverage by Jim Hightower's progressive radio show, based in Austin. He called her nearly every morning and interviewed her as she walked. This brought her to the attention of Ross Perot and many others. Though not a member of Perot's Reform Party, and not in line with much of its philosophy, Ms. Haddock was invited by Mr. Perot to address his party's national convention, in Dearborn on July 23, 1999. She took a brief diversion from her walk to do so. She gave two speeches, as the Party had split into two and was meeting separately. Both groups asked her to speak, both gave standing, shouting, foot-stomping ovations, and one of the groups, in fun, nominated her for the vice presidency of the United States. She declined.

Thank you. There are always a few questions about whom I am and what I hope to accomplish by walking from the Pacific to the Atlantic at the age of 89. Who I am is an old reformer, and I feel at home in this room. [A great and sustained cheer arose.] I have been involved in reform fights through most of my adult life, but I have saved the most important for my last hurrah.

It is my belief that every American ought to be able to run for a public office without having to sell his or her soul.

Fundraising muscle should not be the measure of a candidate. Ideas, character, track record, leadership skills: these ought to be the measures of our leaders.

Ladies and gentlemen, it is my belief that the hundreds of thousands of our dead, buried in rows upon rows in our national cemeteries, sacrificed their lives for the democracy of a free people, not for what we have today. It is up to each of us right now to see that these boys and girls did not die in vain.

With the support of my dear children, grandchildren and great grandchildren, I began my trek and I will see it through. I am doing it to bring attention to the fact that ordinary Americans like me care desperately about the condition of our government and the need for campaign finance reform.

I have traveled as a pilgrim, and Americans have taken care of me through each of my 1,800 miles so far. If you knew, as I know from these last seven months, what a sweet and decent nation we live in, you would be all the more determined to raise it out of this time of trouble, this sewer of greed and cash that we have slipped into.

Ladies and gentlemen, I have come quite a way across our land, looking at every inch and meeting everyone I can.

Please imagine that you have sent me out to walk across America so that I might, this evening, report to you some findings to help you in your deliberations.

Friends, I have walked through a land where the middle class, the foundation of our democracy, stands nearly in ruins. Main streets have given way to superstores. Towns have died. Family farms, family businesses and local owners have given way to absentee owners and a local population of underpaid clerks and collection agents. People are so stressed in their household economies, and in the personal relationships that depend on family economics, that they have little time for participation in the governance of their communities or of their nation. They struggle daily in mazes and treadmills of corporate design and inhuman intent. They dearly believe their opinions matter, but they don't believe their voices count.

They tell me that the control of their government has been given over to commercial interests. They cheer me on, sometimes in tears, but they wonder if we will ever again be—and for some, finally be—a self-governing people, a free people.

With the middle class so purposefully destroyed—its assets plundered by an elite minority—it should not surprise us that the war chests of presidential candidates are grotesquely overflowing with cash while children go hungry and elders must eat pet food to survive. I have met these people. The wealth of our nation is now dangerously concentrated. The privileged elite intend to elect those who have helped them achieve this theft and who will help them preserve their position of advantage. That is what accounts for the avalanche of big checks into presidential campaigns.

Walk through this city—Dearborn and Detroit—and mark the doors of the families who cannot afford to give a small fortune to a presidential candidate or a senator or two. For those who live behind these millions of doors, we do not have a democracy, but an emergency—a crisis that deeply threatens our future as a free people.

The thousands of Americans I have met are discouraged, but they are not defeated—nor will they ever be. They know that the government and the social order presently do not represent their interests and are not within their control—that American democracy is nearly a fiction. But the flame of freedom that no longer burns in public, burns securely in their longing.

It is said that democracy is not something we have, but something we do. But right now, we cannot do it because we cannot speak. We are shouted down by the bullhorns of big money. It is money with no manners for democracy, and it must be escorted from the room.

While wealth has always influenced our politics, what is new is the increasing concentration of wealth and the widening divide between the political interests of the common people and the political interests of the very wealthy, who are now able to buy our willing leaders wholesale. The wealthy elite used to steal what they needed and it hardly affected the rest of us. Now they have the power to take everything for themselves, laying waste to our communities, our culture, our environment and our lives, and they are doing it.

What villainy allows this political condition? It is the combination of two viral ideas: that money is speech and that corporations are people. If money is speech, then those with more money have more speech, and that idea is antithetical to democracy. It makes us no longer equal citizens. This perverse notion, and the general, unrestricted participation of such money in our elections, must be and will be stopped if democracy is to survive. That removal, that riding out of town on a rail, was done a century ago when Republican president Theodore Roosevelt pushed corporate money out of politics. In his absence, and in the absence of backbone in the parties and in the Congress, the slick operators have slinked back into town, and in many cases have been invited back or even coerced back into town by elected leaders who have the gall to think that the democracy our children died for is no more than a dirty bag of barter for their enrichment. They are traitors to everything good that America stands for, and it is time for us to get out that rail again. Here is what Teddy Roosevelt said in 1907:

"...Our government, national and state, must be freed from the sinister influence or control of special interests. Exactly as the special interests of cotton and slavery threatened our political integrity before the Civil War, so now the great special business interests too often control and corrupt the men and methods of government for their own profit. We must drive the special interests out of politics. That is one of our tasks today... The citizens of the United States must effectively control the mighty commercial forces, which they have themselves called into being. There can be no effective control of corporations while their political activity remains. To put an end to it will be neither a short nor an easy task, but it can be done," he said.

Teddy Roosevelt said it well. Business corporations are not people. They are protective associations that we, the people, allow to be chartered for business purposes on the condition that they serve the community and will behave.

We must look to whether we can still afford, as a people and as a planet, to give these little monsters a birth certificate but no proper upbringing, no set of expectations, no consequences for antisocial behavior.

We are simply tired of the damage they do and we are tired of cleaning up after them. If they are to be allowed to exist—and they are indeed important to us—they must agree to be responsible for their own activities, start to finish, without requiring public dollars to be used to clean their rooms up after them. The era of corporate irresponsibility must be ended immediately, particularly in regard to the degradation of our political and cultural and natural environments, while we still have the power to act. Parents know that there comes a time when infantile behavior persists, but the child is too large to do much with. We Americans still can act in regard to the corporations we have given birth to, but not by much of an advantage. Our advantage will evaporate early in the 21st Century if we do not act soon.

Friends, does it matter if it is Rupert Murdoch or another such, instead of Marshall Tito or Nikita Khrushchev, who owns everything and decides everything for us? The soul of democracy is diversity, not concentration. Diversity requires the human scale, not monstrous scale. It is all quite enough to make us mad, but let me advise you, on the eve of your meetings, that we cannot afford to act out of anger, if we desire to win.

Politics today is quite too characterized by anger and even hatred; so let's have none of it here.

If you have true enemies in politics, pray that their lives are filled with anger, for no one so filled can win for long. Anger drains your energy and makes you incapable of endurance or of creative leadership. If you win, your victory will be short-lived. Ask the failed leaders of the so-called Republican Revolution if I am right. Negativity is negativity, and it has no place at the helm of a democracy. It doesn't know what to do with power when it gets it. Only joy and optimism—and love, really—can win in the long term because only they can serve.

General Eisenhower said, "Pessimism never won any battle" He was right. Pessimism visualizes defeat. What we visualize, we bring forth. Carl Sandburg wrote: "Nothing happens unless first a dream."

To the reformers, then: learn optimism if you would have the endurance to succeed, and endurance is required.

Where to find optimism? Well, I have found it for you out on the road, and I give it to you now. It is this:

I give you the Americans I have met. Without exception, they deeply love the idea of America. It is an image they carry in their hearts. It is a dream they are willing to sacrifice their lives for. Many of them do. There is no separating this image of democracy from their longing for personal freedom for themselves, their family, their friends. To the extent that our government is not our own, we are not free people. We feel a heavy oppression in our lives because we have lost hold of this thing, this self-governance that is rightfully ours, because it is our dream and our history. But the spirit of freedom is strong in the American soul, and it is the source of our optimism and joy, because it will always overcome its oppressors.

On the road so far, these Americans have taken me into their homes and fed me at their tables—shown me the children for whom they sacrifice their working lives and for whom they pray for a free and gentle democracy. And I will tell you that I am with them. I am with their dream and I know you are, too. We are all on this road and we must stay on it together, forgetting our minor differences until, together, we achieve the necessary objective of restoring democracy for individuals, and allowing each individual an equal voice in the civil discussions we have as a self-governing people.

We must end our American Century with the optimism and clear purpose and high ideals with which it began. We must visualize this goal clearly, and work to make it so.

Yes, it is a long road ahead. But who thinks they can stand in the way of our need to be free, to manage our own government, to be a force for good in the world, to protect our children and our land? Who thinks we are not willing to sweep away before us any who try to turn our sacred institutions of civic freedom to their greedy purposes?

On the road so far, I have seen a great nation. I have felt it hugging my shoulders, shaking my hand, cheering from across the way. I am so in love with it. I know you are too. Thank you, all.

Remarks the same day to Reform members who had split off:

Thank you. As you begin this convention and these next critical years of American political reform, let someone who has fought many battles and won most of them eventually give you two bits of advice.

The first is obvious: If your cause is righteous, never give it up and you shall never be defeated. Keep at it. Hold the truth up before you and its power will never fail you. Defeat is reserved for those who give up. Even our death does not stop the stubborn advance of the truth, once we have put it in motion.

Now, never giving up may be the secret to victory, but how does one find the energy and the force of will to never give up?

The key to that endurance is to be happy in warfare. Let me explain.

Politics today is characterized by anger and even hatred. If you have true enemies in politics, pray that their lives might be filled with anger and hatred, for no one so filled can ever win for very long. Anger drains your energy and makes you incapable of creative leadership. If you win, it will be short-lived. Ask the failed leaders of the so-called Republican Revolution if I am right. Negativity is negativity, and it has no place at the helm of a democracy. It doesn't know what to do when it gets to power.

Only joy and optimism—and love—can win in the long term. General Eisenhower said, "Pessimism never won any battle" He was right. Pessimism visualizes defeat. What we visualize, we help bring forth.

Now, I have told you that you must not give up, which is easy to say. And I have said that endurance is the product of optimism, which is also easy to say. How does one stay optimistic and full of love in a time such as ours?

You must keep this in mind. Life anywhere is a great adventure. But life in America is very special: America is a great— and, let me tell you, large—laboratory of the soul. We are a restless people, moving about, destroying our lives and starting over again, living several lifetimes in the space of one, while people in other reaches of the globe live comfortable or miserable half lives by comparison. We are a mess, a disaster, a social wreck, but we are alive and learning and experimenting with life in a way that is quite new to the world and quite expanding to the soul, which is the very goal of life. The rest of the world knows this about America, and many of them wish they were here to joyfully suffer with us.

To know that we are the lucky participants in this privileged experiment ought to give us, whether friends or opponents, a secret camaraderie, a secret wink and smile across the battle lines, through the smoke and danger of our battles. In our political wars, let us keep our tongues therefore a little in our cheeks, understanding that the other fellow is not a villain, really, but just someone responsible for the defense of a different hill. We are a rich nation and can afford to be generous of spirit in the conduct of our politics—even where our battles involve life and death matters.

Take it as a fact, please, that anger in your heart is a signal from your brain that something or someone is not understood. The Stone Age reaction might be to get rid of that confusing thing, or strike out at it, but if we are civilized we might instead try harder, and harder still, to study the thing and understand the thing until our anger turns to understanding. From that place, one can see the creative path to victory. This work is hard work. It is what goes on in a good university. It is what goes on in a good mind. It is the essential work of a creative leader.

I don't mean to suggest we should put away our swords and declare a picnic. There is certainly a difference between good and evil, which are real forces. The force of good is, like gravity and like magnetism, a force that brings people together. The force of evil, like the force of explosive bombs or suburban sprawl or ethnic cleansing, is that which separates people and sets them against each other, makes them intolerant and, finally, demagogic or sociopathic or both. We need to be clear about the real nature of good and evil, and we must act with swift instinct to promote and save the good, and to repress and weed-out the evil in our political life. But we must not see people as evil, even if they are evil's captive agents for a time. We need to save them from that captivity as best we can, within the limits of courtesy and democracy.

So, yes, we take on our great political fights and we do so with the great smile that shines from the very soul of truth. Love, one might say, is our secret strategy and motive. Why else would we want to change the world, if not for love? We must remind ourselves of this because this joy, this optimism, is the key to energy, endurance, persistence and victory. We need that secret key because we are at the dawn of our greatest battle yet in our long effort to advance America's freedoms and preserve its democracy. We had better be of right mind as we enter battle. If we enter with bitterness, or with pessimism, or with anger and hatred, we will not have the nearly superhuman strength we now need.

So I advise you, this week, every week, elevate the debate, respect the opponent, and always assume honorable motives on the other side, even against all evidence. It is hard to do so. I slip into name calling many times myself in the heat of rhetoric. It is draining and bad form, and it harms our own cause. If one intends to win, one is cheerful and generous. Good humor and generosity of spirit are the flags of unbeatable armies.

I said that we are facing a great battle. It is a battle of mythic proportion. It is this: America is losing its middle class, which is the foundation of its democracy. It is no surprise that the war chests of presidential candidates are exploding with cash this year: that is a simple reflection of the new concentration of wealth at one end of our population, and a reflection of the intent of the privileged class to preserve its position of advantage. Drive through this city and mark the doors of the families who can afford to give $1,000 to a presidential candidate and a senator and other officials, so that the family's needs might be served. For all the unmarked doors, we do not have a democracy, but an emergency—a crisis that deeply threatens our future as a free people.

My effort is to get big money out of our elections, and I believe that the McCain-Feingold soft money ban will be a good start—but only a start. In the long run our politics must again be the speeches at the Fourth of July picnic again, and the moneychangers must be swept out of the temples of democracy. It's time to get money out of the room so that we can be equal citizens once again, and that means dramatic changes to the way we communicate—freely communicate—political information in our society.

Once we return control of our politics to individual people, I think it will be possible to restore the vitality of the middle class. Right now our local economies, our family businesses, our family time and family savings and family farms, our civic time, our public spaces, are being destroyed. The reins to all that are political reins, and we have to grab them back by forcing money out of our politics.

There are no villains in our midst not of our own making. We have been making them, building them up for a century now, and they are getting too big to handle.

At the beginning of this century, Theodore Roosevelt, that great Republican, worried that businesses were getting out-scaled, and that the family farmer and the family business would be crushed by the great corporations then forming. He instituted anti-trust laws and he pushed corporations out of politics with strong laws that protected us until some holes were punched in these walls during the past twenty years.

Like a frontier family threatened by a shutter blown open in a blizzard, we must struggle to get that opening closed again before our democracy dies in a blizzard of money of selfish intent.

Where are we at this present moment in the history of America? I will tell you what I find as I walk across it. I find communities separated by income, where there is no sense of true community. I find families splintered by the demands of careers, because the companies they work for have no regard for the time and pay it takes to be a proper family, the resources it takes, or the geographic stability it takes. You may argue all day long about whether or not it takes a village to raise a child, but I will tell you that it at least takes a family, and by that I mean grandparents and great-grandparents and uncles and cousins and family friends. The brutal disruption of families by corporations, and by families that put the dollar chase above the other needs of their family members, means that children are growing up almost as street children. They are angry and alone, and they are being pushed to antisocial tendencies. They need their families. The great experiment of this century, the experiment that you can scatter families to the wind, that you can scatter communities out into the fields, that you can scatter races and income groups into enclaves of their own, is an expensive disaster. And yet, there are great industries profiting from our misery and dedicated to our continued strife.

There is only one way out for us, and it is a long shot. Walking across America I have seen a people to busy, to stressed in their everyday lives to be members of a community. If parents are thus antisocial, pulled and pushed as they are by the demands of a wholly commercial culture, is it any surprise that their children will be antisocial too, or that they will joint supremacist cults and do violence? It is hardly surprising at all. It is how they have been shown to live by parents who have no time for their communities, their neighbors, their own family members.

I have seen retired people so caught up in their hobbies and motorhomes that they have no time for their families, their communities or their country. They think they have paid their dues and can relax. Well, no, that is what heaven is for. We all have work to do while we are alive, and if we do not do it people suffer. Things don't get done. Children don't get cared for. Single mothers don't get help. The hungry don't get fed. And, all the while, doing these right things is more fulfilling than anything else that can be done in this life.

So, yes, be the conservatives you are, but work to conserve what our democracy needs to survive and prosper. And in your political fights with others, even those in your own party, act with great courtesy and respect for the other person's views. Only that will give you the joy to keep going, and winning is about keeping going. Thank you.

Unsocial Media

Doris Haddock's campaign was one of the first web-based grassroots political campaigns. At Common Cause in D.C., webmaster Nicco Mele watched the operation with admiration. He soon would take some of what he learned into the Howard Dean campaign, co-creating "DeanSpace." That, in turn, would inform the organizing model for the Obama campaign. Ms. Haddock's Internet trailblazing was not without slings and arrows: She hit a nerve over 1999's Forth of July weekend, when she suggested that too much money was being raised for presidential races. A Reuters story followed, generating a flood of email messages to her website, all of which she patiently answered. A sampling:

FORT WORTH, Texas (Reuters) - A great-grandmother walking across the United States to demand campaign finance reform said Monday that it was "obscene" that Republican presidential hopeful George W. Bush had raised a record $36.3 million for his White House run. "We don't know anything about his ideals or what he stands for. Apparently he stands for being able to raise a lot of money," she said.

Email responses to her website:

GET LOST! John Harkins

Dear Mr. Harkins, Thank you for your brief note. If you knew how many wrong turns I take you would be cheered to no end! Yours, Doris Haddock

Madam, are you serious? You castigate Mr. Bush for LEGALLY raising money, and I've heard nothing for you and your ilk condemning the Democrat party and their union sycophants for all of their illegal practices. I can only conclude that the reason for this is that your problem is not that Mr. Bush has raised a lot of money but that he has done so and is politically opposed to the socialist agenda the Democrat party advocates. I work 60 hours a week, have four children and pay taxes and I have never given to any political candidate, but the fact that people like you are criticizing Mr. Bush has moved me to donate to his campaign... My advice to you: if your walking motivates more working Americans to give to Mr. Bush, I say, keep walking sister!!!! Patrick J. Morgan

Dear Mr. Morgan, Thank you for writing to me. I will take

your advice and keep walking. I admire your hard work on behalf of your family, and I agree that we must always have the right to support our favorite candidates. If you will take a look at the McCain-Feingold bill in detail, I think you will be happy to see that it addresses the union sycophants and the corporation sycophants equally, which I think is fair play (though unions give a pittance compared to corporations and the wealthy). I thank you for introducing that word to my day. I always have liked it. As to Mr. Bush's millions, my comment was not that he was breaking the law. My comment was that being a good fundraiser does not make one a proper candidate for President, yet that is the focus of media coverage. I would make that comment against the press coverage of any candidate. And the money is indeed way out of hand, which I think you will agree in your heart, as only the voices of millionaires now count for much. If you are one, I do not mean to offend. Yours, Doris Haddock

Mr. Morgan responded: *I have to withhold any good wishes pertaining to your cause. In all other things, I wish you God's blessings.*

To Whom it May Concern: If the article is accurate, is Granny D senile or just a propagandist who is willing to distort the truth for her own agenda? Where is Granny D in regards to Al Gore accepting illegal campaign contributions from Buddhist nuns? If I recall, the individual donations there were greater than $100,000. I sincerely hope the article is inaccurate. If not, shame on you Granny D, either for not getting your facts straight or for lying. Best regards, Dan Schuring

Dear Mr. Schurin, Thank you for taking the time to write to me. I answer "a little guilty" to all your charges, except that I had nothing to do with Mr. Gore and the nuns. I can't be everywhere! Yours, Doris Haddock

I note that Granny D is in a tizzy that "big business" money finds its way into political campaign war chests. I wonder whether she is just as angry that illegal money from the Communist Chinese somehow found its way into Bill Clinton's campaign coffers during his 1996 re-election campaign... Joe Braddy

Dear Mr. Braddy, Thank you for taking time to write to me. If someone in Mr. Bush's campaign is suggesting that I am a friend of the illegal Chinese contributions, I hope you will set them straight soon before I have to answer this same email too many times more. Please be my emissary in this and tell the fellows that I am not in favor of illegal campaign contributions of any kind. I am walking across the U.S. for campaign finance reform. Perhaps there is another woman out there who is walking in favor of illegal and improper campaign contributions. She is the one you must get to... Sincerely, Doris Haddock

What a load of crap. Bush didn't brag about the fund raising, it was all in the form of 1,000 donations and what would you propose instead of corporations? Communes? Jim Dalrymple

Dear Mr. Dalrymple, I don't want to do away with corporations; I want them to make our cars, however, not our laws. Yours, Doris Haddock

In Percy Malone's Drugstore

Monday evening, August 9, 1999, Arkadelphia, Arkansas: Percy Malone invited members of the community to come into his drugstore to meet Doris. Percy's computer was the brains of Bill Clinton's massive "Friends of Bill" email list that helped fuel his rise. When a tornado wrecked the town in 1997, Clinton called to see how everyone was doing... and the computer. He cut red tape to help rebuild the town quickly.

I'm here—and thank you Percy—just to meet you all and to hear what's on your minds. I know the people here have a special relationship with the current president, but I'm sure you have opinions about the flood of big money into politics and other things relating to our democracy, so I'm all ears, and I have rather big ones. John Rauh, here with me, has been telling me about the public financing of election campaigns as a way to cut out the fat cats, and I'd like to know what you think about that idea. Dennis, also here tonight, got that program passed last year in Arizona, so it's not just some liberal idea from my New England, it can fit the politics anywhere.

I was talking to a couple of you a few minutes ago about what's going on in Yugoslavia and America's foreign policy, but I'm no expert on that and you all know more about it than I do. I know many people want to see us cut back our involvements overseas, and just be more hands-off. My only thought on that is that, while we Americans don't like the idea of empires—and we truly don't want to be one—history after the last world war has pushed us into that position. There is a dark side to it, as we have been guilty of undermining democracy in some countries and supporting dictators and letting some of our companies push in like private empires, but the other side of the coin is we have given the world an image of freedom and justice that influences their dreams for themselves and their own countries. In addition to what we have given the world in the way of stability and protective organizations, we are indeed an empire of aspirations, and we have often been the grownups arriving in places where chaos and cruelty needed to be addressed and wrangled into order and fairness.

The worst thing an accidental or intentional empire can do is to imagine it is not an empire, because the vacuum it leaves as it turns away threatens every man, woman and child, and the environment, of course, because irresponsible people are always waiting to take power when responsible parties turn away.

But let me get to the things I am walking for, and let me

ask John and Let's discuss how the public financing of elections might work here, so that you'll have proper representation, even when you no longer have a friend and neighbor in the White House.

Together at the Table of Power

Ms. Haddock's was invited to deliver the sermon at Little Rock's First Baptist Church on Sunday, August 22, 1999, as she walked through Arkansas. From Salon Magazine: "Aug. 26, 1999 | LITTLE ROCK, Ark. - When Doris Haddock finishes a speech, you find yourself wishing she'd run for president, or something. True, at age 89 she's off to a rather late start. In Little Rock, Haddock spoke at Central High School, site of the 1957 integration crisis, as well as in a church pulpit where Dr. Martin Luther King Jr. preached in the 1960s. The congregation initially eyed Haddock with some skepticism, but by the time she was finished speaking, they were cheering and surrounding her..."

Dear friends, it is a great honor to stand here in your midst, to stand here speaking where Dr. Martin Luther King, Jr. once stood and spoke. Here was a man—and we feel his presence in this place—who came into this world to speak the truth. Some people listened and understood, and some did not.

And the truth was this and remains this: that we are brothers and sisters; that our struggles to overcome injustice and unfairness, cruelty and oppression are only successful in the long run where our method is love—love of one another, love of our enemies.

When we hate our enemies we stop praying for them. And when we stop praying for them, how can we ever hope to turn them around?

We all have known family members who were on the wrong path and who created turmoil and pain in our families. We pray for them, in love, in the hope of turning them around. Well, America is a family, too. And our struggles are family struggles, where love is the greatest power and, in the long run of history, the only enduring power. Look at the best things—the lasting things—that America has done for itself and for the world in the centuries of our history: they are changes motivated by love, by a dream of equality, by a dream of peace and justice. The changes wrought by hatred fall away, while the changes wrought by love endure.

The use of love and truth to bring forth justice nonviolently was brought to this nation by Dr. King, and we thank him for it. He studied it and learned it from the writings of Mr. Gandhi. Mr. Gandhi learned it from the writings of John Ruskin and Leo Tolstoy, who learned it from American nonviolent abolitionists Frederick Douglass and William Lloyd Garrison, who learned about it from the Sermon on the Mount.

Thus, the great need for justice and freedom in America, the need to end slavery, resulted in a ripple of thought that spread and grew across the world, and came back to us in our time of need, thanks to Dr. King. He brought that teaching here, to this place, this room. Such is the enduring power of the Sermon on the Mount and of love itself in the world.

Nonviolent political action is, according to the instructions of Gandhi and the practices of Dr. King, a five-fold technique that we must always remember. It should be taught in our schools. It should be remembered wherever people gather with the intention of improving their communities or their world. Here are the five steps:

Number One: Determine the truth of a situation before taking a strong position. If it is an injustice, can it be clearly documented? Bring in the experts if you can. Be sure what you are advocating is actually and demonstrably the truth.

Number Two: Communicate your findings, your position and your request for change in a respectful and achievable way to the people who have the direct power to correct the situation. Don't ask someone for something they don't have the power to give. Don't shout on the sidewalks if you have not yet communicated respectfully with the parties in authority and have respectfully waited for a reply.

Number Three: If the response does not come, or is insufficient, bring public attention to the issue. Work openly so the thinking process of the entire community can be engaged. Gandhi and King were accused of staging events for the media. Of course they did. Social change is a public process, and it does not happen for the good when it happens in the dark. Engage the community openly so that they can be a part of the debate and the decision. This consciousness-raising works easiest in a democracy, but few governments, no matter how authoritarian, are wholly immune from public sentiment.

Number Four: If those in authority will not correct a very serious situation that must be resolved, despite an open airing of the issue, then the advocates must be willing to make sacrifices to demonstrate the seriousness of the matter. When King marched forward toward baton-swinging policemen in Selma, he showed that the issue was important. When Gandhi led marches and gave speeches that he knew would lead to his imprisonment that day, and when his followers stood in long lines to be clubbed by security forces standing in the way of their rightful path, the world stopped its daily routine to inquire about the injustice that motivated the self-sacrifice of these people and what, in fairness, should be done. And here is the difficult key to success: It is in the endless willingness of the advocates to make a continuing sacrifice that guarantees their victory. Few injustices are powerful enough, or have enough supporters, to stand against the flow of such generosity.

"You have been the veterans of creative suffering," Dr. King told his followers in the "I Have a Dream" speech. Well, creative suffering is something we all have the power to do. Along with aggressive and creative moral leadership, it is one of the most powerful forces for change in the world. It is always in our pocket, ready for the call of our conscience.

There is a fifth step, made necessary by the fact that the non-violence technique, when properly practiced, nearly always wins. The fifth step, as developed by Mr. Gandhi and as practiced by Dr. King, is to be gracious in victory—to remember that your enemy is your brother, and that you should therefore settle the dispute kindly, accepting some compromises and granting as much face-saving courtesy as possible to the other side. You will meet again, after all, and why not as friends? Gandhi said on many occasions that we have to love and respect our adversaries because they are our brothers and sisters, and also that they are parts of ourselves and of our God. He meant it.

Here is a passage from his autobiography:

"Man and his deed are two distinct things. It is quite proper to resist and attack a system, but to resist and attack its author is tantamount to resisting and attacking oneself. For we are all tarred with the same brush, and are children of one and the same Creator, and as such the divine powers within us are infinite. To slight a single human being is to slight those divine powers, and thus to harm not only that being, but with him the whole world."

Dr. King believed much the same, and you can hear it clearly in the "I Have a Dream" speech, where he calls us together as "all of God's children."

These are the five steps that gave India its freedom and which gave America its second revolution of independence at a moment when it could have devolved into a full race war. In the moment when King left this world, the violence that could have been ours all along showed itself in Watts and Detroit and a hundred other cities and towns. There is no courage in a thrown bottle of gasoline, especially where an innocent person is harmed or a family's life work is burned to the ground. True courage is what we saw in the buses arriving at Little Rock's Central High School and in the Selma march. Sometimes, irrepressible anger moves politics toward justice, but the truer and surer course is given to us in the Great Sermon: Love works. Love wins. Love endures. It is the foundation of our religion, and it must be of our politics.

In my walk across the country, I speak against the idea that those individuals and those corporations with the greatest wealth should be able to buy our elections and our candidates and our representatives, diverting their attention from the needs of the people, and preventing honest candidates from winning.

That we have a problem, that money has become more important than ideas in our political debate, is a proven fact. That this huge, national influence-peddling scheme results in a mass diversion of the public wealth from where it is needed to where privileged people would have it for their own use, is no longer a debatable point. When I walk with this message, I have the advantage of speaking the simple truth, proven by every major research institution, on both the right and left of political life, who have taken the time to investigate the issue.

We have asked those in power to remedy the situation, and they have refused. We have asked them again, and again they have refused.

We have engaged the press of the nation to shine a great light on this cancer, and still there is no movement by the leaders. Transparency is no cure for the metastasized cancer of political corruption.

And so, step four: we must reveal the depth of our concern. We must make a sacrifice of ourselves to demonstrate the serious nature of this problem, and this injustice. All great political change requires pain. Mr. Gandhi and Dr. King advised us to take that pain upon ourselves, not to inflict it upon others. And that is what we must do: sacrifice and stand more and more forcefully in the way of this injustice. If we fail, it will because we did not sacrifice sufficiently. We showed up only on Saturdays when it was convenient for us, even though Congress was out of town.

We made speeches to ourselves about ourselves instead of

into the hearts of our countrymen about their own freedoms and futures. The side that wins in politics is the one with the greater empathy, even if it does not look like empathy—call it the greater connection to the great mass of our people.

The message we must convey is simple: that there is no true equality in America so long as only the rich are represented at the table of power. That is not democracy. There can be no true justice in America so long as only the privileged make the rules and build the jails for those outside the rooms of power. That is not democracy.

Only when we all sit together at the table of power can we do the right things by our communities.

We need quality preschools, affordable or free, for all our young families. We will not get them if we are not all at the table of power.

We all need affordable health care. We will not get it if we are not all at the table of power.

We need quality public schools that will inspire and raise up our children to their highest potential, not suppress them and lead them to despair and trouble. We will not get such schools if we are not all at the table of power.

We need programs so that dropout rates evaporate to nothing and so that every child has a positive vision of his or her future in this nation. We will not get those programs if we are not all at the table of power.

We need to make a college education as affordable as a high school education, because those who do not go on are doomed to poverty in the economy of the coming century. Moving from high school to college should be as automatic as moving from grade school to high school, and it is in the clear national interest of America to make it so. But it will not happen if we are not all at the table of power.

We need to make sure that the rising wealth of America is felt first, not last, in its poorest communities, with a new wealth of personal opportunities so that parents can provide for their children and have time left over to raise their children—and so that children can see a happy future. This will not happen if we are not all at the table of power.

In this new era of electronic communication and commerce, we must include all our children and all our families. We are divided enough already, and we don't need a digital divide to further separate us. We need to provide connection to all our people. This will not happen if we are not all at the table of power.

We need employment and training programs to provide real access to all groups, all races, all people, to every rank of every career. We need to turn renters into homeowners, and open up the capital markets that enable family businesses to start and grow.

We can insist on such changes when we all sit together at the table of power. If we are separated we are not equal.

This is an agenda of love. For, when we are in the same room, looking eye-to-eye and speaking heart-to-heart, it is hard for us to deny each other justice and equality as Americans. If I tell you what my children need that I cannot provide, you will help me provide for them. If you tell me what your children need that you cannot provide, I will help you provide for them. That is the essence of self-government in a free land. The trick is to get us all in the room, all at the table, and campaign finance reform is one of the keys to making that finally happen.

We do have the ability to publicly finance our elections, to make them as free as the candidates' speeches at a Forth of July picnic. And we must do it. We own the airwaves, after all. The billions of dollars we save by eliminating the corporate welfare that flows from today's corrupt campaign system could fund the public financing of elections, with nearly $50 billion left over each year. How we could better take care of our children with that!

We are a free and equal people—in theory and in law. But I don't believe we will have real equality, practical equality, and I don't believe we will have democracy—practical democracy—until the influence of billionaire money is reduced in the elective process and people can run on the strength of their character and ideas. To take money from those you regulate was bribery a thousand years ago, and it is bribery today. And while our leaders take campaign bribes with one hand—bribes that deprive us of our democracy—with the other hand they falsely pledge allegiance to the great dream of America—the dream so many have died for.

"They promise them freedom, but they themselves are slaves of corruption; for whatever overcomes a man, to that he is enslaved." (Second Book of Peter, Chapter 2, verse 19).

And from Psalm 26:

"Gather not my soul with sinners, nor my life with bloody men, in whose hands is mischief, and their right hand is full of bribes. But as for me, I will walk in mine integrity: redeem me, and be merciful unto me. My foot standeth in an even place: in the congregations will I bless the Lord."

I bless the Lord in this congregation and thank Him for .

bringing me safely to this place. I thank you for the honor of being able to address you here, under the Lord's roof and in the presence of Dr. King's spirit. I pray for those in this country who have the burden of responsibility for leading us. I pray that they shake off the chains of unrighteous obligation that tighten around them through the present campaign finance system. I pray that they will have the courage to do the right thing for themselves and for their fellow Americans. I know they are not happy with the present situation, nor are we, the people.

I hope the campaign finance reform movement and the civil rights movement can join hands. Either the common people will rule this land, or they will be ruled. Either justice and loving mercy will be the condition of our communities, or the present harsh regime will continue to erode our lives and foment conflict and alienation within our communities.

We are walking together on the high road of history. We are on even ground, now, because so many sacrifices have been made behind us. We have nothing to lose that we care about, and our shared freedom to gain. We are walking in love, our successes sparkling behind us, and we cannot be stopped so long as our souls are alive, and our souls live forever.

Thank you. Please join me in Memphis on September 7th if you can, to keep walking where Dr. King fell, and then on to Washington through the winter.

To the Apologists of Corruption

Ms. Haddock's remarks from the balcony of the Lorraine Motel in Memphis on September 7, 1999 — the first of two speeches she made from that historic balcony (the other was in 2004). She walked to the site with Dick Gregory and members of the sanitation union who walked with King on his last day.

We are on hallowed ground. The petty affairs of the day fade away at this place, where the courage and pain of a righteous life suddenly transcended to the eternal. And with that transcendence, the light from above that shows us the way to justice and love became, for all time, one soul brighter. Did King die here? The part of him we love, his soul, will never die. And so his voice still rings in our ears and he still implores us to make brotherhood, love and self-sacrifice our own tools for change. We hear you, Dr. King.

In this place, it is easy to remember that our brothers and sisters of every color have sacrificed their lives to advance our shared dream of a land of equality and plenty. We have not made these sacrifices in order to separate our people into rich and poor, privileged and oppressed. Dr. King was in this very place because he believed that equal economic opportunity is the partner of political equality.

Our people are more economically divided now than they were when King walked this way. The tax and labor and business laws of this nation drive that division, and those policies are held hostage by a corrupt Congress and its system of campaign finance bribery and billion-dollar political favors. These favors are paid at the expense of programs that could make our society fairer and less troubled.

Whole parts of our society, stripped of other opportunities, have fallen into illegal markets to survive. A young generation of urban poor is in jail or in the justice system. Our families are working too many jobs and too many hours to be able to raise their families properly.

It is the duty of leaders to shape society so that the great masses of its people can work to provide decently for their families and their futures. Our leaders, distracted by the corruption of the campaign finance system, are failing that duty.

They pass laws that destroy the jobs and lower the protections for workers, that segregate the people into rich communities and communities of despair, that provide jails instead of education, shelters instead of decent housing, and toxic pollution instead of healthy environments for our children. They do it to favor the wealthy elite who underwrite campaigns to keep them in power.

We must replace this bribery with the full public financing of our elections, so that candidates may speak as freely to the community as they did in the days when publically-funded candidate debates in the park sufficed. We must get big money out of politics before it destroys us utterly.

Americans are disheartened, but we reformers must not despair. We must help bring forward the day when ordinary people can speak as equals at the table of power to decide the affairs of our government.

Our democracy is sacred ground. It is red with the sacrifices of our people. We are here today to honor those sacrifices, not with our words, but with our deeds.

To the apologists of corruption in Congress, like Mr. McConnell of Kentucky, understand, sir, that, just like those who stood atop the school steps to block the historic arrival of desegregation, you cannot stand forever atop the Capitol steps, your arms folded against the American people's longing for a democracy worthy of our national sacrifices.

I thank Mr. Dick Gregory and the Memphis sanitation workers who have walked with me today. I hope you will walk with me again in January in Washington. By then I might need a hand up the Capitol steps, and I hope that we, as American brothers and sisters, might go into that great temple of freedom together, with Dr. King beside us and in our hearts. Thank you.

If Ye Break Faith with Us

On October 8, 1999, Ms. Haddock, accompanied by U.S. Senator Russ Feingold and U.S. Representative Zach Wamp, arrived by foot in Nashville, stopping at the steps of the State Capitol to greet citizens. She was 2,200 miles into her walk to Washington.

I want to thank Representative Zach Wamp, who helped lead the successful campaign finance reform effort in the U.S. House for the second consecutive year, and Senator Russ Feingold, who has shown great courage by putting his own reelection on the line by refusing soft money contributions.

I have enjoyed walking through your beautiful, green Tennessee. It has been an honor for me to walk through the land where so many great Americans have lived and walked. I would like to take this occasion to honor just a few of them. I am carrying with me today the names of Tennesseans who served our nation with great courage and distinction. They each received the Medal of Honor for their military service. Some lived to receive the medal, others did not. Please join me in remembering them here again: *(Ms. Haddock named the recipients.)*

For each name, there are thousands of other Tennessee men and women who have dedicated their lives—and sometimes sacrificed their lives—to advance and protect our freedoms.

These sacrifices were not made so that special interests and big money might take control of our institutions of self-governance. If we indeed let that happen, then we are not honoring the price that has been paid for our freedoms.

"If ye break faith with us who die, we shall not sleep, though poppies grow in Flanders field," as the poet McCrae wrote.

For those in the U.S. Senate who refuse to sweep special interest money out of Congress, we hold up this list to you [Senator Feingold did so] and ask you to do your duty as Americans. You stand on the shoulders of free men and women who have come before, who held their courage against all fears and all temptations.

It is time to be adults, and not children. It is time to be courageous, and not greedy. It is time to toss away the flimsy rationalizations that have been set up when no real and mature arguments can stand.

Do the right thing, Senators. Pass this bill that Mr. Feingold and Mr. McCain have put before you and that the common men and women of America long for. Be brave against your financial needs. Be brave against your party's needs. Do what your mother and your grandmother would have you do in the name of your family members who sacrificed so much for our freedom.

The Corner-Posts of Democracy

On October 9, 1999, Ms. Haddock addressed activists in Nashville.

It is a great pleasure to be here this evening. It gives me the ability to publicly thank so many of you who have made my trek through Tennessee a joy and a success. And I thank you all for your steadfast support of good government reform. I know the work seems never-ending, but democracy is a better verb than a noun—it is a work in progress; it is what free people do. We are fortunate, then, that the forces of greed and deception are always busy out there, giving us the gift of a good fight, which is exactly our purpose on this Earth.

After a while, of course, we reformers are liable to start boxing at every shadow. It may become difficult to distinguish the critical fights from the meaningless ones. But we must make those distinctions—we must pick our fights carefully—if we are to succeed in the vital areas.

To do that, we must be able to visualize a healthy democracy. We must understand the architecture of a good civic life, and focus our repair work strategically.

What indeed are the corner-posts that hold up our democracy? I would like us to take a brief walk together around this great structure, poking here and there and making a brief list of needed repairs.

The founding corner-post of our building is a stately—if somewhat chipped—Corinthian column called Education. It is impossible to have proper self-governance if our people are not educated to the task. I am speaking of a "liberal education." The word "liberal," of course, refers to the liberation of the mind to think for itself. If our people cannot think for themselves, we cannot sustain ourselves as a free people. It is not enough to give our children trade school educations if we would have them be a people capable of self-government. To participate properly in self-governance, people must understand the nature of human beings and they must come to love them in all their complex diversity. That requires a good dose of Shakespeare and Tolstoy and Cervantes and a hundred other writers, historians, geographers, philosophers, theologians and poets.

Today, there is no point and no future in ending a person's education at high school. We have publicly-funded grade schools and high schools, and now we must extend that to the college years. And we must insist that schools turn out human beings of the highest order—nothing less will do in a world so balanced on the edge of disaster.

You are wondering if I am getting off my subject, that perhaps I should stick to campaign reform and let others look to other issues such as education. But I tell you that we must help each other to strengthen all the corner posts that keep this house up, or it will surely fall.

Holding up another corner of our democracy is a great post that we can visualize as a farm silo, for it represents the harvest plenty. Not only must we be free to think for ourselves, we must each have leisure time and a modest financial surplus. Democracy thrives best in nations where there is a healthy condition of wealth spread throughout a broad middle class. Wealth is not defined by high consumption, but is a condition of surplus, of plenty. From plenty and power over one's circumstances come security, confidence, brave outspokenness, and the ability to participate generously in a family and in a community. The lack of power over one's circumstances brings anger and division.

In my trek I have seen many people who are too abused by long working hours and long commutes and short paychecks and credit-based living to be able to properly take care of their own families, much less take care of their communities. Living paycheck to paycheck, they cower in private places, bowing to computer and television screens, unable to risk the contribution of even a common sense opinion, for fear that it might land them on the street. Regardless of its technologies, a society that lives fearfully is not wealthy. Even the super-rich, if they are fearful and always stressed for time, always shortchanging their families, are not wealthy in that best sense.

Our democracy was founded in more agricultural times, when the harvest plenty gave families the security of knowing that, if they worked hard, they would probably have sufficient resources for their families and their communities. Self-reliance also made them free with their opinions, and the rhythms of the seasons gave them the surplus of time to be engaged in the civic realm. Our elections are still held after harvest time.

Today, large corporations have replaced the family business, and, for many working families, there is no surplus of resources or time. This is a critical problem for the long-term survival of our democracy, and one that we must address creatively.

We may fight our campaign reform battles and think that labor unions and social justice activists will hold up their end of the building, but if all reformers do not stand together to fight for improvements in the working lives of Americans—to fight for a grand new expansion of the middle class through a reemergence of small businesses, fair labor practices, lifetime education, better urban planning, and corporate employment policies that enable people to have lives outside their offices—this democracy we love cannot stand.

At another corner stands a double-pillar called Equality and Fairness. As we fight for a broad new middle class, we must continue the hard and sometimes frustrating work of bringing all Americans along together. If we pretend that minorities do not operate with tremendous psychological and economic handicaps in this society, and if we do not take steps to affirmatively overcome those unfair handicaps, we are sowing the seeds of our own failure as a democracy. Yes, we are individuals and we have the right to individual fairness and equality. But, yes, we are also groups, and we must be prepared to bring groups into equal status for the good of our best dreams for our democracy. Simple minds cannot balance these competing ideas. Mature, well-educated minds can indeed—and they must prevail if we are not to slip dangerously back into a cruel and unstable past.

The most valuable asset that Americans enjoy—after each other—is our Constitution. A system of fair rules—of justice—is what preserves us from the storms of history in the world around us. We have to fight that fight, too. We cannot let others or ourselves be victimized by those who would use the power of scale or wealth to undermine our equality, muffle our voices, or separate us by income, race, age or tenure here. If we are not daily defenders of social justice issues, we have no legitimacy as reformers.

And the final corner of our great building is supported thus: Democracy is a marketplace where ideas and the powers of the people come together. We can visualize a great kiosk holding up the forth corner of our building, with great and colorful posters of candidates and ideas in profusion. If a democracy is a free market of ideas, the ideas must all be seen and heard and understood by all.

When I was a little girl, there were great political speeches in the parks at election time. We heard all the speeches. Just as our towns once provided the stages for those debates and speeches, we now must provide modern ways for candidates to have free and equal access to our ears and eyes at election time. Since we can no longer all fit in the park, we must provide a public financing system, at least for candidates who wish to take part in it.

Otherwise, only those candidates and ideas will be heard who have already sold themselves to power, and they are not honestly offering themselves to us—they are already sold.

Regardless of the outcome of the current battle to get corporate money out of our elections, we must rebuild our ability to communicate political ideas to each other freely as free people. Democracy cannot afford dollar signs—it has no place for them.

These may seem like dark days for democracy, but it always seems so. We are always in deep trouble. Thank God for that. Thank God we are each given such important work to do in our lifetimes for the survival of our people and of our still brightly shining aspirations of equality and mutual freedom. It is supposed to be like this. We are supposed to give ourselves body and soul to our beliefs, and we cannot do so where there is no challenge, no fight. Dark clouds are simply the proper backdrops for our best exercise of courage. Where but in battle, or upon its eve, can we feel such friendship and brotherhood—as many of us do in this room tonight!

In the coming weeks we have an opportunity for a great victory or a great defeat in Congress. Let's not conserve or spare ourselves. Let's do all that we can to fight for what we believe.

And throughout the coming year and into the new century, let us not specialize too narrowly in our concerns. Let us support each other's work, financially and with our volunteerism. Let us work together to keep all the corner-posts of our democracy in good condition, by working as great friends, and in great coalitions as fellow Americans and as fellow citizens of the nation and of the world. Thank you.

Your Answer, Mr. McConnell

On Saturday, November 6, 1999, Ms. Haddock walked into Louisville and assembled a rally of 160 people outside the office of Kentucky's U.S. Senator Mitch McConnell—the principal opponent of campaign finance reform in Congress. As with most of her speeches, it was widely covered by local newspapers, radio and three television stations. This particular speech was run in its entirety in the newspaper, with a favorable editorial comment. People Magazine also covered the event. Senator McConnell's effort to stall the issuance of an event permit was discovered and defeated, allowing the event to take place legally. "We would have done it anyway," Ms. Haddock told a reporter, "the Constitution is our permit."

Thank you for this welcome. I have so enjoyed walking through Kentucky—the beauty is overwhelming. This is a wonderful state, filled with great people. Today, I want to speak about one great Kentuckian in particular, and that is Senator Mitch McConnell, whose office I have come to after 2,400 miles of walking.

He is on the other side of the battle lines in our effort to return American democracy to the human scale—our effort to get the $100,000 check out of politics. But he is a most worthy opponent.

He fiercely represents his beliefs and the interests of Kentucky in Washington.

He sits as chairman of the Senate Rules Committee, which has jurisdiction over federal election laws and the administration of the Senate. He is the chairman of the Foreign Operations Subcommittee, a key foreign policy committee, and is a member of the Agriculture and Appropriations committees. These positions of leadership indicate that he is held in high esteem by his fellow Senators. He is also the chairman of the National Republican Senatorial Committee, which means he is responsible for supporting the campaigns of Republican Senate candidates in every state. In 1997, he raised millions for these campaigns from corporations and from wealthy contributors. He is raising more for the upcoming election.

When he speaks on the Senate floor, his arguments are well reasoned and a delight to listen to. They make good reading, like the orations of Cicero of ancient Rome. He defends our Constitution—as he sees our Constitution—with a vengeance.

You are waiting for me to say something unkind.

In fact, I have come here to do him a favor, and to ask a favor. I will scold a bit, but I am not here to vilify him.

He asked a question on the Senate floor recently, and got no answer. I have, on foot, brought him his answer today.

In the recent campaign finance reform debate in the Senate, he rather sharply attacked Senator McCain, when Mr. McCain had the audacity to suggest that the hundreds of millions of dollars being spent by special interests to influence the passage of laws in Congress might indeed be influencing the passage of laws in Congress. Mr. McConnell thought that was an outrageous assumption, and asked for the names of any Members of Congress so low as to bend their votes toward the interests of contributors, like flowers toward the sun. Specifically, he said this:

"I ask the Senator from Arizona, how can it be corruption if no one is corrupt? That is like saying the gang is corrupt but none of the gangsters are. If there is corruption, someone must be corrupt."

He also said: "It is astonishing. We have here rampant charges of corruption and yet no names are named..."

Mr. McConnell demanded the names of those who were corrupt. Mr. McCain, for reasons of friendship, courtesy and the dignity of the Senate—such as it is—did not name names.

But Mr. McConnell persisted, demanding that Senator McCain give a name. Mr. McConnell was like a reverse-Diogenes, searching the dark corners of the Senate chamber with his lantern for one dishonest man.

I have come here today to answer the question asked by Mr. McConnell, and to end his long search.

Lately, Mr. McCain has been accused of having a temper. But he did not answer Mr. McConnell's question in anger on the Senate floor.

Nor will I answer it in anger here, though it is true I can get a little testy, too. My feet do hurt sometimes and need to be taped so that I can walk. I wear a steel corset to help my back, and it can sometimes make my words a little sharp toward the end of the day. Torture, even a little of it, does make you testy.

I have come a long way to address great men like Senator McConnell and tell them what Americans are saying about the condition of our democracy, and the role of big money in that democracy. The road wears on me sometimes and I am tempted to say in anger what all America seems to know except a few sheltered men and women whom we care for in a special room in Washington and who do not seem to notice deterioration when it comes over them slowly, or corruption when it becomes the water they swim in.

The answer to your question, Senator McConnell, is

elementary.

You ask, "how can it be corruption if no one is corrupt? If there is corruption, someone must be corrupt." You are right, of course. Your analysis is pure genius. Someone must be corrupt. Who can it be?

Perhaps it is the bagman who shakes down American industries in return for protection in Congress and for special tax breaks from the party in power, while average, working Americans struggle mightily to make ends meet. Have you seen such a person, Senator McConnell?

In 1997, Senator McConnell, when you took $791,945 from insurance interests who needed protection from patient rights efforts, and $602,885 from oil and gas interests who needed a free flow of tax benefits and protections against pollution laws, and $597,915 from communications interests who wanted free access to the digital spectrum and a free hand to merge into giant monopolies, you might have seen such a bag man in their offices. He's the man you were asking about on the Senate floor.

When you let a Ukraine group host a fundraiser for you in 1996, and you used your position as Chairman of the Appropriations Committee to provide a $225 million appropriation for development programs in Ukraine, did you see another fellow there, trading money for public policy? That's the fellow. He is at such meetings and making such deals almost daily, year in and out.

More to the point, Senator McConnell, though I admire your abilities and your achievements, and the hard work you perform for this state and for all of us, you are the man you asked Senator McCain about. And you are not alone. The House and the Senate are full of some of the best minds and most caring hearts in America, and they are being ethically destroyed by the financial demands of campaigning in the modern age.

We must do something, Senator McConnell, and you must help us. I have poked hard at you in these remarks, but I do so with a grandmother's love and the certain knowledge that we Americans are good people at heart who must be encouraged sometimes, and scolded sometimes.

Senator, we need your help.

We must move quickly toward the public funding of state and national campaigns. We must make the airwaves—which are public property—available to candidates without charge if they will restrict their other expenditures.

The news media must do a much better job of reporting local and national campaigns, so that the necessity of expensive advertising is reduced.

Senator McConnell, I do not doubt that you are a great American. I know that you are. Let us drag ourselves from the noxious fumes of this poisoned house and breathe the free and clean air of true democracy. Let us stand up and measure ourselves against each other, not against the size of our friends' bank accounts. Let us return democracy to the human scale, where it belongs.

Join us, Senator McConnell, in calling for the public funding of campaigns. Join us in demanding that broadcasters who use the public airwaves provide a public benefit at election time. Join us in ending corporate contributions to political campaigns, for corporations are not people, and democracy is. Thank you all.

Trickle-Down Democracy

To a gathering on the campus of Ohio State University, Columbus, on Saturday, December 4, 1999:

Thank you for the great honor of speaking with you today.

It has been an interesting week in the news. Tens of thousands of people have traveled to Seattle to protest the policies of the World Trade Organization. They particularly demand that trade policies should not be allowed to sidestep or gut our environmental laws, should not be allowed to work mischief upon the already dire condition of workers and children around the world, and that the organization should end its practice of secret meetings. These demands are clearly reasonable and hardly debatable. It is remarkable that these thousands of people should have had to suffer the expense and personal risks associated with this protest movement.

What the WTO is rapidly becoming, of course, is the commercial version of the United Nations, but one without open, democratic processes or a balanced view. It is dominated by the interests of multinational corporations who achieve their place at the table, to our exclusion, through the corruption of politics. In our country, that corruption extends to the highest officers of the land, who have become the handmaidens of corporate interests at the expense of human rights, of our environment, and of the stability of our middle class.

There is no question that an open world is better than a world of walls. The challenge before us is to open the world in a humane, intelligent and fair way. The commercial interests and their political puppets now driving the process have no such intentions, and can only promise us a brand of trickle-down environmental protection, trickle-down human rights, trickle-down working standards, and trickle-down democracy. That is a fiction and a fraud, for what is really happening is a leaching-up of environmental degradation, a leaching-up of worker exploitation, and a leaching-up of the secrecies and exclusionary practices that are the antithesis of democracy.

The protests this week are a part of the struggle between the human scale and the monstrous scale of overlarge commercial enterprises and their hired governments. In the 20th century, we can trace this battle of scale back to Gandhi's struggle against English industrial oppression of India, and we can trace it through the frightening fundamentalist uprisings in the Mideast and elsewhere, which are, at heart, a rejection of commercial values where they threaten traditional, local values and identities in a time of climate change.

We see the people of Chiapas, Mexico revolting against the commercial forces that the North American Free Trade Agreement has set against them. And now, in Seattle, and in uprisings in Europe, we see the spirit of Chiapas spreading.

It is an extension of the old battle that Theodore Roosevelt fought and lost at the beginning of the 20th Century. He fought against over-large businesses enterprises. He defended the family farm and the small business against those damaging monopolies and trusts. The Republican Party was split between the small business and big business factions within its own ranks. The big business element won the day, and Teddy Roosevelt's brand of politics went underground, poking up from time to time in various populist uprisings. It reemerges now at the end of the century, demanding satisfaction, if it can get it.

It reemerges at a time when large-scale commercial institutions rule the Earth like aliens in some science fiction story.

Seattle may be the beginning of action. I think the new century can be a time of human values, of the reassertion of the human scale in all things, and a time when large organizations cannot hold together against the forces of decentralization introduced by new technologies and renewed human concerns; but it can certainly go the other way.

We do need a balance. We cannot survive without large institutions, just as we cannot be free without small ones. Large institutions can be our tools for fairness and peace and productivity. The larger the institution, however, the more it must be rounded by the participation of a wide range of people and issues. The breaking of that simple law is what makes multinational corporations and organizations like the World Trade Organization so dangerous. The keeping of that law is what makes our constitutional government and organizations like the United Nations so valuable and so worth our efforts to preserve and improve them.

So, let us continue our work to clean corporate money out of our elections, so that our democratic institutions can effectively represent the values of the American people, whose deepest values are indeed sound. Let us improve the United Nations so that it will be known one day for its efficient and intelligent reach into the problems of the world, including trade policies for an open and free world.

As a planet, and as a biological system, we can no longer afford an ineffective United Nations, any more than we can afford a U.S. Congress owned by commercial interests with short term, selfish goals.

The opening of this new century is a good time for each of us to do what we can to improve and advance our human institutions. We must all take our part in the shaping of a more just, more democratic, more peaceful, and more sensible new era. It must be a sacred promise to our children. Thank you.

The American I Haven't Met

Arriving in Clarksburg, West Virginia, January 1, 2000, one year on the road, after climbing the Appalachian Range in blizzard conditions:

Thank you for this wonderful welcome to Clarksburg. The road has been snowy, and I'm glad to be in such a warm and beautiful place. I began my walking journey in California exactly one year ago today. Clarksburg marks my 2,895-mile mark. I expect to get to Cumberland, which is my 3,000-mile mark, on January 24th, my 90th birthday, snow and ice permitting. I will reach my goal of Washington, D.C. on Leap Day, February 29th, and I will indeed leap for joy to again be able to sit down in my own living room in New Hampshire—for a few minutes, anyway. This is an important election year and I don't think any of us should spend too much time in our easy chairs. What's the point of having a democracy—what's the point of all the blood sacrifices that have been made to advance and preserve it—if we sit and just watch other people muck it up?

Some people do wonder if I have taken my activism a little too far. They ask me what on Earth I am doing, walking across the country at my age. I can tell you I am not doing it for my health—though it has done me no harm, and perhaps a brisk walk across the country is something every American should do. I am sorry I waited so long for my first crossing, as there is no better way to fall in love with this land and its people—they are so kind and bright and interesting, and so dedicated to the aspirational dreams of America.

In my long walk I have indeed seen quite a bit. I have crossed the Mojave Desert that I thought would never end—its dust and sand swirling around me. I have landed in a hospital and a rodeo—my first—and in more than a few parades. I have slept in the modest homes of Native Americans in the Arizona desert and walked with children and senators, mayors and vagabonds. I have met elderly women who have pressed their precious food into my hands, though they themselves must buy pet food to stretch their budgets. I have cried with them when we parted. I have watched Texas cowboys and cowgirls break horses in the cool dusk under Texas stars. I have cut my way through weeds and waded across rivers. I have walked with the great leaders of the American Civil Rights movement through the South, and even found myself preaching government reform from a pulpit where Dr. King once preached. I have stood and made speeches here and there, on the steps of senator's offices and in the tiny meeting rooms of so many little communities along the way.

I have met and walked with so many wonderful people of every race, age, income and political persuasion. But through it all, I have yet to meet one person who believes we should hand over our democracy to those who would use their big dollars to take it from us. I have yet to talk with the one man or woman or child who wants their senator to be beholden to the special interest check writers who step in line in front of us all, stealing our representation. As a nation, I tell you we are of one mind on the matter of special interest, big money politics: We are through with it.

I did not walk across the United States of America to tell anyone how to vote, but let an old woman advise you to look closely at how your Congressmen have voted for or against corruption, for or against graft, for or against the stealing of our democracy by special interests.

It is usually a mistake to vote for or against someone on the basis of a single issue. But campaign finance reform is the master issue. If we do not get the poison of big money out of our system, we have no representatives, and no democracy. You may like your representative. He may have done you a lifetime of favors. But we are at a time in the history of our nation, and in the fate of our world, when a line must be drawn between those who will stand with the people and those who instead sell themselves to the high bidders.

I am honored to be in this beautiful, 230-year-old community. I know Clarksburg is the home of many great Americans. I know you have it in your history and in your blood to fight this fight. An old woman can't do it alone. Thank you.

Our Town

January 3, 2000, also in Clarksburg, West Virginia, more with young people and other residents, as opposed to her entry speech, which included the mayor and officials:

Thank you. It is a great pleasure to be here. Clarksburg is a beautiful community, and I know how you love it. Your people have been here for centuries, surviving deep snows and wide floods, and you have watched your children grow and your friends grow old. You, yourself, are still looking fine, however.

I know about the magic of being from a good town, and loving it.

There is a stage play that I'm sure you know, entitled "Our Town," by Mr. Thornton Wilder. It is about life and death in a small New Hampshire town. More exactly, it is about all the beauty we can miss if we are not fully awake to the brief magic of life. Mr. Wilder wrote the play while residing in the New Hampshire community where I live. Ages ago, I got to play the lead role of Our Town when the play was new and so was I. We of the region take his play as a correct description of the heartbreaking beauty of life in a caring community of decent people. The area is called Dublin and Peterborough and Keene, New Hampshire, just west of Manchester and along the skirt of Mount Monadnock.

Now, Mr. Wilder was careful not to start any arguments about where the real Our Town might be, and whether some of the characters might therefore have real counterparts. In the very beginning of the play, he therefore cites the longitude and latitude of the town. If you go to a map, however, you will see that the coordinates he gives describe the middle of Massachusetts Bay, quite a ways out in the water. So, respecting his wishes, we do not claim to be the true Our Town. We do, however, live and die as he described, and we understand the emotions that stirred within him as he wrote.

He wrote in an area of 32 little cabins set up for writers and artists by Edward and Marian MacDowell. At the MacDowell Colony, Mr. Wilder wrote his play, and America's great music composer, Aaron Copeland, wrote much of his masterwork, Appalachian Spring. Virgil Thomson wrote Mother of Us All. Leonard Bernstein completed his great symphonic Mass.

Over 4,000 artists and writers have taken their turn working in that beautiful and harmonious setting, including Edwin Arlington Robinson, Milton Avery, James Baldwin, Willa

Cather, Jules Feiffer, Studs Terkel, Alice Walker and many, many others.

I spent most of my weekends for a half century at another such colony, called Dundee, several hours up the mountain, where we spent our leisure hours with great thinkers and artists, and where we prepared our big meal together each evening, and put on plays for each other in the theater built for just us and our children.

This all may be something of a revelation to many people who have grown up in big cities or towns under clouds of oppression. They may not have imagined that humans can form happy and creative communities—that they can make something of a heaven for themselves here on Earth. It can be done. I have done it all my life, and I assume that many of you have, too.

For those not so fortunate—if they would like to find their way to a community of love and courtesy where the purpose of living is to reach one's full potential as a creative human being and help others do the same—I have some advice.

There is a secret to the creation and nurturing of true community. Once people know the secret, they can create community anywhere they choose—any place they happen to find themselves.

The secret is to take the world as your own—to take full responsibility for it. Once a person steps into the circle of those who take responsibility for the happy operation of the community, once someone decides that they are not a customer of government, but government itself, the magic of community begins, and, as long as we are breathing and thinking and our hearts are beating, the world is ours to shape according to our values.

There are many people who would like us to believe that the world is theirs, not ours, so that they might steal our world from us—steal our lives from us. They would like us to be their little slaves, mindlessly working for their happiness at the expense of our own, and accepting all the evils of the world as somehow necessary. That is nonsense.

More and more, I am seeing homeless people along my walk. If a man or woman or child is on a street with no place to go, it is not only a great affront to their dignity and safety, but also to yours, though you are but driving by. That homeless person is a billboard statement to you from the financially powerful members of our economy, who indeed have the resources to shelter everyone in a decent home. The intended message is that you are at risk too, if you are too often late for work, if you are too troublesome with your demands for justice of any kind. The misery of others is thus used as a weapon against us all. It is a statement that says, "this is not your community; you do not have the power to impose your humanitarian and other values on this place." And so our answer to that must be to help everyone and make safety nets of our own devising, so that no one will fear to live free and the community will be a true reflection of our values. It will be Our Town.

When some people accept the "them versus us" divide between the people and the government, they are buying into the lie that destroys democracy. They need to wake up, and, frankly, we need to wake each other up from that hypnosis from time to time.

The violence in our society is a symptom of that hypnosis. A real citizen, a person who takes responsibility for the community, is not someone who returns poison with poison, rudeness with rudeness, violence with violence—for to do so would be playing but a bit part in a minor play. When someone can return rudeness with concern, poison with understanding, violence with peace, they are not being ruled by others. They are free. The world is theirs, and it begins to turn their way, toward their higher values, because they are not giving rudeness what it needs to survive, nor violence what it needs to grow. They are spreading their consciousness over the larger view and taking responsibility for the workings of their community.

In our land, the rise of violence is held as a mystery. It is no mystery to me. It is what happens when people, young and old, no longer feel responsible for their communities. There is a great, and now global, corporate-political complex at work to strip people of their ability to feel responsible for their communities, of their ability to feel connected with its needs and valuable to its operation.

In my long walk, I am trying to get some new laws passed that will make it easier, I hope, for people to be responsible for their own communities and their own government. I worry that the influence of very rich companies and very rich people make it difficult for regular people to feel that they are in charge of their own affairs. We need to get the big, $100,000 special interest contributions out of our elections. Those contributions shout down you and me, and there is no true free speech nor true political equality so long as this condition persists.

I would not be on this path if I did not believe that America is my responsibility; I am responsible for its workings, as are you.

Even in the very act of trying to help, I find my happiness and I find a creative community of people. In this way, we have already won. We always win if we will only wake ourselves from the hypnosis some would impose on us, and take responsibility as the happy leaders of our communities, our land and our Earth.

In this generation, the fate of our natural environment, and of our democratic environment will be decided. Only great leadership, and great love, can get us through the times ahead. We must all take our parts in this great drama. It is more than politics; it is a struggle of the soul, and it is exquisitely personal to each of us.

I have talked long enough for someone who is supposed to be out walking. But let me say that I take my town with me. Our Town always travels with each of us. The longitude and latitude of it cross upon our hearts. We bring the good community into being with our love and our relentless consciousness. We mustn't fail to appreciate the magical moment of life, and to fully participate in it joyfully and constructively, never giving an inch to injustice, unfairness or inequality, nor ever forgetting the long line of people we have known and loved in the great circle that extends well beyond the world we know.

Thank you for listening to me today, and thank you for your very warm hospitality along a cold and snowy road.

Morning Morgantown

Ms. Haddock's remarks in Morgantown, West Virginia on January 8, 2000 after a greeting downtown by the Mayor and a small parade:

Some years ago, Joni Mitchell wrote a song about beautiful Morgantown, and I have always assumed it was this great university town, although Morgantown, Pennsylvania, is also lovely. I have always wanted to come here since hearing the song. I am many years late, but I see the beauty has waited for me. In the song, Ms. Mitchell wrote and sang: *"We'll find a table in the shade / and sip our tea and lemonade / and watch the morning on parade / in morning, Morgantown."*

I never imagined, of course, that I would be that little morning parade, but life is full of magic. My little parade is a political mission, of course, on its way to Washington, but here, not Washington, is where America is most beautiful, most authentic and most honest. Here is where we expect fairness from each other, and where we expect and demand clean government. Here, in beautiful communities like Morgantown, is where we learn to care about, and for, each other.

We need to live in communities that reflect our highest values. We need a national government, too, that is a reflection of our highest values, not our lowest. Things have gotten a little turned upside down in Washington, but as a people we are up to the task of setting things straight, beginning with the work of getting the big, special interest contributions outlawed from our elections.

Thank you for this welcome. I am very honored to be here.

The Efficacy of Sacrifice

Delivered later the same day in Morgantown, at West Virginia University:

Thank you for being here to welcome me. It is an honor to be here with you in Morgantown. It may seem odd to you that an 89 year-old woman—almost 90—should walk across the country for an issue like campaign finance reform. It sounds like something CPAs should worry about, not old folks from New Hampshire.

Nevertheless, on January 1st of last year, I began my walk in Los Angeles and I have been walking ever since, usually ten miles a day. It has been a great adventure.

That you might better understand how this kind of protest works, let me describe what has happened to me again and again on my walk. When I got across the Mojave Desert in California, I found myself at the Arizona town of Parker, on the Colorado River. The mayor of that lively town is a wonderful woman named Sandy Pierce. Now, I don't know if Sandy cared too much about campaign finance reform before I got there, though she well may have. But after we met—and after people congratulated me for crossing that big desert where many others have died, and after Good Morning America and National Public Radio interviewed me—people were very curious about campaign finance reform. Sandy understood immediately what I was talking about. Within a few hours, she was introducing me all over town with a little speech like this: "Now I would like you to meet Doris

Haddock. She has just walked here from Los Angeles, through the Mojave." People's eyes would open a little wider. She would continue: "She is doing it to publicize the need for campaign finance reform. She is upset that big money interests are calling the shots in our elections, and we no longer have much of a say. She thinks that is a huge problem for us all. She says that all the people who have died in wars to defend our democracy would want us to defend it now, from those who are buying it from under us."

Well, all I would have to do after that was smile and shake hands. People would immediately see that what I was doing did, in fact, relate to serious issues that disturbed them, too.

Then, of course, the local newspaper reporter would want to know about campaign finance reform. If someone would walk so far across that desert for it, it must be important. And so I would explain how there are laws limiting what a person can give to any one candidate, and that these laws are meant to preserve the health of the democratic system. I would explain that there is a soft money loophole that gets around those laws. The loophole allows corporations, unions or wealthy individuals to give unlimited amounts of money to parties. The parties can pass those dollars along to candidates. What is the point of contribution limits, if you can just use this back door?

Well, reporters are quick studies by trade. So wherever I have gone, reporters have quickly learned about the issue and written about it. Large newspapers have looked anew at the issue, and some have changed their positions, including big papers like the Dallas Morning News, now demanding campaign finance reform. Now, could I have done as well if I sat back in New Hampshire and wrote letters to the editor? Probably not. People respect serious and sincere sacrifice, and they will listen to you on account of it.

Having newspaper reporters and editors who understand and care about campaign finance reform is very bad news, indeed, for anti-reform Members of Congress who were later interviewed by those same news people.

Now, back to campaign reform for a moment. Some of your friends may ask, why shouldn't they be able to spend as much money as they want on a candidate? It is a free country, and that is a part of free speech, isn't it? Well, tell them this: If money is speech, how can we be equal citizens? If money is speech and we are all in the same room, trying to run a democracy, then some of us are mute and some richest of us have bullhorns. It is reasonable to put some limits on the money going into campaigns, if only to make it so that all can be fairly heard.

As you know, big corporate money has taken up residence in Washington in a very serious way, and has now taken over the process. If you decide, as a free citizen of America, that you believe we need to do a better job of reducing greenhouse gasses, or of protecting natural resources, or any other cause you believe in, and you go to Washington to press your case, I ask you: will you be talking to those Senators and Representatives, and will they be listening to your arguments and making decisions based on the best facts and the best interests of our country and our world? Today, they will not, and that is the tragic condition we must not allow to persist. They are all running on high-speed treadmills of fundraising that only give them time to listen to big money lobbyists, and then to do their bidding. They rationalize it, of course, thinking that, in the big picture of things, they are doing the best for America. They are lying to themselves, and to all of us.

K Street, where the biggest corporate lobbyists have their offices in Washington, is the main feeding trough for this piggery. The big lobbyists put money out in the troughs each morning on K Street, and then the great oinking starts up on Capitol Hill. Soon, members of Congress are all nudging each other at the troughs. It's enough to make you a vegetarian.

I am walking to Washington, but I am not going first to the Capitol building, as that is only the puppet theater these days. I am walking first to K Street, the true center of power, where we will show Washington to itself for the shameful place it has become.

Enough negativity. Let me tell you that, for every negative thought I have had along this long walk, there have been a thousand beautiful moments. Americans are truly kind, interesting, odd, beautiful and smart people. I recommend that, someday, when it is not escapism, you don a backpack and go see it all for yourself. I don't think you should wait until you are 90. I expect that most of you younger people will live 150 years or more, so you might think about doing it twice: once through the north, and once through the south. And leave time for the rest of the world, too.

On your walks, you will see how important political leadership is in the lives of the people. When we do not have leaders that care about fairness, and health, and the fulfillment of the educational potential of each person, what we get is what we have gotten: poverty, illiteracy, dysfunctional communities, a disappearing middle class, widespread emotional depression and political anger. I am not saying that it is the government's role to run our lives; I am saying we are the government, and we run this country for our mutual benefit, unless powerful interests get in our way, stealing our common resources and our very lives.

When that happens, we must act, and that is what I am doing for myself, and what you must do for yourself. For this is your land. It is not someone else's. This is your life, not someone else's. Your freedoms and your position of responsibility as a member of a self-governing community have been paid for in blood by the people who came before you. You owe it to them, and most of all to yourselves, to sweep away anything that gets between you and your rightful place as the free member of a free community.

Up the road a ways, near Cumberland, I will mark mile 3,000 and my 90th year. I am almost finished with this walk, but I am far from finished with this work. In Washington, we will make a determination regarding who in Congress is for reform, and who is too busy with their snouts in the sludge to make a commitment to reform. On the basis of that determination, I will be active in the states in the coming election year to try to defeat some Members of Congress who stand in the way of reform. We only need a few more votes in the Senate to achieve a good start.

So this is serious and long-term work, but I am up for it, and I hope you are, too. Our democracy, and even the biological survival of our planet are in the balance. And aren't we fortunate to live in a time when so much is at stake—when we each of us have such a fine challenge to our souls? Thank you all.

A Modest Proposal for Sacrifice

Ms. Haddock's remarks to friends and supporters via email on January 17, 2000, in remembrance of the birthday of Martin Luther King, Jr.:

In my walk across America, I have met, in so many faces, the clear-eyed sense of fairness and equality that has guided our nation's slow but steady progress. This sense of fairness has a big, farmer's handshake and a direct preacher's voice. When you are in the presence of it—when it shouts a friendly hi across a road to you—why, you know you have not walked too far; you are still in the land of Jefferson and King, Whitman, Steinbeck, Susan B, and ever so fortunate you and me.

I met a gentleman in Arizona, Mr. Eddie Basha, a grocer of proud, Lebanese descent. In the early 1950s, Eddie was on a high school football team in an Arizona farming town. A local restaurant owner promised the team a steak dinner if they would win the big game. They did, and the team showed up to claim their dinner. One of their team members was Black. The restaurant owner said he could not serve him. Eddie, knowing nothing yet of the simmering Civil Rights Movement, but knowing plenty about fairness, told the restaurant owner that he was being unfair. Eddie organized a boycott of the restaurant until the owner finally agreed to serve everyone of every color. The other restaurants in town soon followed, not wanting to see those linebackers and eloquent Eddie on their sidewalk next.

To nurture that sense of fairness, and to bring it to life with acts of personal leadership, are what we must be about as parents and community leaders. As always, we must teach by example. Fairness and leadership are everything to the life of a democracy.

A simple sense of fairness is the great genius of America's enduring aspiration. That is what drives our equal rights movements and our politics, courts and councils. It used to drive our Congress, too—I remember that time, before big money bought it out from under us.

We will change it back, for we are good at fixing up this old democracy.

Raising the level of fairness in our society is always painful and often dangerous. Martin Luther King, Jr., as a student and teacher of nonviolent protest, followed the example and writings of Mr. Gandhi, who was himself instructed—indirectly through Ruskin and Tolstoy—by American Quakers. Dr. King brought this teaching back to our Nation at a dangerous time, when we most needed it. He told us we must take the pain of moral progress upon ourselves, rather than inflict it upon others— what an amazing and ethical concept! And more amazing still, is the fact that it works better than any other method of social change.

If we would be successful, we must suffer the batons, not wield them. We must suffer hunger and cold, not inflict them. The political and cultural changes which have come about through self-sacrifice tend to be good and lasting changes. Changes wrought by violence are often filled with unanticipated evils.

Dr. King looked out upon mid-Twentieth Century America and he did not have to look far to see that his enemy was massive, institutionalized unfairness—rooted so deeply that many could not see it or imagine the world any other way. But he saw it, and gave leadership to mend it, taking the pain upon himself.

I walk for campaign finance reform, which we surely need if we are to have a democracy of self-governing, free people—not the wage slaves of a corporate state. And while we fight, we must have ground to stand on, and that ground is a broad mountain called the middle class. We cannot have a democracy without it. It is that city of hard working, equal brothers and sisters that Dr. King could see on the mountaintop. Well, we have indeed come a ways up toward equality, but let us not take this day as a time of self-congratulation while the whole mountain slips into the sea, leaving nothing but deep water between the very rich and the poor.

Where are our leaders and our representatives at this critical moment, when the shape of our economy and our jobs are in the balance, and when the health of our environment is in the balance, and when everything to do with fairness and equality that Dr. King and so many others lived and died for are in the balance? Where are our representatives? They are sold and gone, I fear. Sold and gone. The lobbyists in Washington spend millions per month for their attention, and you know where that leaves you and me, don't you?

What cause do you care most about? Go to Washington to press your case, I ask you: will you be talking to your representatives, and will they be listening to your arguments and making decisions based on the best interests of our country and our world? Today, they will not, and that is the tragic condition we must not allow to persist. They are all running on high-speed treadmills of fundraising that give them time to listen only to big money lobbyists, and latitude to do only their bidding.

For a people who have given their sons and daughters to the defense of freedom, this is unfairness on a grand, new scale. We rise against it. Fairness compels us.

Can we fight it like we fought segregation? Where are its buses and lunch counters, so that we might bravely go like Rosa and do what must be done? What sidewalks can we stand on with Eddie Basha and say, Stop, brother, there is an unfair situation here? How shall we proceed to enforce our values and our love?

We will do it as we must: peaceably and relentlessly. First, we need to get big money out of politics by outlawing soft money contributions—those huge, $100,000 checks that are funneled to candidates through the parties and special committees. We can do that simply by demanding that our senators and congress members do the right thing this year when the matter comes up, which we must insist upon.

Second, we must get involved in the congressional election campaigns this year, and we must work as hard as we possibly can to get rid of those incumbents who continue to resist the outlawing of soft money. I will help every way I can, in every state where there is a close election, and I hope some of you will, too.

Third. I will tell you where to find the sidewalks where we can stand with the likes of Eddie Basha. Would we walk past Eddie and go eat in a restaurant that had grossly unfair policies? None of us would, I hope. I have made a list of the thirty dirtiest companies that no longer merit the business trade of good Americans. They have betrayed our most deeply held values by circumventing our campaign laws and giving huge amounts of soft money to the senators and representatives who are supposed to be representing us, but are now their overweight puppets. We rise against these companies: Fairness compels us.

This list includes companies to which you may be loyal. I am asking you to make a sacrifice—to take the pain of political progress upon yourself. I would like you to stop buying from them and from their subsidiaries. I would like you to send the list to your stockbroker, if you are fortunate enough to have one, and tell them to move your investments elsewhere. When we get these thirty companies to swear off the dirty habit of undermining democracies, we will go after the next thirty.

Now, life is complex today, and we sometimes have to do business with firms we do not like. A drug company among the dirty thirty may make a drug you need. But on the list may be some firms where you do have a choice in your purchases and your investments. There are surely several opportunities for your action and modest sacrifice.

If you say we cannot clean up the system, I tell you we are still free enough people in two areas, where we vote and where we spend, to shape our future. Fairness to our fellow citizens, fairness to our families, fairness to ourselves, and fairness to those who sacrificed their lives for our freedoms compels us to do so. Thank you.

The Disruption Economy

Ms. Haddock at the Cumberland, Maryland, Rotary Club on January 25, 2000. The response was wildly enthusiastic.

Thank you very much. In my walk I have seen countless main streets in hundreds of towns, and it is heartbreaking to see the boarded-up windows and empty sidewalks. Other than homelessness, of course, it has been the only sad thing I have seen, not counting quite a few armadillos and foxes and other animals that did not make it across the road as they had planned. It is sad that the economic life of our towns can be listed among the road-kills.

You, however, have done so much with your beautiful downtown, and there is such a sense of vitality in Cumberland, that I can talk about the issue here without it being a criticism. It is not your problem here, except that we are all Americans and we must all care about the vitality of Main Street America, for it has historically provided the strong middle class soil for the flourishing of our democracy.

There is an advertisement currently running on television showing a man coming to work in the morning on a New York subway and sitting down in a small cubicle and making his first telephone call of the day to a client. He is a stockbroker. The announcer says, "If your stockbroker is so smart, why does he still have to work for a living?"

Well, that may seem like a good question, but it really is not. Working for a living is a fine idea. It is perfectly fine to make a living serving the needs of others. It is perfectly fine to manage investments so that they grow carefully over the years. It is not essential that everyone buys penny stocks and becomes billionaires overnight. A stockbroker does not have to be incredibly wealthy to be incredibly worth his or her salt. That is obvious.

So what is really behind this ad, which of course was for an Internet stock trading service, or should I say, a casino? The Internet is only the latest tool that allows big, distant companies to put middle class business people and professionals entirely out of business and to deny their clients their wisdom and caution.

Here we see an attack on the very legitimacy of a stockbroker. Who is safe from such an attack? Surely not insurance agents, real estate agents, travel agents (poor dears), retail store owners, pharmacists, bookkeepers—anyone. We are all competing with automated systems and with 25-cent an hour labor on the other side of the world. Which members of our middle class can survive? And how can our democratic society survive without a strong and stable middle class? As that television ad shows, the demonization and undermining of our local professionals and our town economies is very much underway and very well financed. Besides purchasing television ads, these Internet giants are buying our elected leaders.

Now, you're starting to understand my direction. You have been wondering, "What does all this have to do with the issue she walks for, campaign finance reform?" Look no further than the pledges the presidential candidates are now making to keep the Internet free of sales taxes—a policy that will make it increasingly difficult for Main Street merchants to compete. Then look at who is funding these candidates, and you will see the names of the same billionaire companies doing business on the Internet.

The computer-based financial management program, Quicken, which controls some 85% of the market for that sort of thing, is now selling every kind of insurance on the Internet, as a part of its software. They will soon be selling home mortgages and they are already selling investment products and banking services. If you walk down Main Street in three years, will any of your neighbors be selling insurance or mortgages? Will there be any banks behind the ATM machines? Not if the mega-corporations have their way and destroy all our middle class jobs. Disruption is not a good thing.

Maybe there is a natural evolution involved here, but it is important for you to know that the new law that enables these companies to pull the rug out from under all the state insurance and banking regulations went through Congress last year on a fast track, greased by millions of hard and soft campaign dollars. If you are in the insurance, banking or mortgage business, ask your senators and representatives how they voted on the big financial services bill last year, and you will know if they can be bought or not. You will know if they represent your interests, of if they have sold you down the river. If they say that the bill was good and necessary, tell them that they might have some credibility if they had not taken the money from the bill's lobbyists.

The biggest problem with the current campaign finance system is that we can no longer trust our elected leaders. We don't know if they are making decisions for the right reasons, or for corrupt reasons. We have our suspicions, and suspicions alone are deadly to a democracy.

In a corrupt environment where public policy is for sale through the campaign finance system, towns and small businesses and family farms, and the people themselves, cannot successfully compete for representation. If that is the case, then a coup of sorts has taken place. We continue to finance the government with our taxes, but it no longer serves our interests or answers to our concerns. This is a change of government and a treachery to those who have sacrificed their lives and limbs for our freedoms.

Those causing this change of government—senators and representatives, lobbyists, corporations and the very wealthy—are consciously and aggressively putting us out of the picture. They are conspiring daily to steal our government from us.

Don't go away from this meeting thinking that I was speaking against the Internet. I do not mean to suggest that it is a bad thing, or that the nature of commerce should not evolve. I do mean to suggest, however, that our elected leaders should be looking to our interests, not those of the highest bidders, and that is in fact what has happened; the power center of our democracy has moved from the Capitol building to the lobbyists along K Street and Pennsylvania Avenue in Washington. I am suggesting that, in this time of rapid change to our economic system, we need our representatives to carefully represent our interests.

Hanging in the balance is the nature of our town economies. What does it matter to a community to have its own businesses owned by its own townspeople or by faraway, multinational corporations?

It is, of course, the difference between a community of free men and women, and a colony—which is rapidly becoming the condition of many American communities. The first president to really see the problem of the small business and the small farm pitted against over-large corporations was that wonderful Republican, Teddy Roosevelt. He broke up the trusts while he was in power. The minute he left power, no leader took his place to defend the human scale of our communities, and to defend the health and breadth of the middle class. This battle has been untended for most of the last century. So we have watched the decline of the family farm, the decline of family businesses, the deterioration of towns, and a growing income gap that leads rather directly to personal stress and family stress and all they bring.

It may seem that I have picked on the Internet a little bit, so let me say something to cheer up the Internet people in the room before I close. There is a dark and light side to every new thing. Yes, it will challenge us to find new ways to be free communities where people own and operate their own businesses, but it allows anyone, including the parent or elder at home and the smallest of small businesses, to provide services or products to a worldwide market. That can help he middle class, if it is nurtured in that way.

Another bright side of this new invention is its potential to provide a new medium for political campaigning: one that can potentially be free of charge to candidates, or nearly so, and a means of collecting small contributions that can overpower the billionaires.

All this can, and surely will, revolutionize politics in America.

The Internet is only one case. There are many new things we can do to move into a better future, but we the people must be in the driver's seat. The interests of ordinary people must be represented, which is not our situation today. If you will go down this hill to Washington without $100,000 in your pocket and try to get your representatives to listen openly and help you on the basis of what is right, why, you are dreaming. I remember a time when you could do that without a penny in your pocket, and they were interested to listen and take action. I witnessed it many times.

Thank you very much, and I do hope you will push your representatives to support the campaign finance bills now before Congress.

Don't Give Up the Ship

Also in Cumberland on January 24, 2000, after a good portion of the townspeople and their children marched with her through town, Doris delivered a speech from the back of a caboose in the town's rail station. It was her ninetieth birthday:

Thank you all very much indeed. What a wonderful birthday this is, here in the exquisite setting of historic Cumberland, Maryland. It is such a treat to be in a place even older than myself.

President Washington, I have recently learned, was here in 1794 to review the federal troops sent here to discourage a little rebellion called the Whiskey Insurrection—a disagreement over the advisability of a tax on distilled spirits levied by the rather new federal government.

President Washington noted this in his diary: "After an early breakfast we set out for Cumberland—and about 11 O'clock arrived there... I passed along the line of the Army; & was conducted to a house, the residence of Major Lynn of the Maryland line... where I was well lodged, & civilly entertained."

Well, I know how he felt.

That residence, by the way, is just over there, across the way where we can see it, still standing, against all odds, to which I can also relate. But we see how the past is cherished and respected in Cumberland.

We must also cherish and respect the institutions that provide, after long and bloody years of defense, our freedoms as a self-governing people. I am headed to a city where those institutions are being sold for scrap—a place far downhill from here.

But before we depart from this place, let us look around at the beauty of America. Let us look at a town where there is no other way for public servants to be except honorable. If a mayor or constable or executive of such a town as this should sell out the interests of his townspeople for the sake of a campaign contribution, a career would be over and shame would come to a family. This is the real America. Down the hill is another America, where there is no shame, and where the buying and selling of America's interests are not called bribery, though that is what they are, and where the stealing of real power away from what we founded as a government of, by and for the people is not called a coup or a treason, though that is what it oozes toward.

So we Americans stand here no longer concerned about the tax on our whiskey. We can bear that; we can even drink to that. But we cannot bear the greater damage that is being done to us by far more intoxicating poisons: power, money, and prestige: distractions that blind the vision and poison the souls of those within the Beltway in an epidemic of disdain for the American People—whom they take as a mere market for their political products—chiefly their darling selves.

A flood of special interest money has carried away our own representatives and our own senators, and all that is left of them—at least for those of us who do not write $100,000 checks—are the shadows of their cardboard cutouts. If you doubt it, write a letter to them and see what rubber stamp drivel you get back. For all we know, they might all have died ten years ago and the same letters continue to be sent out.

Now, standing here on the back of this charming caboose, why would I spoil my own birthday party with a bunch of politics? Well, because I love politics, and this is my party.

I love it to death and I shall love it to unto death. It was the dinner table meat and potatoes of my wonderful, 62-year marriage. It is what we talk about in the town halls of our communities and on Tuesdays in my reading group, which we call the Tuesday Morning Academy. It is what self-governing Americans must hold in steady fascination and endless conversation, if we are to be free.

My husband, Jim, died several years ago after a ten-year struggle. At the end, he said that he was ready to go and that he did not want any more food or water. It took him eleven days and nights more, before he was successful. My son, Jim, my grandson Raphael, sat with him at night and I held his hand during those last heartbreaking days. After ten years of caregiving, it is difficult for an old wife to adjust, especially when the mate was such a sparkler—such a person of light and life and red-blooded activism. He was fun. And how do you wake up each morning in a world where the fellow you would run to with a new thought to share is nowhere to be found and where he does not answer your call through the house?

My dear friend Elizabeth died too, shortly after Jim, and also after a long period of caregiving that did wear me out.

I am not trying to make anyone feel sorry for what happens in a long life. All things end. But I want to say something important about it, and that is why I bring it up. I stand here on the tail end of a caboose. And so it was when Jim and Elizabeth were gone. Life seemed very much over—all the picnics, all the hikes, all the frosty ski trips. I was deeply depressed and I know that many people today are in that same place. And what I want to say to them, and for all of you to remember for that day ahead when you think you are standing at the end of your life, is, damn it, don't give up the ship.

I know I am mixing my transportation metaphors with trains and ships, but it is my 90th birthday and I have just walked 3,000 miles and I shall mix metaphors as I please.

For those of you who have lived a long life and think your are finished with it, I tell you that, if you will pray for courage and look to the needs of your community rather than yourself, a great energy and happiness will come to you. Indeed, your community needs your wisdom and your patience. Your family needs you, too, whether or not they believe it. And your country needs you.

Friends, look at this country, our genius republic—this great sailing vessel we have built that we might find our way to the future together as free and equal citizens, as friends and partners in self-governance. Though it is two and a quarter centuries old, the paint still smells new some days, and the flags still snap in the wind. But what a price we have paid for it! I do not have to remind you of the rows upon rows of marble stones that mark the sacrifices our friends and our children and our forefathers and mothers have made to build this great craft and keep it safe, do I?

But now, in a time when people are so stressed in their lives and are so unaware of what it means to truly live well—to live free, to live with enough leisure and confidence to be the stewards of their own lives and communities—in this time, we strangely find ourselves having to explain why it is a bad thing if multinational corporations control our elections, and why it is a bad thing if our elected leaders no longer represent the interests of the people.

I know that some of these people just need to be awakened. We can do that. We can show them a future they will want. But there are others who know very well what has been lost in this nation over the last few decades and they have lowered their fists slowly in despair. To them, to my generation and the generations younger, I cry to you, please—don't give up the ship.

Work with us to return our self-government to the human scale. Help us defeat those Members of Congress who will not take even the first step toward reform, which everyone with a brain and a soul knows is the simple act of outlawing the huge money contributions that now flood our elections—special interest dollars with special interest obligations.

We care nothing for the taxes on whiskey, because they are nothing to us anymore. But we pay billions of dollars each year in extra taxes or inflation because tax breaks are being sold for campaign contributions—we pick up that tab.

Where do we march to make a fight of this? Not against our government, but against those inside and outside of it who have set up their cash registers in our temples of democracy. Where are they? Downhill from here in a place that smugly dismisses the rage of Americans.

Let them become suddenly uneasy. Let them notice that the birds are strangely silent and the dogs are barking. Something is brewing, and it is called an election. Thank you for helping me celebrate one of the great days of my life—I know that many of you have come a very long way. Let's adjourn now to make our plans for Washington and have some cake.

Note: The largest blizzard in 40 years rendered the road from Cumberland to Washington impossible for walking. Ms. Haddock used her cross-country skis to complete the 184 miles to Washington, using the snowy towpath of the historic C&O Canal. It would bring her all the way into Georgetown.

As Senator McConnell, her nemesis, had said that campaign reform would pass Congress when "hell freezes over," Ms. Haddock asked organizer Nick Palumbo to take a photo of her on skis in the deep snow and have John Anthony and Matt Keller of Common Cause, who, like Nick, had both been of service to her throughout much of her journey, deliver it to the Senator with her compliments. Ken Hechler found her with in the snow and asked her to speak the next evening to the students of a nearby college, Shephard.

Casting Self-Interest Into Oblivion

"Sitting outside O'Hurley's General Store, eating pizza, 90-year-old Doris Haddock feels so strongly about her cause for campaign finance reform that she is walking across the entire country. Haddock, better known to her grandchildren and now half of America as Granny D, has walked 3,000 miles, meeting and greeting Americans that believe in her cause. She arrived in

Shepherdstown on Feb. 14, less than 60 miles away from her goal: the steps of Washington's Capitol Building. While in Shepherdstown, Granny D took a break from her massive trek to speak on Wednesday, Feb. 15 at 7:30 p.m. to a full Reynolds Hall audience... When the winter weather arrived, Granny D broke out her skis and began cross-country skiing along the C&O Canal. Despite emphysema and arthritis, Granny D keeps going, one way or another." — From The Picket, the newspaper of Shepherd University, by permission.

Ms. Haddock's remarks at Shepherd University (then Shepherd College) in Shepherdstown, West Virginia, on the evening of February 15, 2000:

Thank you. I am honored to speak to you all today on this truly beautiful campus. My walk across America has taken me through many fine communities and put me in the presence of unforgettably grand people, and now I am so pleased to meet you.

I am walking for the issue of campaign finance reform. I speak wherever I go of the need to remove from our elections all money that has unhealthy strings attached. We are a wealthy nation, and we don't need to let our elections and our leaders be sold at auction. The right things for us to do, I believe, includes the outlawing of what is called soft money contributions.

You see, we have good laws already in place that limit the amount of money any one person can give to a candidate, just so that candidate will not feel undue influence from that donor. And we have good laws that prevent corporations from giving any money to candidates, for the same reason. What we also have, unfortunately, is a big loophole that allows wealthy individuals and corporations to give any amount of money to a political party or to a special committee, which can then pass that money along to support or oppose a candidate. That unregulated money is for some reason called soft money. It is not soft in its impact. It is a loophole that makes all our carefully crafted and constitutionally approved laws useless. Closing the loophole has proven to be very difficult, because soft money has quickly become like heroin to both political parties, and they fall with knives upon any bill that comes close to closing the loophole.

The measure that would close the loophole has been presented several times in Congress. On the Senate side, where it comes closer to passage every year, it is the McCain-Feingold bill. On the House side, where it has twice passed, it is the Shays-Meehan bill. All four of the bill's sponsors have been kind enough to walk with me or visit with me from time to time during my walk. I honor what they are trying to do.

After we close the loophole, I believe we need to take the next step and enact programs to provide public funds to candidates who agree to refrain from other fundraising. There are four states with such programs already in place for statewide and state legislative candidates: Arizona, Maine, Massachusetts and Vermont. We need to push the program into a few more states every year.

If we can do that, then, in ten or fifteen years, many of the people in Congress will be from states where public financing is the norm, and it will be what they used to win, and I think we can then see public financing at the federal level. We can all get a big tax relief when that happens, because we now all pick up the tab for billions of dollars in corporate welfare that Congress enacts to pay back the fat cat campaign donors. Public financing will cost a fraction of that. In fact, every dollar of public financing saves about ten dollars in corporate welfare.

Think of public financing in this simple way: Imagine that America is a small town, and that we have a meet-the-candidates picnic on the 4th of July. The town pays for the stage, the public address system, the promotional fliers, and even has a copy machine so that people can get copies of the candidates' resume's and statements. That is a fine way to run an election, and we must make it happen on the larger scale if we are to keep our leaders unfettered by shadowy obligations.

There. Now you know what my big issues are. I don't know what your big issues are, but let me tell you that if you are interested in any big thing—from the environment to human rights, farming, business, health policy, science policy—you will sooner or later have to knock on the door of Congress, if you are to go very far with it. If you want that doorway to be open, you had better help me first to get that fat cat out of the way, because right now he will not let you in. Today, your senators and representatives have no time for you and no interest in your ideas unless you walk in with a $10,000 check. We simply cannot afford, as a people or as a planet, to let that condition persist.

I do hope you have a vision of your own life that includes a great deal of political involvement in the big issues of the day. We are a free people and we each have a responsibility to understand and work and provide leadership in important areas. If you don't think that is true, then you have been brainwashed by those who want to take that power and that responsibility away from you. Don't let it happen. Don't get so wrapped up in consumer spending and careerism that you forget that you stand on the very same ground as the founders of our nation and Martin Luther King, Frederick Douglass, Caesar Chavez, Tecumseh, Susan Anthony and so many others who cared about the life and freedom of future generations—and that is you.

How long do you think democratic government has been the sacred tradition of the soil that you tread every day—on your way to class, on your way to free meetings, on your way to church services, on your way to wherever you freely choose to go?

You may think it began in 1776 or with the subsequent ratification of our Constitution, but those Founders were latecomers to this land of democracy.

The Iroquois Constitution, the memorized document that ruled this very soil hundreds of years before the rest of the world arrived, was the very model of fairness and balance that helped inspire Jefferson and his contemporaries. It was the law here for a very long time, and it continues in force and influence even now, in the way Native Americans govern their nations and in the forms and symbols of the U.S. Government.

The animal symbol of the Five Nations of the Iroquois was the eagle, like ours, perched high with its eye looking out for any danger to the peace.

Another important symbol of the Five Nations was the cluster of five arrows. Look at our One Dollar bill and you will see our newer cluster of thirteen arrows, one for each original state, in the iron grip of the eagle. The Iroquois Constitution says this: "As the five arrows are strongly bound, this shall symbolize the complete union of the nations. Thus are the Five Nations united completely and enfolded together, united into one head, one body and one mind. Therefore they shall labor, legislate and council together for the interest of future generations." Unquote.

Well, that would be us, and they, too, are our forefathers. In times of trouble we should take their council. They had wise laws. The men had all the power in council, but the women had the power to choose the men who would lead. A reasonable balance, perhaps, for their time. The men and the women had their own, highly democratic council fires, where concerns could be voiced and presented for action to the nation.

They had quite an elegant disarmament policy, which went like this:

"(We) now uproot the tallest pine tree and into the cavity made thereby we cast all weapons of war. Into the depths of the earth, down into the deep under earth currents of water flowing to unknown regions we cast all the weapons of strife. We bury them from sight and we plant again the tree. Thus shall the Great Peace be established..." Unquote.

They had two houses of legislative deliberation, plus an executive and judicial branch, more or less, and veto powers, impeachment, and a fair justice system that respected the dignity of every person. We should not admire that history as outsiders, but should embrace it proudly as our own history, accepting its wisdom and humanity.

We would do well to install our new senators and representatives in the same way that we Americans did when we were the Five Nations. Here is a part of the ceremony, addressed to any new representative arriving at council:

"Your heart shall be filled with peace and good will and your mind filled with a yearning for the welfare of the people. With endless patience you shall carry out your duty, and your firmness shall be tempered with tenderness for your people. Neither anger nor fury shall find lodgment in your mind, and all your words and actions shall be marked with calm deliberation. In all of your deliberations in Council, and in your efforts at law making, in all your official acts, self interest shall be cast into oblivion."

In all your official acts, self-interest shall be cast into oblivion!

Their confederation broke down from the pressures of change from abroad, as we know. They were cast into warfare and anarchy. We must ask ourselves if we are being swept away: Is our modern rule of law breaking down? I can show you very fine laws against bribery that sit high and dry, even as an incredible flood of influence-buying money sweeps away our democratic representation and our history as a free people.

Let us remember who we are. Let us remember that a good government can fall away unless we forever give ourselves to its defense, and unless, in all our official acts, we cast self-interest into oblivion. Our planet and the people of the world now depend very much on our ability to keep control of our government and rule it with the wise hand of love and reason, and not greed and profit.

The Framers of the U.S. Constitution took the Iroquois Constitution very consciously as their model. Have you been taught that in school? Well, at least now you have, tonight.

Here is how the Iroquois instructed their leaders to begin their great meetings. I will end this meeting now with this language from, truly, our first Constitution:

"Offer thanks to the earth where men dwell, to the streams

of water, the pools, the springs and the lakes, to the maize and the fruits, to the medicinal herbs and trees, to the forest trees for their usefulness, to the animals that serve as food and give their pelts for clothing, to the great winds and the lesser winds, to the Thunderers, to the Sun, the mighty warrior, to the Moon, to the messengers of the Creator who reveal His wishes and to the Great Creator Who dwells in the heavens above, Who gives all the things useful to men, and Who is the source and the ruler of health and life."

Let me say finally that you are being raised in a culture that ever tries to trivialize your life. Your life is not trivial. It is not designer-labeled; it is not on-line or virtual; it is real. You are a free person in a land of free people who have served each other, in the main, with dignity and sacrifice for many centuries. Do your duty to those who came before you. Do your duty to your own freedom and to the freedom of Americans and all people to come. Cast your self-interest into oblivion and see, through the progress of the soul, what a magical world this is! Thank you.

> *Email note: "Dear Ms. Haddock, Happy, happy birthday! We will bake a cake in our house to celebrate your birthday and your march, which excites all of us to action. I have some old bananas and a handful of walnuts, so banana bread birthday cake it is! I am an activist in my own hometown—we constantly fight the special interests of deep pockets, but what really concerns me is that those folks get the rubber stamped approval from our government. We must see an end to special interests running amok, and a beginning to campaign reform. Thank you for every step. I can't tell you how much strength it gives me to carry on what probably would seem insignificant to you, in my small town, but knowing that grass roots efforts can be truly effective is what it is all about. You are quite a grand woman. Take good care of your feet. Love, Jennifer and girls, Heather, Sarah and Megan, and husband, Michael*

Entering Washington, D.C.

On February 29, 2000, Ms. Haddock was met by approximately 2,300 people at Arlington National Cemetery, where she began her final miles to the Capitol Building by way of K Street— Lobbyist Row. Progressive reformer Jim Hightower, equipped with a bullhorn and high spirits, helped guide the big crowd across town, hopping onto the bases of convenient statues to lead the cheers. Mr. Hightower is behind her in the photo, in the cowboy hat. In the shirt and tie is John Anthony, her volunteer press advisor. In the dark shirt, with his fist in the air, is Nick Palumbo, her volunteer road manager. On K Street, it was surprising to see a "Go Granny Go" banner hung from a high window, and several young women cheering from on high (see previous page). Before K Street, Ms. Haddock paused at the Lincoln Memorial to give the following remarks:

The beauty of this memorial we take from the ancient Greeks. Inside this temple of democracy, however, sits no god of Olympus, but a man of Illinois—a country lawyer with a talent for self-government, which we all must share if a government of the people and by the people and for the people is not to perish from the Earth.

We all have our own religions to guide us, but we share a common civic belief, and this is a temple of that shared belief—the belief in our ability and our responsibility to manage our own government as a great people. It is our belief in the proper human scale of things. We have sculpted Mr. Lincoln large in stone, but only so that this solitary man might not be dwarfed by the columns of our institutions, and only so that we might remind ourselves that those who would overwhelm any of our individual voices in matters of our self-governance with their money or with the very power we have granted them, are the opponents of all good things represented in this place.

If our experiment in self-government is to survive in reality as well as in name, we must defend the position of the individual. That is what we march for today, and Mr. Lincoln's enduring optimism for his people encourages us onward. So let us now go to our own Capitol, just up the hill from here.

On the U.S. Capitol Steps

Ms. Haddock's arrival remarks, delivered on the East Steps of the U.S. Capitol to the 2,300 people who walked the final miles with her; Tuesday, February 29, 2000, after welcoming remarks by many Members of Congress and reform leaders:

Thank you. Before the days of the Civil Rights Movement, a senator might have said that the millions of oppressed people were happy in their condition. But now, after so much history, after so much painful growth, we see the insensitivity and ignorance of such a statement. How did anyone dare think that the oppressed and abused were happy in their condition?

Before the rise of the Environmental Movement, a senator might have looked upon a polluted Hudson River and said that the old river is simply paying the inevitable price for progress. But now, after so much sickness endured, so much new understanding gained of our fragile network of life, and after so much effort by so many, we see the insensitivity and ignorance of such a statement. How did anyone dare think that our beautiful land stretches itself out for companies to ravage for their profit and our misery?

Before the Campaign Finance Reform Movement, which grows every day now with such power that it shakes the political parties to their foundations, a senator might have advised his fellow member to not worry about voting down campaign reforms, because the people don't care. That is, in fact, what Senators McConnell and Lott did say—and that is what precipitated my walk. I have come to tell them that they are wildly mistaken, and I am glad to have you along to add your voices to mine.

This morning we began our walk among the graves of Arlington so that those spirits, some of whom may be old friends, might join us today and that we might ask of them now: Did you, brave spirits, give your lives for a government where we might stand together as free and equal citizens, or did you give your lives so that laws might be sold to the highest bidder, turning this temple of our Fair Republic into a bawdy house where anything and everything is done for a price? We hear your answers in the wind.

What might we call the selling of our government from under us? What might we call a change of government—from a government of, by and for the people, to a government by and for the wealthy elite? I will not call such a change of government a treason, but those more courageous shadows standing among us, whose blood runs through our flag and our history, and whose accomplishments are more solid beneath us than these stone steps, why they might use such a word in angry whispers that trace through the polluted corridors of this once great Capitol and slip despairingly through the files of correspondence and receipts in this city of corruption.

Senators, we speak for these spirits and for ourselves: No, you may not have our democratic republic to sell. What our family members died for, we do not forget. They died for our freedom and equality, not for a government of the rich alone.

Along my three thousand miles through the heart of America, which I made to disprove your lie, did I meet anyone who thought that their voice as an equal citizen now counts for much in the corrupt halls of Washington? No, I did not. Did I meet anyone who felt anger or pain over this? I did indeed, and I watched them shake with rage sometimes when they spoke, and I saw tears well up in their eyes.

The people I met along my way have given me messages to deliver here. The messages are many, written with old and young hands of every color, and yet the messages are the same. They are this: Shame on you Mitch McConnell and those who raise untold millions of dollars in exchange for public policy. Shame on you, Senators and Congressmen, who have turned this headquarters of a great and self-governing people into a bawdy house.

The time for this shame is ending. The American people see it and have decided against it. Our brooms are ballots, and we come a-sweeping. We will visit every state where anti-reform Senators are up for reelection and bring with us the long lists of your corruptions, and I will be with them. You will try to buy your way out if it with expensive advertisements. But we will take such spending as further proof of your corruption, for Americans pay ten dollars in extra taxes for each dollar you receive for your campaigns from special interests.

While we are here to speak frankly to our representatives, let us also speak frankly to ourselves: Along my walk I have seen an America that is losing the time and the energy for self-governance. The problems we see in Washington are problems that have been sucked into a vacuum of our own making. It is not enough for us to elect someone, give them a slim list of ideas and send them off to represent us. If we do not keep these boys and girls busy they will always get into trouble. We must energize our communities to better see our problems, better plan their happy futures, and these plans must form the basis of our instructions to our elected representatives. This is the responsibility of every adult American, from native to newcomer, and from young worker to the long retired. If we are hypnotized by television and overwrought by life on a corporate-consumer treadmill, let us snap out of it and regain our lives as a free, calm, fearlessly outspoken people who have time for each other and our communities. Let us pass election reforms and anti-corruption measures in our towns and cities and states, winning the reform wars where they are winnable, changing the national weather on this subject until the winds blow even through these old columns.

Now, Senators, back to you. If I have offended you speaking this way on your front steps, that is quite as it should be; you have offended America and you have dishonored the best things it stands for. Take your wounded pride, get off your backs and onto your feet, and go across the street to clean your rooms.

You have somewhere on your desks, under the love letters from your greedy friends and co-conspirators against representative democracy, a modest bill against soft money. Pass it. Then show that you are clever lads by devising new ways for a great people to talk to one another again without the necessity of great wealth. If you cannot do that, then get out of the way—go home to some other corruption, less harmful to a great nation. We have millions of people more worthy of these fine offices.

So here we are, Senators, at your doorstep: We the people. How did you dare think we do not care about our country? How did you dare think that we would not come here to these steps to denounce your corruptions in the name of all who have given their lives to our country's defense and improvement? How did you dare think we were so unpatriotic to have forgotten all those rows upon rows of graves that mark how much we, as a people, care for our freedom and our equality?

The People of our nation do care. They have told me. They laugh with disgust about you on the beaches of California. They shake their heads about you in the native village of Hashan Kehk in Arizona. In Toyah, Texas, they pray for deliverance from your corruption. In Little Rock, they understand in anger how you undermine their best dreams for our society. And in Memphis and in Louisville and in Chillocothe and Clarksburg, through Pennsylvania and Maryland and into this city today, the people see you for what you have become and they are prepared to see you another way: boarding the trains at the great train station down the street. They are ready for real leaders, unselfish and principled leaders who will prove their worth by voting for meaningful campaign finance reform this year.

The time has come, Senators, for reform or for some new Senators. Tell us which it will be, and then we will go vote.

In the name of the people who have sent me along to you, and in the name of the generations before who have sacrificed so much for the sanctity of our free institutions and who stand with us in spirit today, I make this demand.

Note: Nearly two years elapsed before the passage of the reform bill. During this time, Ms. Haddock covered the nation with her speeches and rallies. At critical moments she returned to the Capitol for direct action, including a four-day, 24-hour walking fast around the Capitol Building in freezing weather.

Taxation Without Representation

Ms. Haddock's spoke to a community audience in Harrisburg, Pennsylvania on March 13, 2000 — she was in town to support a reform bill in the state legislature. Though she was ready to go back to New Hampshire for a rest, she agreed to this important detour.

Friends, we taxpayers find ourselves shouldering the burdens of the nation while wealthy special interests are able to avoid paying taxes, shifting their share, plus many of the costs of their own businesses, including environmental cleanup, onto working people. This goes quite beyond taxation without representation, for the problem is not so much that our interests are being neglected, but that our interests are being squarely attacked and damaged while we subsidize our attackers. It is un-American in all its aspects.

The dark heart of this treachery is the current campaign finance system, where special interests simply buy public policies aimed against us with their campaign donations. This is not the normal condition of our political history. This is not inevitable. It is now being practiced on an open, brazen, and massive scale, and it is cancerous to the underpinnings of a fair, free, and civil society.

One way or another, of course, we publicly finance our elections. Under the present system it is a fact that, for every dollar commercial interests invest in political campaigns, they receive in excess of ten dollars, provided by taxpayers, in the form of special tax breaks and subsidies. That clearly is a public funding system—just not a good one from the taxpayers' point of view. There is nothing to say they will not take all of our tax money someday, as they settle in to their power.

If we instead will directly fund our political campaigns, on the theory that the citizens need information about the candidates, then we can save nine out of those ten tax dollars, for we will not have to provide all the tax loopholes and special benefits that commercial campaign contributors now demanded from lawmakers in exchange for their donations to candidates.

It might occur to you that another approach would be to find a new class of candidates who cannot be bought. We must, however, understand that the very best of us are soon co-opted and then corrupted by the horrible expenses of political campaigning. We must stop putting good people in ethically corrosive environments until they become, like Senators Santorum and Specter—financial monsters who rail against reform and care only for the next grotesque donation of blood money to keep themselves half-alive. They do not represent their people anymore.

We have allowed this horror to happen. It is up to us, you and me—for that is what we mean by democracy—to design elective systems that will bring out the best in our people. It doesn't matter if our systems are a little expensive. There is no reason why we should pay more for our roadways and our parks than for the institutions that provide us fair representation, freedom and equality.

Those are my thoughts on public funding, which I hope, if you do not agree with, you will at least think about. Now let us briefly consider soft money donations. Friends, how would you feel if you were involved in a lawsuit and you found that the other side was making big financial contributions to the judge just before the ruling?

How would you feel if you were a baseball player in the World Series, and you found that the other team was making big financial contributions to the umpires?

How would you feel if you were a citizen in a free democracy and you found that the person elected to represent your interests was receiving huge financial contributions from people outside your district whose interests were completely opposed to yours and those of your community?

Is there a fundamental difference between these situations? I don't think there is.

And now, would it matter if the contributions to the judge were not made directly, but were instead made to the judge's family foundation and passed back to the judge?

Would it matter if the political contributions were made to the elected official's party, and then passed back to the official?

Well, in the last example, those unregulated, or soft money political contributions tend to be in very high amounts— quite beyond the reasonable limits imposed on donations made directly to candidates. Even a child can see that this back door approach is wrong and unfair. And there is no reason, so long as the Supreme Court says that contribution limits are legal, why such deceptive practices should be allowed under the law.

That is the clear logic of it, and here are the feelings I carry to this issue in my heart. I have lived long enough to see great sacrifices made by a great many people to preserve our freedoms in a nation of equal citizens. People who try with their wealth to steal our representatives from us are attempting to steal our freedom. For this we have gone to war and have sacrificed the lives of our children. Do they think we will permit it now for some reason? We will not.

Maintaining our freedom is constant work, and it is our business here today. Some, like Senators Santorum and Specter, will stand in our way. But they stand against our history as an equal and free people, and they stand against the tide of this reform.

In this reform battle, you and I fight for the position of the individual, for ourselves, for our friends, family and neighbors, and we fight so that those who gave their lives to the defense of our equality and freedom did not do so in vain.

I support the important work you are doing here. You are patriots to the cause of the American experiment in self-government, and I urge your fellow citizens to join you.

Note: Associated Press story by George Strawley, 3/16/2000: DATELINE: HARRISBURG, Pa.... Doris Haddock, a longtime activist nicknamed "Granny D" who trekked from Los Angeles to Washington to show that everyday people were interested in changing how political campaigns are funded, put in an appearance Monday on behalf of the bill. And on Tuesday, the House reversed an earlier vote and approved the bill to allow taxpayers to "check off" their approval of publicly funded campaigns for governor and lieutenant governor... Wearing a straw hat decorated with a turkey feather and a vest adorned with pro-reform buttons, the 5-foot Dublin, N.H., woman climbed the Capitol steps with legislators and addressed television cameras inside the building. Longtime advocate Sen. Allen G. Kukovich, D-Westmoreland, said it was the most attention he has seen given to a reform-related event in years. The proposal approved Tuesday calls for a system of public financing.

Independence Hall

Ms. Haddock collected enough keys-to-the-city from mayors across the nation to fashion an impressive wind chime — she took it down, however, as it just clunked unmusically in the wind. Here are her remarks in Philadelphia at one such key ceremony, March 21, 2000:

Thank you very much. The citizens of Philadelphia have the right to determine what their common needs may be, and they have the right to use their common resources to address those needs, as they together and fairly decide. It is a process we call self-governance, and it is the essential activity upon which all our freedoms depend. If others decide what is important for us, if others decide what is to be done with our wealth-in-common, then the citizens are not free, and those who gave life and limb to protect that freedom are dishonored.

If citizens organize to remove big money special interests from their municipal elections, they are acting to preserve their rightful freedoms. They are acting to defend a system of self-governance that thousands of your Philadelphians have died to defend around the world.

If you think the citizens do not have the right to spend their own tax money to assure clean government, your argument is bizarre and it stands against the fact that the most expensive and wasteful kind of government is government based on the solicitation of great wealth for political campaigns, and the corrupt payback expected by the wealthy. The payback comes in the form of special treatment at the taxpayers' expense. Careful research regarding large political donations by commercial interests shows a ten to one return on the donor's dollars—which is paid by taxpayers. So we are better off by far, saving nine of the ten dollars, if we pay the campaign costs directly, cutting out the participation of special interests.

The money you have wasted on city campaigns, in the face of so many unmet human needs in this city of love, is a crime against the hearts of your people.

I hope you all are mature enough and practical enough to move into a more sensible future—one that moves everyone out of the way who stands between the people and their rights of collective decision-making.

To the Philadelphians who dare oppose huge special interests and who have committed themselves to the work of restoring the participation of the people, I congratulate and encourage you. To other Philadelphians who have considered coming to stand with these people, I urge you to take the next step today and join them in this great work. For, in this generation, our democracy and our planet are at stake in history's largest power struggle, and the battles are local. We need good people to join our ranks, and we can promise you only a great battle. Thank you very much for this honor.

Good to be Home

At a welcome home event in Peterborough on Saturday, April 1, 2000:

Thank you. It is good to be home. My long walk took me through so many landscapes and communities that I often could not imagine that the parade of them would ever end.

America is a very large place indeed, and yet it is a small town. We are a close people—closer in temperament and bound by a deeper friendship than we give ourselves credit for. We love being Americans more than we love being of any town or city or state. We have not only our history in common, but our dreams. And our idea that we can all be free, that we can treat each other fairly with justice under the law, and that we might all find some happiness and prosperity together, while it is not unique to America, is certainly not the common condition or attitude of the world.

So I come home full of new admiration for our American family.

I am thankful for the encouragement of my townspeople and family, who supported the idea of my walk without regard to my age and who allowed me to take my own risks. Some of you went to great trouble to come walk with me, which was such a joy.

I have not come home to die. I have come home to live robustly, pursuing my civic interests and my dream of a democratic republic where ideas, work and honorable service are the currencies of exchange, and where bribery is shamed into near-extinction.

Wherever I went across America, people were so glad to meet someone who just simply cared. They were happy to meet someone who listened and who had something to say, but who was not running for something or trying to get some personal advantage from it.

If any of you would like to ever run for office, I will tell you that if you will cast self-interest into oblivion—to use a phrase from our original Iroquois Constitution—people will follow you anywhere. What they are tired of, in all departments of life, is selfishness. There is no reason why an old lady walking down the road should have been so well received, except for the fact that it had been a long time since any of these people could go meet someone who was not a callow, self-promoting, snakeoil-selling political promoter. They wanted to shake my hand and wish me well, not because they thought I was something special, but because I was someone like them. Americans are not selfish. They are kind and full of a great spirit. They want and they merit leaders who will cast self-interest into oblivion.

We Americans are idealists, but we are practical. We are not waiting for Gandhi to come walking down the path to represent us with perfect, unselfish honor. We will make the best of who we have, as we always do. We have no perfect neighbors, no perfect family members, no perfection in ourselves, and we mustn't expect it in our leaders or our candidates. Yes, we must accept the fact that they do not suffer from low self-esteem. We must take them on as a project—like a woman takes on a man with potential—and we must make something of them, especially if they will at least express their willingness to learn and to improve, and to deepen and widen their political souls.

But for now, I am just glad to be home. Thank you all very much.

Her additional remarks in the Dublin Town Hall, up the hill from Peterborough and walking distance from her home in the woods:

Thank you. Coming back home after my long journey fills me with thankfulness. I am thankful for the love you have extended to me during my time away. No distance, it seems, is so far that the heartstrings of home cannot find us and comfort us. Your willingness to encourage me, write me, come walk with me, and to come here today and welcome me back into the bosom of our town is an act of love that touches me deeply.

I am thankful to my family members who made my adventure possible in so many ways. I especially thank my son, Jim, who did not dismiss my idea as some further sign of my aging, and who in fact set out to make my dream a possible one. All along, he provided, like Dorothy's ruby red shoes, my magic way home if things should have gotten too hard. But, thanks to him, they never did.

I am thankful to the memory of my husband and my friends, whose spirits and memories urged me on and who now stand among you to celebrate me home. I am thankful for so many kind Americans and visitors from other nations whom I met along the way and who sheltered and fed me and shared their lives with me. You simply cannot imagine the moral richness of this land. We are blessed in many ways, but mostly with the company of our fellow Americans.

I am thankful to our God, who let a million sleepy-eyed drivers see my small frame on the margins of dawn roads and Who sent me good weather or at least tolerable weather each day. He never sent me anything He had not prepared me for as a woman of New Hampshire—even the snow.

Yes, I am indeed thankful to New England, for it raises its children with business-like severity so we might be a little tougher and more courageous, and so we might become, after long years here, great connoisseurs of beauty in everything.

My travels for my political issue are not over, but I soak in this homecoming and I delight in this exchange of our neighborly love and friendship.

We Are Problem-Solvers

Ms. Haddock's remarks to the New Hampshire House, in their chamber, April 18, 2000:

Thank you very much. I want to honor the pragmatists in this room. It is easier to be a political idealist, and to refuse to budge because you know you are right… Idealism always sounds better than it actually works out. Pragmatism, if it is based on love and mutual respect, usually takes us to the happier place.

Just sitting there and being idealistic requires no further work. In politics, it is the best excuse for laziness and the easiest road to finding useful enemies, against which you can raise money and votes from the similarly narrow-minded.

It takes more maturity to be pragmatic. In fact, I believe the very definition of maturity is the ability to accept and even embrace a lesser evil so that life can move forward.

Now, this principle could apply to any of our most difficult political issues today, for many people are willing to let a great deal of harm go forward so that they can defend the absolute rightness of their opinions—opinions that are usually better argued in a holy place than in a public place.

But I would like to apply the principle today to the public financing of our elections.

I know it rubs many people the wrong way. But let's be practical for a moment and consider our circumstances. Yes, we all believe in free speech. As a people, it is our most cherished freedom. That does not mean that we tolerate speech that causes a crowd to panic or speech that is wrongly and purposefully damaging to a person's reputation. We have a pragmatic approach.

Public financing, some say, might damage free speech in elections. If we are pragmatic, we can prevent that from happening. We can have voluntary programs that do not compel people to participate, for example. If the program allows more candidates to participate and to get their ideas out to the public, that is a net gain for political speech and worth the work of developing a program that suits our main concerns. In the states and cities that now have public financing as an option, the number of candidates is increasing. As they will not have to be on a fundraising treadmill after they are elected, they will be freer to speak their own mind, and they will have more time so that their constituents can speak freely to them. Those are huge net gains for free speech in a democratic republic.

But some people may oppose it because public dollars are being used to support political positions they might not agree with. This is also true, of course, when a town has a speakers' stage built for the candidate forum in the park, or when a ballot is printed up, or when an incumbent is allowed to send newsletters to constituents, and on and on. Just as our streets are not built to bestow a benefit on any one person who might happen to be using them, so a system of information about candidates is there to serve the larger goal of a well-informed electorate. Surely we can be pragmatic about this. The candidate's picnic in the park, sponsored by the town, can be our mental model, though we use the more modern public address systems now provided by television, radio, newspapers and the Internet.

Now. Let's honestly look at how our fellow citizens now regard government and political leaders. To a certain extent, we always hold our government and our politicians at a disdainful distance. That may be part of our defense mechanism that allows us to maintain our personal freedom and our objectivity as voters. But if it goes too far—if too many people are up in the canyons with their ammunition and their direct satellite links to God or Rush Limbaugh, then we risk losing those freedoms by backing away too completely from the fact that we are supposed to be a self-governing people who are, ourselves, the American government. Some pragmatic space in the middle is necessary. How do we make more of our people feel connected to the processes of self-government? Can public funding of elections be a tool for that necessary task? Well, the pragmatist inside you is saying, "possibly so," and that it the right answer.

The day may come again when ordinary people can afford to advertise their campaigns without spending a fortune, and the day may come when broadcasters and newspapers do a better job of telling us all about the people running for office. In the meantime, we pragmatists are confronted by the fact that it is too expensive for most people to proceed upward as our community leaders. They must sell their souls or spend their children's inheritances, and neither is right. If we want freethinking and accessible public servants, we know that we must take all this money out of the way. It stands between us and our representation.

I congratulate you on your practical approach. More and more states and cities are solving this problem by creating public financing systems that address most people's concerns.

As New Hampshire people, we have a tradition of free speech in our town halls and in these rooms. Let us be among those states that look to the future with pragmatism and with a love for the very idea of political speech unfettered by financial strings. Thank you very much.

We Are Peaceably Assembled

After a short rest at her home, Doris Haddock was again on the move: On Good Friday, April 21, 2000, with her lawyer's phone number inked on her palm, she entered the U.S. Capitol Rotunda as part of a protest that linked campaign finance reform with the environmental movement.

She was joined by 29 distinguished authors and leaders of the American Environmental Movement, including Bill McKibben, John Moyers, John Passacantando (Greenpeace), and the leaders of the campaign finance reform movement.

The protest involved standing beside each other in the Rotunda as Ms. Haddock read from the Declaration of Independence. Her statement to the group before they entered:

We are here to celebrate Earth Day by asserting our roles as a free and self-governing people. Americans by an overwhelming majority want their elected leaders to protect our environment. We have elected our representatives to do this difficult work. We are here to make their work easier, by removing the difficult task they all face in regard to the financing of their next elections. We do not want them to spend their days and nights collecting money from people who have in mind the purchase of public policy.

If there are some here who do not want to be freed to do the people's business, then I ask them to look into their hearts on this Earth Day and reconsider their positions. I ask them to join the majority of Americans who want serious campaign reform.

Some may be opposed to radical changes such as the public financing of our election campaigns. But we already publicly finance these campaigns. We pay with tax loopholes traded for contributions, and, in this way, we pay ten dollars for every campaign dollar donated.

Cannot Congress do better for the taxpayers than that?

Can we cut out the middlemen and save those nine lost dollars? Of course we can. We can declare independence from the special interests that now hold our system under chains of corrupt obligation. We are here to say we, as a people, know how to declare our independence. Let us go inside and again do so.

Her remarks inside the Capitol Rotunda, as tourists applauded:

Friends, the First Amendment to the Constitution says that Congress shall make no law abridging the freedom of speech, or of the press, or the right of the people peaceably to assemble and to petition the Government for a redress of grievances.

We are peaceably assembled here, in this our hall, to freely speak, to petition our Government. Our grievance is that we no longer have proper representation. Our elected leaders are consumed by the need to raise election funds from special interests, and they no longer are able to represent the needs of the people or of our ravaged Earth.

We must declare our independence from the corrupting bonds of big money in our election campaigns by reforming our campaign finance system. We must alter our government. As a people, we know how to declare our independence and authorize alterations of our government. Here is how we did so in Congress, July 4, 1776:

"We hold these truths to be self-evident, that all men are created equal, that they are endowed by their Creator with certain unalienable Rights, that among these are Life, Liberty and the pursuit of Happiness. —That to secure these rights, Governments are instituted among Men, deriving their just powers from the consent of the governed..."

While she was reading from the Declaration of Independence, Ms. Haddock was arrested and manacled by Capitol Police. Tourists seemed shocked. She was taken to jail with 29 supporters.

Her later court pleading:

Your Honor, the old woman who stands before you was arrested for reading the Declaration of Independence in America's Capitol Building. I did not raise my voice to do so and I blocked no hall.

The First Amendment to the Constitution, Your Honor, says that Congress shall make no law abridging the freedom of speech, or of the press; or the right of the people peaceably to assemble, and to petition the Government for a redress of grievances, so I cannot imagine what legitimate law I could have broken. We peaceably assembled there, Your Honor, careful to not offend the rights of any other citizen nor interrupt the peaceful enjoyment of their day. The people we met were supportive of what we were saying and I think they—especially the children— were shocked that we would be arrested for such a thoroughly wholesome American activity as respectfully voicing our opinion in our own hall. Any American standing there would have been shocked. For we were a most peaceable assembly, until Trent Lott's and Mitch McConnell's police came in with their bullhorns and their shackles to arrest us. One of us, who is here today, was injured and required a number of stitches to his head after he fell and could not break his own fall. He was detained for over four hours without medical care. I am glad we were only reading from the Declaration of Independence—I shudder to think what might have happened had we read from the Bill of Rights.

I was reading from the Declaration of Independence to make the point that we must declare our independence from the corrupting bonds of big money in our election campaigns. And so I was reading these very words when my hands were pulled behind me and bound: "We hold these truths to be self-evident, that all men are created equal, that they are endowed by their Creator with certain unalienable Rights, that among these are Life, Liberty and the pursuit of Happiness. —That to secure these rights, Governments are instituted among Men, deriving their just powers from the consent of the governed, —That whenever any form of Government becomes destructive of these ends, it is the Right of the People to alter or to abolish it."

Your Honor, we would never seek to abolish our dear United States. But alter it? Yes. It is our constant intention that it should be a government of, by and for the people, not the special interests, so that people may use this government in service to each other's needs and to protect the condition of our Earth.

Your Honor, it is now your turn to be a part of this arrest. If your concern is that we might have interfered with the visitor's right to a meaningful tour of their Capitol, I tell you that we helped them have a more meaningful one. If your concern is that we might have been blocking the halls of our government, let me assure you that we stood to one side of the Rotunda where we would not be in anyone's way. But I inform you that the halls are indeed blocked over there.

They are blocked by the shameless sale of public policy to campaign contributors, which bars the doors and the halls to the people's legitimate needs and the flow of proper representation. We Americans must put an end to it in any peaceful way that we can. Yes, we can speak when we vote, and we do. But we must also give our best effort to encourage the repair of a very broken system. We must do both.

And the courts and prosecutors in government have a role, too. If Attorney General Reno would properly enforce the federal bribery statute, we would see lobbyists and elected officials dragged from the Capitol Building and the White House, their wrists tied, not ours. I would be home in New Hampshire, happily applauding the television news as my government cleaned its own house.

In my 90 years, this is the first time I have been arrested. I risk my good name—for I do indeed care what my neighbors think about me. But, Your Honor, some of us do not have much power, except to put our bodies in the way of an injustice—to picket, to walk, or to just stand in the way. It will not change the world overnight, but it is all we can do.

So I am here today while others block the halls with their corruption. Twenty-five million dollars are changing hands this very evening at a fundraiser down the street. It is the corrupt sale of public policy, and everyone knows it. I would refer those officials and those lobbyists, Your Honor, to Mr. Bob Dylan's advice when he wrote: "Come senators, congressmen, please heed the call. Don't stand in the doorway, don't block up the hall."

Your Honor, the song was a few years early, but the time has now come for change. The times are changing because they must. And they will sweep away the old politician—the self-serving, the self-absorbed, the corrupt. The time of that leader is rapidly fading. We have come through a brief time when we have allowed ourselves to be entertained by corrupt and hapless leaders because they offer so little else, and because, as citizens, we have been priced out of participation and can only try to get some enjoyment out of their follies. But the Earth itself can no longer afford them. We owe this change to our children and our grandchildren and our great grandchildren. We need have no fear that a self-governing people can creatively and effectively address their needs as a nation and a world if the corrupt and greedy are out of their way, and ethical leadership is given the helm.

Your Honor, to the business at hand: the old woman who stands before you was arrested for reading the Declaration of Independence in America's Capitol Building. I did not raise my voice to do so and I blocked no hall. But if it is a crime to read the Declaration of Independence in our great hall, then I am guilty.

Court pleading of Jim Haddock, her son:

Your Honor, I am here because my mother, who is ninety, and who has stood up for fairness and justice all her life, is determined to spend the last years of her life working for the reform of our corrupt campaign finance system.

When she told me that she wanted to walk across the United States to bring attention to this issue, which was then not a high profile issue, I reminded myself that she is no less a fighter at 90 than she was as a fifty year-old when she and my father traveled to Alaska to stop the destruction of a fishing village by the atmospheric testing of hydrogen bombs. She stopped six hydrogen bombs, so I didn't expect that I could stop her from walking. I did what I could to support her walk across the country. It has been the greatest experience of my life, as it has been for many, many people.

I say that because I have met so many wonderful people across the nation, and I have learned what a caring and patriotic people Americans are. They despair of their democracy now, as it seems so lost to the corruption of the large campaign donors.

Americans responded with instant love and attachment to my mother. I have now an uncountable number of unofficial brothers and sisters across America, and I feel very enriched indeed by the friendship of these special people.

I cannot tell you how many people of very modest circumstance entrusted my mother with their message to Washington. They want an ethical democracy that looks to the needs of the people and the environment, to justice and fairness. They speak eloquently and from the deepest parts of their hearts. They have given sons and brothers to the defense of a democracy that they insist remain a government of people, for people.

So I was honored to stand silently near my mother as she read from the Declaration of Independence in the Capitol building. She was sent there by America itself, and I am witness to those thousands of conversations and teary-eyed handshakes and hugs.

Those people feel they no longer have representation in their government, so they sent Doris to speak for them. If you lock her up for stating the truth in a hall that is by the Constitution a protected place for a citizen to freely speak, the people will send another. If you lock me up for standing silently in my own Capitol, then I would rather be there anyway. Thank you.

Judge Hamilton's sentencing remarks:

"As you know, the strength of our great country lies in its Constitution and her laws and in her courts. But more fundamentally, the strength of our great country lies in the resolve of her citizens to stand up for what is right when the masses are silent. And, unfortunately, sometimes it becomes the lot of the few, sometimes like yourselves, to stand up for what's right when the masses are silent, because not always does the law move so fast and so judiciously as to always be right. But given the resolve of the citizens of this great country, in time, however, slowly, the law will catch up eventually. So it becomes my lot to apply the law as it is at this time—perhaps not as it should be, but as it is. With every confidence that, to the extent that it is lacking in righteousness, it will reach that point eventually given the resolve of her citizens to make it right." (He sentenced them to a few dollars and time already served—the better part of one day in jail—and released them. He asked to meet with them in his chambers. He shook Jim's hand and gave Ms. Haddock a hug.)

Note: an email: "I have just read this account. I am a French citizen, but I was moved. It feels like a Capra movie. That is the America that the world wants to love, the America we French went bankrupt helping win the War of Independence. Years ago, when I was serving my 12-month tour as a conscript in the French army, I was posted in a mid-18th Century building that once housed the Ministry of the Navy. It is on Rue de l'Independance Americaine - American Independence Street - right across the street from the great Palace of Versailles. History has its addresses, and sooner or later they will whisper in your ear. God bless Doris Haddock and the true ideals of America. – Philippe Dambournet

A More Affordable System

Delivered on the Connecticut State Capitol steps, Thursday, April 27, 2000:

Thank you. I am speaking to you here present, friends, as witnesses only, as my remarks are directed to Governor Rowland.

Dear Governor Rowland: You are in an awkward position, but that is the very position where leadership shows itself and history is made. You are faced with the decision to sign or veto an historic bill that promises to place Connecticut in the forefront of representative government reform, yet it is a bill opposed by many in your own party.

This bill, which provides for the public financing of candidates who choose to say "no" to all special interest campaign donations, comes at a time when citizens believe that their voices in government are drowned out by floods of special interest money, and they are right. No one seriously argues that point anymore. The flood is too great, and the preoccupation of candidates and officials with fundraising nears its completion, fully eclipsing the interests of everyday constituents.

So here is a bill, finally, that provides a dramatic and fundamental correction to the system, yet it is unpopular with your party, and for several reasons. Let us look at these reasons.

First, it is argued that the taxpayers' money should not go to candidates. After all, many of the candidates are people we could never vote for, so why would we want to support their campaigns with our tax dollars? Of course, we support all kinds of people we do not approve of with our tax dollars, starting with our prison budgets. We do not support them; we support a system that provides for a functioning society. Our tax dollars print the names of our political foes on our ballots. Our tax dollars provide for the primary elections of parties we disagree with. We do all of this in the name of democracy. It is an expensive affair. It is the infrastructure of our decision-making system.

It is like financing our road repairs. Our tax dollars cannot serve our own interests unless they serve the interests of all. So we must not worry that some of our tax dollars go to help candidates with whom we do not agree. We support them with our tax dollars after they are elected, and we can do so in the election process as well—especially if it means taking the special interests out of the driver's seat.

Governor Rowland, you must understand that financing our elections by its very nature means financing the good candidates and bad, providing the public with as much information as possible about each candidate and their views, so that we can make a well-informed decision. The expense of getting this information to us is a proper public purpose.

Secondly, I would make the point, Governor, that public interest groups on the left and right, from the Cato Institute to Common Cause, agree that, for every dollar given to a candidate by a special interest group, over ten dollars in special tax breaks are given in return. This is nothing less than full public financing, but it is a poor system of public financing. By instead directly providing for the expense of campaigns, we can eliminate nine of the ten dollars paid by taxpayers—now paid in the form of tax loopholes for special interests.

Governor, if you are a true conservative, will you not trade a corrupt system of public financing for a clean one that costs the taxpayers one-tenth as much? Is that not the essence of smaller, more efficient government?

Governor, surely you see that the arguments that the taxpayers should not fund the vital business of free elections is not a good argument. Surely you can see that it is put forward by those who now own the system by virtue of the dark contributions they make and take.

But how can you do the right thing and not alienate many members of your party?

Can they not be persuaded to conduct a bold experiment in this time when citizens are disengaging from civil life and from voting? Can a leader bring them around to break some eggs and make something new and exciting in the face of this despair and apathy? That is the essence of enterprise government, is it not?

And can your party members put on their most practical hats and realize that, henceforth, if this bill is vetoed, all future scandals and all future news of special interest influence will fall at the feet of this governor and this party? Is it not best to let the experiment run and let it fail of its own devices, if it is flawed?

That is the practical approach. There is no advantage to being the man who stopped reform in a day when reform's time is upon us. That would typically mark the end of a career, not a beginning.

Finally Governor, let me address you as the leader of this state's police and military powers. It is you who must call men and women to fatal duty to defend our system of government. Would you send the Connecticut Guard off bravely to defend a system of corrupt special interest influence? To do so would tear at your heart, I believe, and I would rather you felt joy and patriotism in your leadership.

To honor these people and those who have given their lives in service, will you agree that the present system of organized corruption can and ought to be set aside for this experiment, born of a love of democracy and a trust in the people's good sense?

Governor Rowland, on behalf of my own generation, most of whom are gone, many of whom have served this country and held high the idea that we are a free and equal people, I ask you with all my heart to give this important American reform its day, its chance to prove itself.

Governor Rowland, on behalf of my great grandchildren, for whom I hope to leave a better democracy, I beg you to do the brave and right thing, as your heart may see it. Thank you.

Note: as Ms. Haddock predicted, a major scandal hit Connecticut in the wake of the governor's failure to sign the bill. It was left to the next Republican governor to sign public campaign financing into law.

The Seven-Layer Cake

Ms. Haddock delivered variations on this speech at a number of schools, mainly in New England. This is the original version, delivered at Franklin Pierce College (now University) in the spring of 2000, following her long walk.

Thank you. I am honored to talk to you all today. I know you have worked hard to get to this moment, and I admire you for that. Life is so much more complex and fast moving than when I went to school, and things were already hard enough then.

I would like to try to give you something of value in my brief remarks today—some piece of useful knowledge that perhaps you weren't taught in school or at home, and something that perhaps is easier to hear from someone who has lived a long time.

It is the simple fact that the world as it was back when I was your age is still with us, and you live in that world, too. And the world of several hundred years ago is also still with us, as is the world of the misty, prehistoric past. We live in a many-layered world, and we are many-layered people. Each era of our history makes a contribution to the way we live our lives, and each era imposes expectations upon us, to this day. Unless we understand that fact, we will have a hard time navigating through the conflicting rules and expectations of life. Think of life as a seven-layer cake and you will do all right.

As an example, I have often overheard young men arguing about how difficult women are to deal with. Are men supposed to open a door for a woman or not, pick up a check at a restaurant or not? Aren't they supposed to now treat a woman as a total equal? They are confused because they don't understand that a person is not one thing. A person is many layered. There is certainly a very old layer where women are princesses and men are princes, and that layer needs to be acknowledged sometimes when the moment is right and a carriage door needs opening. That layer is still with us and it glows under the moon. There is also of course a modern workplace layer, where men and women are colleagues or employees and where they treat each other in a businesslike way, without reference to gender, and where it is a great sin to open a door for someone instead of an opportunity.

And there is, of course, an ancient, biological layer that compels a man to seek a mate and compels a woman to find the resources for a safe and respectable home. This is just one layer, but it must be acknowledged and given its due. And because it is one of the oldest layers, it is the first one you come across as you approach maturity. Though you may not believe me, there is more to life than that layer.

There are also layers, of course, from our own childhood, still intact, still demanding comfort and security and the freedom to creatively explore.

So you must look at a person and see all of this, if you are to see truly—which is to say, wisely.

When we make snap judgments about people based on some single quality, we dehumanize them, and that is a moral crime, indeed. I know you have probably had the experience of being in the same activity with someone and getting to know them, even though you never might have talked to that person on your own. But you became good friends or at least you came to respect each other. That happened because you got down a few layers with that person.

Most people are worth knowing, if you will take time to understand them. Unfamiliarity with other people, ignorance of other people, is what makes war possible and violence possible, and it drives all the social divisions in a school or in a town or a nation or a world. When you understand people well enough, you can't help but love them, even if you hate them, too. If you think those are incompatible emotions, I remind you to think about your relationship with almost any close family member.

Understanding people is loving them. Hatred is what we feel when we do not understand.

Are there some people so over the top with their evil deeds that they do not qualify for this sweeping statement of mine? Some people may take more understanding than we are capable of summoning. We must accept our own limitations.

One of the most difficult and important tasks we have as humans is to regularly, and sometimes without cause, forgive each other and move ahead with our lives together. If one layer of someone's personality flares up and causes us harm, we must try to put it in perspective among all the other layers of that life.

A long marriage requires the willingness to do that, time and again. No relationship can long survive on the basis of what happens in just one or just a few of those layers. Understanding and forgiveness require a view of the whole person.

That whole view can also help us to forgive ourselves. It is a great act of maturity, I think, to not condemn yourself or define yourself by what goes on within just one of these different layers, some of which are intensely biological or set down in cement in early youth. Sometimes we are given to suddenly see with great clarity an amoral and reptilian side of our own motivations, but it is wrong to think we have suddenly discovered our true self. That one layer is no more important than the layers of loving kindness, so long as the negative layer is not given free rein.

Emotional maturity is the ability to stay balanced, not letting any one layer dominate our lives. I do not mean that we should fiercely suppress the darker layers, for to do so causes us to transfer our fear and loathing onto other people. But we must give every layer an opportunity to go for its walk at a time when it will do least harm. And our more positive layers we must of course encourage and put in the company of like souls, for the most important thing we can do for ourselves is to surround ourselves with people we respect for the best reasons—we simply cannot help but become like the people around us.

After acknowledging and coming to understand the layers of life, a gentleman may finally come to know when to open the door for a lady and when to share a check. A woman may come to know that a fellow is more than the polygamous forest creature he sometimes seems—he is also the artist and the prince, the poet and the friend. It is not easy, of course, to negotiate through all the layers lain down through the eons of evolution and the rise of civilization, but if life were easy it would be a bore. Life is that seven-layer cake, and so are our hearts.

It has a layer of icing, by the way; the icing on top is not youth or victory or wealth, but a smiling measure of enlightenment and love that comes as we live with our eyes and our minds and our hearts wide open.

I wish you a happy life. I hope you have a high opinion of yourself, that you understand that you are worth the trouble you have invested in yourself so far, and that you are worth a continuing investment in a future that begins always at this moment.

If you feel alone in the world, or at work, or at school, or at home, here is something you can do: approach someone you thought to be unapproachable and ask them how they are doing today. See what happens. Our alienation, which is the greatest danger to us all, is not so hard to overcome with a little honest curiosity about the situation and the feelings of the person just over there.

I hope you will look to the people around you—in your family and your community, and your nation and the world—with an open heart and an active curiosity, so that you may not condemn but, instead, better understand and befriend them, and so that your friendships may mature into love. Thank you very much.

Like Mr. Roosevelt in Milwaukee

Ms. Haddock speaking before the Alliance for Democracy meeting in Davis, California, July 14, 2000:

Thank you. I should like to make some observations regarding what I see as our immediate opportunities for reform, and I should first like to provide some perspective.

If I need a strong post to tether my line of argument, I would do well to choose that great reform president, Theodore Roosevelt. He was a Republican, of course—a Lincoln Republican. We may have forgotten what that meant, so let me give you an idea of it.

My father was a Lincoln Republican. Abe Lincoln was only twenty-five years gone when my father was born. That means Papa grew up at a dinner table where Lincoln was remembered and honored. You can't imagine how Americans idolized and mourned Lincoln—northern Republicans, anyway. If you are old enough to remember how America felt after John Kennedy's death, or how England felt after Diana's death, you will have but the smallest sense of it.

You must remember that there was no television or radio or Internet to change the subject back then. The much longer attention span meant that there was time for everyone to read all about Lincoln's life, hear countless speeches about him at the civic meetings, countless poems and odes at afternoon teas, and time to form opinions about his best writings and his best decisions. Many writers simply made a career of writing about Lincoln. The words Lincoln left hanging in the air for people to ponder were words of democracy and tolerance, even when spoken on a fresh battlefield: "a government of the people, by the people, and for the people...," and, of course, so immortally from his second inaugural address:

> "With malice toward none; with charity for all; with firmness in the right, as God gives us to see the right, let us strive on to finish the work we are in; to bind up the nation's wounds; to care for him who shall have borne the battle, and for his widow and his orphan...to do all which may achieve and cherish a just and lasting peace among ourselves and with all nations. ...."

Now, who can do better than that? These words were a spiritual meditation for America to think upon for many long years. They certainly helped America inch forward toward democratic and social reforms.

In 1912, when I was two years old, former-president Roosevelt was deciding to get back into the game. He had served out McKinley's term, been elected to one of his own, during which he had pushed through anti-trust, pure food & drug, forest conservation, fair labor standards, and many other reforms. When his second term was over, he went on a long safari and wished Taft, his successor, well. When he returned, however, he found that Taft and the Republican Party had backpedaled on many important reforms at the behest of big industry. The soul of the party was in the balance. It was Main Street, family businesses and farms against the big railroads, oil, steel, and the rest. I think you can guess who won.

For that reason, Roosevelt ran against Taft in 1912. He rounded up enough delegates to take the nomination away from Taft, but backroom backstabbing at the convention gave the nomination to Taft. Roosevelt's supporters walked out, quickly forming a rump group: the Progressive Party.

Roosevelt had to be talked into running as a third party candidate under that banner. He finally agreed to it. The split in the Republican Party assured victory to the Democrat, Woodrow Wilson. That didn't bother Roosevelt too much, for Wilson was also a great reformer. The First World War, however, soon changed everything, dampening much of America's reform energies.

But when Roosevelt was campaigning as the Progressive "Bull Moose" candidate, he traveled to Milwaukee to make a speech to a civic group.

Under the leadership of Governor "Fighting Bob" La Follette, Wisconsin had become America's great incubator of Progressive reform ideas. Brilliant and brave La Follette, with his cabinet of state officials and a kitchen cabinet of professors from the University of Wisconsin at Madison, were the clear-thinkers behind the Progressives. Much of what we like about modern American democracy came out of their collaboration, including the citizens' ballot initiative, the referendum, the direct election of U.S. Senators, a civil service system to replace cronyism, regulation of trusts, consumer health protection, social security and social welfare systems and much more. So Roosevelt was preaching to the choir in Milwaukee that day. He hardly gave his best speech—he rambled and repeated himself, going on for an hour and a half. Now, if a public speaker goes on for an hour and a half, repeating himself and rambling, you might think just he's asking to be shot. In Roosevelt's case, however, he already had been.

A fellow named John Schrank, who had been following Roosevelt around the country waiting for the right moment, pulled out a pistol and shot Roosevelt in the chest as the ex-president was getting out of an automobile and about to walk into the meeting hall. The proper thing to do under the circumstances would be to make one's way to a hospital. Roosevelt, however, insisted that he give the speech first, as the audience was waiting, and he had come a long way himself. It is entertaining to imagine the state of mind of the Secret Service men. There was a stenographer in the meeting room who took down his every word, and I have a copy of it. His speech started thus: "Friends, I shall ask you to be as quiet as possible. I don't know whether you fully understand that I have just been shot; but it takes more than that to kill a Bull Moose. But fortunately, I had my manuscript, so you see I was going to make a long speech, and there is a bullet— there is where the bullet went through—and it probably saved me from it going into my heart. The bullet is in me now, so that I cannot make a very long speech, but I will try my best."

From time to time during that speech, particularly when he began to ramble and drift and look unsure on his feet, there would be a scurry of officials behind the rostrum, but Roosevelt would wave them off. Half way through the speech he said:

"I know these doctors, when they get hold of me, will never let me go back, and there are just a few more things that I want to say to you."

He spoke for another forty-five minutes, laying hard into Mr. Wilson for posing as a reformer but doing nothing to repeal the charters of the most abusive corporations. Many of them were based in New Jersey, where Wilson was governor.

Near the end, just before he finally allowed them to help him out to an ambulance, he clearly described the great divide that had come upon the Republican Party. He said:

"When the... bosses in control of the Republican party, the Barneses and Penroses, last June stole the nomination and wrecked the Republican party for good and all—I want to point out to you that nominally they stole that nomination from me, but it was really from you. They did not like me, and the longer they live the less cause they will have to like me. But while they don't like me, they dread you. You are the people that they dread. They dread the people themselves, and those bosses and the big special interests behind them made up their mind that they would rather see the Republican Party wrecked than see it come under the control of the people themselves."

The Republican Party had set a course in favor of bigger business, leaving the main street merchant and the farmer behind, where they would occasionally pop up in a populist third party.

Mr. Roosevelt lost the election, but history went his way. America got the 40-hour work week, an end to child labor, a right to organize unions, food and drug safety laws, civil service, securities laws, anti-trust laws, regulation of railroads and utilities, conservation of forests, social security and much more. The federal government had been marshaled for the purposes and goals of the Progressives, and that would continue right up until the Reagan presidency.

At its heart, populism is the uprising of we the people against the wealthy elite. It can go in the direction of better government and more democracy, or it can go toward scapegoatism, demagoguery and dictatorship. All those elements are always visible in America's reform community, and are always cause for vigilance and caution.

The Progressive Movement certainly had a fine fist-waver in the form of Teddy Roosevelt, and he was too much dedicated to the causes of fairness and legality—at least in his domestic policies, not his foreign adventures—to have ever considered becoming a dictator. Fairness—the Square Deal—was the tenor of Roosevelt and the Progressive movement generally.

The rest of the world was not as fortunate, as strongmen and their cruelties began to rise up in Europe and elsewhere, during and after the First World War. We watched it happen, my generation, with such broken hearts!

The branches of reform in America today agree that an oversized monster is stalking the land and ruining our lives. But if you set the reformers down with police sketch artists and ask them to describe the giant, half will describe transnational corporations, and the other half will describe government itself— these sad people have stockpiled guns and ammunition in the childish idea that they could successfully oppose today's military and intelligence capabilities.

These dears have been subjected to a constant demonization of their own government. Just as they have been robbed by the chess masters of our new Gilded Age of their local stores and factories and Main Street communities, they have also now been robbed of their country itself. For a country at its core is a community of positively cooperating people, not just a flag, not just a love of militarism or a particular race or religion, not just the country's initials shouted with raised fists. As men and women without a country or an economic future, they pour their anger into every political crack, until democracy itself is poisoned and frail.

The two groups are on a collision course. It might however be possible for them to agree on a common enemy: the control and expansion of government as a direct result of corporate campaign donations. If they can join hands just long enough to force corporate money out of politics, they will at least have a democracy to fight over. For that reason I spoke at the Reform Party's convention, but my one voice will not be enough. We need leadership like the kind that stood and delivered, no matter the cost, with the force and endurance, like Mr. Roosevelt in Milwaukee.

As today's Progressives, we are the remnant of those Lincoln Republicans and Teddy Roosevelt Bull Moose Republicans who saw government as our common tool of community action. Our very conservative friends are the remnant of the Taft Republicans, who have been fed hallucinogens by TV blondes working for billionaires—fed to fear only the expansion of government and fattened for slaughter by tax laws and corporations.

The thing we share in common is that we defend the position of the individual against oppression and exploitation. Despite that common agenda, we split our votes, as we shall tragically do this fall among the Progressive Democrats, the Greens, the Reforms, and the Libertarians.

But the fact that over-scaled corporations are now controlling and expanding government gives us an opportunity for joint action among all the reform branches. This joint action is the unfinished business of the 20th Century. You can see that fact when you read Teddy Roosevelt's words spoken in Kansas in 1910, which could have been spoken yesterday:

> *"Our government, national and state, must be freed from the sinister influence or control of special interests. Exactly as the special interests of cotton and slavery threatened our political integrity before the Civil War, so now the great special business interests too often control and corrupt the men and methods of government for their own profit. We must drive the special interests out of politics. That is one of our tasks today...The citizens of the United States must effectively control the mighty commercial forces which they have themselves called into being. There can be no effective control of corporations while their political activity remains. To put an end to it will be neither a short nor an easy task, but it can be done."* Unquote.

It can only be done, I believe, by getting the reform groups and parties together to work on a few of the problems that separate us. Perhaps is it madness to think that people more comfortable at a Sierra Club meeting can break bread with people who would be more comfortable at an NRA-Libertarian militia weekend? All I can say is it would be a most interesting time, and I would be most entertained to be there and watch. If it isn't done soon, I worry that the divide will be too wide.

Can it be the role of a group like yours to approach these groups and work with them to find the common ground? I think it could.

Certainly we can go forward on the certain knowledge that all these groups respect the position of the individual, and we should assume, whether or not we have a right to, that they respect the principles of a fair democracy. That is common ground enough to go after the forces that now conspire against the position of the individual.

Nothing will shake the major parties more deeply to their bones than to see such an effort. And nothing less will motivate them to shed the influence of the corporation. We have the public speakers and the communicators among us to make a go of it. It will not be easy, as TR said.

I met a fellow on my walk who stopped his garbage truck to wish me well. As a victim of AM radio, he said the biggest problems we face today are the inheritance taxes and the capital gains tax, according to the religious radio station he listened to religiously. I asked him if those problems were important in his own experience; he looked confused, and then changed the subject. The fact is, very powerful players who do not want people to focus on the real problems of our lives or our planet, have redirected attention in ways that favor the interests of the wealthy elite. We need to win these people over without dismissing them.

And frankly, although we are secure in our opinions, we stand to learn something from being in a long and friendly conversation with people who have a different take on politics. We could all deprogram each other and come out the better for it. Thank you very much.

A button from her 2004 U.S. Senate campaign

Second Arrest Statement

Several months after her first arrest in the Capitol Rotunda, she returned with environmental activists on July 10, 2000, to read the Bill of Rights. They were arrested. Her August 9, 2000 court statement:

Your Honor, all Americans are protected by our Constitution, which says, at the very top of our Bill of Rights, that "Congress shall make no law... abridging the freedom of speech, or of the press; or the right of the people peaceably to assemble, and to petition the Government for a redress of grievances."

That is the highest law in the land, is it not?

Under what legal authority, then, was I dragged away from my Capitol Building in shackles, when I entered peaceably, and peaceably did nothing more than read, word for word, that very Bill of Rights in a calm voice? What country is this, Your Honor, where we do not have the right to peaceably assemble, where we do not have the right to petition the government for a redress of our grievances, and where we are not allowed speech in our own hall?

The grievance I was there to stand against is the fact that ordinary citizens are no longer represented in Congress, because special interests have bought and paid for our elected representatives and corroded the process of free elections.

We are taxed without proper representation, and the graves of millions Americans who died under our flags are being spat upon by those who think our democracy is theirs to sell to the highest bidder.

You honor, I have pled guilty because I do not dispute what is charged: I spoke freely in the halls of what used to be my own government. Thank you.

The Bribery Coast

In the company of politicians, musicians and reformers, Ms. Haddock' spoke on the West Steps of the U.S. Capitol on September 19th, 2000. Following her remarks she marched with Georgetown students from the Capitol to the Justice Department, where she pasted a copy of the existing federal bribery statute on its front door. Her remarks on the West Steps:

Thank you very much. Do you think there are enough of us here, that if we all wished the same wish, it might come true? Well, let us try. Let's imagine that we could pass a law that could work some magic. It would get big money out of the way of our democracy.

The law would read as follows:

"Whoever directly or indirectly, corruptly gives, offers or promises anything of value to any public official with intent to influence any official act; Or, being a public official, directly or indirectly, corruptly demands, seeks, receives, accepts, or agrees to receive or accept anything of value personally or for any other person or entity, in return for being influenced in the performance of any official act, shall be fined under this title or not more than three times the monetary equivalent of the thing of value, whichever is greater, or imprisoned for not more than fifteen years, or both, and may be disqualified from holding any office of honor, trust, or profit under the United States." Unquote.

Now, how hard must we wish to make that law the law of this land? Humor me, please, and close your eyes tightly and click your heels together three times. One, two, three.

You have done it. The law I read to you, condensed somewhat, is indeed the law of the land. It is United States Code, Title 18, Chapter 11, Section 201: Bribery of public officials.

18. 11. 201! Under the crystal clear provisions of this law, most of the people who make laws in these buildings should be in jail. Under the unambiguous provisions of this law, political parties that extract protection money from industries are in violation of federal bribery law, and they require prosecution.

I ask our Attorney General to investigate the sale of public policy by the elected leaders of our nation, to investigate the purchase of public policy by the great lobbying operations that have set upon our temple of self-governance like great vampire bats.

18, 11, 201! The law is there to be enforced, and the evidence drips from every window of K Street, flows down every hallway of Congress, rises waist-deep in the fundraising ballrooms of every luxury hotel in this city, washes in waves from the Bribery Coast that K Street has become.

How many good men and women have died for our freedoms as a self-governing people? Go across the cold river to Arlington and see! The spirits of the dead, and the hearts of the living are filled with sorrow for what now happens in this, our own Capitol, home of our democracy.

Title 18, Chapter 11, Section 201! That must be our demand at the door of Justice!

Ms. Haddock's Local Walks

Ms. Haddock walked across cities and states from 2000 until her death in 2010 to promote local reform initiatives. Her September 2000 remarks during a walk across Missouri to support a state campaign reform bill:

Thank you all very much. Missouri is a very large and beautiful state, and I do enjoy walking across it. I am doing it of course for one reason: to show how much I, as one person, care about the reform movement now underway in America to remove special interest money from our elections. Missouri citizens are now making one of the most important efforts in that battle, in the form of Proposition B, and I could not stay home on my porch when there was such great work being done here. Plus, I was invited, and it would have been rude, I think, to refuse an invitation to walk across one's state.

I hope Missouri citizens will look to the four states that already have approved similar measures, and I hope they will agree that the time has come to sweep the moneychangers from the temples of Missouri's democracy.

It is the very least that we can do for the many people who have dedicated their lives, and given their lives, so that we can remain a free people. We cannot remain so without fair elections, free of undue special interest influence.

For the thousands of Missourians who have dedicated their lives to the advancement of our freedoms, I dedicate this walk

I Want My Congressmen Back

Her speech in Jefferson City, the midpoint of her walk across Missouri in September of 2000:

Thank you. If I had a hundred dollar bill I would hold it up to you. I would do that because it is such a lovely thing to see, and many of us do not see too many of them.

But I would like you to imagine that I have stacked around me, right up to my straw hat, stacks of hundred dollar bills. In fact, imagine 140 thousand hundred-dollar bills. You would not be able to see me at all, and you might not care to.

Well, that is the number of hundred dollar bills that went to Missouri legislators and other politicians from special interest political donors in the last election, and it is indeed enough of a pile that the legislators cannot see the individual citizen or her needs.

Where do these hundred dollar bills come from? They come from tobacco, big oil, chemical plants, alcoholic beverages, gambling and on and on.

As a citizen, you may have an idea or two regarding what the laws should be, but you are not part of this great and happy celebration of money, so you might as well write down your opinion on a leaf and let it go in the wind.

I was in the town of Sugar Creek recently, up near Kansas City. The people there are trying to get a major oil company to clean up their horribly polluted environment. That oil company has spilled contributions all over the Missouri Legislature, and it is hard for the men, women and children of Sugar Creek to swim against that flow. Special interests pollute our political system just as they pollute our very air and water and soil and future.

Research groups on the left and on the right agree that, for every special interest dollar donated to a campaign, the special interest receives about $10 back in the form of special tax breaks and other considerations. That means that, for every dollar that goes into these political campaigns, ten dollars in extra taxes comes due to each of us. That is not a free election.

Further, that money controls who runs, who wins, and how they vote. If we still believe in the kind of self-governance that so many of our countrymen have died to preserve, we must not allow this sale of public policy—which gets worse every election—to persist. It is corruption writ large.

Now, the citizens of some states have decided to put an end to this kind of special interest politics. They have programs providing advertising funds to candidates who agree to not raise or spend any special interest campaign money. The system is working.

That is why, when election reform leaders in Missouri invited me to come walk for Proposition B, which will do exactly that in Missouri, I couldn't get my shoes on fast enough. I am here. I am walking across all of Missouri to show you that I care deeply for this reform you are considering.

I am an old Yankee who remembers when our Congressmen were our representatives, not the front men for special interests. I want my Congressmen back, I want my Democracy back, and I want to again be able to walk past a veterans' cemetery without having to feel ashamed about the way we have allowed special interests to degrade the democracy they died for.

I hope you will join me in supporting Proposition B. Let Missouri lead the way in bringing real reform to the heartland of America. Thank you.

Corporate Leadership

At the suggestion of Bill Moyers, the group Business for Social Responsibility invited Ms. Haddock to speak to their 800 members in New York City, November 8, 2000. It was not strange for her to be in their company; she had been New Hampshire's highest-paid woman executive in her time.

Thank you very much. I am delighted to be in the presence of so many people who care deeply about the serious issues of our day and who are striving to make important changes.

I believe the brightest business leaders—those capable of planning three or four chess moves ahead—are reformers by necessity, for there can be no sustainable commerce without a sustainable Earth, and there can be no free enterprise and no enjoyment of the fruits of enterprise without sustainable democracies to guarantee those freedoms.

I set out on my walk across the United States at a time when the leaders in Congress were saying that no one cared much about campaign finance reform. I wanted to demonstrate that I indeed cared, and I hoped to meet others along the way who also cared or who might become interested. That was indeed what I found.

Not very many people understood the term "campaign finance reform," but nearly all of the thousands of people I met felt and still feel that they no longer have senators and congressmen who represent their interests.

They believe that wealthy special interests have taken away their opportunity for a representative democracy. And many, many people got teary-eyed or they cried outright about it. They sent me on my way with a prayer for success for all of us, and many of them—over 2,000 of them—came to join me for the last mile in Washington, D.C. That was a joyful day, but despair, sadness and anger were the typical emotions I encountered along my way.

On that last day of my walk, we started from the graves of Arlington—rows upon rows of white stones that mark the sacrifices that have been made for the idea of freedom and self-governance. I felt those honorable spirits walking with us to the Capitol to demand an end to the political bribery that now dominates Washington. The present bribery nicely calls itself campaign finance—much as prostitutes might wish to be called personal companions—but it is what it is.

We gave witness against it on the Capitol steps and later from the very Capitol Rotunda, where some of us were arrested and jailed for peaceably assembling and petitioning our government for the redress of our grievance. I had very good company in jail, by the way, including young people from some very notable families, as Mr. Moyers may be aware.

My long walk was a 14-month, 3,200-mile opportunity to think about what cures might apply to this corruption. Time and again, people agreed that the full public financing of our campaigns is the only real way to insure that ideas and character will count again in our politics. I was surprised to hear this opinion voiced from progressive California to conservative Texas, Arkansas and West Virginia. People are so truly sick of the present system of special-interest-dominated politics that they are ready for that change.

I was surprised to learn about the public financing of campaigns during my walk. I was not informed about it when I began. People along the way convinced me that there is no other chance for real reform.

Four states have already embraced public financing of campaigns. A candidate for the Arizona legislature, for example, needs to find 200 people living in his or her district who will contribute no more or less than $5 each. All further campaign funds are provided by the state clean elections fund. No special interests need apply. It worked beautifully in the election cycle that concluded yesterday.

In Arizona and in Maine, Massachusetts and Vermont, the citizen listening to a candidate at a neighborhood forum can now, for the price of $5, be the one and only fat cat in the system. That is a breath of fresh air for democracy, isn't it? It is a victory for the human scale.

I am certain that public financing will also come to our federal elections. We have it in a modified way now for our presidential elections, but the presidential candidates who take the federal funds are not restricted from raising and spending other funds, which is a problem.

What else will drive the success of this reform? Well, the continuing damage to the weather system, to the healthy diversity of nature, and to the healthy diversity of local economies, I believe, will create a rising demand for effective leadership and proper representation without interference from selfish interests unconcerned for the future.

I know you are here because you are reformers. I am sure it gives your efforts some urgency when you hear that the polar ice cap is a third thinner than it was in 1980, and that animals are dying off at a rate that qualifies our age as the planet's sixth major extinction. I am sure that you must be ready—if you have not already done so—to add your own voice to those demanding serious action on these fronts. I doubt that you would waste you time on window-dressing issues while these fundamental issues of global consequence are filling the streets and the jails with young and old protesters around the world. We do not want to repair our representative democracies for the fun of it; we see urgent issues that are not otherwise being addressed properly.

A young carpenter from Chicago, Nick Palumbo, who helped me across a good many states in my recent walk across the U.S., and who more recently helped me across Missouri in my walk there for Missouri reform that concluded last week, was one of the many young people who peaceably protested in Philadelphia during the Republican convention. He cares deeply about non-violence, and went all the way to India to study its principles from the followers of Mr. Gandhi. He was nevertheless jailed in Philadelphia for no good reason, and held for ten days under purposefully brutal conditions. If you want to know why many Nader voters would not compromise to support Mr. Gore, it is because an entire generation is becoming radicalized against corporate-dominated politics, and it is just beginning. It grows with every change of weather, and it grows as every big-box discount store destroys another Main Street of family businesses—and I walked through hundreds of such ruined communities. It is the human scale resisting the scale of the monstrous, and history has shown that human scale always wins in the end...

There has been a power race between business and government, and neither side can afford to unilaterally disarm. So you may feel the need to own a few dozen senators, because the government can make or break your business. But the game has gone on now to a point where half the people don't vote and the other half aren't too happy either, because they don't think it's a democracy so much as it is a rigged game of special interests. That is what sends people to the streets instead of the ballot boxes. How do you step back from this brink without putting your company at risk?

You do it with courage. If you need a role model, Arnold Hiatt ought to do fine for you. He was the second largest individual political donor in the 1996 election. But he saw that, long term, political giving is a losing game.

Let me quote him exactly; Mr. Hiatt said:

"Breaking the link between candidates and big donors would inevitably contribute to a more equitable, and efficient, allocation of our country's ample resources. Wasteful subsidies that serve narrow economic interests rather than the national interest—like the $500 million a year subsidy that goes to the sugar lobby, or the tax break for ethanol producers that has cost taxpayers more than $7 billion since 1979—would wither away. Instead, government would probably find the money to subsidize, for example, every child in need with high-quality day care: many studies have shown that every $1 spent in quality day care saves $7 in later remedial costs."

He continues: "Such changes in our spending priorities would help create a healthier and more productive work force, and a better climate for business in general. I've seen this occur with individual companies and I'm convinced it can occur on a wider scale. This is not only a moral imperative—it is good business sense. The well-being of a company cannot be separated from the well-being of society." Unquote Mr. Hiatt.

I agree with every word he said. Further, the less involved corporations become in government, the easier it will be to reduce the size and cost of unnecessary government.

Now, in the shorter term, if you are concerned that your withdrawal from political participation will allow other business interests to take your place, let me remind you that you can head them off by supporting the full public funding of elections.

Now, I'll bet you thought you had outlived or divorced all the old women who would dare nag at you like this. But I love free enterprise at the community scale and all that it brings to a free world. We all, whether we are major stockholders or customers in line, have an interest in a healthy system of commerce. We have that in common.

Further, you and I share a deep feeling for all those who have given their lives to defend our freedoms and our government of, by and for the people. We know these brave souls—many of whom we knew and loved—did not die so that special interests might steal away our representative democracy. Part of you cares more about that than your business profits, and I tell you that you must listen always to that valiant voice within yourself.

When you are my age, it is the only voice still worth listening to.

Thank you for the privilege of meeting you and speaking with you, and good luck in your meetings here today.

Beyond the Shouting

Ms. Haddock's remarks to the "Citizens' Army" of New Jersey Common Cause, on November 14, 2000, were a mild rebuke to the expanding idea of forming special political groups outside the political parties to push reforms:

Thank you very much. When I climbed the steps of the U.S. Capitol after my walk across the United States I was accompanied by several thousand other people who walked those last miles through Washington with me. We did not arrive as an angry mob at the castle gate. We are Americans, and we are talking to ourselves when we demand reform. We are the government.

The worst kind of politics is the politics of division—demagoguery. We know how that played out in Europe before and during the Second World War, and we know how it has played out in Yugoslavia and Rwanda and so many other places. There is always some political advantage to be had by saying there are two kinds of people: them and us, good and bad.

Good politics, honest politics, is the politics of gathering, inclusion, cooperation and mutual respect—love versus fear. It is about assembly, growth and life, versus division, decomposition and death.

In our effort to reform American politics at the local and national level we must keep in mind the fact that we are the government.

What, therefore, should we do? Well, I think it means that we should be active in the political parties that best represent our civic values.

Over the past thirty years or so, Americans have become involved in special interest political organizations that represent certain issues or reforms, instead of investing their energies more directly in political parties. We have thereby divided our energies and ourselves. I think we must not divert our reform energies away from the political parties. We must bring our passion for reform into the heart of the daily work of the parties.

If we stand too far outside the circle of real action, we are accepting the dangerous idea that there is a "them versus us" division in our politics. We are taking the part of the mob at the castle gate, rather than accepting the fact that we, indeed, are a self-governing people.

We each have a high personal responsibility to be involved as candidates, supporters, voters, and as those who give wise testimony to the councils of our government.

I'm a Democrat, and our party is sometimes frustrating to deal with. The state parties for the most part need cleaning out. Their stuffiness and general incompetence need a wave of fresh activist members, young and old.

So let us raise no pitchforks against ourselves, remembering instead that we are the government and its parties. Let's go courteously but forthrightly into the parties, into the town councils, into the legislatures as fellow citizens who care for the common interests of our communities and of our nation and our remarkable planet. Be involved. Stay involved. Understand what it means to be an American. It means to take responsibility.

In a world where the polar ice is thinning daily and Earth is warming, and in a world where the divide between the very wealthy and the very poor is growing rapidly, we must assume responsibility. We must take our place at the table of power, even if we must do so boisterously—though there is no shouting that will save us if we cannot lead by responsible example in our homes and our communities.

Therefore, if you are organizing as a "citizens' army," as you say, let it be an army that sits at the table, not one that shoots arrows from outside the halls of self-governance. Thank you.

Freedom from Anger

Ms. Haddock's remarks to a massive gathering on Dupont Circle in Washington D.C., Saturday, January 20, 2001, the morning of George W. Bush's first inauguration:

Thank you. There are many angry people in America these days, and there are many things for them to be angry about. Anger is the normal and healthy reaction to unfairness, criminality and injustice.

But, as I am young enough to yet see with my own heart, let me tell you that there are sufficient injustices in the world to keep us angry all the time, unless we give ourselves some freedom from anger, and it is only with that freedom that we can truly improve the world.

As I am old enough to have seen and felt a third of our nation's history, let me tell you that there has always been a sufficient supply of raw deals to keep us toasty warm with rage, if we are only capable of rage instead of action.

So, if you find yourself one day in charge of a company or a community or a kingdom, and you discover that you now have enemies who would try to bring you down, here is your best strategy: keep them angry about little issues so that their energies will be spent before they get to the big issues that could truly threaten you.

You can lead a revolution from anger, but you cannot lead or govern a democracy from anger. You will fail miserably and create great harm.

Anger is not the engine of our democracy. Our imperfect Union, our ever-wobbling Republic, beset as it is by occasions of demagoguery, corruption, assassination, poor judgment and faulty elections, moves generally forward toward greater human kindness, greater fairness, greater equality—all riding on the shoulders of brotherly love.

Our nation moves upward despite all its errors and deficiencies, because it is a society founded upon an inspiring common dream that has proved durable. The dream has moved us forward. Indeed, America is a fairer, more just place than it was 91 years ago, when I was born.

What is the real issue today? It is the fight to hold to that dream of representative democracy, for how can we serve each other's needs and preserve our very Earth if we are not at the reins of our own democracy? There's the issue, friends: not the theft of an election by one Supreme Court justice, but the larger theft underway of democracy itself through the financial corruption of political campaigns...

Let us fight to win, but with only as much anger as we need to sharpen our resolve.

We shall do it for all who have given themselves to the betterment and the defense of our great idea: a government of people, for people. We shall do it for our children and grandchildren and great grandchildren, who need for us to be brave and take action at this critical moment.

You know from your own experience that, once you step onto the street to oppose a great injustice, a joy comes over you because you are representing your deepest values. That joy is at odds with your anger. So let the joy win the battle; joy is more powerful than anger in changing things.

And change things we must, so that our great Capitol building might be filled with the warm light that ever streams from the hearts of our people. Thank you.

This, My Government

On March 19, 2001, a year after her arrival speech on the U.S. Capitol steps, Ms. Haddock returned to Washington to picket the Capitol Building as the Senate began debate on the McCain-Feingold bill. She decided more drastic action was in order, and so planned a 24-hour walking vigil around the Capitol Building for as many days and nights as the debate might continue through the following week. The weather was not cooperating: freezing rain in the 20s was predicted for the coming days, and she was asked by those traveling with her to cancel the walking fast, especially as her emphysema had been giving her coughing fits, and pneumonia was a clear risk. "Well, I'll certainly need a good Mackintosh," she replied, and took a cab to an army-navy surplus store, where she bargained for a heavy one. She then sent this message to her supporters:

Friends: Mr. McConnell and some other senators are of the opinion that Americans do not care about campaign finance reform. It is true that many people are unfamiliar with that term. They are quite familiar, however, with the fact that their government has been sold out from under them by wealthy special interests. If they seem uninterested in the selling-out of the very democracy their friends and family have died to defend, it may only be because they despair of a solution, given our present Congress.

I do not despair. I think these men and women who serve in our Senate are capable of doing the right thing—of lowering the boom on soft money and holding the line on hard money. We know that many of them care. We have seen them working hard on this matter these past days.

If the senators need some encouragement—if they need to know that Americans indeed care—then let the few of us who can afford the time to be here do more to show we care. Let us walk continuously around our Capitol, day and night, while the Senate struggles to free our democracy from the corrupting clutches of big money. While they are doing their best, we will be doing our best with this walking vigil.

Those at home, I hope, will call their senators again and demand the passage of McCain-Feingold in a way that will outlaw soft money—huge contributions given by corporations to parties, who then pass it to candidates—and preserve the existing $1,000 limit on hard money contributions—the money given directly by individuals to candidates. Yours, Doris

> *On March 24, 2001, the Saturday before the planned Monday action, she met with a group of 25 college students who came to Washington to lobby for campaign finance reform as a strategy for protecting the environment. Here are her remarks to them, delivered on the West Steps of the Capitol. Her speech draws upon an earlier speech given in Little Rock during her long walk. After the meeting, the students joined her in picketing the Capitol Building.*

Members of the press and many elected leaders say that the people do not care about campaign finance reform. Mitch McConnell says most people care more about static cling.

Part of my mission in walking across the country was to see if this is true, and if it indeed was, to talk to people to help them to understand the seriousness of our situation as a people.

What I found was that very few people knew what I was talking about when I used the term "campaign finance reform," but nearly everyone agreed that they no longer have representatives in government, and that their representatives have been bought away from them by big-money interests. So they do care a great deal about campaign finance reform—often they care to the extent that their eyes fill with tears; but they did not have a name for this abandonment they feel so deeply.

Now, good political reform work requires that we look deeply into our reform issue and see how it connects to basic cultural values.

For example, if you have a great-uncle who was killed in the Second World War, or an uncle who was killed in Vietnam, you might wonder if their spirits are angry when they see the country they fought for moving from a democracy of the people, to an oligarchy where the interests of only the elite are served. Of course they did not die to protect the interests of the super-wealthy and the corporations, while school children go unfed and innocent people rot in corporate jails.

So as I walked, I connected campaign finance reform to the memory of these people. I think I first did it in the little desert town of Salome, Arizona. I recited the war poem, In Flanders Field.

Now, what we are talking about is the element of sacrifice. You rarely can have successful reform politics without an element of sacrifice. Here I was in Salome, talking about the sacrifice of others. But, about eighty miles earlier in my trek, as I finished walking the Mojave Desert and arrived in the river town of Parker, Arizona, the mayor (Sandy Pierce), took me all over town talking about the sacrifice I had just made, and that made people interested in my cause.

In the same way, it was hard for me to get signatures on my petition at the very beginning of my walk as I stood on a sidewalk near the ocean in Santa Monica, until a kind woman joined me and told passers-by about the sacrifice I was about to make. That made them care enough to stop and sign.

Gandhi and King taught us, of course, that we must take the pain of social change upon ourselves, if we are to change society. If we inflict it instead upon other people we have not changed the world for the better, and we shall only generate short-term and very unpredictable changes. It was King's nonviolent work that gave us the voting rights bill and other civil rights bills, for example. All the riots and other violence gave us short-term programs that did more harm than good in the final analysis.

So our own willingness to demonstrate the importance of the issue, by inconveniencing ourselves in a dignified way that our fellow citizens can relate to, is our most powerful tool for change.

Sometimes you have to be willing to get arrested, but there is no percentage to be gained by harming anyone or anything, as that goes beyond what the people can accept and see themselves doing. The whole point of reform politics is to attract, not repel, the supportive thinking of the people.

The teaching of nonviolent political action is a five-fold technique that we must always remember. It must be remembered whereever people gather with the intention of improving their community or their world. Here are the five steps:

Number One: Determine the truth of a situation before taking a strong position. If it is an injustice, can it be clearly documented? Bring in the experts if you can. Be sure what you are advocating is actually and demonstrably the truth.

Number Two: Communicate your findings, your position and your request for change in a respectful and achievable way to the people who have the direct power to correct the situation. Don't ask someone for something they don't have the power to give. Don't shout on the sidewalks if you have not yet communicated respectfully with the parties in authority and have respectfully waited for a reply.

Number Three: If the response does not come, or is insufficient, bring public attention to the issue. Work openly so the thinking process of the entire community can be engaged. Gandhi and King were accused of staging events for the media. Of course they did. Social change is a public process, and it does not happen for the good when it happens in the dark. Engage the community openly so that they can be a part of the debate and the decision. Openness works easiest in a democracy, but it also works in authoritarian regimes, so long as there is visibility between the action and the public. Few governments, no matter how authoritarian, are immune from public sentiment.

Number Four: If those in authority will not correct a very serious situation that must be resolved, despite an open airing of the issue, then the advocates must be willing to make sacrifices to demonstrate the seriousness of the matter. When King marched forward toward baton-swinging policemen in Selma, he showed that the issue was important. When Gandhi led marches and gave speeches that he knew would lead to his imprisonment that day, and when his followers stood in long lines to be clubbed by security forces standing in the way of their rightful path, the world stopped its daily routine to inquire: what injustice motivates the self-sacrifices of these people? What, in fairness, should be done? And here is the difficult key to success: It is in the endless willingness of the advocates to make a continuing sacrifice that guarantees their victory. No injustice is powerful enough, or has enough supporters, to stand against the flow of such generosity.

"You have been the veterans of creative suffering," Dr. King told his followers in his "I Have a Dream" speech. Well, creative suffering is something we all have the power to do. It happens to be the most powerful force for change in the world. It is always in our pocket, ready for the call of our conscience.

There is a fifth step, made necessary by the fact that the non-violence technique, when properly practiced against moveable opponents, always wins. The fifth step, as developed by Mr. Gandhi and as practiced by Dr. King, is to be gracious in victory—to remember that your enemy is your brother, and that you should therefore settle the dispute kindly, accepting some compromises and granting as much face-saving courtesy as possible to the other side. You will meet again, after all, and why not as friends? Gandhi said on many occasions that we have to love and respect our adversaries because they are our brothers and sisters and also that they are parts of ourselves and of our God. He meant it.

Here is a passage from his autobiography:

"Man and his deed are two distinct things. It is quite proper to resist and attack a system, but to resist and attack its author is tantamount to resisting and attacking oneself. For we are all tarred with the same brush, and are children of one and the same Creator, and as such the divine powers within us are infinite. To slight a single human being is to slight those divine powers, and thus to harm not only that being but with him the whole world."

Dr. King believed much the same, and you can hear it clearly in the "I Have a Dream" speech, where he calls us together as "all of God's children."

These are the five steps that gave India its freedom and which gave America its second revolution of independence at a moment when it could have devolved into a full race war. The moment King left this world, the violence that could have been ours all along showed itself in Watts and Detroit and a hundred other cities and towns. There is no courage in a thrown bottle of gasoline. Courage is what we saw in the buses arriving at Little Rock's Central High School and in the Selma march, not the riots of so many cities. Good changes, like the voting rights act and the opening of universities and public facilities, came from King's work. Poor changes, temporary changes, came from the anger of riots.

Love works. Love wins. Love endures. It is our religion, and it must also be our politics.

In my walk across the country, I speak against the idea that those individuals and those corporations with the greatest wealth should be able to buy our elections and our candidates and our representatives, diverting their attention from the needs of the people, and preventing honest candidates from winning.

That we have a problem, that money has become more important than ideas in our political debate, is a proven fact. That this huge, national influence-peddling scheme results in a mass diversion of the public wealth from where it is needed to where privileged people would have it for their own use is no longer a debatable point. When I walk with this message, I have the advantage of speaking the simple truth, proven by every major research institution, on both the right and left of political life, who have taken the time to investigate the issue.

We have asked those in power to remedy the situation, and for a long time they refused. We sacrificed. We gave ourselves up for arrest. We—thousands of us—kept the pressure on, thought it cost us time and energy and our meager incomes to do so.

And this coming week we shall see something for it. It will not be much. We will get rid of soft money. We will take that hill, thought we will pay a high price for it, as I am sure they will try to raise hard money limits in the process. We will do what we can to limit that damage. Thank you. If you will lend me a sign, I will join your picket of this gorgeous building of ours.

As the McCain-Feingold Bill debate began inside the Senate on Monday, she launched her action with a small speech to a gathering of Members of Congress and her supporters at the Senate "swamp:"

Thank you friends. The fact that the American government is my government is a joy to my heart, even if it does not always feel like my government. When it is, it is a part of me and I am a part of it. I help direct its actions according to my civic values, through the work of my representatives in its powerful councils. In this way, through them, I can better fulfill my responsibility to do good for my countrymen and for others around the world. If I cannot fulfill these responsibilities, a soul sickness comes over me and over the land itself.

There is a high price paid in America and around the world when Americans, whose values are profoundly fair and generous, are not in control of their own government and when they do not believe they are indeed a self-governing people.

Some of you have never known the feeling that it is your government. Some, by income or race, have been denied that feeling through all their generations. But I have been lucky—privileged is of course the better word—to often feel it was my government.

And so, some may think I do not see the same world as do they.

They may say, "Doris, did you not see how the credit card industry bought a bill last week?"

I saw that. All America saw that.

Or, "Doris, did you not see how manufacturers stopped

the worker safety bill, or how the coal lobby has undermined our nation's ability to stop the destruction of the Earth's climate?"

Yes, I see that. I agree with you—the challenge is great. Indeed, there may have been uglier Congresses in our history, or less competent, but there have never been more fundamentally corrupt Congresses than these in our time. Certainly democracy had a better chance of survival in the darkest days of the two world wars than it does today, at the hands of the campaign corruption from within.

But I am not worried: I know we shall overcome this time of destruction.

It is a bit early to celebrate. I do hope that, at the end of this present battle for reform, we can say the day is ours. But we are small and the forces against us are strong and unprincipled in battle. Before this week is out, they may take our best garden tools for reform and twist them into blades to dig corruption even deeper. They may make a nice plum pudding of the McCain-Feingold bill. In any case, it will be something to watch.

They will cry into their million-dollar campaign troughs over the idea that any real reform might tilt the playing field unfairly, though it doesn't matter how the field it tilted if no team is playing for the people. The playing field is tilted up beyond the moon now, and it matters very little to ordinary Americans whether it is tilted in favor of the credit card party or the coal party, as neither is playing for us.

But I am not discouraged. We the people can afford any losses and yet always overcome. We are the millions. Ours are those who have happily died to defend this country and its idea of a government of its people. We the people are generous in our sacrifice for democracy, and no one is rich enough or cruel enough to stand forever in the way of our sacrifices and our aspirations for our country and our world.

It will be written in history that America came into a dark time when its leaders became corrupt—so dishonest they could not admit it even to themselves.

And history shall further record that a dedicated band of people sacrificed the best years of their lives to set their people free from the bondage of corruption. Let history say they did so, or that they died trying.

I know these heroes by name and many of them stand around me now, and I know that the spirits of those who sacrificed everything for democracy walk behind us—bandaged, on crutches, but each wearing a determined smile because they understand that we are not interested in forgetting their sacrifices for self-government. They walk with fife and drum, reminding us that heaven may be our work tomorrow, but America is our work today. And as long as any one of us is left standing to claim these columns, to claim this, my government, then we are not defeated.

Thank you, and join me now—those of you who can and are dressed for this weather—as I begin my walk and vigil.

As she walked around outside of the Capitol Building in the hard weather, Matt Keller, John Anthony, Dennis Burke, Claudia Malloy, Nick Palumbo and others worked the halls of the Senate, urging Senators to meet with Ms. Haddock, "so we can get her out of the cold." In this way, she met with half the Senate, usually asking nicely for their vote but sometimes offering to walk across a senator's state to oppose them if they voted against the bill. At least one vote changed on the spot, and others changed due to the pressure of phone calls from Ms. Haddock's now-thousands of followers—she had also been on national television, urging viewers of NBC's Today show and ABC's Good Morning America to call their senators. The 24-hour fasting walk continued for four days. She stopped only for brief respites in a brownstone behind the Supreme Court, home of Bill Moyer's son, John. She would consume only vitamin water suggested to her by Dick Gregory, a veteran of many political fasts. In that way—Gandhi's way of self-sacrifice—she helped get the bill passed by the Senate. She was called by Senator McCain to stop walking and be in the gallery when the final vote was taken. It still had to go to the House, but it had now passed the Senate—over Mitch McConnell's energetic efforts to defeat it.

Witness report by Ben G. Price, national organizing director for the Community Environmental Legal Defense Fund, writing in the Alliance for Democracy newsletter (used by permission):

It was a blustery, rainy gray day in Washington, D.C. We were joining Doris Haddock, better known as "Granny D," as she continued her 24-hour walking vigil around the Senate.

While the hundred senators debated the McCain-Feingold bill that would ban "soft money," Granny D walked around the Capitol grounds to emphasize her outrage over the selling of democracy by its supposed representatives. She had walked 3,200 miles to demonstrate her commitment to reform; now she was circling the Capitol, day and night. When I caught up with her she was out there in a cold rain, her signature straw hat with its feather on her head, planning to continue her walk until the Senate voted for reform.

Lou and Patricia Hammann, of the Alliance For Democracy, were with her when we arrived. Patricia, concerned about Doris's health, asked her to consider ending her vigil.

"When I started this I knew it might do me in," Doris said. This was the day—Thursday—that the opposition would have its last chance in the Senate to kill McCain-Feingold outright. Senators Bill Frist (R-Tenn.) and John B. Breaux (D-La.) had proposed an amendment to invalidate the whole bill if any section, phrase, or word of it was found unconstitutional.

By invitation, Granny D took a break and entered the Senate gallery to witness the proceedings. We joined her, gaining entry to the mezzanine just as Senators McCain, McConnell, and a few others were making the final arguments. Then the roll was called. Lou and I tried to keep track of the votes as they dribbled in. As we watched the senators appear and disappear from the cloakroom, the tally trickled in, running two to one for the deadly amendment.

Across the gallery from us sat Granny D. After all the miles, all the footsteps, all the aching joints, there down below her, in the theater of the Senate, these men and women would decide whether she had walked in vain.

At last, the decision was in: 57 senators voted to kill Frist-Breaux and 43 senators voted in favor. Mitch McConnell took the floor, obviously shaken. He saw the adoption of McCain-Feingold as the demise of political parties, since they could no longer command the huge slush funds called "soft money." Passing the bill, he said with his usual arrogance, was "a stunningly stupid thing to do." If the bill finally passed, there would be a court fight at once, "and I will be the plaintiff," he told the emptying chamber.

Even if McCain-Feingold is passed by the House and signed into law, it will be an imperfect bill. It does not guarantee the primacy of citizens as sovereign in the electoral process. It simply eliminates the grossest forms of obvious impropriety in the funding of election campaigns. But for the first time since 1974, something had happened.

Think For Yourself

Ms. Haddock delivered the Franklin Pierce College (now University) graduation address, New Hampshire, Sunday, May 13, 2001:

Thank you. We have these ceremonies in the spring. We do so in order to celebrate a successful ending, yet we call them commencements. Endings indeed commence new life, new worlds. The overture and opening act of your personal story is done; from here, the main action of your adult life begins. Good luck to all you darlings.

In the end—and it will end—your life will seem to have sped by like a fleeting dream. Much of your story will be the age-old but ever joyful human experience: romance, family of one kind or another, satisfying work, and happy completion. I wish you a great fountain of successes. You will also be provided with all the failures and tragedies necessary to deepen and widen your soul—sufficient, I hope, to make you wise and forgiving of our human frailties. I pray that these necessary troubles will never long crush your optimism nor your love for this magical life.

The greatest danger before you is this: you live in an age when people would package and standardize your life for you—steal it from you and sell it back to you at a price. That price is very high.

You have already been selected for this program. You have its credit cards and designer labels already expensively around you. In the months ahead, you will find yourselves working long hours, too exhausted for community life or even good friendships—too compromised to take a stand against the abuses of the system you serve. A great treadmill has been devised for you, and its operators do not care much if it wears you out or kills you. A system is in place to steal your life from you, if you will let it.

Don't let it. Read, study, meditate and think for yourself. Let your most serious education now commence, if it has not already done so. Refine and hold your own values, and pay the high price necessary to live those values. Decide what is important to you, and hold your ground against all temptations and tortures. From the pink granite of your own values, build a fortress against the world's ethical compromises, or you will soon be among those dead of eye who stand next to you in elevators but who are not alive. Don't let them steal your life.

This is the only warning you will receive.

While on my long walk across America, a young carpenter from Chicago came to walk with me for many months. He and a friend in college had pledged to each other that they would, all their lives, spend at least one day a week doing something they thought important to the world or to their communities. Nick has been arrested protesting what he believes to be America's immoral training of brutal army squads for South American regimes. He has protested for social justice and for clean elections. He was arrested at the Republican Convention in Philadelphia last year, just calmly walking down a street. He rotted in a cell for two weeks where people were severely abused by the police.

Nick is a free man in a land where few people have claimed their freedom to live a life that represents their values.

I am not suggesting that you all need to be protesters and to get arrested to be free, but you need to stand up for your values, and you will be surprised at the trouble that will get you into today. I was arrested for reading the Declaration of Independence in a calm voice in the U.S. Capitol Rotunda—and again reading from our Bill of Rights. You will be surprised at what happens when you dare to be free. But you will never be sorry you dared to do so.

For it is where true happiness is to be pursued and found. Nick and I and so many others are happy when we meet. We have stories to tell. We are free people in a land that is free to us, because we have dared to be free in it.

The fate of the Earth's environment is at risk in your generation. Prison industries are spreading over the land. A new kind of colonialism of our towns and cities is afoot by companies that can and do crush our local businesses and buy our elections and destroy our natural environment. You will participate in these and a hundred other issues, on one side or the other. Fight hard for whichever side you choose. All I ask is that your decision—your life—is the product and the strategy of your deepest values.

As your generation begins its turn at the helm, my generation fades away. We have done what we could, imperfectly, for each other and for democracy. Endings commence new life, new worlds. From here, the main action of your adult life begins. Good luck to you and to your friends and your countrymen. Thank you!

The Monster at the Door

Ms. Haddock's remarks in Florida, June 16, 2001, to a voter rights meeting of young activists in Tallahassee:

Thank you. Born in 1910, I lived through 90 years of the previous century: two world wars and uncounted smaller conflicts, massacres, tortures and atrocities. Over one hundred million people died in those years due to the abuses of power that arose because governments had become disconnected from the basic human values of their people.

Our imaginations are not dark enough or twisted enough to fully comprehend the mass horrors that have been perpetrated upon the people of the world—men, women and little children; if we knew it all and remembered it all we could not draw another happy breath.

In America we are more blessed. We have come to expect that our neighbors will not be rounded up en masse and shot. We have come to expect that we will not ourselves be dragged out of bed and sent away to death—though these things do happen here, especially to our immigrant neighbors. While we may distrust an election or a party, we have—most of us—not lost faith in the good intentions of our democracy, writ large. It is balanced between left and right, and between politician and bureaucrat, and we mostly manage.

We look around the world. We understand that it is the absolute power of institutions out of balance that allows atrocities, because force is the opposite of sensitivity and accommodation. Force is a monster, a man-eating, woman-eating, child-eating beast that we keep in check but never really kill. In America, our dear Constitution is the amulet we wear to preserve ourselves from its teeth.

Our Constitution gives us our democratic republic, which has as its intention the fragmentation of power, keeping the exercise of force as close as possible to the human scale, and letting its power accumulate only where absolutely necessary for the common good of the people. The parchment document of the Constitution is not enough—we also require supportive institutions and customs; we need these five things:

1. We need fair and accurate voting systems that we can trust beyond a shadow of doubt;

2. We need worthy candidates who represent our interests and values and who are free from compromising financial or other obligations;

3. We need a free press that takes as a sacred trust its duty to inform the citizenry on the great and small issues of the day;

4. We need to be an unhurried society, with each of us given the time and resources to be active citizens, not hamsters on corporate treadmills;

5. We must be an educated people, forever students of the vital issues before us and of the history, art and literature that shapes our human sensibilities and our civic and cultural values. We require all that if we are to be a wisely self-governing people. Our schools must produce citizens. Our immigrant arrivals must be made into informed citizens.

In many of these five areas we are now in trouble. The stakes are very high, for the monster of force is never far from the door. It comes in quickly. If I told you that an unrepentant U.S. Navy seriously roughed up a Member of Congress because he was peacefully protesting, or that a building full of people who were making political puppets were summarily arrested and taken away, or that people walking calmly down the street near a political convention were arrested and brutalized for two weeks, what country would you think you were in? If I told you that I was arrested for calmly reciting the Bill of Rights in the U.S. Capitol building, and that I cried when the police tried to pull from my finger a wedding ring that had not been removed in sixty years, where would you think you were? All these things—and many more—have happened under the American flag within the last twelve months.

If I told you that a man would be in the White House who lost the popular vote, what country would you think you had landed in?

It happens quickly and moves swiftly. It is nothing for the forces of raw power to discredit the proper law enforcement agencies and set up new ones, run by political cronies, and with prisons and police of their own to suppress and arrest those who dare investigate or protest. It is nothing for raw power to thumb its nose at the interests of world peace or the Earth's environment for the sake of power and plunder. It is nothing for raw power to mistake the flowering of political ideas and dissent in a democracy as a dangerous tangle of garden plots and disloyalties. It can happen quickly. It can happen in America. We must have our eyes open for it and our voices ready!

Those who speak out first—the leakers, whistleblowers, activists, patriots—will be vilified, jailed, or worse. Stick up for them. Oppose the autocrat at every turn. You will be among a new generation of American patriots putting yourselves at risk to preserve our dream of individual and civic freedom. Nothing is more important than this work, as the history of the previous century shows us—clearly written as it is in the blood of one hundred million people.

To those who died for democracy, we owe a sacred trust. For those who died for lack of democracy, we owe our efforts to make a world worthy of their memory. American democracy is worth a great deal of trouble and all our human strength. Thank you.

The Weather Forecast

Ms. Haddock spoke to Common Cause in Washington D. C. and accepted an honor on June 20, 2001. Her remarks:

Thank you very much. The weather forecast is in. We are in for great hurricanes, droughts, floods and rising sea levels that will erode our coastlines. Earth's sixth major extinction of species is underway. As my friend Bill McKibben said on the day when we were arrested in the Capitol Rotunda, this is not an act of God, but an act of Congress.

Indeed, what happens in the government of the most powerful nation on Earth profoundly affects the environmental fate of our planet.

Is Congress in the hands of we the people, so that we can protect the sustainability of our world? Presently it is not, as we know. The problem is the corruption of our politics by corporations and the greedy rich.

Let me share my favorite quote from Teddy Roosevelt. He said this in Kansas on Aug. 31, 1910, the year I was born: "The citizens of the United States must effectively control the mighty commercial forces which they have themselves called into being. There can be no effective control of corporations while their political activity remains. To put an end to it will be neither a short nor an easy task, but it can be done."

The only thing that has changed since he spoke those words is that the stakes are now much higher.

So, what do we, as reform-minded citizens, propose to do about it? What is our strategy for getting corporations out of our politics? Certainly, the public financing of elections, as has been won in Maine, Vermont, Massachusetts and Arizona, offer important ways to outflank excessive big donor influence. Does the reform community have an integrated plan to achieve similar reforms in the remaining states and in Congress? I think we need one, and we all need to see it so we can decide where we can each help best. I know you are organizing to take these victories to other states.

Are we documenting the present system of bribery in a way that the U.S. Attorney General and her counterparts in the states will be forced to make arrests? I have seen little action on this front, yet there is a fine federal law against accepting bribes of exactly the kind being offered.

If all we are doing is trying to get a flawed bill through a corrupt Congress, do we really have a plan for success, or is it just about the self-perpetuation of the reform organizations.

Finally, are we putting our bodies in the way of an unjust system in the way that King's followers did in the segregated American South? Certainly the Civil Rights Movement would have not gotten very far if King restricted his actions to the release of reports about the harmful effects and unfairness of segregation. Documenting the truth is important, but it is only useful as the justification for action. If you do nothing but document the problem and cry about it, you only serve to lower people's expectations of government, which damages the cause of reform. And if the only other thing he did was plan protest rallies in D.C. on Saturdays, when most the Congress was out of town, there might still be segregation, even in this city.

Now, I got in some trouble with some of you when I made a speech in Boston suggesting that reform battles are best fought in the states, and that Washington is only useful as a place where the peace agreements are signed. I will not belabor that point today. Today is a day to remember. I remember coming to meet some of you before my walk, when I think you were trying to be careful not to encourage an old woman to walk to her doom. I was not encouraged, though you promised that you would notify your members in the states along my walk so that they might help me. You did that, and I am very thankful to you and to the supporters who responded.

Those supporters, I know, gave the national office a hard time, because they saw the needs and opportunities of my trek at first hand, and thought that Common Cause might lend some material support. I understand, I think, why that never happened. I was told that, by someone on your board, that Common Cause leaders were worried that my successes on the road would not be taken seriously if politicians and the press thought I was a creature of Common Cause, and not of the people. Well, that rather says that Common Cause does not consider itself a representative of the people anymore, which is a shame. I tell you that you do represent the people, and you need not fear supporting people who make extraordinary efforts to push for reforms. If someone wants to sit in a tree to make a point about political corruption, please send them up a little birdseed from time to time.

I am grateful to those Common Cause staff people and volunteers who walked with me and who helped get my message out. It was, and it continues to be, a great pleasure to work with them, and I think we have together done some good in moving campaign finance reform into higher public profile and so that people will respond emotionally to this issue. Matt Keller and Claudia Malloy have made a real contribution to my effort and to this larger historical development, and Scott has quickly become the voice of America's conscience on campaign reform. On the road, John Anthony, Dennis Burke and Nick Palumbo also made great contributions in defining and delivering the message of reform to hundreds of communities and to the national press. If you weren't out there, you have no idea how wonderful it has been, and how deeply Americans thirst for true reform. They look to you.

Thank you very much for this honor, and I look forward to many fine arguments and adventures with you in the future.

Old Elijah's Tree

Ms. Haddock's June 24, 2001 remarks at Dublin Community Church, where she was asked to deliver the sermon—her first, not counting her speech in Little Rock's First Baptist Church; the Bible verse of the day was 1 Kings 19:

Good morning. Much is expected of us. We have not been sent into this theater of the soul to watch passively. We are not the audience but the players in this drama, writing our parts as we go, so that we might learn something—both as individual souls, and together as the fragile web of consciousness that sparkles over God's creation. It is all evolving, we hope, toward some unity with the Divine.

This life is not a test or a drill or an accidental light opera: Much is expected of us. Some days it is quite too much, indeed.

Some days everything we love is suddenly gone, or has turned against us. We look at our life and our meager accomplishments and we sense that the game is lost; the play has run; we have no more to give; we have no interest in fighting on.

So it was, so many centuries ago, when Elijah sat down to die under a desert broom tree. His own fear had chased him into the wilderness. He had fought hard and well against the enemies of the Lord, but the altars of his beliefs lay in ruins and he was the lone prophet facing heartbreaking work ahead. He had fought so long and given so much strength to his calling that there seemed nothing left inside him. When Jezebel threatened his life, he broke and ran.

And any young person who has tried to do well in school or on the field, and any parent who has tried to be saint and provider to a family, knows Elijah well, as do I. We have often sat down with old Elijah under that desert tree, just wishing it were over.

As Elijah slumbers under the tree, the Lord sends an angel twice to nourish him with bread and water and encouragement. "Get up and eat, for the journey is too much for you," said the angel. The Lord did not send solutions to Elija's problems—only enough sustenance so that the show might go on. For much was expected of Elijah, as much is expected of each of us.

Deep in a cave, which is where we indeed go when we have had enough, Elijah listened to the voice inside him that he knew to be the voice of the Divine. He prepared himself for the approach of the Divine itself. The wind blew until the mountain nearly fell in around him—the rocks crashing into bits. Then the earth rumbled and a great earthquake rolled Elijah in his cave. But he did not feel the presence of the Divine in those signs, just as we do not feel much but fear and horror as our world crumbles around us now.

But then Elijah felt the presence of God in a gentle whisper. God asks him what he is doing there. God certainly knows the answer, but Elijah needs to remind himself who he is and what his work is. And so God makes him say it aloud. "I have been very zealous for the Lord God Almighty. The Israelites have rejected Your covenant, broken down Your altars, and put Your prophets to death with the sword. I am the only one left, and now they are trying to kill me too." Ah, Elijah thereby remembers: "That's who I am. That is what I am about. I can do this, even if it kills me to do it."

You may have said aloud in the privacy of that little cave called your car: "I am a parent of two teenagers. They both hate me and they do the opposite of whatever I say and I am terribly worried for their safety and their futures. I must express love instead of anger, yet I am screaming inside and incredibly lonely in this work. I am exhausted." Well, yes, Elijah, life is tough all over. It is supposed to be, or we shouldn't learn a thing and our souls might not grow an inch deeper or wider, as they must.

Much indeed is expected of us. But we shall always be given enough bread and water and encouragement to struggle through, if we will but rest under the Lord's tree. And a whisper may come to us; to remind us who we are and what work we have come here to do.

It is no secret among my friends in this church that, when my husband, Jim, and then my good friend, Elizabeth, died, I was quite depressed. God did not forget about me. He kept my son Jim and my daughter-in-law Libby at my side to give me encouragement and sustenance.

And there was a whisper in my ear—you may have heard me tell the story: Jim was driving me down to visit my sister in Florida. Along the road, as we sped by, was an old traveling man out in the middle of nowhere, just standing there. Soon, he was far behind us.

"Well, Doris," he nevertheless whispered, "what are you doing here?"

"Well, Sir, I have become an old woman. My husband and my dear friend are dead, but my son and daughter are alive. I used to travel with my husband as we journeyed far to help where we thought we could be useful. We drove to Alaska to stop atomic testing, you know." The old man knew.

And in saying it all, I remembered who I am, and I saw that there was still a great deal of work for me to do. And why should I care if it kills me, if doing it is my business on this Earth?

And so the questions and queasiness that I had been struggling with, looking for a way to express my concern for our democracy—so polluted as it is by big, special interest money— came suddenly into focus. I stepped out of the cave of my depression and began to plan my work—my job.

I decided to go on the road to talk to people about our democracy, and what we might do to help it survive. Every door opened to me. My every thirst was quenched, every hunger satisfied. Whenever I needed a special kind of person for the work at hand, they appeared as if by magic. When it rained too hard, there was some earthly angel with a great, plastic tarp to walk with me. When the snow was too deep for walking, a beautiful ski path, nearly 200 miles long, presented itself. You must never doubt that you will be given what you need for this show to go on, once you accept the idea of who you are and what you must do.

Much is expected of us, but everything needed is given us, if we but have faith in the Divine importance of our lives.

We have hard work to do in this life, and it can get very discouraging. It is hard work, loving each other, helping and forgiving each other, protecting the people and the ideas we care about, preserving nature, helping the millions of people who need our help, taking care of our own needs. It is hard work. Let us meet from time to time under Elijah's old tree and rest our bones. God will give us what we need to carry on.

Bribery Bob

Ms. Haddock returned to Capitol Hill regularly to keep up the pressure for passage. Her July 10, 2001 remarks follow. They were made on a sidewalk prior to a picket march around the House office buildings in support of Shays-Meehan, the House version of the McCain-Feingold bill, just as House debate on the bill was beginning. She mentions Rep. Bob Ney in her remarks; she would later set up a podium and then commence a "filibuster" in the waiting room of his Capitol Hill office, reading from his list of compromising donors until she was ejected. Ney later resigned when he pleaded guilty in the Jack Abramoff bribery scandal.

Thank you all for coming! A great Republican said this on Aug. 31st, 1910: "Our government... must be freed from the sinister influence or control of special interests (which) corrupt the men and methods of government for their own profit. We must drive the special interests out of politics... The citizens of the United States must effectively control the mighty commercial forces that they have themselves called into being. There can be no effective control of corporations while their political activity remains. To put an end to it will be neither a short nor an easy task, but it can be done."

Who said that in 1910, the year I was born? Teddy Roosevelt said it. And it is truer today, for now the fate of the living Earth is in the balance.

We are here today to drive the million-dollar, sure-as-hell corrupting political contribution out of the system. Some Members of the House are on the side of reform. They will vote for Shays-Meehan, as-is.

Some Members of the House are content to be the handmaidens of corruption, and they will vote for the Bob Ney bill. Bob Ney represents the people of a coalmining district in eastern Ohio, and yet he takes more money from huge coal corporations than any other member of the House. How, then, can he fairly represent the human beings of his district? Is this corruption? It certainly has the appearance of corruption, for his political survival depends upon staying in the good graces of the giant companies he ought to be regulating. If he is not swimming in shame, he should at least be swimming in fear, for no honorable public official should allow himself or herself to be in that impossible position. He should be the first member of the House to demand reform, to demand passage of Shays-Meehan, not the first to offer a counterfeit reform bill that would preserve corruption as usual.

But, "Oh, my," these poor dears in the House do cry, "How shall we be reelected without these millions of soft dollars?" That question is the siren song of corruption, the self-deluding whine of bribery itself. The better question is, "how shall we end this shame and find an honorable way to fund our elections? There are such ways, as Maine, Arizona, Vermont and perhaps Massachusetts have shown us—the public financing of public elections. That is the simple solution to the problem.

But for today, we are here to remove the cancer of money from the body politic.

I am asking my friends to support, door-to-door, the candidates who vote aye for Shays-Meehan as is, and I ask them to work door-to-door to help defeat those Members of the House who vote this week to preserve corruption as usual, as represented by the bill of Bob Ney, the Bribery Guy.

Those who vote like Ney must be sent packing from Congress. We will use Earth Day of next year entirely for that organizing purpose. Hispanic, African American, Asian, Native American, White and all kinds of volunteers understand that we cannot preserve the living Earth and we cannot improve the conditions of justice upon this Earth until the dominance of government by greedy special interests is ended.

Good luck to all of us this week. As Teddy Roosevelt said, it must be done and it can be done. Thank you.

My Friend Berta Begay

Remarks to the Alliance for Democracy in Minneapolis, August 2001:

I would like to first thank you very much for your generous donation of funds to facilitate the activities surrounding the completion of my walk across the country. You provided the funds so that we had the banners and signs and food for the 2,200 people who walked with me. I want you to know that we obtained the food, which was excellent, from a non-profit agency that trains homeless people to be chefs and caterers, so your contribution did double duty. We kept nothing for ourselves.

I think the way we arrived made an impact on the campaign finance reform debate, and it has helped elevate our struggle toward the status of a movement. Your help in that is so very much appreciated.

If I were a rich, I would have brought to Washington all the beautiful Americans I met along the way, who would have loved to walk with me in Washington if they could have afforded it.

I will introduce you to one of those people in these remarks.

In the old railroad town of Toyah, Texas, where the ruins of a once-beautiful main street stand like a western movie set, we knocked on the door of a friendly looking house and asked for shelter. Berta Begay answered the door. As it happened, she owns an extra little house across the road that she keeps for special visitors, usually affiliated with her church. The house has linoleum floors held down in strips with upholstery tacks to the wavy wooden floor, cooled only by the open doors and the overhead fans. The yard is dirt with a little grass, and everything about the house is well ordered and clean. She said I would be welcome to stay there for as long as I needed, if I would give her a chance to first clean it and make sure the linens were fresh. That would be my evening home for the next several days as I walked the final miles to the Pecos River, which marked my completion of the Far West.

Berta, a lovely Native American and Hispanic woman, would each evening bring over a basket of bread and other wonderful dishes, and would tell me about her family. Her daughter, whose name is Misty Moon, was about to graduate from college as an agricultural scientist, and her son, whose name is Dearheart, is a medical assistant at a community hospital. Her husband, Steve, is an expert machinist for an auto parts dealer in

Pecos. Berta is the postmistress of a nearby town. She is rightfully very proud of her family, as they have come a long way in one generation.

There is a collection of antique bottles in the little house where I stayed. Berta collects them in the desert as her mother did before her. The pharmacy in Pecos, thirty miles away, has a nice collection of them also, from the day when Berta's mother traded bottles for medicine for the children. Berta took my hands and said that she understands my mission. All other reforms depend on cleaning up the system, she said.

Berta helped introduce me at Toyah's tiny city hall, which also serves as a church for the town. The two women clerks there invited me to speak the next evening, and as I walked into town the next day at the end of ten miles, there were posters up at the gas station and general store on the highway, promoting my talk. Government moves fast in Toyah.

Many townspeople brought snacks to the evening event. Berta brought delicious cold snacks made from prickly pear cactus paddles—I had some for breakfast the next morning. So, if I ever doubt that I am a tough woman, I can remember that I had cactus for breakfast in Toyah, Texas. It is like a very tart and tasty melon, by the way.

After my talk at the city hall, which included a chart I made to show how influence flows from campaign contributions to public laws, there were heartfelt comments from the townspeople about how they could no longer defend their town and how it was suffering.

At the end of the evening, Berta folded a letter into my hand. It was a long and beautifully written letter about her religious beliefs and about her town. The letter detailed how political corruption was literally dismantling her town, selling off the beautiful historic buildings for their bricks, and diverting the rail service that was the lifeblood of the town. Her letter concluded:

"I must tell you that at first I was somewhat apprehensive, but now feel privileged that you sought us out. God has a mission for all of us, though we often don't know the details, so therefore we trust. When you pray, please remember this little town." Well, I do indeed remember in my prayers this community of kindness and reverence, and I remember also Berta and her family and neighbors.

Let me tell you a little about her religious beliefs, because you will find them interesting.

She told me about her beliefs because my walking

companion through that area was Martha Fleisher of Connecticut, whom Berta correctly surmised was Jewish.

Berta told us that her church, which is Protestant, believes that the Jews are indeed the chosen people, and that it would be wrong to try to convert them. They take a subscription of the Jerusalem Post and pray each Sunday for the Jewish people, whom they believe have a central mission in God's design. Yes, it all may be about the Apocalypse, but they are acting with great kindness. They raised $600 this past year—and this is a very small and very poor church—to help a family of Ukrainian Jews immigrate to Israel.

I tell you all this because it is impossible to otherwise describe the capacity of Americans for kindness and tolerance without such examples. These are people deserving of great leaders, for they are a great people.

We cannot have great leaders, of course, so long as our system is in the stranglehold of selfishly corrupt money. We all have a duty to resolve that problem as quickly as we can.

What Berta feels, and what so many people along the road feel, is incredible loneliness in the area of cultural leadership. They feel abandoned by those who have the skills, education and resources to lead.

With all the progress we have gained during the modern era, let us not think that we are necessarily better off than the tribal village, whose elders gather at the council fire at evening to discuss the needs of the village and its people, and to manage the common resources of the village to best serve the people's needs. Where now is our council fire? The right wing, anti-government people will tell you that it is at your church and in your home, and that is correct. There should be council fires there. But Berta and a thousand people along any road will tell you correctly that the community, too, needs a council fire, and very few have one. The New England town hall form of local government provides good council fires, as do the town councils of many good places. But it is becoming increasingly rare for a town or city to have such a place were citizens come together as a community to study and solve their needs in common.

They therefore do not have the power to manage their common resources, and those who do in fact have the power— who have taken it over the years—often misdirect those resources for their own and their friends benefit. That is the feeling. That is what brings tears to people's eyes when they tell me how they feel about that loss of power, especially in the way it applies at the national level.

An old woman, obviously in very impoverished circumstances, pressed a can of government-issued food into my hands. She did not think I looked hungry, but she wanted to give me something to help me on my way to Washington. So did so many people want to help me say something for them in Washington.

Of all their troubles, the unkindest is abandonment by a political system that has been captured by the wealthiest of the wealthy elite. That is what they perceive. There is no one for them to complain to who will listen, except a crazy old woman walking by.

So what must we do? We see it already, as campaign-financing reforms spread state-by-state, pushing out the systems of corruption. It is also how the progressive reform movement spread across the nation at the beginning of the 20th Century. It is happening again. I am glad to be a part of it. I will ask you for more help, so that I can do more projects in more communities.

I think we have a long road yet to walk, and I ask you to stay with me, as I will stay with you.

A Season of Blood

Ms. Haddock emailed this message to supporters September 14, 2001, three days after the 9/11 terrorist attacks:

Dear Friends: In the space of an hour, thousands of Americans had their lives snuffed out by acts so cold-blooded that we cannot wrap our imaginations around what has happened. I have three grandchildren who, until Tuesday morning, worked near the World Trade Center. We held our breath until they found their ways to telephones and finally, on foot, to bridges and home. Many of their dear friends must be among the less fortunate.

It is a nightmare from which we cannot wake.

As we emerge from our pain, as we begin to accept the dimensions of this loss, we will of course resolve as a nation to make our world safer.

Whenever we suffer a tragedy we ask ourselves, how can we prevent this in the future? In answering this question, all Americans must participate and add what they can to the discussion and the plan. It is an opportunity for the political left and the political right to respect each other's point of view and their differing interpretations of history.

Those who see the attack as a military act of war are like the cancer surgeon who must find the tumor and kill it. Some minds indeed have become cancerous in this world and they threaten our survival. They are just as emotionally capable of exploding a homemade radioactive weapon in our cities, or of poisoning our air and water with biological, chemical toxins. What we saw Tuesday morning, horrific as it was, was essentially the loss of several large buildings and thousands of their inhabitants, while we risk the loss of whole cities of millions of people in today's charged international environment.

While the surgeons will cut, others will look to a deeper question: how can such cold-bloodedness arise in the hearts of our fellow men? As the nutritionist examines the lifestyle that may lead to disease, we begin to ask: What can we do in the future so that love and respect are nurtured in the place of hatred? Surely we cannot kill our way to love and respect, which is where our only true security rests.

The surgeons will undoubtedly have their way for a time. The news shows (that incidentally are never interested in covering the reasons why so many people are angry at American policies) are now full of swaggering militarists who are looking, please, for someone to kill for peace. They will have their way, for the emotions of our nation are running full red.

But those who seek true security must not stand aside in silence. Those who know that international justice is the only road to international peace must continue to speak their minds. It is not un-American to do so. It is, on the contrary, un-American to fall into a state of fascism, where our civil liberties are forsaken and the human needs of Americans and of people around the globe are forgotten.

The secretaries and file clerks and young executives in the stricken office buildings, and the children and mothers and fathers and sisters and brothers aboard those four airplanes would not have been the targets of hatred had we Americans better expressed our highest values throughout the world—had our government expressed in all its actions the fairness and generosity that characterize our people. That disconnection between our people and our government does not excuse the cold mass-murders committed by terrorists, but it helps explain it, and we cannot stop it if we do not understand it.

There is much we can and must do to regain control of our own government and to stop its participation in cruelties around the world. That is our best road to long-term security for our own people. There will always be breast-beating generals to lead us into further horrors. Let us pray that some of our leaders are wiser than that, and can see that the real road to security does not lead us to places like Kabul with our missiles and troops, but to places like the CIA headquarters at Langley with our mops and brooms—and also to the mammoth political fundraising events where our representatives are bought away from us and from our values.

Many media pundits glibly say today that America will be less free from this point onward. If they mean that we will have to have our luggage examined more closely, we can all agree to that. If they mean that we will all have our telephones tapped and be rounded up if we criticize our government—that we must be enslaved to be free—then they are wrong.

From my long walk across the U.S., and from my everyday experiences, I know that Americans are kindhearted and do not wish to colonize and exploit any other people on Earth. Our central question—the question that will determine the security of our cities in the future—is this: can the values of the American people yet be expressed by the American government? Can we be more a government of our people? Can we get the greedy, shortsighted interests out from between us and our elected representatives?

Our struggle for campaign finance reform and other democratic reforms will now take a back seat as a season of blood has its day. But until we clean up our government we will all be the targets of rising international rage, and our children and grandchildren are not safe. Yours, Doris

A few emailed responses:

Doris, Thank you. I felt more peaceful and focused when I read it than I have since the destruction. One of my friends of like mind burst into tears when he read your message, and again when he read it to his friends on the phone. I hope it cheers my 22-year-old son who has been worried and distressed at the mindless chauvinism everywhere. Many of us feel alone at times like this "when the best lack all conviction and the worst are full of passionate intensity." Thanks for the reminder that, although sometimes we may be few, we are not alone. —Burt

Doris, It has seemed to me that we should flood our friends who have too little with goods that they need: seeds, equipment for farming and building and establishing water

resources. An enlarged Peace Corps effort... Naive, I suppose, but as long as we puff ourselves up as we consume a disproportionate amount of the resources of the planet, it is not difficult to see that when you add political/religious fanaticism to the mix, revengeful acts becomes more likely. —Maxine

Granny D, When this kind of thing happens we realize that we are all family, despite the differences despite those within our own country that try to divide us along the lines of race, religion, gender etc. We must be careful not to preach anger towards Americans who have a different style of dress or worship in a different way, or speak differently. The beauty of this country is that this is a country where ALL are welcome to participate in the experience of freedom and democracy. Let us all remember this as we pray for the families who are suffering at this time. —Kit

The Four Freedoms Today

Ms. Haddock spoke in Unity, Maine on September 22, 2001, eleven days after the 9/11 terrorist attacks. Her remarks received harsh criticism in several conservative newspapers, but she fearlessly repeated the theme in subsequent speeches, especially as the run-up to the Iraq War took shape. As she and several of her organizers were at the Capitol during that time to push election reforms, they saw the situation at first hand, even getting to know the main arms inspector who came to the Hill to say that Iraq, in fact, did not have weapons of mass destruction, and that he and his American inspectors had free access to every corner of Iraq. The Senators who would not meet with him understood very well the fraud the Bush Administration was committing, yet they went along. This upset Ms. Haddock.

Thank you. It is hard to think clearly as we yet rock in the wake of terrorist attacks on our cities and our people. But think clearly we must.

Politics is a serious business. Not everyone cares to listen when people argue about the policies and practices of our political leaders. Americans would rather be painting their houses or going to ball games than listening to speeches, and that is not a bad thing. We wouldn't get much done if we just argued politics all the time.

But there is a time for it, and this is that time. Our neighbors and children are being killed in great numbers because Americans are not in control of the American government, and haven't been for some time.

And now we are being killed by our own airplanes, just as we were killed in our African embassies in 1998 by our own explosives, which we gave to the Islamic fundamentalists so that they would please kill our then-enemies, the Russians.

Our subcontracting of death has never done us much good, with examples still bleeding in Central and South America, Africa, and in Southeast Asia.

The Coca-Cola Company has been accused of financing the death squads in Columbia that kill union activists among the plantation workers, so that our Coca-Cola is affordable to us. Wherever our large mining companies extract the value from foreign lands, we have a CIA and a military working to keep any leaders in power who will guarantee us a cheap labor supply and cheap mining products, at the expense of local people and their efforts toward democracy.

This is not who we want to be.

If you ask the common American to describe the America he or she wants us to be, you will here a version of this: *'We are the country that represents freedom, opportunity and fairness. We use our strength to help people around the world. We oppose brutal regimes and work toward world health and justice and democratic participation of all people. The Statue of Liberty's torch is our beacon of promise to the world.'*

The ordinary American wants the American government to be exactly that, every day and in every corner of the world.

The ordinary American would never answer: "America is this: We use our powerful military forces, intelligence forces, and our huge financial power to extract from weaker countries what we need for our own, affordable lifestyle. We will support any brutal regime so long as they provide us with the cheap labor and materials and profits we need, and so long as they keep any competing political systems out of the region. We will finance the massacre of peasants and workers, the torture of journalists and clerics, and the rape of nature and the sky itself so that we may live pleasantly, however temporarily."

The ordinary American feels ill at such words. And yet, that is the vision of America that many people in the world carry in their angry hearts. They see their miserable lives and their precious children and their land being sacrificed for our luxury.

They see our US-made helicopters and jets and guns and rockets blowing up their wedding parties. They celebrate when we are made to suffer.

The disconnection between their perception and ours is profound: Our people are stunned at the idea that we are not universally loved.

In classrooms all over America this week and last, teachers and professors asked their students, "Why do you suppose that some people around the world are so angry at us?" Many students no doubt suggested that differences in religion make some people intolerant and fanatically homicidal. What other reason could they have?

In a West Virginia college classroom last week, a friend of mine, a former member of Congress, had something different to say.

"Look at it like this," he said to a classroom filled with honor students who couldn't imagine why America was under attack, except for reasons of religious extremism.

"Imagine that West Virginia was a Third World country," he said. "We have all this valuable coal, but there is one country, far away, that buys it all. They are the richest nation in the world, and they stay that way by taking our resources from us cheaply. They use their wealth to buy-off our government officials, and to kill or torture any worker here who tries to organize a union or clean up the government. How mad would we be toward that distant country, and just how innocent would we think its citizens are, who drive around in luxury cars and live in elegant homes and buy the best medicines for their children, and otherwise live life in sparkling skyscrapers—a life made affordable by the way they get resources from us and turn their blind eyes to what their government and their corporations do abroad?"

The classroom was silent. "Well," he said, "that's pretty much what we do all over the developing world."

Someone at the back of the room said, "Well, we may not be perfect, but this attack didn't come from Central America or Africa or Southeast Asia, it came from wealthy people from the Mideast, for religious reasons."

The class soon remembered that the C.I.A. had arranged a brutal coup to install the Shah of Iran, so to better protect the oil profits of Western companies, who had just been nationalized by Iran's democratically elected leader. The brutality of the Shah led to the rise of the Ayatollah Khomeini and the camp of violent Islamic fundamentalists, of which Bin Laden was a product. Bin Ladin's career, too, was financed by the CIA in the years when we used him to fight the Russians. The class was silent again. Then they began to discuss our problem, and now they were in a position to come up with real answers.

So must all Americans see America as the world see us, so that we can strive for justice and the peace that comes with justice. It's not so much about religion. It's about poverty and undeclared colonialism.

And do we do good things abroad, too? Indeed we do. It is nearly immeasurable, from the loving toil of Peace Corps volunteers to the massive aid programs of every kind.

But the politics that killed thousands of people in New York last week is the politics of Mideast oil, the politics of the Shah of Iran and our support for him and his torture police—supported so that we might secure oil profits for our elite and an anti-Communist puppet—at any price to the local people, and at any price to their democracy. The Shah did not deliver peace or safety, but instead he delivered into the world the Ayatollah Khomeini and the present wave of violent Islamic fundamentalists—who are no more Islamic in their practices than America's radical right are Christian in their practices.

This is not a time for all good Americans to forget their political differences and rally behind the man in the White House. The man in the White House should apologize for the most serious breach of internal security in the nation's history, not disguise his failure in calls for war. Can he hope that the fiery explosions in New York and Washington and Pennsylvania will be more acceptable to us if they are placed in a larger context of explosions of our own making? I do not rally around that idea. It is "wag the dog" taken to an extreme, for he is not covering up his failure with a fake war, but with a real one.

He has taken every opportunity to make the world less safe, first in North Korea and then in the Mideast, and in Russia and China. He needs a dangerous world to sell his military vision of the future for a "new American century." He is getting it. We must not go along with him.

We and the international community may soon have to rescue the Afghan people from the Taliban just as we had to rescue Europe from the Nazis, and rebuild it and let it find its way to self-government, but that is not the same issue and that will not resolve international terrorism at its roots.

Sixty years and eight months ago, Franklin Delano Roosevelt delivered his "four freedoms" speech to Congress as he prepared the nation for war. In it, he laid down the sensible and humane preconditions for future world peace and democracy.

If Mr. Bush insists on preparing us for his war against evil, let him learn from that great speech. Let me read you the final paragraphs:

"In the future days which we seek to make secure, we look forward to a world founded upon four essential human freedoms. The first is freedom of speech and expression—everywhere in the world."

Now, Mr. Bush, do not tell us that we must prepare to lose our free speech rights and our rights to privacy so that you and your corporate-military complex can continue to abuse the world safely. Do not take away our first freedom.

"The second, FDR continued, is freedom of every person to worship God in his own way—everywhere in the world."

Do not, Mr. Bush, let your vision of good and evil and your friends on the religious right overpower the other religions of America, which are religions of peace and justice. Do not take away our second freedom.

"The third," said FDR, "is freedom from want, which, translated into world terms, means economic understandings which will secure to every nation a healthy peacetime life for its inhabitants—everywhere in the world." Unquote FDR.

We cannot live peacefully if we do not work every day for the people, not the despots, of the world—and for justice, not for banking arrangements and trade agreements to fatten our already fat banks and corporations. Do not deprive the third world of this third freedom, for none of us are free if some of us are economically enslaved.

"The fourth," said FDR, "is freedom from fear, which, translated into world terms, means a world-wide reduction of armaments to such a point and in such a thorough fashion that no nation will be in a position to commit an act of physical aggression against any neighbor—anywhere in the world." Unquote FDR.

Let the U.S. stop selling the weapons of death throughout the world. We have fallen far, far from the vision of a peaceful, unarmed world. We are now the principle source of arms and high-tech weapons for all the despots of the world. Mr. Bush, you can only give us freedom from fear if the people of the world are free of fear. This the ordinary American knows in his heart.

I remember Roosevelt's speech well. My husband and I discussed it at the dinner table. We had already been married eleven years at the time.

I hope I speak for many common Americans who cannot see our flag without getting emotional with love for it. Our dream is that it should always represent the best that human beings can do on this Earth. This is a time for us to rally around its best values and its highest aspirations.

To the terrorists themselves, misled by power-hungry leaders into thinking this is about religion, here is my message: You are not martyrs, but cowards. Your selfish, egomaniacal greed for a place in heaven is childish. Heaven cannot be purchased with the death of innocents. Look across the Khyber Pass toward the land of Gandhi, who taught us that violence makes justice harder to come by, not easier. Today in America, the work of terrorists makes the work harder for those who want reform America's policies and practices. You do not want to change American policies, or you would be using your millions to bring your message to us in ways that we can understand and act upon. You want only your shortcut to heaven. We have the same great God, the same Allah, and he shakes his head in sad disbelief at your spiritual immaturity.

"The ultimate weakness of violence" Dr. King taught us, "is that it is a descending spiral, begetting the very thing it seeks to destroy. Instead of diminishing evil, it multiplies it... Through violence you may murder the hater, but you do not murder hate. In fact, violence merely increases hate.... adding deeper darkness to a night already devoid of stars. Darkness cannot drive out hate; only love can do that," he said.

Terrorism makes it hard for us to do the right thing, but do it we must.

Old "Fighting Bob" La Follette, the great reformer, said, "war is the money-changer's opportunity, and the social reformer's doom." But we will not accept doom. We will keep going. It is a time for all of us to speak the truth with courage and hope. America is, despite all, still the best hope for the world. But we are a work in progress, and we all have some work to do right now. It is the work of peace, of frank education, of making our lives and our communities more sustainable and less dependent on the suffering of others, and of cleaning up a campaign finance system that has allowed our elected leaders to represent not our interests and values, but those of international corporations who are set on world domination and who have the resources to buy our government away from us if we will let them. But we will not, so long as we live and so long as our freedoms are our guiding lights and inspiration. Thank you.

The Road to Freedom

Ms. Haddock speaking on Boston Common on Saturday, September 29, 2001, at a reform rally and march for clean elections.

Thank you. Freedom is what we walk for today: the freedom to elect candidates who will represent us in the halls of our government, not represent the wealthy special interests whose puppet strings bind and twist our government and our society. We want representatives who don't have to spend all night raising money and all day paying favors. We want people who will listen to us, who will represent us and our needs, our values, and our future.

I know that the Clean Elections Law has been under fire in Massachusetts by politicians who would rather fund their campaigns with the same old special interest bribery. But the times have changed, and they had better listen very carefully to what I am about to say.

Much of the money that is given to parties by corporations, and then filtered down to the campaigns of politicians, is given by organizations that are increasingly owned by people around the world. It is their asset to give, most certainly, but it is global money, not American money. We can no longer have corporate money in our elections unless we will accept the idea that people from Asia, the Mideast, Europe, China and elsewhere are influencing our elections with their money. No, let us keep our elections for ourselves, and tell those anti-reform politicians to get with the program—the Clean Elections program, funding it fully with Massachusetts money and nothing else.

More important than the source of the money is the effect of the money. It buys our representatives away from us at a time when we need them very dearly.

For, what happens when we lose control of our own government? What horrors rain down upon us when our government does not represent our values, but instead those of greedy interests who do not vote here and therefore should not influence elections here?

We walk today for our freedom. But we walk, too, for the peace and justice that comes when our government is in the hands of the people—we the people. The road of equality and justice is the road to freedom and peace. Thank you.

The Real Danger

Ms. Haddock's remarks to a gathering in Louisville on October 11, 2001, a month after the 9/11 attacks:

Thank you. We live in strange times—especially so after the recent terrorist attacks. We will never be able to fully digest those events. The ultimate act of dehumanization is murder, and mass murder is mass dehumanization—of the dead and of us all. We have no place to put this experience, no labeled shelf in our minds for such things. Being dealt with in so wholesale a manner disorients and disquiets us.

We are dehumanized from time to time by the powerful earthquakes of history, but each of us holds the even greater power to re-humanize the day and the world. Our humanity is found at the personal scale. When we place a flower in a heartbroken space, when we give a helping hand to a homeless family, or share good food and music with a friend or a lover in a romantic little restaurant, we again have done that.

Have you noticed how kind we have all been to each other since the attacks? We are re-humanizing our cities and towns.

The human scale is the thing we must preserve and defend. It makes no sense for our globalized marketing machinery to use its advertising and its entertainment shows to try to shape all the world's cultures into one mass market for our products. That, too, is a monstrous act of dehumanization that will provoke terrible resistance.

In our own democracy, preserving the human scale means preserving the human connection between citizens and their elected representatives. When those representatives need millions upon millions of dollars to get elected and re-elected, the personal relationship with constituents is, by necessity, abandoned in favor of relationships with donors. The human occasion is lost. The constituent no longer has someone to represent his or her values and needs. It's even impossible to get a phone call returned, unless a large donation precedes the call.

That is our condition today. Most Americans now believe that their own interests take a back seat to the needs of special interests in Washington and in most state houses.

So we have tried a number of laws to limit the problem. There are laws to limit what a person can give to any one candidate. The Supreme Court has ruled, in Buckley v. Valeo, that such laws are fully constitutional when they are needed to preserve the ethical health of government. We have tried laws to limit what a candidate can spend.

But a loophole called "soft money" was devised. The rich give their money to the political parties, who then spend it in ways that benefit the candidates. The McCain-Feingold bill, when it passes, will make it harder for this to happen, but we are not naïve, and we know that special interest money flows to candidates like lava to the sea, and so we will need new approaches in the future, I am certain. To use another metaphor, the rats always find their way through the maze to the cheese, so we must constantly rearrange the maze.

The McCain bill will also require groups that advertise right before an election in a way that clearly benefits or hurts a candidate to register as campaign committees, divulging their donors. The bill does not prevent a group from advertising, as many opponents of reform claim, but merely asks people who are acting like campaign committees to properly register as such.

Every aspect of the McCain bill has been reviewed by the top constitutional scholars, and they agree that the bill is fully constitutional. If you care to see their report, it is available from the Brennan Center for Law at New York University, on their website.

I have found that most people who claim that the bill is unconstitutional have never read the bill and never read the constitutional analysis of the bill. Ignorance is not bliss; it is mean-spirited and dangerous to the future of our democracy.

The McCain bill, in any case, does not solve all the problems. It is only a beginning toward reform, if we can get it and keep it.

Imagine a day when candidates don't have to raise huge sums. Imagine that they spend their time talking to constituents and learning about solutions to problems rather than running from donor event to donor event.

It wasn't that long ago, in my experience, when money was not such a drag on our democracy.

Some states are creatively solving the problem. In Arizona, for example, if you want to run for election or re-election to the legislature or state office, all you need to raise is a $5 contribution from a certain number of people qualified to vote for you. That demonstrates your level of community support that then qualifies you for public funds for your campaign advertising.

It involves some public money, but it is much, much cheaper than having a legislature full of people who must pay off the special interests with multi-million-dollar tax loopholes and other expensive public benefits.

We do have a public funding program for our presidential campaigns, but it has some defects that we must fix. It needs to be modified so that, if a candidate chooses to use that money, they cannot raise and spend other money from special interests, and it needs to match the competition.

What these reforms do is return our politics to the human scale.

It is fun to go to a public meeting in Arizona and see the candidates making their speeches, trying to persuade their neighbors to fork over the $5 donations. That $5 is all you need to be a fat cat in those states. That is an important return to the human scale of democracy.

Does it really matter, or should we leave things well enough alone? Should coal company money elect the senators from the coal states? Is that how we best protect our people and our resources? Should pharmaceutical companies and military hardware manufactures and oil companies control who gets elected and how they vote on our laws?

What is your opinion of that? Are you for reform, or do you like being an outsider in what is supposed to be your own democracy? Are you for campaign finance reform, or are you among those who have been brainwashed by the corporations and their elected puppets into thinking that our constitution is best protected by destroying real democracy with inhuman amounts of special interest money?

We are in strange times. Our position as a self-governing people is at grave risk. Not so much from terrorists—we are bigger and tougher than any group of murderers. Our risk is in our hearts and in our lazy willingness to let our democracy slide from under us.

Are you for reform, or are you worried that corporations, owned by people from around the world, might have their free speech rights abridged if they cannot buy any politician they choose?

Do you think the brave people under the graves of Arlington and a thousand other military cemeteries died to protect the rights of special interests to destroy our democracy? Or do you think they died to protect the idea of a government of the people, by the people and for the people?

There has been a lot of flag waving in the past weeks. But let us look at the real thing our flag stands for: It stands for our freedom and our responsibility as a good and self-governing people. If we are really for that beautiful flag, if we care for the sacrifices made for it, we must be a part of the effort to remove all barriers, especially the slimy money of special interests, between us and our representatives.

And so, are you for campaign finance reform, or not? If you are, it is up to you to re-humanize our politics. Support the enactment of the public campaign financing models in this state. Support McCain-Feingold in Washington. Use your own voice, your own ideas, to move reform forward. Inhuman forces oppose us, but we will win this, one neighbor, one friend at a time. Thank you.

At the Toadstool in Peterborough

A remnant of Ms. Haddock's February 2002, remarks in her hometown bookstore, after the campaign finance reform bill had passed the U.S. Senate, but before the House vote:

Thank you all, very much, and thank you Nell for the wonderful food. Now let me begin:

When I walked the final miles to the U.S. Capitol building, some 2,300 people were walking with me and having a wonderful time.

Until you walk America, you cannot understand its beauty and you cannot begin to understand the kindness of her people.

In Cumberland, Maryland, the people of the town heard I was coming and that it would be my 90th birthday. They marched through their streets with me, waving American flags and singing "This Land is Our Land." They boosted me up on the back of a caboose in their lovely train station so that I could make a birthday speech. The America that you might fear is long gone is in fact still there, waiting for you.

If I have any single message for you, it is that it is never too late to get in shape. It is never too late to do a great thing. It is never too late to go in search of your deepest values and your wildest dreams of brotherhood. Everything still awaits you. Everything is still laid out in front of you. It isn't even over when the fat lady sings, for I have had more than a few of them sing to me and have had hundreds of adventures since.

Now. I want to soon get to any questions you might have,

but finally let me tell you that the issue I walked for is far from resolved. The Senate has approved the McCain-Feingold bill, but there is a good chance it will die in the House of Representatives, or that they will change it so much that it will have to go to a Senate-House conference committee, where the anti-reformers will let it die. We are working to avoid these fates and I will go back to work the House very soon.

Here is our national problem: The cost of our elections has sent our senators, representatives and presidents running away from us in every direction to raise money. The interests of Americans of modest means and the interests of a healthy planet have taken a back seat to the demands of multinational corporations and billionaires, who now control our elections. That situation is worth walking across the country at any age, and I am glad I did it. I'm sure that if you fought in a war to defend democracy, or if you have lost relatives or loved ones in that constant effort, you will agree with me that our freedoms fundamentally depend upon our ability to choose people at election time who will represent our interests and values. I hope you will agree that we must return our elections to a proper human scale.

I walked for one main reason. So that I might ask the people I met, and I do not exempt you, to make one phone call to your U.S. Representative and demand passage of the campaign finance reform bill, and to pass it in a form that will not require a Senate-House conference committee. Please do this for me. I cannot imagine anything further I can do in the short time remaining to earn the right to ask that favor of you.

Pressure Campaign in the U.S. House

By February of 2002 the only hope for the passage of the campaign reform bill was a "discharge petition" in the U.S. House, forcing a floor vote. It was ultimately successful, partially because Doris toured the country to put pressure on House members. She gave the following remarks at one such rally and march, in Chicago, organized by her friend Andrea Raila (who later organized Ms. Haddock's voter registration walks through Chicago's underserved neighborhoods, including the Cabrini Green housing project). The details in this speech reflect the fact that, in the search for possible swing votes, she conversed with Senator McCain before naming names.

Thank you all very much. I have come to walk with you because this is about all we Americans can do these days. Our representatives in Congress, with whom we should be able to call up and discuss our health care needs, and who should represent us in the formulation of health policy, are no longer available to us. They do not have time for us unless we come with $10,000 checks, like the lobbyists for HMOs and drug companies when they come calling on Congress. Our so-called representatives do not have the ability to vote for programs that we need, for they have sold their votes for cash. So we walk. We walk because sometimes that's all we can do to get the word out, to get the truth out, while they have millions of ill-gotten advertising dollars to drown out any honest competitors and to drown out the truth of what they themselves have become.

Some of your Illinois Congressmen talk a good game of reform, but are a mile short on the delivery.

Republican John Shimkus of District 20 voted for final passage of Shays-Meehan in past sessions, but has yet to distinguish himself in this session by signing the discharge petition or insisting on fair rules of debate.

Republican Tim Johnson of District 15 was glad to have John McCain campaign for him, making the critical difference in his 3% win. Now it's time for Mr. Johnson to do what he told Mr. McCain he would do: vote for reform, and that must include signing the discharge petition so that there can be a vote on the Shays-Meehan bill. Among the Republicans there are men and women of principle who see the line in the sand, who are trying to get the corruption out of a corrupt system so that we can have health reform and the other reforms we the people need. On the other side of that line are the party hacks, trying to hold on to every slimy, special interest dollar they can prostitute themselves for. Tim Johnson needs to decide which side of the line is for him. If the people of District 15 will call him and encourage him to be a man of character and do what he told McCain he would do, then all America might benefit by the passage of real reform. A few votes can make the difference, and a few phone calls can make the difference.

Democrat William Lipinski of District 3 signed the Shays-Meehan discharge petition in past years, when it didn't matter as much because the reform was certain to die in the Senate. Now it has passed the Senate and he's not so sure he's a reformer. But he talks a good game: His official House of Representatives website quotes him on the subject of the Shays-Meehan bill. He says: "The Shays-Meehan legislation will improve the current system by actually limiting the influence of major political donors and the power of soft money. This bill will ban solicitation of soft money from inside government buildings. And, more importantly, this bill will ban direct or indirect foreign national contributions, including soft money, in connection with any election. Foreign influence has no place in American campaigns and elections."

He is right to note that foreign money and foreign influence will come into our elections even without the protection of Shays-Meehan. Is he willing to stop that foreign money from coming into our elections and into his own campaign treasury? He will show his true beliefs by signing the discharge petition or by refusing. If he refuses, the voters of Illinois have a right to ask him why he is allowing foreign money to come into his campaign and into campaigns all over the U.S., and why he is unwilling to show the backbone necessary to clean up the system. Does he need that foreign money to win? If so, he shouldn't run. He needs to sign the Shays-Meehan discharge petition. Call him and tell him to do the right thing—he knows what that is.

Ask any of these candidates if they take any party money. If they do, it includes foreign money meant to influence our elections. The only way they can get themselves off the hook with us is to sign the discharge petition and get the Shays-Meehan bill passed. That will get the foreign money and the other special interest money out of the system—our system.

I am honored to walk with you. I hope you have enough energy left to go visit your Congress members in their local offices—and do take your figurative pitchforks with you, because our democracy has never been in such danger—not even during the great wars—and we all need to raise our voices together now. Thank you all.

Valentines for Congress

The Shays-Meehan Bill, which was the House version of McCain-Feingold (more formally, the Bipartisan Campaign Reform Act) that Ms. Haddock walked for, finally passed the U.S. House on Valentine's Day, February 14, 2002, and went without delay back to the Senate for final approval and then to the president for signing into law. In freezing and subfreezing weather, Doris and volunteers had been picketing the House office buildings for days with large banners that invited Member of Congress to redeem themselves from the Enron scandal by voting for campaign finance reform. Ms. Shays, wife of one of the bill's sponsors, prepared hot tea for Doris and her comrades on the sidewalk.

Doris and friends made and then delivered handmade "Don't Break Our Hearts" valentines to each Member of the House. Doris invaded a resistant Member's office and began reading a list of his shady campaign donations until she was ejected.

But House members soon had enough.

On the Afternoon of the 14th, Minority Leader, Dick Gephardt, sent word for Doris to come up to his office. He told her they now had the votes and she should be in the gallery that evening. It passed. She was given salutes from the floor. After the vote, near 2 a.m., she waked out into the dark and down the East Steps with Mr. Shays and Mr. Meehan.

"It was not just what you said in your speeches," Mr. Meehan told her as they said goodbye, "it was how you sacrificed."

Her remarks the next day via email to supporters:

On behalf of the tens of thousands of people I have met over the last few years who have said they pray for the day when their government again responds to their concerns and needs and values, rather than solely those of wealthy special interests, I thank those whose personal courage and political willpower has started us on a journey out of this dark time.

I thank of course Senator McCain and Senator Feingold, Congressman Shays and Congressman Meehan, and also their families and their staffs—dedicated people who made it a matter of personal mission that this victory must be won.

I now pray for one thing more before I go home. I pray that the president will sign this bill into law. Perhaps those of us inclined toward prayer ought to pray together this Sunday for that signature. For if he fails to do so, we are in for a great deal more work, and I will have to go shopping for some new shoes. But no one should ever think that we will not win this thing—now, tomorrow or the next day.

And once we have won it, we shall move on to other reforms.

When I began my walk, the issue of money in politics was considered the linchpin to other needed reforms. I still believe that is true, and I have become a supporter of the public funding of our elections and the health of our global environment.

But during this last year, many Americans have also become concerned with the health of our Bill of Rights—our very status as a free people. I sense that we are entering a time when great political and personal courage will be necessary to fight against dark forces that have long been lurking behind the curtain, as Mr. Eisenhower warned us many years ago.

Those dark forces may have emerged in what will become greatest historic battle for America's soul. This battle today between big money and the position of the individual in our self-governance may be but an opening skirmish in that larger conflict.

But for now, let's relish this battle won.

With Senators McCain and Feingold

Be Like Laura

Doris Haddock speaking on campus at The American University, Washington, D.C. on Friday, April 19, 2002 — an Earth Day pre-event:

Thank you. This is a rather strange Earth Day weekend, isn't it? A strange dream we find ourselves in, where danger is seen coming but we seem unable to do much about it. We are oddly distracted by the most bizarre sideshow of horrors in the Mideast and in our own cities.

Yes, it is quite an Earth Day. The poles of our earth are melting and our mad addiction to oil and coal are distorting our international politics, leading us to do great harm to other people around the world, and prompting the destruction of our own mountains, streams, air, jobs and communities. We come to a time now when our planet and its atmosphere and its oceans and rivers and its fragile web of living creatures are most at risk and yet our leaders are remarkably and nightmarishly unwilling to lead us with creativity or even with simple sanity.

It is an Earth Day of monumental distractions, and, indeed, how easily we are distracted!

I am here to remind you to keep your eye on the ball—the beautiful blue-green ball that runs around the Sun in the company of Venus and Mars: this ball we live upon and that our children and grandchildren may or may not live beautifully upon.

Yes, we must fight for justice here and fairness there. But in these battles, we must not be distracted from the larger struggle. We must not forget to fight at a high and strategic level for the defense of life itself, the earth itself, and for love itself.

There are several strategic approaches we must consider.

One is democratic reform. So long as the people who are elected to serve as the stewards of our lives and of our environment are beholden to rich special interests who pay for their election campaigns, we will have a continuation of the present mind-boggling chronic scandal. It has eviscerated our middle class, flattened millions of acres of our once-beautiful mountains and rivers, pushed the limits of our atmosphere to the breaking point, strangled our oceans and created an unsustainable lifestyle of pressure, expense, credit, and relentless exploitation for the great majority of Americans and for others around the world.

There is indeed a small and effective class of very selfish, very brutal and very shortsighted operators who have stolen much of our democracy and our wealth away from us and, if we don't get both back from them, we will have neither a democracy nor a living planet.

Friends, they carve off the tops of the mountains, fill in the valleys—covering hundreds of miles of fresh streams with toxic sludge and rubble for the next million years. The plants and wildlife and people are pushed out. Horrific floods soon follow, killing all nature. The coal itself is burned for a cheap energy fix, though it is the largest contributor to global warming and toxic air pollution.

So we must fight for justice at every turn and fight for fairness every day—but also keep our eye on the big picture for the blue-green ball.

The Middle East and Venezuela and Afghanistan and the sky above us will all be friendly territory if we no longer are the mad addicts clawing the world over for another pound of coal, another barrel of oil. Keep your eye on the blue-green ball and make a personal promise to yourself and your children that you will do what you can in the next days and months and years to end this fossil fuel dark age.

The New York Times reported yesterday that pollution from coal-based utilities east of the Mississippi causes 6,000 early deaths a year. That is twice the toll of the World Trade Center attack, and this is one we can see coming, again and again.

Now what do those deaths really mean? It comes down to a young mother standing out in her lawn and tiny flakes of something fall from the sky and she knows she must do something to protect her family and her world. That's the way it was for Laura Forman as she stood in front of her little farm in Kenova, West Virginia. Let me tell you something about Laura so you will never forget her. Let me put this little picture of her in your head: Here she is, a little redhead growing up in Upstate New York. Her father is mowing the yard, but it is taking him a very long time, as it always does. Why? Because little Laura crawls in front of him to save the little creatures, the tiny frogs and other fellows, who live in the lawn.

As a teenager, she would sometimes go down the road to clean up areas of the forest near her home, taking away litter left by campers.

She loved the birds so much that she married the closest thing she could find to one: an air traffic controller and bird lover named Mike.

Mike and his small son—Laura's small son—stood the other day in front of the Corps of Engineers office in Huntington, West Virginia to continue a protest where Laura had fallen last

December. She had made her demand that the Army Corps of Engineers stop issuing permits for the obliteration of the mountaintops of West Virginia and Kentucky. Then she slumped to the ground, dead. Later, her friends went to her little office over the antique shop and found the puppy she had rescued from a roadway a few days before. She had fought so hard and worn herself out, trying to protect her mountains and this world from the ravages of King Coal. People told her to take some time off— to get away from the fight for a while. She couldn't. And her heart gave out. She also had several cancers, it was later learned— probably from living in the ashfall of a coal plant near their home.

But in her short life she helped stop some bad projects and she encouraged many a hero in the coal fields to stand up and do the right thing, and they are doing the right thing today, and they surely need your help.

Mike recently made a list of some of the things Laura loved. I am going to read it to you because it will help you know Laura and know how much Mike loved her. Here is what Mike said. I want you to listen to every word and hear a human being come through—a human being like you.

He said, "*If you knew Laura, then you must have known she loved these: Her family and her pets; Being a mommy—she took motherhood seriously; Her friends; Animals; Her work. And she loved chocolate, especially truffles; And travel-—she dreamed of an African safari; A good book by Denise Giardina, Barbara Kingsolver, Rachael Carson, or Wendell Berry; She loved an honest-to-God liberal—bless you Ken Hechler; She loved being Home; The Simpsons; Cleveland Amory; Ben & Jerry's Cherry Garcia; A good bottle of Cabernet; Mahalia Jackson; Picking out clothes for Donald to wear in the morning; Old movies—the older and sappier the better—It's a Wonderful Life, To Kill a Mockingbird; She loved bed & breakfasts; Mozart; Roller coasters; Poetry; Alice Walker, Walt Whitman; her sister Lynn's poetry; Jimmy Carter; A night out with the girls; Boston the city, not the band; Bob Dylan; Christmas; Reading to Donald before bed; Art—Laura was a member of the Huntington Museum of Art; Otters; Taking pictures— Laura was a published photographer; Outdoor markets; Mel Gibson; Chinese takeout; Martin Luther King; Scary movies; West Virginia's Blackwater Falls, Dolly Sods, Cranberry Glades; to be on top of a mountain in the southern coal fields with Larry Gibson; the New River; Brooks Mountain, Coolfont, the Greenbrier Valley, and Salt Rock; Doing stuff in bed—reading, shopping online with her laptop and snuggling; John Lennon; Dried Flowers; Jessye Norman; Buying gifts; The X-Files; Granny D; Antiques [I think she may have put me in that category]; Breastfeeding Baby Donald; Food cooked on the grill; Sailing—we dreamed of touring the Galapagos Islands by sailboat; the song Any Day Now; Alaska; Redford; Going to the Symphony; California; Camping in a tent; Hanging plants; 60 minutes — the piece on mountaintop removal that she put together with Mike Wallace was one of her proudest moments; Japanese food; Pottery; Lois Gibbs; Looking good — I can't remember a time when she didn't; A big bowl of cereal; Scotland; Georgia O'Keefe; The power of email and the Internet; Enya; Hiking in the woods; Yoga; meditation; Jane Goodall; Candlelight vigils.*

"*For those of us who were engulfed by her loving spirit,*" Mike continued, "*we'll always remember that she loved what she stood for. She walked the walk. Laura was 24-7 zealous and incorruptible. She didn't back down — she sent the bullies running for cover... I will continue to teach Donald Roy what Laura taught me: The Big Picture. The 3 R's-- Reduce, Reuse, Recycle. Protect Mother Earth. Think globally and act locally. Love animals and remember that all living things deserve respect and protection. Demand social justice. Stand up for the oppressed. Curse out the bad guys — to their faces, on their home turf. Tell it like it is. Give back more than you take. Make a difference. Love your friends. Let your hair down but not your guard. Walk the walk.*"

So wrote Mike Forman.

And so, to the extent that any person can make a dedication, I dedicate Earth Day 2002 to Laura Forman and to Mike and Donald and to their friends in West Virginia who are fighting the bad guys, the greedy, the corrupt, the powerful. God bless Laura Forman, because people like Laura provide the real homeland defense for all of us. They are not distracted. They have their eye on the blue-green ball.

Homeland defense starts with our air, our water, our mountains, our communities, our Bill of Rights. Homeland defense means we protect our children from rapacious polluters and their politicians. Homeland defense means we defend America the Beautiful and its highest values here and around the world.

Don't think any of these fights are little fights. West Virginia coal operators, for example, have a lot to do with your life. Not only because they are destroying your planet, but because their campaign cash was responsible for bringing George Bush the one more electoral vote he needed, so they might continue raping the mountains and burying the rivers with total impunity. So don't ever think that by going into the dark of a distant fight you are not going to the front lines of the battle for the world itself.

And in every fight, work happy. Work in love. Laura was one of the most joyful people I have known, despite the fights she led. Don't let the forces of darkness drain you or divide you. Whether your life is long or short, you will have loved every minute.

Don't walk away because you are confused or because it is difficult. We have entered an amazing time, when each of us has an important role to play. It is the best time ever to be alive on this earth, because everyone matters. Everyone is needed if we are to survive—your creativity, your love, your courage—all of it. As the smoke of political battle swirls around you, smile, for it is a privilege to be alive in such a time.

And please don't hide in self-effacing modesty—be a hero of this great planet. Be like Laura, full of love and energy. Follow great people, and lead great people and always, always keep your eye on the blue-green ball. Be like Laura, always letting your loving heart be your strength and your guide. Be like Laura, always remembering that we cannot do for the world what we cannot do first for our friends, our family and the loves of our lives. Thank you.

Note: Larry Gibson, of Kayford Mountain, was helped in his advocacy by Laura and other coal country mountain advocates. Marybeth Lorbiecki, Larry's biographer, wrote that she was at a Washington D.C. meeting of the Sunrise Movement, when Sunrise leader Will Lawrence said he met the late Larry Gibson up on Kayford Mountain, surrounded by the ruination of mountaintop removal coal mining. "He changed my life," Will told the group. "He's why I'm here. We went to visit his mountain, and he said, 'If I show you my mountain and you don't do something, then I've wasted my time. You have to go back and do something.' So my friends and I went back to Swarthmore and started the divestment movement.'" From that point, Bill McKibben of 350.org became involved, as did the Global Catholic Climate Network, worldwide. Then Will and his friends organized the Sunrise Movement to fight for a livable climate by advocating for "a green new deal." He traced it back to Larry, who began his advocacy to protect his mountains when Doris Haddock walked through West Virginia on her way to D.C. in 2000. He met her and became inspired, first for his own walks across the state to educate people about mountaintop removal mining, and later with actions that landed him at the United Nations, in the lecture halls of major universities, and in jail. He was in regular communication with Ms. Haddock for all but the last two years of his life, as Doris passed before him.

Take Your Heroic Part in Life

Ms. Haddock was honored at the May 2002 commencement at Franklin Pierce College (now University). Her remarks:

Thank you very much for this honor. After I finished my 3,200 mile walk across the United States to speak out for campaign finance reform, I was often asked to share how I prepared for this walk, and to share what I learned from all those miles and all those many, many towns and people. I did learn something, but it is more for the proud parents and grandparents in the crowd today. So I speak today to them.

What I learned—and I hope you will not take this too personally, mom and dad—what I learned is that it is never too late to get in shape.

It is never too late to dust off the dreams you may have for yourself and for your community and your country—and to do something about them.

It is never too late to have another great adventure, make a few thousand new friends, and, well, if you like—it worked for me—to march on the Capitol and get arrested.

Not all of my new friends cared to get arrested—many marched to the Capitol and then treated themselves to gin and tonics and pedicures. This is a wonderful country and there is something for everyone.

That is my advice to you forty-and-fifty-year-old kids in the parents' bleachers. You haven't even yet lived out the first halves of your lives. Take a heroic part in life. Follow your heart.

For you graduates, I have no advice. You know everything there is to know, and you now have the paper to prove it. Over time, of course, you may forget some of it and then we can talk. If I am still kicking when you have room for some advice, come over to my place in Dublin and I will try to fill you up with some subversive ideas.

The main idea will be this—that we must take personal responsibility for our communities and our country. We must live in communities that do not pollute the world with greenhouse gases or other toxins. We must not have stores full of cheap prices if those bargains come from the suffering of other people anywhere in the world. We must gain the ability to elect leaders who represent our values, even if that means we have to upend the political system so that good people can run and get elected, and serve without undue influence from special interests that today distort their actions.

Those are subversive ideas. But don't think another hard thought today.

I give you all my deep respect for the self-respect you have shown by investing in yourselves in order to come to this day. You are responsible people—just what the world needs. Good luck to us all.

Fight Like Hell

Ms. Haddock spoke to the Arizona reform community on July 29, 2002. Her remarks:

Thank you. I am glad to be among my Arizona friends again. The last time I was here, I walked here. Many of you walked with me and helped me. I have come back to thank you. Some of you were also with me when I arrived in Washington, D.C. We are all a part of the effort to get corporate money out of American politics.

Arizona is a reform state. It didn't just start with your Clean Elections victory, by the way, or your open meeting laws or your lobbyist gift ban or your campaign finance laws that limit maximum donations and require full disclosure, or with your groundbreaking anti-gerrymandering Citizens Redistricting initiative. No, you have been a reform state from day one of your statehood. You were denied that statehood for several years because you were born in the era of the great Progressive Movement, and your proposed state constitution gave the people the power to legislate by initiative, referendum and recall. That seemed pretty dangerous to President Taft and others. They turned you down.

But Teddy Roosevelt came out to Arizona to dedicate the dam that you named for him. You got that dam, by the way, because he got most of his Rough Riders for the Cuban War from Arizona and New Mexico, and so, when he was president, he made sure that Arizona got the first big reclamation dam in the new federal water program.

So, while he was here to dedicate the dam, he told you to drop the populist stuff from your constitution, get admitted to statehood, then put them all back in, and that it would not be unmanly to do so in that fashion, as it was just politics. And, bless you, that's just what you did. And you have, ever since, been a laboratory turning out good reforms and bad governors.

The Progressive Movement, by the way—in case you haven't noticed—is back. I am glad to have lived to see two of them.

At the turn of the 20th Century, it was the abusive practices of banks and railroads and other corporations that swept reform across America. Farmers and small business people didn't do that for any other reason except that their livelihoods were fully at stake.

What happened as a result of that uprising, in a nutshell, was that the powers of government were expanded to keep the powers of the corporation in check—to keep corporations from overwhelming our human values and our ability to provide good lives for our families as free people.

What has happened in the last few years, in another nutshell, is that the government's ability to prevent corporate giantism and its abuse has been undermined and nearly emasculated for the benefit of the corporations who underwrite the political careers of their puppets in Congress, in the White House—Democrat and Republican White Houses—and in the state houses.

The crisis this time around is more dangerous, for not just our ability to prosper is at stake, but also our ability—and nature's ability—to survive at all.

Alaska's glaciers are melting. Seas are rising. Droughts and their fires sweep across our purple mountains and our fruited plains. Any mountain with coal under it is being sheared off and dumped in the next valley. More explosives are used against our mountains every day than we used in all of our recent wars—and why? So we can burn more coal in an already carbon-saturated environment. No respected scientist any longer doubts that we are destroying the planet rapidly. We have an obligation to our children. We will have to stand in front of our Maker—will we not?—and explain how we properly cared for the great gift of life we were given—the birds and fishes and flowers of this Eden.

Even in this solar state, where is your solar energy? Your utilities are now opening another giant coalmine, this one across the line in New Mexico. What kind of madness is that? Isn't it enough that you are destroying the lives of Hopis and Navajos up on Black Mesa—destroying their land and draining their water— so that you can heat your pools and cool your doghouses?

This kind of cultural and environmental injustice and madness follows naturally from the presumption of corporate leaders—they are as shortsighted as they are greedy, and yes, I'm talking to the presidents of Salt River Project and Arizona Public Service—Tucson Electric is perhaps trying harder.

Let's pick on APS. They should be ashamed of themselves. They generate one megawatt of solar energy. That is it, of their 8,000 megawatt total. And they ballyhoo in environmental fairs and their green-this and green-that programs how valiantly they are trying. But in their annual reports they say how wonderful it is that demand is growing and that they are burning coal for nearly half their demand.

Perhaps we need to revisit the idea that utilities should ever be for-profit corporations. Maybe they are killing us. SRP isn't better, and is leading the way in coal mining. Do they get away with this because there is no political leadership, here or in Washington? Where, indeed, are the leaders?

If we had any, we would expect that they might come to us and say, "Well now, we must all conserve these resources. We must stop burning coal, which is the largest contributor to greenhouse warming, and we must move rapidly to solar and wind and other sustainable energies. We must make better cars and design cities that people can move around in without trashing the planet." These leaders of ours would tell us that our children's lives are in the balance and that we must all pull together with sacrifice and creativity, and they would remind us that there are more new jobs in a green economy than in a dying carbon one.

How can it be that this has not happened?

There is only one possible explanation: that there are people so greedy and so assured that their vast wealth will always find them a safe and comfortable place on a dying planet that they think they need not worry about the costs of their rampages, and that these people have, through distortions of our political process and real thuggery, taken over the top positions where they can use every crisis as a new opportunity to further their position and advance their power over us—stealing our freedom, stealing out common wealth, misrepresenting our values around the world and bringing us accelerating harm and misery.

Is there another explanation?

Where are the leaders who will move us toward a healthy, sustainable future?

Who will defend the health and extent of our middle class—which is the necessary foundation of our democracy? Where are the leaders who will say, "Dear People, our democracy rests on the solid ground of a strong middle class, and so we must find ways to eliminate the financial exploitation of our families—

we must help them to rise, not cause them to fall."

Surely the leaders who represent our values and our interests would say this and would care about this. They would point to the big-box retail stores that destroy all the family businesses throughout a region, turning its people into greeters, and they would tell us, "The money you save at these stores is destroying your lives. Don't be bribed into destroying your towns and your fast-receding middle class."

Is there an explanation for why our leaders are not telling us this truth?

Who can lead us to a time and place where we have power over our own lives, the resources and time to care for our friends and family, and the leisure to live proper lives under God's sun and moon?

Well, I know you are fighting these fights. But they can wear you down, as they never seem to stop coming. I want you to understand that the American Dream is not a leaky old boat that always needs fixing. It is not an old house that always needs repair. No, this high-reaching society of ours is not in trouble from its own age or infirmity. It is in trouble because it is under attack. The holes are not from age but from flaming ordnance. We are engaged in a cultural war, and we had better wise up to it and get rid of the leaders who are very clearly not on the people's side.

The corporate elites who have declared war on us give no quarter. They will shut down the factories we need without blinking. They will refuse us the medical care we need without blinking. They will burn coal when the sun is all around us. They will push for growth when they should be pushing conservation. They will finance the careers of politicians who will make nice speeches to us but will participate in our destruction without blinking.

Dear friends, we have our families to save. We have out planet to save. We have our water and our air and all the creatures of nature—including ourselves and our friends—to protect. What a great and glorious fight we are in! But let us believe we are in it. We did not declare this war against corporations and their wealthy elite, but they have declared it against us. Let us go for victory. Let us limit the size of these beasts, limit their political participation and limit their ability to ruin our family business and our needed jobs. They act like dictators, not only to their own employees, but to all of us. They are a hazard to us and they must change or go.

Can we survive without the little darlings? Yes, with some inconveniences, of course. Can we survive if we let them continue on as they are? Clearly not. What do you do with a villain who trashes your world, threatens the peace and happiness of your town and family, and sends your children off to its selfish wars? You put its picture up in the post office among other villains. You go after it until this public enemy is caged and the world is at peace with leaders and institutions that represent the people's highest values and aspirations.

I suspect you will have to talk each other into running for office before you will have such leaders. So do it. And work for your friends who are indeed running for office. Some of them are in this room, and this is your opportunity to do something that matters. Say you will help.

And keep Arizona's assembly line of reform ideas moving. Get going on instant runoff voting or proportional representation. Those reformers are here with a booth today. Go say hello. Go learn about what that reform can mean to you and your children in Arizona.

I know it's hard sometimes. Americans are tired, overworked, underpaid and sometimes we are filled with despair over the condition of our government and the institutions of American business. Can we save our American Dream and the free democracy that powers it? Sometimes we doubt that we have the energy to do it. We doubt that our efforts will make a difference. We are like the nearly unconscious man in a house full of gas fumes. He knows he must crawl out to survive, but he is tired and tempted to just close his eyes. But we cannot do that.

Too many wonderful people have given their lives for this democracy, this garden planet, this dream entrusted to us today. We have to find the time. We have to find the energy. We have to find the optimism to get up, stand up, and defend our Bill of Rights and the rest of our Constitution and our planet.

Let me say one more thing: I am an old woman. I have seen a lot of bending and twisting of our dear Constitution. Thank goodness we always had, until now, an honest Supreme Court to set things right. But we now have reason to worry in this country.

A year and a half ago, our new president swore to uphold our Constitution. The Constitution gives to Congress the power to declare war. It does not empower the president to put people in jail without attorneys or without the right to be reasonably charged within a reasonable time. It does not provide that American citizens can be deemed enemies of the state and deprived of their rights. It does not provide for the setting of some Americans against others with an elaborate snooping campaign. If we are indeed at war, then our enemies are soldiers who have rights under the Geneva Convention. If we are not at war, then citizens have rights.

And are we torturing people? Are we arranging to have them tortured by other countries? What do we call all of this except by the dreaded name that I hesitate to say aloud? Are we in danger of becoming a fascist state?

Here is a man in our White House who was not properly elected but who calmed us by assuring us that he would bring us together. He brought us together all right. We come together to fight him so that we can save our world's environment and world peace. We have come together.

In future years, historians will write in amazement that the present administration, after colossal incompetence that allowed a historic crime to take 3,000 American lives, took that crime for his political advantage and brought America into its moment of greatest danger. It will be called the time when America almost lost itself, its values, its soul, and almost lost the courage of its Constitution, which remains the First Wonder of the Civilized World.

I'm not afraid to die for my freedom. Mr. President, don't make me safe from terrorists at the expense of my freedom. I gladly accept risks for my freedom. I have the courage of my Constitution, because I owe a debt of courage to all who gave their lives for my freedoms. I fear you, Mr. President—not Osama, not Sadam—but you. You are the threat to America and its Constitution.

If any of you out there are tipster spies, make a report on what I just said and send it on. Let them put me in jail. It won't be the first time, and I always meet interesting people there. They have jails enough for us all, you know.

But we will fight to keep our Constitution. We must do that in the short term, and we must all very soon go to Washington and march to stop a trumped-up war that will have as its first victim the remains of our Constitution.

And in the longer term, we must defend the health and wealth of our middle class against the neocolonialism of today's corporate elite, and we must defend our right to elect people who will represent our interests, our values, in the halls of our government. We must rise up and do this by electing a great new generation of courageous leaders.

We must manage our own lives and our communities in responsible ways that do not require the exploitation of other generations or other parts of the world.

I am proud to be with you Arizona reformers, because I

know the good you do. Your reforms, including public financing of elections and the creation of an independent redistricting commission, have spread to other states. I ask that you let your energies continue to join with others around the nation and around the world in a new progressive wave to save our democracy and our planet while there is yet a chance.

Be bold about it. Fight like hell for your values and our common dream of brotherhood and sisterhood on our garden Earth. Thank you.

News Media and Our Communities

Ms. Haddock speaking as the guest of Pete Seeger at a Grassroots Radio Conference in New York's Catskill Mountains, August 10, 2002:

Thank you. What a beautiful evening. Don't we pray that all the people of the world might have such peaceful evenings in peaceful places? But there is no peace in so many places, here and abroad. Only a well-informed American citizenry can right things here, but, if we must rely upon our traditional news media, we may be in trouble.

Our locally owned daily newspapers and broadcasters have been bought out from under us, and the flow of truth to us— always a problem—has been dramatically eroded. We simply can't have healthy democratic institutions without a well-informed citizenry.

On a local level, we are losing the community and cultural leadership from those grisly old bears who once ran our newspapers and stations. Though we often disagreed with them, they were from among us, and they nurtured great professionals to act as the conscience, the eyes and ears of our communities. But the old bears and their cub reporters are mostly gone.

The best editors and reporters are driven out when a major newspaper chain takes over a city's newspaper. Thirty inch stories, which are barely sufficient to give citizens the background they need to make intelligent decisions and to develop wise opinions, become ten inch stories and then four inch.

Seasoned journalists are being forced out in favor of low-wage rewriters of wire stories.

The important news of the day is not something that

comes into a city like a parade that can be reported by simple observation and description. Good reporting is complex and dependent on research, experience and wide reading, rather like a doctor's ability to diagnose.

Real news is not found solely by attending council and board meetings—it is the careful collection and assembly of sometimes subtle facts; it is the rising up of truth and conscience and outrage—it is the stuff that boards and councils and legislatures must then confront. Yes, reporters can take down notes when things hit the fan in public meetings, but journalists also include the slightly rumpled and red-eyed scribblers at the back of the room, whose long dedication to their beats happen to have helped drag the issues into the room. They did it for the people, and for justice, and they get no respect by the media chains that discard them.

Wherever the big corporate media giants go, we are losing these rumpled heroes. Increasingly, therefore, the only local news items getting to the people are the cherry-picked agenda items decided by board commissioners and mayors and woefully uninformed, marketing-oriented editors, who may have very little passion for the truths that the people need to know, but who do know what gets seen on the Internet.

We are talking about the rapacious exploitation of our communities. Some newspaper chains expect a twenty to forty percent operating profit from their newspapers and stations. That is colonial exploitation. It takes but does not give back to a community.

We cannot survive without high journalism—not if we are to have any chance of being a self-governing people, and not if we are to be well balanced in our civic considerations and in our selection of leaders and in our support for domestic and foreign policies.

So what to do? As to the work of taking corporations out of our elections, the recent campaign finance reform law was no cure-all, though, if we can keep it and if we can get proper enforcement, it was worth the battle.

The rise of independent media came into importance in the last year of that battle for campaign reform, and it was an important factor in our success. Your radio stations, webcasts and independent media centers are rapidly filling the vacuum created by the ever-shrinking newspaper newsrooms. You know what you are doing, and, while I have no wisdom to offer people like my brilliant friends Amy Goodman and Juan González of Democracy Now!, I will comment gently from the margins:

First, I urge you all to reach out to the good journalists in your community, some of whom are working under horrible constraints at the big newspapers and television stations, and offer them a regular guest microphone so that they can tell the deep stories that they can no longer otherwise report.

Second, I urge you to be even more aggressive in getting to high school-aged young people, letting them learn the reporting ropes. You have the technology and the dramatic missions they crave. They will never become the robots of the system if you enlist them in the cause of truth at an early age. Do go out and find those special teachers, often teaching history classes, and get them involved with your station so they will bring the young people into the fold. Put them on the air. Remember what your own high school life was like, and think of how an indy media center could have saved your pimpled life.

Third, I think we do not do enough to outreach to new audiences. If you have not already done so, I urge you to read "Nickel and Dimed," the story of working at Walmart. Some community radio stations should consider a weekly call-in show for such employees. You could promote it with little bookmarks tucked into the sweaters they have to restack at the stores. Use the Norma Rae image to get people standing up for their rights. This is not a niche market. The largest employer in some states is now Walmart. Before they will join Reverend Billy's Church of Stop Shopping—and Reverend Billy is here today and has baptized me in the waters of anti-consumerism—before they will join, they must come to understand that they are in the same boat with sweatshop workers around the world.

Which brings me to my fourth piece of unsolicited advice. It is not enough to tell people how messed up everything is. If that is all you do in this rising movement of independent media, the largest opportunity will be lost. The most powerful force for reform is always the positive image of the better way of living. Can you communicate what it will be like to live in the world you propose, the first of it beginning each new day?

Most people are realists. Even the men blowing up the mountains of Appalachia for more coal to give us more global warming know that what they are doing isn't a good idea. They say this to us: "Please, I'm just playing by the rules I found. I need to provide for my family. Our happiness depends on money, and here's how I can get it. Change the rules if you can. I would like to be able to provide happiness for my family in ways that are not destructive. What do you propose?"

What indeed do we propose? What is our creative vision

for life on Earth in the 21st Century? We have to project that in realistic ways. From that image will come the passage of laws and the changing of buying habits—our two biggest levers for change. Reform is driven by dreams. Effective revolutionaries know that. Use a good part of your bandwidth for the positive.

Well, that is enough pontificating on a night that should have less preaching and more banjo playing from Pete Seeger—look, he's just standing around when I should shut up and let him play.

But one last thought: We all have a special job to do in the weeks and months ahead. Our Bill of Rights and the other remains of our Constitution are under attack. When I walked across the U.S. for campaign finance reform, in hundreds of speeches to groups large and small I appropriately mentioned that the rows upon rows of our war dead were men and women who loved life and did not go off to defend a corrupt system of legalized bribery, but they died for an American dream of fairness and freedom and individual rights. What is it if not a treason against their memory for an elected leader to purposefully destroy the Bill of Rights—the right of habeas corpus, the right to face your accuser, the right of privacy implied in the Preamble—for there are no Blessings of Liberty if we are not free of surveillance, and on and on—the freedoms that so many have worked for and died for? We must steadfastly connect and contrast what is going on now with basic American values, and we must do it in our news stories and speeches and in our private conversations with our friends and neighbors. We have the patriotic high ground, and we had better use it.

In the 1950s, Joseph McCarthy and Roy Cohn rolled on and on, destroying people and the ethical ground under the U.S. Senate, until Joseph Welch and Senator Margaret Chase Smith finally spoke up to put them in their place. We don't have too many senators worth piss anymore, but we can do that shaming ourselves if we must, and I guess we must.

Not everyone will feel the same way about these things. We must invite them to come argue as friends. As an American, that is my favorite thing—the fact that we can hash it out peacefully and each come to a better understanding, which will inform the way we think and vote. We call it democracy, and, for all our worries, we've still got it.

Thank you all, and goodnight.

Like a Tree Standing By the Water

Ms. Haddock in Seattle on August 24, 2002, nearing the first anniversary of 9/11:

We have come to a time for communal remembering. We will see the images again of 3,000 fine people dying a year ago. We will see again in our minds those crematory clouds that overwhelmed the sun and all our sensibilities.

The horror of September 11 was not only the horror of 3,000 deaths: We were all victimized, all dehumanized by seeing our fellow human beings killed in so wholesale a manner—as if ants.

Since that morning, in more than three thousand ways, we have tried to re-humanize the city and our lives. We said, "I love you" in public parks. We placed flowers in harsh places. In small cafés by candlelight we rekindled torches of human love and, like resolute townspeople suddenly of one mind, we carried these torches against the monstrously inhumane oppressions and abstractions of modern life.

As a democratic people we require the support of our political representatives in that effort—their jobs are to serve as the agents of our common dreams. We had an opportunity to make those deaths mean something. We had an opportunity to honor those individual hearts by bringing more humanity, more love into the world in vivid and heart-moving forms. We had an opportunity to defeat the forces of hatred—that sick product of the spiritually immature mind that reduces humans to abstractions. For a moment, we looked at life with the same amazement that I'm sure those who died share from the other side. Do they stand around us yet, hoping that we do not fall back into the hypnosis of exploitation—hoping that we can still imagine love and be fully conscious and amazed in the world?

Instead, their memories have been harshly abused. We got

an inhuman response that yet grows—a sickening cloud that yet darkens the American sky and the world's sky. And to Ashcroft's and Rumsfeld's and Cheney's and Bush's false alarm manipulations of the childish news networks and the pushover Daschle Congress, we say, for God's sake, men, if you aren't smart enough to see the positive opportunities for the world at this moment, at least sit on your hands and do no harm. This is no time to repeal the Bill of Rights, or to renounce America's citizenship in the world. Don't do all that because you think we fear a few madmen enough that we will give up America's freedoms.

Yes indeed, there are people intent on killing us who are as dedicated as they are spiritually deformed. What indeed is more childishly selfish or more spiritually immature than to love your religion so much that you would ask someone else to die for it? But there are things in this world worth dying for honorably. And one of those is real political freedom for our loved ones.

I am from New Hampshire and our state motto is, "Live Free or Die." I never thought much about it until recently. But I tell you that we must all now have the courage of our Constitution. I will take the risks of living in a free country. I will risk the danger of terrorists. I often carry a heavy purse and can defend myself, and if that is not enough, so be it. I will NOT stand idly by and allow my government to commit treasons against our Constitutional Bill of Rights.

Get a grip, Mr. Ashcroft, Mr. Cheney, Mr. Rumsfeld, Mr. Bush: this is America, where we live free or die. Go visit a military cemetery to remind yourselves that we are a courageous people and that we mean it when we say Liberty or Death.

Whose dark cloud is it that darkens our Constitution, our Bill of Rights, our national soul, our responsible position in the world community? It mustn't be a dark cloud of our own making.

Would you have thought a year ago that people in America could be arrested and held without charges, without lawyers, without any rights? Would you have imagined that America would be running detention and maybe torture camps, holding people secretly for months or years, and with the corporate media cheering them on?

Would you have imagined that the government would reorganize around the idea of becoming something of a police state, and that soldiers would be patrolling like policemen and that your email and that the posters on your bedroom wall would put you at risk of all this machinery of snooping and detention and isolation and perhaps torture, and with the corporate media cheering them on?

Could you possibly have imagined that any American could be stripped of all his or her rights by being named with no proof as an enemy combatant, an enemy of the state? Could you have imagined that permanent war would be declared against nobody in particular and that it would be used to de-fund every social program the radical right ever didn't like? Could you imagine the idea of our elite troopers being authorized to go anywhere in the world, without invitation, to kill anyone they pleased, and with the corporate media cheering them on?

Could you have imagined we could fall so far so fast under this dark cloud?

These dark clouds from the towers, if they darken our Constitution, are clouds of opportunism. The wealthy bullies behind the radical right never miss a trick in manipulating our own fears into a mass capitulation of our freedoms. The maneuvering to undermine our Bill of Rights by a fraudulent pursuit of public safety is as un-American as anything that has occurred in my 92 years. These un-American usurpers of our election and of our freedoms do not represent us in the least.

We have the courage of our Constitution to live free on our garden Earth as brothers and sisters—to live free or die. And together as the human community we stand for love and its courage and against death and its fear. As agents of life, we are the tree standing by the water, and we shall not be moved.

The responsible course for America is no secret. Our only real safety lies in crafting an American success story that does not rely upon the repression of the world's people and the destruction of their systems of self-determination for the sake of our industrial needs. Otherwise, a state of constant war is indeed inevitable. We know that. We choose against it.

Our only real safety lies in the crafting of an American success story that does not rely upon the trashing of America's and the world's environment for the sake of our convenience and corporate profits—profits that are used to pay political protection through our corrupt campaign finance system.

Otherwise, there is no America the Beautiful for our children or life on Earth for our grandchildren. We know that. We choose life and love, and we shall not be moved. The blue haze that often keeps us from seeing our mountain majesties, and that heats the Earth and threatens our survival, is the product of a domestic political terrorism that harms us far more than any cells of terrorists. In the Northeast alone, where the Hudson River Valley is now blanketed in coal pollution coming from as far as the Midwest, twice as many Americans die each year from the loosening of environmental standards on coal plants as died in the twin towers.

To get that coal, a thousand times the explosive might of the Oklahoma City bombing is used each day against the mountains of Appalachia by the president's coal friends, who help finance his career. Every four days, the explosive power of the entire Afghanistan campaign is used against Kentucky and West Virginia mountain ranges we once called "almost heaven,"—all while the president rejects any effort to conserve energy. What kind of patriotism is that? It is none.

Yes, we also have a war to stop. We need to organize massive peaceful demonstrations in Washington and in our state capitols. The trumped-up war in Iraq is power madness and pure stupidity. The fact that it is monstrously immoral, and based on lies to the American people and Congress, ought to also count for something. But beyond our necessary efforts to stop these destructive things, we must, in our own creative ways, show— with the courage of our Constitution—how to live free on our garden Earth as brothers and sisters—living free until we die. Thank you.

Be Open to Your Own Genius

On September 5, 2002, Ms. Haddock spoke to the incoming freshmen at Franklin Pierce College (now University), New Hampshire:

Thank You. I know you all are grateful to be on campus and finally, safely away from all your grandparents and aunts and uncles who have been asking you what you will major in, what career you have chosen, and where you plan to retire and be buried. Older people are stuck in a view of the world that is quite rigid. You go to school—according to this view—learn a trade or profession, get married, get a house, raise kids to take your place, have a well-attended funeral, and then do your part to increase New England's insufficient topsoil. The great New England schools like Franklin Pierce are so reliably longstanding that they create a mirage of constancy, when in fact the world is changing rapidly and the world of your parents and your aunts and uncles is being swept away.

For you, college will be a lifelong affair. You cannot learn enough here in four years to get you through your entire life. Your life will be about constant learning and growing through a number of related or unrelated careers, and that is a dramatic improvement in the condition of human beings—if life is about maximizing our potential, which indeed it is.

You will have a number of personal relationships in your life. I am glad to have had one marriage to one husband, but your life may well be quite different. While I recommend loyalty, I know the statistics.

The bright side of this difficult emotional terrain is that you will have the opportunity to experience enriching pain and you will have the advantage of essentially living several lives, to my one.

Of all the shifting sand your tent will be pitched upon, perhaps the condition of the Earth's ecosystem and its democracies will present the greatest challenge. If the great present division persists between the world's poor and rich, I assure you that you will live in a violent world.

If the great exploitation of the Earth's resources persists at the expense of sustainability, you will experience the flooding of Venice and other great seacoast cities and treasured beaches, and you will curse the generation before you that let it happen without trying harder to end the corruption and the selfish misuse of resources. But you will learn to adapt and to fight for the planet's survival. Your career and your life will be about this struggle, one way or another.

Yours may be the most privileged generation to ever live on Earth. I don't mean that you have soft advantages, but that you find yourself in a time when your individual contribution will have a heroic importance to the world. This may sound overblown. It may make no sense to you for an old woman to stand here and tell you that you, personally, are the hero or heroine whose actions will decide things for a troubled world. But I think that may indeed be the case. Our lives are more beautifully linked than you can imagine, and the genius of one life—and yours is a genius life—can affect all the others in unimaginable ways.

You must become the hero of your own life in any case, and that is enough for your happiness, regardless of any extension into the world.

Finding your genius is sometimes a hard trick. Sometimes it is easily spotted, embraced and nurtured. But some of you will not find it until you are old and gray. Some of you will never find it, though it was always there for you to find, I assure you.

Sometimes we see it and do not want to find it quite where it pops up. "Well, yes, I happen to be very good at that, but, Dear Lord, I don't want to be that for life."

Indeed, you may turn away from your own genius many times before it comes knocking with a baseball bat on some dark night of the soul.

Be open to your own genius. Try everything fearlessly. See what gives you energy instead of taking your energy away. Discover the things that keep you joyfully up until 6 a.m. Sex, of course, doesn't count, because we are all geniuses at thinking about that. It's a given.

If you can't get excited about anything in the way of a first career, don't despair. Keep exploring. You are on a Grail quest, and your quest will be rewarded if you keep combing through life, looking for the thing that sparkles for you. It is there, believe me. It is your soul. It is your life's work.

Finding your soul is the great project. But it is not the only happiness to be enjoyed in your life—especially in these glory days of your youth. Take time each day to look at the beautiful lives around you. Look with love at these lives, and be a force for good in them. We all need each other very much. There is no better way to find your own heart than to look with kindness to the needs of others. We cannot find ourselves except though friendship and love and serious respect for the lives around us.

So, the big question is, "what are we to do with our lives?" And the answer is this: we are to look at this life with eyes of love and find for our hands those things that bring us the most joy and curious interest. That is a simple prescription for a happy life and a happy college career. Thank you.

How The Takeover Artists Took Over

Ms. Haddock speaking before the peace group Citizens for Participation in Political Action (CPPAX), Boston, September 27, 2002:

Thank you. I want to begin by congratulating you for all the work you have done over the years. I know peace and justice work is often frustrating. Through the vision of your values, you see ahead to a world of cooperation and peace—a world of justice and sustainable economies and meaningful democracies. You wonder why others cannot or will not see these things or reach out for them, and why they in fact oppose the obvious good—why they take the part of the oppressors or the blinkered warhorses.

I would like us to take a few moments to consider why this work is so hard, and what we might do to move toward our common dreams more rapidly and with greater joy.

Some of you may be old enough to remember the Reagan Administration. Mr. Reagan and those around him believed in a very new kind of American hero. This new hero was a business hero—not the fellow who built up a family furniture store on Main Street and supported the Little League and the Scouts; this new hero was not the woman who worked late hours to create a successful travel agency, nor was this new business hero anything like any of the hard-working Americans who built-up our middle class, advanced our standard of living and gave us the resources and leisure for the proper civic life of a democracy with its leagues and Rotaries and Lions and Elks and VFWs and party conventions and all that glory.

No, the Reagan business hero was the corporate takeover artist.

Any regulations that might get in the way of these ruthless new capitalists were removed so that reptiles of uncommon greed and brutality might rule the Earth, which they now nearly do.

What soon happened was that all publically traded corporations of medium or larger size had to look over their shoulders. How did a corporation protect itself in this environment from a hostile takeover? It had to close down any factories that were not earning obscene profits. Never mind that a factory had served a town well for a century, or that it provided a healthy and regular profit for its stockholders. If it seemed to be underperforming by the new hyper-greed standards, or if it could be closed in favor of opening a foreign plant that provided an even slightly higher rate of return, then, in this new atmosphere, the company was considered derelict in its duty to its stockholders if it did not ruthlessly act.

Perfectly good and profitable factories were closed. Benefits to employees everywhere were eviscerated, and staffs were downsized, outsourced, computerized, downsized again, outsourced again to temp agencies that paid no health care or retirement, and on and on until America became a very different place. The gap between rich and poor is now wider than at any time in our history. It began with the corporate raiders and takeover artists celebrated and enabled by the Reagan Administration and the Republicans.

Ours is still a wealthy nation for many people, but poverty is on the rise, and those with jobs find themselves so overworked trying to make ends meet that there is little time for family or for the joy of living. Indeed, there is very little joy left in American work life. Workers are not loyal to their companies, because companies treat them like expendable slave oarsmen, with no dignity or assurance that hard work will result in advancement or security. We are living in the harsh world invented by a handful of corporate raiders whose values were completely foreign to the fairness and moderation that had so long served as the proper foundation of American success and the American dream of plenty for all. They were not a new kind of person, for there have always been among us a few dark hearts of uncommon greed. What was new was the political permission they received for their rape and rampage, which continues.

And so a new world devolved as if from a virus. The new business hero, a Horatio Alger on crack, did very well. The new model CEO derived from that moment—the ruthless mercenary who would come in to reorganize a company and render it takeover-proof by rendering it inhumane, or who would ruthlessly save it from massive debts created by a takeover. This executive was worth millions per year, we were told. In this way, a Darwinian system of corporate survival assured that the most carnivorous, rather than the most responsible, would rise to lead our most powerful commercial organizations. It became expected that, since the taken-over, debt-loaded companies needed warrior CEOs worth their weight in gold, then all CEOs should be paid to this new standard. This would require cutting wages and benefits and job security to all others below the CEOs, but so be it. Even public universities and professional ball teams would need these salaries, as they were the new standard.

As these mostly men—raiders and CEOs—moved to secure their wealthy status, they started buying up our politicians of both major parties. They joined the wealthy who had destroyed America's small businesses with their big-box stores, the Internet, and other machines of monopoly.

They together came to control Congress and the White House and state houses.

To survive and move up in these organizations, one must be like the boss. In Fox News, even reporters in local regions are told how to slant each story hard to the right, to satisfy the reptilian big bosses. There is very little remaining pretense of journalism within that organization. And many people stuck in those jobs, who got into journalism with the idea of doing legitimate journalism, are sick to their stomachs every working day. They would leave except that journalism jobs are shrinking; so they live in hope of better owners.

In this way, the right-wing leanings of a few people have distorted entire industries, including television news and radio networks. Political leaders are quickly infected in this trickle down reptilism—trickling down from the people who write the checks for political campaigns and who control enough of the political news to get them reelected.

It all trickles down further, to the weaker minds listening to talk radio and to those silly enough to spend time watching Fox News—listeners and viewers who buy the lies, who are simply suckered into forking over their own political best interests to the billionaire con artists who attempt to pick their pockets at the same moment they are pointing out others who, they say, are the real trouble makers.

Some percent of our people are susceptible to this kind of con, and they then give us problems by standing against any reasonable reforms. They have been spiritually twisted by the cheap poison of a hundred Rush Limbaughs into the angry, unthinking robots of the superrich.

On my long walk across America, a man driving a garbage truck told me that the biggest problem facing America today was the inheritance tax. I didn't have to ask him if he had a radio in his truck.

I remind you of all of this because it is important to know that the reason our reforms are difficult is not because Americans are split into two camps, conservative and liberal. It is not like that at all. There are lots of conservatives and liberals in America, but we are not the two sides of the divide. True conservatives in our country don't have many political leaders to look to with respect right now. Barry Goldwater may not be our favorite politician to remember, but even he believed that the government had no business in our bedrooms. He believed that a woman and her doctor didn't need the government's help in deciding her important issues. He would have laughed and become angry at Ashcroft's attacks on the Bill of Rights and his citizen-against-citizen snitching system. Goldwater believed that the only issue of importance regarding gays in the military was whether or not they could shoot straight, and he said so.

What we are seeing now from the far right is not conservatism at all; it is fascism: the imposition of a national and worldwide authoritarianism to enforce a narrow world view that enriches and empowers the few at the expense of the many, and that gives no respect or honor to other cultures, other ways of living, or other opinions. To call that conservatism is a crime against the memory of America's true conservatives, who might think that government ought to be less involved in life than we old liberals would concur with, but who nevertheless stood for certain values that today's right wing leaders undermine at every opportunity.

If we Americans are split into two meaningful camps, it is not liberal versus conservative, but rather politically awake versus the angry hypnotized—hypnotized by television and other mass media, whose overpaid Svengalis dangle the swinging medallions of packaged candidates and oft-told lies.

It is done to prolong the open season on us all, as the billionaire takeover artists and their complicit minions bag their catch for the day. And in their bags are our freedoms, our leisure, our health care futures, our old age security, our family time, our village life, our family-owned businesses on Main Street, the middle class itself, our position of honor and peaceful leadership in the world, and the livability of the world itself. It will likely get much worse before we rise to make it better.

When we understand what we are up against, and where the meaningful dividing lines truly run, then our lives as reformers can be easier, because we shall know how to proceed.

And here is how it is best done:

Pull any contractor out of his white pickup truck, turn down the talk radio blaring from it, and ask him, "government good, or government bad?"

His glazed eyes will widen. "Government bad!" he will say. Ok, good; you found one to play with. Now ask him what the town might do to make it safer for kids to get to and from school, and around town when they're not in school, without getting killed by traffic or getting in trouble. He will have a million ideas. Good ideas. He has no clue that he is being government—if government is what happens when we get together to solve our common problems and to make life better for our communities.

You have broken his trance with the elixir of participation in decision-making. As evidence of this, we see progressive ballot propositions passing in presumably unprogressive states. Why? Because people are problem-solvers at heart.

Government agencies, of course, have often been the communitarian's worst enemies. Anything that smacks of bureaucratic rudeness or pushiness or counterproductive stubbornness does nothing but damage the idea that government is we the people, where we act together to solve our problems as fellow citizens. That corrosion of government really needs to be brushed out wherever it shows its pinched, gray face. Would it be possible for Progressives to organize a way to encourage government courtesy and efficiency? After all, if we are looking to promote the idea that government is the place where a community takes action to solve problems, shouldn't we improve the product that we are trying to sell? Who will step forward to organize this?

That really should be done to prepare the ground for what could come next, which is a new engagement of citizens with issues of interest to them in their communities. We should begin in our high schools. During the years from 13 to 19, lifelong civic values are formed.

We should work with the popular history and civics teachers in our high schools to bring the issues of the day and the issues of the town into the classroom—not to propagandize but to openly invite students to learn, research, and offer advice to the community on a wide range of issues. This is where the hypnosis falls apart. This is where democracy finds its feet again.

This summer I asked America's independent and community radio stations to get involved with those same teachers in our high schools, to make students into community reporters and commentators. I reminded these independent news stations that they have the technology and the dramatic missions that young people crave. I said young people will never become robots if they are enlisted in the cause of truth at an early age.

What we do in schools, we must also do in colleges and then in the general community. But if we only have the means to focus on the high schools, that will be enough. These young people will be voting in only a few years. If we support their increased civic engagement as they move through college and into the community, we will have raised an army of citizens immunized against corporate hypnosis. Our victories for needed reforms will come naturally. With an engaged and informed citizenry, who knows what good we might do, and what great civilization we might yet again move toward? The crashing climate will organize young people soon, but we can and should advance the schedule.

I urge you to think young, to link with moderates on the other side of the fence, and to approach the schools and teachers who can help you connect your young, rising citizens to the issues that will shape their lives.

If you believe that human beings, in addition to all their other instincts, want to help create and live in a happy, sustainable, just, creative and cooperative world, then you must believe that people are to be trusted in their politics, so long as they are encouraged to study everyone's experience and study the competing points of view—and so long as they are raised with enough love and security to be capable of empathy. We need not force a liberal agenda on our society, any more than we need force our political opinions on our children. We can enjoy life instead of banging our heads against the old walls. If we encourage an awakened thoughtfulness, democracy and justice will have all the victories our hearts can handle.

We should never let up in our efforts to protect young children from poverty and other abuses. We should support young parents so they will raise their children well. This is not only the right thing to do, and therefore the proper goal of political action, but we must understand that one of the credible theories of the divide between the political left and the right is that those on the right have a deeply-seated belief that people are basically selfish and bad and in need of authority figures who will straighten them out. Those on the left have more of an innate trust in the good of people, and they therefore look to remove the stresses and abuses that would corrode that naturally gregarious and cooperative sense of sharing and goodness—empathy, to put it in a word. And what makes a child fear others, distrust others, have a bad opinion of people in general? It is a rough childhood where the security children need has been stripped away by a culture that overstresses the parents. So, let us care about how children are raised, for it determines whom they become.

I began this talk with a view of the corporate takeover artists who shaped our present world. To reshape it now will take a new kind of takeover artist, whose guiding value is not greed but love. It will take artfulness, strategy, energy and resources to do what now needs doing. Thank you very much.

Big Institutions Need Big Democracy

On October 3, 2002, Ms. Haddock received an award at Shenandoah University. A portion of her remarks:

Thank you very much. I like being on a college campus because I love learning new things. A college campus is somewhere between a temple and an amusement park—a place dedicated to wisdom and our curiosities and also our childlike sense of wonder. The college campus should be our model for life generally, and for our cities.

People of all ages should feel at home here, because the adventure of learning and the *ah-ha!* of a sudden new understanding of the old world is a lifelong romance with the divine.

Have I learned anything new lately? I think I may be coming to understand better the nature of democracy, power and the proper human scale of things.

Look around the world, and look at all the bright young students who are concerned that overlarge corporations and overlarge global trade banks and control groups are damaging human affairs. I think they are very right in their concerns, and I admire them very much for their bravery and energy in taking a stand, so long as they follow Gandhi's peaceful prescription for social change.

But I do not think these young people will be successful in reducing the scale of corporations or of the controlling organizations that seem to do the corporations' bidding. It may be possible to enforce an ethic of human scale, but I think it is far more possible to pursue the adoption of a new way of thinking about large organizations in a way that will make them less toxic to our planet and our lives.

I think we have learned this: that the larger the institution, public or private, the more genuine and thorough must be its internal system of democracy, and the more intimate must be its connections with the needs of the society it serves.

Man and earth can no longer afford our corporations to be little private fascist regimes, with Mussolini-like CEOs living like total despots over the thousands of people under them, underpaying them, forcing them to move here and there, and stealing the value from their work so that the few at the top can live better than any kings or dictators in history.

No, the world cannot afford that. A corporation is, or should be, a community of people who spend much of their lives together, and they should have systems of justice and fairness to make their lives and careers decent, civilized, secure and fruitful. As there are tremendous benefits for all of society if that kind of organization should flower, we must create great incentives in our tax codes and other laws for organizations that will adopt that kind of corporate charter. We as consumers could encourage it too, by doing business with them, and not the old kind.

The principle, as I say, should be this: the larger the organization, the more democratic should be its internal structure.

A second principle, relating the size of institutions to the needs of the societies they serve, is just as important. The new or revised charter of any forward thinking corporation should require a thorough connection of the corporate goals and culture with those around it in the community, the nation and, for the largest organizations, the world. We cannot afford corporations that ride roughshod over our communities, especially if corporations are to be as large and powerful as some nations—which is already the case.

We the people give life to corporations by issuing charters. We must look at what has become of these creatures, and we must now make some adjustments that will benefit people and the earth. No corporation, after all, can long prosper unless we the people prosper.

Thank you.

Let Us Name Names

Ms. Haddock in Oklahoma City, October 26, 2002:

Thank you very much. I am a New Englander from New Hampshire, and we New Englanders are, by tradition, fairly good business people. For example, there is a fellow who lives about an hour and a half south of me who buys-up state legislatures for profit, including yours here in Oklahoma.

His name is Harry Bresky, and he lives in the suburbs of Boston in a very nice home.

His name might ring a bell with you, or perhaps not. In any case, you should know about him because he is what you have instead of a true representative democracy.

Mr. Bresky has set himself up as a poster boy of corporate welfare. That is to say, you all pay him millions of Oklahoma dollars for the privilege of smelling his factory hog farms.

The Federal Government, four years ago, was paying out about $125 billion a year in corporate welfare nationally. And now, special corporate tax breaks have more than doubled it. They get that landslide of our tax dollars—billions more than is paid to alleviate poverty in this country—in exchange for their campaign support of key legislators in Congress and in statehouses. The conservative Cato Institute has estimated that campaign contributions from fat-cat donors are returned ten-to-one in corporate welfare payoffs.

Mr. Bresky has a little company called Seaboard, which includes flourmills in Ecuador, Guyana, Haiti, Mozambique, Nigeria, Sierra Leone and the Democratic Republic of Congo. He has feed mills in Ecuador, Nigeria and the Congo. He has 3,000 acres of shrimp ponds in Ecuador and Honduras; 37,000 acres of sugarcane, 4,200 acres of citrus; a sugar mill in Argentina; a winery in Bulgaria; agricultural interests in Chile, Colombia, Costa Rica, Guatemala and Venezuela. He owns electric-power-generating facilities in the Dominican Republic; shipping companies in Liberia, and has containerized cargo vessels running between Miami and Central and South America. He also, as you may know, has hog farms in Oklahoma, Kansas, Texas and Colorado, and poultry-processing plants, feed mills, hatcheries and 700 contract chicken growers in Alabama, Georgia, Kentucky and Tennessee.

Now why would this busy, busy man take time to write checks to members of the Oklahoma Legislature? Why does he pepper the members of the environmental regulation committees with generous donations? I suspect that he is just a good government booster, don't you?

It could be that he feels a little guilty for squeezing millions out of a tiny Minnesota town and—after cutting wages, importing strikebreakers, and refusing to properly dispose of massive wastes—eventually leaving the town with an environmental and social disaster. Maybe he is trying to do better here.

He abandoned Minnesota to come to Guymon, in Texas County, Oklahoma. The town and the state put together an economic incentive package worth $21 million for Mr. Bresky's benefit. The county raised taxes on its people, many of whom were already hurting, to front $8 million to Mr. Bresky. The state granted a $4 million, 10-year income tax credit. The state spent $600,000 to train Seaboard's workers. The company received grants and low-interest loans to finance a waste-pretreatment plant. The company was excused from paying $2.9 million in real estate taxes. The package was $21 million altogether.

When it was time for the public to get some of that back, no dice. The company protested every tax bill, finally whittling it down to about 17% of what was due.

Oklahoma taxpayers picked up the unpaid portion. And the social costs of a large, low-paid workforce are piling up, as is the stink and goo, driving long-time residents to despair.

Now. How on Earth does that happen? How does it go on and on?

Well, here are a few people you might ask to explain it. Ask your candidate for governor, Steve Largent, why he took Harry Bresky's thousands and how those dollars might influence his policies, if he wins.

Ask Kelly Haney, who serves on an important environmental committee in the legislature, if those thousands he received from Harry will affect his decisions.

Ask Fred Morgan in the House about the thousands he took from Harry in 2000.

Ask Brooks Douglas, Johnnie Crutchfield, Bernest Cain, Gilmer Capps, Billy Mickle and Kevin Easley. Ask Cal Hobson, Danny Hilliard, Jim Covey and Terry Matlock why they took Harry's money.

Are they bad for doing so? No. But, is it harder now for them to do the right thing in their legislative work? You bet it is, and they know it.

People like Mr. Bresky are paying off your politicians and thereby picking your taxpayer pockets.

Every day that passes without the passage of a clean elections program in Oklahoma is a very expensive day for taxpayers. It is simply much, much cheaper to publicly finance our political campaigns than to let special interest fat cats buy our representative out from under us. We must be our own fat cats. We the people must own the hearts and souls of our elected representatives.

I urge you to forge ahead. It is the right thing for Democrats, Republicans, independents, Greens and Reforms. Get the big money bullies out of your politics and breathe the fresh air of real democracy again.

The seemingly countless gravestones in our military cemeteries do not mark lives given for the defense of special interest politics. They mark the sacrifices made for our freedoms as a self-governing people. From time to time we must chase the moneychangers out of the temples of our democracy. This time has come in Oklahoma. Thank you!

How to Not Split the Vote on the Left

Ms. Haddock's remarks to a political science group at Penn State, November 2, 2002:

Thank you. Peace in any family requires fairness, kindness, honesty, shared financial and physical security, a positive and creative view of the future for each individual, and real respect for the things that sustain us. When those basic conditions are not present, happiness fails and bad things begin to happen. Bad behavior begins to happen.

Peace on any planet requires fairness, kindness, honesty, shared financial and physical security, a positive and creative view of the future for each individual, and real respect for the things that sustain us. When those basic conditions are not present, happiness fails and bad things begin to happen. Bad behavior begins to happen in civic and national life.

In other words, peace is not the product of force, no matter how well-meaning may be our 500-pound bombs, no matter how enlightened may be our cruise missiles, no matter how sensitive and caring may be our antipersonnel cluster-bombs. Peace is not the product of war. Death and dismemberment, orphans and anger are the products of war. Peace is the product of fairness, kindness, honesty, shared financial and physical security, a positive and creative view of the future for each individual, and real respect for the things that sustain us.

I repeat myself intentionally because our White House and Congress have it all wrong and we need to keep reminding them of the truth.

So let me say it in a way our president might understand: If you want peace and safety in America and the world, you must work to make fairness and kindness and justice and economic security the common condition of the world. If you want terrorism, then drop bombs, support dictators, steal resources, use all your weapons and develop more, instead of your people.

"The ultimate weakness of violence" Dr. King told us, "is that it is a descending spiral, begetting the very thing it seeks to destroy. Instead of diminishing evil, it multiplies it... Through violence you may murder the hater, but you do not murder hate. In fact, violence merely increases hate.... adding deeper darkness to a night already devoid of stars. Darkness cannot drive out hate;

only love can do that," he said.

For here is our new reality: The world is now too small for us to do harm over there and hide over here. The world has found us. We have to base our international policy now on fairness, kindness, honesty, shared financial and physical security with a positive and creative view of the future for each individual and respect for the things that sustain us all. We don't have a choice, and thank God for that. Thank God we are constrained to now have to do the right thing to others in order to survive, ourselves.

We know morally what we must do—but how can we do it politically?

Both of our major political parties need saving. We must save them, even though we might like to let them go.

The Democrats are often useless because they have learned from Mr. Clinton that victory lies in the mushy middle, and so they stand now for mush. They stand for mush in a time when real leadership and real courage is required to save the very planet and to preserve our free democracy. They do not have it in them, as we saw most recently in the Iraq war vote.

The Republicans, too, are mostly useless, because they have forsaken their honestly conservative rank-and-file members in favor of a brand of right-wing extremism that we must call the American Taliban, in that it is so virulent. It has nothing to do with authentic conservatism. It has nothing to do with Lincoln the Republican, Teddy Roosevelt the Republican, or even Barry Goldwater or John McCain the Republican. It is a kind of fascism, if fascism is the merging of state and corporate control to extend, by force, their narrow interests worldwide, subjugating the people of the world into sweatshop workers, McDonald's feeders and Wal-Mart greeters, and all of it fueled by oil and coal ripped from a gasping and ill planet by an ever-more privatized military.

How are real Republicans to be saved from this—real Republicans who believe that government should be less powerful, not all powerful; who believe that government should be out of our lives, not in our bedrooms, and not spying on us from every street corner camera?

Both parties need the same medicine. They need competition.

The Republican Party will not straighten out until they have to face John McCain, running as an independent and splitting the vote.

The Democrats already know what's in store for them with Mr. Nader and the Greens splitting their vote.

Now. Let's be Democrats for a moment and find our way

to happiness.

Here's our problem. If we adopt all the Green Party positions, we may or may not lose the middle voters, if middle voters even exist anymore. And if we don't adopt sensible Green positions, the Greens will split our vote again. What should we do? And what should the Greens do, now that they may have in their hands the ability to grant or deny Mr. Bush a second term?

I happen to love Ralph Nader. I consider him a friend. Another friend, historian and founder of the Alliance for Democracy, Ronnie Dugger, recently went over to Ralph's office in Washington to ask him to not run in 2004. Ronnie, whom I first met in jail, is of the opinion that we are facing a national emergency, and that our nation is at risk of losing its free democracy. I fully agree with him.

Ronnie supported Ralph in the last election, but he does not want to see a second Bush term. I'm sure Mr. Nader would not like to think of a second Bush presidency, either.

It is not for me to say what Mr. Nader said in confidence, but I will say that we have a problem.

The American left may be so fully cracked in half that the Democrats will suffer a long string of defeats to the unified Right.

What would you do if you were, say, Terry McAuliffe, the national chair of the Democrats? I first met Terry, by the way, by crashing a very fancy fundraising party where they were raising millions of corporate dollars. I told him that I was opposed to corporate campaign donations. He said he was too, and then offered me some hors d'oeuvres, which were delicious. You know, Gandhi and King taught us that we must sometimes put our bodies in the way of injustice, and I think we must all do more to crash these parties and eat these hors d'oeuvres before they reach the mouths of our elected representatives.

But I digress.

You are Terry McAuliffe. You dab your mouth with your napkin and think how you might avoid another split vote in 2004.

Well, what do you do in an impossible conflict? You negotiate a truce.

As Mr. McAuliffe, you call up Mr. Nader and the leadership of the Greens. You offer a four year truce, during which time two things happen: One, the Green Party members are welcome at the Democratic convention and at local and national Democrat meetings, to make their case and influence the party planks. Two, the Democratic Party agrees to push multiple-choice voting though as many state legislatures as possible, and even through Congress.

With multiple choice, or ranked choice voting, you vote for your first, second and third choice candidates. If your first choice candidate is not elected with a majority, your second choice applies, and so on. With choice voting in place, the Greens can build their party because people will not fear that a vote for Greens is a vote for Republicans. The true strength of the Greens can finally be measured at the polls, and that will dramatically influence Democratic and national policy.

And the Democrats will prosper because, in the final tally, the vote will not be split.

Now, will the Democrats be able to deliver choice voting during the truce? Can they get it approved in the statehouses and perhaps in Congress? They certainly can, with the help of the Republican Party. And why will the Republicans want to see this reform enacted? Because John McCain, we'll now imagine, is running as third party or independent candidate. Let's further imagine that Colin Powell is his running mate. That's why the Republican Party would suddenly help to get it passed.

And then, by God, we'll have something of a democracy, or a chance for it.

So I take this occasion to ask Mr. McAuliffe to please call Mr. Nader and set up a little meeting with the nice snacks that seem always near him.

And I urge Senator McCain to see what the Reform Party folks are up to these days, and to have a little sit-down with Ross Perot and company, or start to put together your independent campaign committee.

Otherwise, we are in for it.

But have no fear. We will never say die until we are dead. This is our democracy and we know how to fight for it.

We the people will someday again know the feeling of having a president that a majority of American actually voted for. We will see our highest values and human aspirations, not our lowest needs and greeds, reflected in the policies of our government—locally, nationally and internationally. We will live on a peaceful and civilized Earth because, over time, we will have created a world of fairness, kindness, honesty, shared financial and physical security with a positive and creative view of the future for each individual and respect for the Earth that sustains us.

We will have thrown the moneychangers out of our temples of democracy. We will have put the military-industrial complex into the psychiatric hospital where it needs keeping. We will be able to look at our children and our grandchildren and say that the world is run by grownups that have put away the things of childhood, the selfishness, the anger and the cruelty.

You, personally, have an important role to play in this greatest drama of our times. I hope you enjoy the fight. It is a grand thing for all of us to be doing. Thank you.

Represent Love in the World

Ms. Haddock speaking to students and reformers in Keene, New Hampshire, January 25, 2003:

Thank you friends. My family belongs to a group of families who, together, provide for the annual income of a local farmer in exchange for the food he produces. It is an organic operation, which not only means that dangerous chemicals are kept out of the foods, but they are also kept out of the soil and the water that flows eventually into the rivers and seas.

How we live shapes the entire world. I am no angel. I have bought clothing at a bargain, and I look at the tag with guilt if it is from some faraway place where the workers may be abused. My part of New England used to be a great textile center, so I also care about those lost jobs.

What we drive, what we buy, the entertainments we choose, the way we use electricity and water—all of these things matter. Our little decisions work for or against our dream of a fair world with nature in balance and with people living well in their local economies. Poverty happens, war happens, imperialism happens, when all the little bad decisions of a nation's people accumulate and find political expression.

Just as an unbalanced mind can accumulate mental stresses that can each grow and take on a lives of their own inside us, so the little decisions of our modern life can accumulate to the point where our society finds itself bombing other people for their oil or supporting dictators who torture whole populations—all so that our unbalanced interests might be served.

When we look at our president and his war machine and his rising campaign against our own freedoms and civil rights, we must think of it as a mental illness that has come over the American mind—and it is our illness. Yes, we must stop it, but we are bailing out our flooding boat with our straw hats if we do not look to the cause.

Sane action would be finding alternative energy rather than blowing up our Appalachian Mountains for their coal. Sanity is in buying bicycles or at least hybrid cars rather than bombing other people for their oil. It is in supporting our family farmers, especially the organic farmers, rather than suburbanizing all our land and turning to factory foods that are more health hazard than nutrition.

We cannot have world peace without peace in our own lives. We cannot attack our planet by the daily way we live, and then go off to a peace rally in our big cars and hope to set right all the imbalance we have caused. Peace is first a private matter. It cannot grow except from there.

I know I will be in jail before this president is out of the White House. I know some of you will, too. I know I will give my all to stop this unwarranted invasion of the world by this disturbed man and his disturbed friends. I urge you to fight as well.

But I ask you to do so not in anger, but in joy; not in frustration, but in peace. Aren't we privileged to live in a time when everything is at stake, and when our efforts make a difference in the eternal contest between the forces of light and shadow, between togetherness and division? Between justice and exploitation? Be joyful that you live in this great and consequential time!

And be joyful because your own house is in order. Your friends have your friendship. Your lover has your love. Your community has your support. Take time for yourself and for your peace of mind. Look to your lifestyle and begin to make the adjustments you think wise and appropriate.

Most of all, represent love in the world. That is more powerful than you can possibly imagine. Thank you.

We Will Not Be Distracted

Ms. Haddock's remarks at a March 2003 Boston rally and march to oppose the imminent Iraq War:

Thank you. The man in the White House believes that, when he starts dropping bombs on faraway people, we will fall in line behind him. But America must become a beacon of justice and peace and self-determination in the world. It is to this idea that we are patriots, and as patriots we must say no to an unnecessary war—for when has an unnecessary war not been a war crime?

The man in the White House believes that, when our American soldiers start coming home to our communities in coffins, that we will rally 'round him—that the bloody distraction will make us forget what he did to our budget surpluses, our Social Security funds, our Medicare, our pensions and stocks, and yes, to our sons and daughters and to the civilians of another nation.

We will not be distracted by the blood of our own sons and daughters, Mr. President. Each drop calls our hearts to oppose you. Your legacy will be one of the shadows on our history.

The president is counting on our patriotism. He is correct in assuming that we are patriots and that we will take our stand for America and for American values. He will be surprised, however, to see what it means when we actually do that.

The president believes that, when the dust settles and the bodies of Iraqi men, women and children are trucked away, we will be satisfied that it is over and that a tyrant has been removed and a people freed.

Saddam is one of the leftover Cold War puppets now getting his walking papers. Is he being replaced in favor of justice and self-determination? Will the people of the region now have the ability to control their own destinies? Is that the purpose of our proposed permanent military bases there? Is that the objective of all the oil executives preparing to arrive in all their little jets? Or is this simply the beginning of another era of repression and exploitation, for which we will reap the whirlwinds of resistance and terrorism?

The people of the Middle East have no illusions as to our purpose in Iraq. The people of Kosovo and Afghanistan have no illusions, nor should we. The difference is, we the people of America have full responsibility for the actions of our government, and we must remove the present gang of oily men who have wrested moral control away from us. We must reform the campaign finance systems and the electoral systems that allow the rich and the corporations to force these bastards on us and to force this war on us.

The president knows that one good missile attack on the world's most historic city is good for an immediate boost in his overnight ratings. He knows that, with the game now begun, we have to choose which side of the stadium to sit on, and we will sit with the Americans and wave our flag. The problem is, Mr. President, that this is not a game, and what you are doing is unlike anything this generation of Americans, though we are no angels, have ever done or ever wanted to do. We are not with you sir, and you bring shame upon our flag and our traditions and our dreams of a better, safer, more peaceful and prosperous world.

Let our president assume that we are patriots, for we are. We pledge our patriotism today. Let him tremble as we do so.

I pledge allegiance to the flag of the United States of America, and to the Republic for which it stands: One Nation under God, Indivisible, with Liberty and Justice for All! How are those not our fighting words? Let us fight for justice for all! Let us be a republic and not an authoritarian regime! Let us be indivisible! Thank you.

Don't Stand in the Way of our Joy

Ms. Haddock's remarks at the Rolling Thunder Chautauqua in Asheville, May 3, 2003:

Thank You. You and I can agree and disagree about many things, and still respect each other as friends and as fellow Americans with strong opinions. We might disagree about the Iraq War.

I was among the many people who thought Mr. Bush should have disarmed Iraq peacefully through the United Nations process that was already underway. But Mr. Bush took the road he took. There was, as a result, a time of killing and looting, and the spoiling of the treasures of an ancient civilization.

It has been interesting to me to notice that, though the leaders speaking on the rally stages of the great peace marches have often spoken with righteous anger, and even though death was hanging in the air before and after this war, and even though the marchers understood, and still do understand, that our American and global environment is also under attack, as are the working poor and our Bill of Rights, that the people in these marches were nevertheless joyful. Did you notice that? Did you feel it yourself, if you were among them? The best smiles I have seen in years have been in these marches. This leads me to think that the peace movement is about something far deeper than the emergencies of the day.

Our own emotions have been conflicted by this war. We peace marchers of course wanted our young people in uniform to come home safely—sooner rather than later. And we now are hopeful, against all wisdom, that the new day in Iraq can be a good day for the people of that region.

Many Americans and others have a happier view of the whole thing, and I think I can understand their point of view. Let me see if I can put words to it.

It is a dangerous world, this line of thinking runs. We have come through the Cold War, where competing superpowers held each other in check and avoided nuclear war by setting up dictators here and there to protect their interests in key regions. Now the Cold War is over and these dictators, who have outlived their usefulness, must be shown the door at the point of a tomahawk missile. It is important to do so now, some strategists argue, because these dictators may develop weapons that can be delivered to terrorists who will use them on us. This rising danger of terrorism and leftover dictators is a prescription for future tragedy that must be defused, both by going after the terrorist networks, and by taking away the possible providers of their most fearsome weapons.

To police the world in this new era of danger, the argument goes, we must be willing to become the policeman in dangerous regions. We must put military bases in key regions, not only to support our vital resource supply lines, but to preempt terrorism in the regions where it is nurtured. At the same time, we must strive to encourage modern, secular democracies to replace fundamentalist religious states. We must do this not only to protect our own interests, but also to advance human values and to protect those who are commonly oppressed or tortured by such regimes, especially women and religious minorities. This is simply the advance of civilization, and we must be prepared for the fact that it sometimes requires a fight and a sacrifice.

Now, if I have been able to get inside the minds of those who have given their unqualified support to the war, let me now ask those people to try to do as good a job getting inside our peacenik heads and seeing things through our eyes. We do respect your point of view and hope for the same in return.

So here we go: The United States, as you have no doubt heard many times, accounts for about five percent of the world's population, but we consume a quarter of the world's oil and approximately that percentage of the world's other resources. If we raise the entire world to our standard of living and of consumption, we run into some math problems rather quickly. There is also the matter of the amount of carbon dioxide that once was so thick in the hot atmosphere that only the most basic life forms could exist. Over billions of years, that carbon was put in safety deposit boxes, away from the atmosphere. It was taken up by the plants of great swamps, and trapped in now deep layers of coal and oil and permafrost and by the sea. If we bring it all up, which we must do if all the world is to have SUV's and 100-watt toothbrushes, we will be back to overheated swamps in no time. Our great coastal cities—Venice, New York, Amsterdam, London, Rio, Hong Kong, will be awash and we will perish in heat and famine and unimaginable violence and anarchy, or unimaginable authoritarianism. And it is not out there in the distant future; it will begin very soon, indeed.

Now it should not take too much effort to see all this, as nearly all the scientists of the world agree that we are releasing more carbon into the atmosphere than the atmosphere can bear without changing, and that will mean a disruption of our agriculture, to be sure.

Don't worry, as I am getting to Iraq and all that in a moment.

For it works like this: The leadership elite of our society is very invested in the idea of continuing with things as they are. They would like a McDonalds restaurant on every beach in Tahiti and an SUV in every pop-up garage in Tierra del Fuego. That's the only way they know how to think. The CEO's of corporations make tens of millions of dollars a year, not on the long-range expectations of profits, but on this quarter's profits, and how those profits affect stock prices. They can't think more than a year out. The real problem is that they also own all the broadcast networks now, and they finance the careers of most of the politicians in Congress and certainly in the White House. These people do not go around the world spreading peace, justice and democracy. They spread credit card debt, cell phones, sweatshop conditions, factory farms for hogs, and not much better for people. They are in it for the money, and they want to economically enslave people, not free them. I will bet that Iraqis will see bills from MasterCard before they see a meaningful ballot. This is a new wave of economic colonialism, and, like previous waves, it is done in partnership with armies and authoritarian rulers.

Did Iraq have weapons of mass destruction? No, it had only what was left of the ones we sold them. Why the change of heart on our part? With the Cold War over, we don't need them anymore and we want some control in the region, as it is key to our business interests.

And terrorism? Was there much likelihood that Iraq would sell or give a bomb to Islamic fundamentalists, their enemies? There was not.

And to the larger issue: How do you stop terrorism? You stop it the same way you have always stopped terrorism: with justice for all the people of the Middle East. Everyone knows that. The war's proponents know that. It is just that war is more useful, and terrorism is more useful, and tragedies are more useful, if you want to take over regions abroad and limit freedoms at home. Why do you want to do all that? It is very, very good for business, and that is ninety percent of it.

So, that is a more complex view of things than the pro-war supporters might entertain. Which view has the ring of truth to you? Or is the truth just too complicated for you? Different people will surely see it differently, but history will decide.

Some of us want America to move toward environmental sustainability so that the world will be sustainable for future generations. We are the conservatives. We want to conserve nature, the atmosphere, our cultural diversity around the world, and our ideas of freedom, justice and happiness. We want America to be safe.

We understand that this security can only come with international justice. We know that, if America is clean energy self-sufficient and less dependent on other foreign resources, we can well afford to be a force for justice in the world, not for self-serving greed. So we have a vision of a better world, and we will work hard to make it so. You cannot protect an open society from the effects of injustice. You can either close the society, as the president is doing, or you can cure the injustices. Which should be the American way?

We know the answer, don't we? We will fight the radicals whose short term, unsustainable vision of the world drives American policy today. We will work in the coming election to move our imperfect candidates to victory. Our victory strategy must be simple but thorough. One. We must hold the left together—please listen, friend Ralph—and connect with the middling middle where we can.

Two: We must split the right, driving a wedge between the neoconservative radicals and the traditional conservatives, who are our friends on many issues, including civil liberties and elder programs. We must do this door-to-door.

Three: We must widen our circle on the left and do so in many languages, connecting with all the people and groups who are being seriously damaged by the neocon social agenda, helping them connect the dots, helping them register, and helping them get to the polls, especially in the swing states, which are many.

Four: We have a very narrow media window, so we must have a narrow message to fit this narrow window. We must fill the gap with door-to-door work, and must recruit respected

American voices of authority to join us in projecting our messages, such as the erosion of personal freedoms and the danger to our Social Security system and health programs.

Who are we to be out there fighting, to be winning elections? We are the people who believe in a world of environmental beauty, of happiness and not exploitation, of justice and not oppression and torture—a world safe for children. We want government budgets that invest in our smart babies, not smart bombs. We believe in international law and cooperative action. We are the opposite numbers to the neoconservatives. If we lose, the world loses its environment, its justice and its happiness. So we must win.

There are many among us on the peace trail that will not support a candidate unless that candidate is perfect on every issue. Politics is about winning. For us, it is about winning to save lives and raise people up from poverty and illness and loneliness and injustice. Those posturing on the left sometimes forget that. Don't tell me that you can't support a particular candidate because of this or that. This isn't about you and your precious political standards. It is about saving nature and our people. We are coming out to win, so please don't stand in our way. When we have reasonable people in power, let us start our arguments again, for we cannot move forward unless we have a decent government underneath us and a Bill of Rights to let us speak freely.

This is great work. Did you, as a child, hope that one day it would be in your hands to save the world? Then rejoice. It is indeed joyful to find yourself engaged in a life of great meaning. For what is life, if not a theater of the soul where we take our part representing love and justice? What better thing do we have to do than to save the world? Thank you.

Be Brave Enough

Remarks to a gathering of teachers and professors in Portsmouth, New Hampshire in June of 2003:

Thank you very much. These are interesting times, to say the least—a time when our most deeply-held ideas are challenged. Many of us have differing views of what is going on in the world, why it is happening, and what we need to do in order to secure a safe and just future for ourselves and for our people and the people of the world.

It is a time when you can be booed and your life can be

threatened—in this country and in this state—for suggesting that peace and justice are preferable to war. It is a time, even in our America, when you can be beaten or taken away to unknown prisons for an indefinite period of time if you are from the wrong part of the world or if you dress a certain way or hold certain religious or political beliefs.

On National Public Radio the other day, experts were debating whether or not torture should and could be used to get information from some of the 1,000 people we have rounded up and held in violation of our Bill of Rights. No one on the program seemed willing to say that torture would be wrong, and that, therefore, we must not engage in it.

Did you think you would live to see such times in this nation?

There is a good deal of flag waving going on now, and I do love our flag and I love waving it and walking with it. But that flag represents courage, not cowardice. Would all those now waving the flag be willing to die for the freedoms that it represents? Would they be willing to risk death to preserve the Bill of Rights?

And how about you? Are you brave enough to smile at an Arab American sitting across the aisle from you on an airplane, or are you so cowardly and so contemptuous of our Bill of Rights and so disrespectful of everything that our flag stands for that you would rather have that other passenger whisked away to a nameless prison than risk any degree of danger? That is not Americanism, if Americanism is the courage to be free, and to guarantee freedom to others according to our Bill of Rights— despite the risks of doing so, despite the danger to life and limb of doing so.

If this new day is some twilight, everlasting war, as some leaders have said, then we are its soldiers defending its flag. We cannot do so without risking life itself to defend what that flag stands for.

Now, you may have gathered that, no matter what risk it may pose to me and my loved ones, I want all people who are arrested or detained in this nation to be advised of the reason for their imprisonment, and to be provided a lawyer if they require one, and that they will have the ability to speak confidentially to their lawyer, and that they will not be detained without the speeding filing of charges and a speedy trial by jury.

You may say that it is not reasonable to grant these rights to everyone today. I understand the problem. We risk our lives to extend these rights to each other. We always have. I pray that we always will, though there are people in power who do not feel the same way, who want to hold people indefinitely without charges filed, who want to deny confidential communication between detainees and their lawyers, and who have no interest in providing speedy trials or clear charges. They have clearly said so, and have thereby declared themselves, in my view, quite un-American and quite cowardly. If this is still America, those who trample on the Bill of Rights should be removed from office, no matter how high that office is, for they swore and oath to defend the Constitution.

Now, I have shared some of my concerns with you, so that you can find points of disagreement with me. I hope you have done so. I hope you have your own, well thought-out points of view that could give us a rousing evening on your back porch or mine.

If this is still America, we will not suffer prison for our different points of view. Though I will be frisked at the airport every time I fly, as is already the case due to my exercise of free speech.

The reason they pull me out of line at the airport these days is that I dared stand in the Capitol Rotunda last year and read the Bill of Rights on one occasion, and the Declaration of Independence on another. At both times, there were tourists and schoolchildren in the Rotunda, taking their tour and learning about our democracy. They cheered my reading, but on both occasions I was arrested, taken away in cuffs, and put in jail. That was long before any concern about Osama bin Laden or his terrorists.

I read those documents in the Rotunda as a part of my 3,200-mile walk across the U.S. at age 90. I made that walk on behalf of Campaign Finance Reform—the effort to get special interest money out of our elections. Making the walk was the only way I could think of to talk to thousands of Americans about the need for this reform, and it was a way to show that people do care about the need for the reform.

Gandhi and Martin Luther King taught us that you have to take the pain of social change upon yourself if you want to change things for the better. So I walked and talked and tried to forget about my pains.

If I had been more successful, perhaps the Congress, in the past few weeks, would have been less interested in paying off their campaign contributors with special tax breaks and more interested in providing sensible security at our airports and in our airplanes. You may have heard that the airlines, which are major donors to political campaigns, resisted the costs of reinforced cockpit doors by having their bought-and-paid-for senators kill the bill whenever it came up.

But now, of course, you're getting your money's worth in airline safety, as they worry about nail clippers and Granny D.

If I seemed to downplay the power of the terrorists, it is because I know the greater harm they can do to our great democracy is to cause us to forgo our defining principles as described in our Bill of Rights. And they cannot do that unless they have helpmates in the highest ranks of our own government, telling us that we must give up our civil rights—America's crown jewels—for a thimble-full of imaginary security.

I don't fear a thousand Osama bin Laden's as much as I fear any politician or judge who turns his back on the essential rights that make America worth defending.

There are great leaders in this nation, and I pray that they will rise up to the hard demands for courage now before them.

I have met some wonderful senators, representatives, mayors, governors and judges on my walk and since my walk.

Judge Hamilton, for example, was the Washington DC judge I appeared before after my arrest for reading the Declaration of Independence.

He looked wise in his great robe, but I did wonder if he would sentence me to six months in jail, as well he might have. Instead, he sentenced me to the day I had already served, and he said this:

"As you know, the strength of our great country lies in its Constitution and her laws and in her courts. But more fundamentally, the strength of our great country lies in the resolve of her citizens to stand up for what is right when the masses are silent. And, unfortunately, sometimes it becomes the lot of the few, sometimes like yourselves, to stand up for what's right."

He gave me a fine hug in his chambers afterwards. His staff members were tearful and I was tearful, and America felt like my own country again.

And so it is. And it is yours, if you can keep it.

And if this is still indeed America, you can yet engage your students in great discussions, debating the pros and cons of American foreign policy, and American civil liberties, without worrying that parents or administrators or newspaper editors will ride you out of town on a rail—they might.

But I know that you must worry about it. You worry that if you raise certain subjects in class, you risk your career. If you ask your students to talk openly and think freely, you will open up a can of worms. So you will, what? cower? neglect the great issues of our day that could truly energize your students and make them want to learn about the world and its people and its laws and customs?

In the greatest universities of America, there is a healthy debate going on about America's role in the world. A thousand questions are being asked: Should America promote solar power and therefore become less dependent on foreign oil, so that our foreign policy might be based on our values instead of our needs? What risks must we run to preserve our Bill of Rights? Is a declared war against "evil," a religious war? And so on. Many freshmen and sophomores, since September 11, are looking at their career goals and modifying them with their newfound concern for the issues of a complex world.

It is a world as richly textured as a Persian or a Navajo carpet, and we mustn't be afraid to study it.

This moment, in other words, is a teachable moment—a great learning opportunity, if you can find a way to use it without getting yourself strung-up by those who react to complexity and horror with knee jerks instead of creativity, and who react to danger by circling their limited mental wagons instead of widening the tent of their consciousness.

How can you educate the next generation of Americans to be soldiers of democracy, defenders of the Bill of Rights, fighters for equality, fairness and freedom? First, by teaching them by fearless example.

To be the next generation of free Americans, they must be free to think. They must be able to empathize with any people, anywhere in the world. In order to do so, they must understand the issues and the points of view. That takes study, imagination, and creativity. How do you teach empathy? You do not. You only create the rich soil for it, hoping it will grow.

Do you remember your first encounter with Ann Frank? You did not have to be a Jew to suddenly understand what the Jews had suffered. You stood in her stocking feet, didn't you?

Where is the Palestinian Ann Frank? The Afghani? The Chinese, Russian, Indian, Pakistani? Do we know what is happening to people in our own country? Do we understand what goes on in our poorest mountain communities and in our prisons?

Empathy does not flourish in a heart too broken by hardship and lack of love. I know that many teachers find themselves giving love in extra doses to children who are deprived of it in all other areas of their lives. That is important, too.

If we can raise our new Americans in love, and with the proper tools of empathy that literature and correspondence and travel can give us, then we need not fear for the future of our nation.

Big work. Huge work, isn't it? How you indeed rock the cradle of our great experiment in human freedom! I admire you for it. I hope you have the courage and the love to do it with all your hearts. Thank you.

The Rich Don't Know Us Anymore

In June of 2003, the Massachusetts Legislature repealed its public financing of elections program. Ms. Haddock was active in the effort to dissuade them from that action. Her remarks on June 7, 2003:

Thank you. We elect our representatives to represent our values and our needs in shaping public policy and allocating community resources. In this work, the regular citizen doesn't stand a chance if elected representatives need wealthy special interests to fund their campaigns—the representation game is over before it begins.

It is nothing particularly new. But in the past, the wealthy lived among us. We shopped in their stores on Main Street and their children went to grade school with ours. We shared the same community interests and values.

We are now talking about inhumane organizations of inhuman scale and transnational allegiance. They care not if our main streets or our families prosper or if they blow away.

And so, we must not have them influencing our community decisions. We must not allow them to provide funds for our candidates, where those funds will deny us proper representation.

We struggle here for the very survival of representative democracy. The people of Massachusetts have seen this problem and they have acted at the ballot box to create a new way to fund candidates, free of excessive influence by wealthy special interests.

But those same wealthy interests have their agents in this state house, and they will destroy what the people have done at the ballot, if they can.

The people have spoken clearly in favor of this historic reform. Did the members of the House not hear them? Do they need for the people to speak again—this time in the coming

House elections?

At the ballot box, the people have provided for the public financing of candidates who choose to say no to all special interest campaign donations. Their action comes at a time when citizens believe that their voices in government are drowned out by floods of special-interest money, and they are right. No one seriously argues that point anymore—the flood is too great Pubic interest groups on the left and right, from the Cato Institute to Common Cause, agree that, for every dollar given to a candidate by a special-interest group, over ten dollars in special tax breaks are given in return. This is nothing less than full public financing, but it is a poor system of public financing. By directly funding qualified campaigns with public funds, we can eliminate nine of the ten dollars paid by taxpayers—now paid in the form of tax loopholes for special interests.

Any true conservative would surely trade a corrupt system of public financing for a clean one that costs the taxpayers one-tenth as much.

Any true American would trade a corrupt system that deprives Americans of their proper representation and therefore of their fundamental political freedom, for a reformed system that makes our politics once again the arena of our ideas, not our billfolds. Thank you.

Later in the morning, a march was held. Ms. Haddock's remarks:

Citizens of Massachusetts, if you contact your elected representatives in state government because you have a problem or perhaps an idea for the improvement of the law, you had better hope it is not an idea that would change how lawyers do their business, because lawyers have visited your elected representatives in this State House a few times before you, with checks in their hands. In 1998 alone, they passed along 14,369 campaign checks, totaling $3.2 million. Your good idea might get a polite nod, but money talks and you will walk, and so you might as well walk with me.

If your good idea is about insurance or real estate, be advised that 8,606 checks and $2.5 million passed in hand from those industries before you shared your opinion. That money talks. They say giving money is protected free speech, and that's what they mean—though it is hardly free, as the citizens pay dearly for it in the form of special interest tax breaks and protective laws that cost the citizens dearly.

If your idea or complaint is about construction quality or development patterns, understand that, before you arrived, 2,837 checks were given to your representatives by the construction lobby. And 5,248 checks from other business lobbies. If you have a problem with the way HMOs or other medical organizations treat you, be advised that 4,509 checks from those companies have preceded you into the room, so you might as well save your breath. These contributions were all in 1998, and they are even higher in this year's election.

Your position as a free person in a self-governing land is being taken from you. You have no real voice, no real representation, and that means your freedom is slipping away, if you let it.

Money talks, the people walk. And so, we will walk until this tainted money is taken out from between "we the people" and our elected representatives.

The voters of Massachusetts have spoken overwhelmingly at the polls. They have had enough of this corruption and have enacted public funding of campaigns. Will they have to speak a second time at the polls, to turn out those members who dare to overturn the will of the people? I think the people might do that, if it comes to that.

In the meantime, money will talk, and we the people will walk. So let's begin our walk.

The walk stopped briefly in Arlington, north of Boston. Ms. Haddock's remarks there:

Thank you. Americans have been traveling on this road for many years—always in the pursuit of personal freedom and civic self-governance. Freedom is what we walk for today: the freedom to elect candidates who will represent US in the halls of our government, not represent the wealthy special interests whose puppet strings bind the actions of so many of our officials. We want representatives who don't have to spend all night raising money and all day paying favors. We want people who will listen to us, who will represent us and our needs, our values, and our future.

We walk on the high road of history this morning, for we are leaving behind a for-hire political system that has become soiled and broken with the weight of too many crooked dollars and too many crooked politicians. We have to reinvent our democracy from time to time, and we are doing it here today, on this historic trail.

Her remarks the same day, on Boston Common:

Thank you. Freedom is what we walk for today—the freedom to elect candidates who will represent us in the halls of our government, not represent only the wealthy special interests whose puppet strings bind and twist our government and our society. We want representatives who don't have to spend all night raising money and all day paying favors. We want people who will listen to us, who will represent us and our needs, our values, and our future.

I know that the Clean Elections Law has been under fire in Massachusetts by politicians who would rather fund their campaigns with the same old special interest bribery. But the times have changed, and they had better listen very carefully to what I am about to say:

Much of the soft money that is given to parties by corporations, and which is then filtered down to the campaigns of these politicians, is given by organizations that are increasingly owned by people around the world. It is their asset to give, most certainly, but it is global money, not American money. We can no longer have corporate money in our elections unless we will accept the idea of people from Asia, the Mideast, Europe, China and elsewhere influencing our elections with their money. Let us keep our elections for ourselves, and tell those anti-reform politicians to get with the program—the Clean Elections program, funding it fully with Massachusetts money and nothing else.

More important than the source of the money is the effect of the money. It buys our representatives away from us, at a time when we need them very dearly.

What happens when we lose control of our own government? What horrors rain down upon us when our government does not represent our values, but instead those of greedy, multinationals and billionaires?

We know what happens because we see it happening, to our horror. Extra doses of real democracy and true international justice are the only ways to stop it.

We walk today for our freedom. But we walk, too, for the peace and justice that comes when our government is in the hands of the people—we the people. The road to freedom is the road to peace.

We Happy Few

Ms. Haddock speaking to a reform gathering in Hood River, Oregon, August 16, 2003; it includes some material from her September 27, 2002 remarks, in Boston:

Thank you. Well, you've often heard the Margaret Mead quote about how you should never doubt that a small group of dedicated people can change the world, and that it's the only thing that ever has. Well, I think it's time we stopped repeating that quotation and took time to decide what, exactly, we happy few might do over the next five years or so. That is the purpose of my remarks today.

There are two kinds of politics in the world: the politics of love and the politics of fear. Love is about cooperation, sharing, nurturing, growth and inclusion. It is about the elevation of each individual to a life that is neither suppressed nor exploited, but instead nourished to its full potential—a life for its own sake and so that we may all benefit by the gift of that life. Fear and the politics of fear is about narrow ideologies that separate us, militarize us, imprison us, exploit us, control us, overcharge us, demean us, bury us alive in debt and anxiety and then bury us dead in cancers and wars. The politics of love and the politics of fear are now pitted against each other in a naked struggle that will define not only the 21st Century but centuries to come. We are the Sons and Daughters of Liberty in that struggle, indeed we are. Let us not shrink from the mission that fate has bestowed upon us, for it has done so as a blessing to all who would want a meaningful life.

This struggle is real. A very close friend of mine, a college student, spent this summer in Guatemala to help small communities prosper in ways that support their local environments. Those villagers and their environments are under siege by international big business, using a captured U.S. Government to push through damaging treaties such as the proposed Central America Free Trade Agreement and the hemisphere-wide Free Trade Area of the Americas. The villagers of Guatemala want global "fair" trade, but the corporations and their captive governments want "free" trade, instead. If fair trade wins, a global middle class will rise, as farmers and craftsmen are paid fairly for their work, and as they gain a voice in their governance and their environments are protected for their future generations. If free trade wins, it is colonial exploitation, torture and murder written in blood across another century, and, in this small world, it will end up on our doorstep.

Do you wonder if it is really an honest difference of opinion as to which policies are best for the people? On July 24, three armed gunmen broke into the home where my young friend was staying in Guatemala, dragging her and another young woman into the basement, covering their heads with blankets. These young women began to count their lives in seconds. For three-quarters of an hour, the gunmen went through the biodiversity files in the office. Big business interests in Guatemala, in league with elements of the military, are trying to push-through the passage of free trade agreements and to do it they must suppress all dissent. Their partner and blood brother is the U.S. Government. Not the U.S. Government that we see, but the U.S. Government that much of the world sees.

The two courageous women escaped and thereby survived, but tens of thousands of others have not, because they are in the way of global business interests. It is not an honest difference of opinion; it is a global struggle of people versus a global crime syndicate that counts taken-over governments and multinational corporations among its members.

There is a term now in common use that is still confusing. It is called neoliberalism, and it is a very dirty word indeed to the brave pro-democracy and fair trade groups throughout the Americas. "Neoliberal" sounds like the happy return of the Kennedys, but it is not. Nor is it about some resurgence of the liberal values of the Square Deal or the New Deal or the War on Poverty or any of those great moments when we called upon our best instincts to cooperatively address our largest needs as a free and self-governing people. The liberation that we meant then when we used the word "liberal" was the liberation from poverty, despair and ignorance, the liberation of the mind through public education, the liberation of the citizen through universal voting, equal rights and equal opportunity, and the freedom to prosper from the fruits of our labors. But that is not the liberal that is meant by neoliberal. It means business interests are newly free to rampage. It means massive corporate organizations are free of government constraint or community responsibility. It means free trade, not fair trade.

"Neoliberalism" refers to the liberation of a giant beast that we, the ordinary people of America—the farmers, the townspeople, the trade unionists—managed to tie down to the earth early in the 20th Century. It is that beast that has now loose again to do great damage to us all. The deadly meanderings of this beast are most apparent in the most labor-intensive regions of the world, but the beast is here, too, and he has brought misery and suffering into your life and mine, stealing our jobs, our water, blowing up our mountains, fouling our air and seas, and stealing our lives and our future at every turn. Neoliberalism is the colonial expansion department of neo-conservatism, and it is bending our own country toward self-colonization.

How did we handle this evil giant before? The Teddy Roosevelt Progressives, and the William Jennings Bryan Populists before him, were part of a somewhat successful effort to tie down the giant. After the Civil War, at the high point of the Industrial Age—the age of railroads, oil and steel—great corporations and trusts were created that towered high over the human-scaled businesses of America's Main Streets and cast dark shadows over human liberty and happiness. These monstrosities treated humans as slaves. They robbed the public wealth and were properly called the robber barons of that Gilded Age. These giants freely stalked, destroying the economics of family farms and family businesses, corrupting our governments with great bribes and corrupt deals, and polluting our food, our land, water and air. They tore our families apart and dragged us into the hardest of hard times, as they have now been liberated to do once more.

I am not talking about all corporations or all big business. Corporations of reasonable size are but groups of people. Beyond some point, however, the humanity falls away from an organization and all that is left is the will to power and profit. They care not that our seas and atmosphere are rapidly changing in ways that may lead to disaster and famine of unimaginable scale. They care not because they are not human and they have moved beyond human values. They do not need the fresh air or the water or the mountains or the birds. They are a kind of virus or a cancer all prettied up with nice logos and television commercials to tell us the most outrageous lies, one after the other. For in reality, they crush us under their boots and they pay off our political leaders with campaign contributions and other bribes. They trample on diversity of all kinds, including human personality, as fewer and fewer kinds of people can prosper in the world they are casting, and more and more of us are marginalized and rendered homeless.

The big corporate empires would be powerless if they were not in league with crooked politicians. I do not mean that the politicians necessarily know what they are doing. The corruption is so immense that they cannot even see it, even when it pays their spouse and finances their reelection. These ethically stunted humans populate Capitol Hill and our state capitols like creatures that have been for generations in deep caves where they gradually lose their vision.

Well, two and a quarter centuries was a good run for this democracy, but a rebirth is long overdue, and it is indeed necessary if we are to save our freedoms and our human values, here and abroad—and if we are to protect the beauty and sustaining graces of nature and operate from positive side of human nature.

What Republican Teddy Roosevelt understood at the beginning of the 20th Century was that, if the rights and fortunes of the human scale were to be protected, if the rights and fortunes of average Americans, small businesses, family farms and Main Street were to be protected from the ravages of over-scaled business giants, then government needed to protect the people. The big business wing of the Republican Party, under Taft, defeated the family business wing of the Republican and that wing's leader, Teddy Roosevelt. It would take another Roosevelt of another party to turn the Square Deal into the New Deal, under which government stepped up to protect the people.

That has not been an altogether happy history, as large government has its own costs and abuses. The Libertarians are our new allies in defending the Bill of Rights from this administration's anti-American attacks on those rights, but they would have us do away with most of our government. Anyone who has paid too many taxes or dealt with too many rude and overly-powerful bureaucrats understands the Libertarian's feelings, but I ask at least the intellectually honest Libertarians— and there are many of them—to wisely see that government, which is indeed a system of restraint—must be matched in strength and scale to the corporate monstrosities that now have the ability and the willingness to destroy us—to blow up the entire Appalachian Range for the profits of coal, as is now happening—or to poison or steal for profit the water supply of whole regions, or to enslave whole regions at low wages rather than allow fair trade—or to move every one of our good jobs overseas. These inhuman and inhumane organizations are stealing our lives and all nature around us.

Only government is large enough and powerful enough to reign-in the corporations whose cold-heartedness trades lives for profits all over the world. Theodore Roosevelt began the buildup of big government solely to protect us from overlarge corporations, so that they might not overwhelm us human beings. In doing so, he created a split in the Republican Party, and big business interests won. Perhaps the rational solution is to scale them both back—corporations and government—and let individual enterprise and individual freedom, and its many middle class treasures and blessings, blossom in the old battlefield. But there is no leadership for that, and governments are being stripped of all regulatory powers by the false religion of a new deity: the unfettered, liberated—or shall we say neo-liberated—market. So, no longer protected by governments, we must fight the battle that is before us: human beings versus monstrous corporations and their body-snatched government puppets. The battle of human scale versus monstrous scale is, very simply, the politics of love versus the politics of fear. Yes, the billionaires and their companies and associations are fearful. What deep neurosis or psychosis is required to turn a person away from the interests of their own grandchildren? Who would willingly send their children into a world of climate catastrophe and failing democracy of their own making, except a very sick and fearful person? The illness goes beyond any Ebenezer Scrooge imagined in past eras.

What is happening now, of course, is that huge military commitments, huge tax cuts to the wealthiest individuals and corporations, and huge budget deficits leave less money for the old New Deal programs like Social Security or newer programs such as Medicare. No money for schools, hospitals, police, fire, veterans—no money for anything but the front lines of a corporatized military and a militarized corporatocracy. A starved government—once our own government—has no ability to restrain the liberated giant or to investigate his abuses or prosecute his crimes.

When did this monster get untied? He did so in the era of corporate raiding, permitted and smiled upon by the Reagan Administration. Reagan admired those cowboy businessmen of the 1970s and 80s—the corporate raiders who engineered hostile corporate takeovers. Allowed by hamstrung regulators, those takeovers caused all large and mid-sized American public corporations to go on a rampage of streamlining, outsourcing, wage cutting, plant closings and job exporting. They did so to make themselves takeover-proof. It was no longer enough to make a respectable profit and serve your community with good jobs and fairly priced goods and services. The new mentality of profit maximization and unlimited mergers and no government control was the untying of the monster and it was no accident.

The ropes were further loosened in the Clinton and Bush administrations, until we find ourselves now with a government of, by and for the corporations. The new model CEO was the ruthless cost-cutter and dealmaker. CEO salaries went unbelievably high, where they have stayed. For every hundred dollars that the average American worker makes, these top CEOs make fifty thousand dollars. It is a moral outrage in the land of so many homeless and struggling and worried people. But the giant does not care if we struggle or worry. The giant does not care that every homeless person we walk by is a humiliation to us, too, as members of a community no longer able to take care of our own. It is a humiliation designed to impress upon us that we are not in charge. That we must do as we are told if we do not want a similar fate. It is police state logic.

A century ago, the ordinary people of America joined together to tie down the giant. The antitrust laws and environmental laws and the rights of workers to organize and collectively bargain for wages and benefits all joined to nurture the restoration of a great middle class—always the bedrock of democracy. The robber barons, the great giants, remained tied down, no longer free, liberated, to do as they pleased in crushing us with their great wealth and political power. And so it was for a time.

But now, loosed again, these giants have taken over some of our television networks and some of our newspapers, turning them against our interests and against the truth itself. These giants send our young people off to fight their commercial wars—great profitable ventures.

How free are we now, friends? Check you bills and your bank account. How much time and leisure do you have to enjoy your life and friends? How is your place in your community as a free and equal citizen? Or are we drones that go to work, go to bed to rest for more work, go to the stores to spend all that we earn and more, and watch television to receive our instructions what to buy the next day, if we have jobs at all? Is that freedom by some other name? It is not freedom by any name and it is wrong to push it on the rest of the world in the name of freedom.

These corporations steal our time with their computerized telephone switchboards and their long waiting lines and few employees, forcing us to be their unpaid employees, serving ourselves. They steal our jobs and our benefits and our pensions. They use fear at every turn to sell us a little protection, and a little more. Did we steal your credit? Let us sell you credit protection. And they steal our senators and congressmen just when our so-called representatives might have earned their keep protecting our democracy.

What shall we do? How shall we get our children home

from their wars and ourselves free from their captivities?

We the people, acting together in the new ways made possible by electronic communication, must become the large counterbalance to these powers. By communicating and acting in concert, we can reward the good companies and keep our money clear of the worst. We can make our demand for fair trade products and provide the shift in market share that will change the practices of those businesses that now exploit our brothers and sisters here and around the world—our buying habits are votes for the kind of world we will live in. By nudging market share, our small group of dedicated people can influence great changes. We have the tools now to do this now.

It will not be an easy task, but we have no real alternative if we are to save the world, and that is what we must do. Let us not be shy about it, for time is short. We stand for love and fairness in the world. That is not gentle work, nor is it painless, as so many people around the world know.

This is, after all, our world and our lives. Do you remember those few weeks after the 9/11 attacks when, as an automatic antidote to the inhumanity of those attacks, we all sought to reassert our humanity again in a million little ways? For that moment we came out of the hypnosis we have come to live under and we saw the Eden of human love and cooperation. We must not fall back under corporate hypnosis again, as it is a waste of our lives. The forces of life and death are in struggle, for those are the other names for love and fear. Let us choose life and love, and happily use ourselves up in loving service to one another. Thank you.

Trust Your Own Values

Ms. Haddock speaking to the Freshmen Class at Franklin Pierce College, New Hampshire, Friday, September 5, 2003; her memoir was required reading for the incoming freshmen:

Thank you. It is a great pleasure to grow old and to be asked to dispense advice and to not have to follow it oneself. In that department, let me urge you to go to bed early, get up at dawn, keep well ahead of your studies, stay well behind your credit limit, refrain from smoking and drinking and wild living. I give you that advice, not because I have ever followed all of it myself, but because life's pleasures are all the more delicious if an old lady has told you to do otherwise.

The fact is, life is a feast of great pleasures and we are rude to our Creator if we do not partake of the beauty and fun and pleasure of this life. So I do hope you will take care of yourself and that you will mind your schedules to the extent that you will not always be behind and worried and stressed and missing out on the joy all around you. The captain of a well-run ship can afford the time to enjoy the breeze and the view. Be that to your own life, starting now with college. It is a challenge, I know, but if you keep at it, you will get the hang of living well in this life.

You will see that some of the students around you are forever behind and worried, and others seem on top of it and have a smile. Your choice, indeed. The moment of truth is when you are tempted away from your resolve. Will you be a person of strong character? Here is the test of it: a person of character stays true to a resolution long after the mood has passed in which that resolution was made. Watch for that: Your conscious overview of your daily life can guide you toward improvements that will strengthen your hold on life and its happiness. Let me warn you more specifically that problems like depression and chronic procrastination are always a good excuse for a visit to the health center where you can get very useful help. The brain is no less fixable an organ than the stomach, and we do get our aches and pains and should go for help sooner rather than later. And be advised: if you come to a point sometimes when you cannot imagine your life working out, cannot imagine getting to a happy future, you are depressed; what you are feeling is not real, and you should go talk it out with a pro.

Now, that is all boilerplate advice. Let me tell you something more interesting. You come into college with the expectation of learning many new things—of becoming an expert in many areas. But there is one area where you are already the expert, and where the professors and the other old birds are not. Young people bring something special and, if you are not fully aware of this superior quality, you might waste it unknowingly.

I am not speaking of your athletic or more personal areas of strength and stamina, though I am sure you are very impressive to watch in action. I am speaking of your view of the world, which in many ways is superior to the view seen by older eyes.

Trust your sensibilities toward justice and fairness and toward the environment and peace. Understand that your value judgments in these areas are better because they have not been beaten down or crusted over. Information overload can make us insensitive. While your eyes are yet wide open—and also your heart—trust what you see. Do not hang back from involvement in addressing the problems of the world, waiting to become an expert. You are expert enough. You are our annual resupply of new eyes and fresh hearts to give our sorry species its best hope for improvement and survival. Take your part in the great dramas and the great struggles now still in their opening acts in this world. It is the part where you storm on stage with a confused but mischievous look and the audience cheers you madly. Don't wait to know the part too well, or the moment will pass.

What is your passion? The right place for you is directed by that passion. Or are you drifting, looking for your passion? Let your curiosity lead you to it. Trust the force of that curiosity. Be brave when your curiosity takes you to places you would rather not go—it knows what it is doing and it has served you well for much longer than you can possibly imagine.

Look around every now and then and wonder what all this life is about. Whom is served by all this life? Whom does life serve? Life serves life, and we are happiest and at our best when we let our full life force—indeed our divine life force—rise within us as we engage our lives in service to the world—to the life around us. We are happiest when we are serving life and adding to its health and bounty. We are simply made that way—made for cooperation and togetherness of every kind.

This is an extraordinary time you have happened to come. What an amazing world! The young woman college student in Iran, wearing her Levis under her burka, is your sister and your friend. The farmer in Central America who is trying to get a fair price for his coffee beans so that he can build a better house for his children is your uncle and a man you deeply respect. The Navajo woman who is fighting for the right to stay on land that has been her family's for generations is your grandmother, and she needs your help.

It is not too much at all. It is all quite beautiful. Cast your heart into this world right now, for your eyes and your heart are open and your senses of justice and fairness and your sense of the right thing to do for the planet that sustains us is fully matured and at its perfect moment to give hope and progress to the world. Don't save yourselves for later; spend yourselves today in love, and your investment will come back to you a hundredfold.

Most of the social progress of the past hundred years has come from students demanding a better world.

A good friend of mine was flying across the U.S. this past week and his seatmates were a young man and woman from Iran. The man was a naturalized U.S. citizen. The young woman had come here more recently. She told my friend how she had grown up under the artillery barrages of the Iran-Iraq War. She described how the Iranians saw that war: that the Americans had built up the Shaw's army to be among the strongest in the region, but that, when he was toppled by the Ayatollah, the U.S. then armed Saddam Hussein in Iraq and encouraged him to take down the Iranian army a few notches. It was in that game that she found herself as a child target of artillery. My friend asked her if she did not resent Americans for that time in her young life. She said that she tried not to hold Americans responsible for the actions of their government, as she hoped she wouldn't be held responsible for the actions of the Iranian government. She said that Americans seemed so kind and so unaware of what was being done in their names around the world, and she said she thought it must be like being the children in a family where the father is in the underworld—that their lives are comfortable, but they know something is wrong. She said that she did not like to tell Americans about all that she knew, because it was kind of a shame to wake them up to all this when their lives were so cluelessly blissful—her words.

Well, she was wrong on many counts. As citizens of a democratic republic, we are indeed responsible for what our nation does in our name. And it is no discourtesy to awaken us into the citizens we must be.

America is a great country and we love it. We love this planet, too. And you young people here today are the bright eyes that must be the open and awake eyes, though still full of joy and honor, love and mischief, duty and courage to serve life in a time when life is challenged by its old foes: fear and hate and ignorance.

May you be a great brotherhood and sisterhood of love and action. Arrange your personal lives so that you have the time and resources to take your part on this great stage. And smile the smile of the peaceful warrior whose weapons are love and light, and ever more love and ever more light.

Thank you and good luck. If it ever gets too crazy, do come down to my porch in Dublin and we'll talk it over, if I'm not away on some adventure of my own. Do call first. Your dean has my number and is to give it to any who ask. Thank you again.

Ms. Haddock feeds alligators, so their regular tender, 18-year-old Jamie, has time to register to vote.

Registering young mermaids at Weeki Wachee Springs, Florida. The events attracted television cameras, and the television cameras attracted county voting officials, who promised to expand voter registration hours and locations.

Working Women Vote Campaign

Having recently received a report that many working women do not vote because they do not have the time to register, Ms. Haddock embarked on a campaign to encourage women and the residents of poor neighborhoods to register to vote. She took over their jobs for a few hours so they might go register.

She walked across the major cities of most the swing states east of the Mississippi, taking over the jobs of working women, as planned. The job switching was done to gain public awareness of the need for easier voter registration. County officials often responded to the public pressure—television cameras often showed up for Ms. Haddock—creating new pathways to registration for working people. Her brief jobs included an alligator feeder at an Orlando alligator park, a mermaid in Weeki Wachee Springs, a barmaid in New Orleans and many others. She registered women in a Tampa strip joint and encouraged them to organize Exotic Women Vote, which happened.

She canvassed for new voters through housing projects, from Miami and Fort Myers to Cabrini Green in Chicago, considered by many to be too dangerous to visit, She registered enthusiastic new voters there.

Molly Ivins in her December 16, 2003 column: "Whenever I get discouraged about the greed and corruption that seems so rampant in both the corporate and political worlds these days, the thought of Granny D always perks me up. Doris Haddock is the priceless activist who walked across the entire country three years ago at the age of 90 to build support for campaign finance reform. She's at it again, this time traveling from one workplace to another registering people to vote, especially working mothers."

Ms. Haddock speaking in Manchester, New Hampshire, September 20, 2003, preliminary to the launch of her Working Women Vote campaign:

Thank you. Well, here we all are again, some of us together for the first time but many of us now getting to know each other rather well. This has been a special time in the history of our nation. Through our anger and our pain we have also found great joy. It is the joy of making our lives mean something—it is the joy of connecting with deep values and worthy dreams.

And in the past few months I have come to understand that human values and truth are winning, as they sometimes do. They are lighting up the political darkness and challenging the politics of fear and lies with the politics of love and truth.

We don't know how many times we will be able to meet together—life is short—so we should savor these moments. We should take a moment to recognize what has been done by the small group of friends here present and so many others around our nation—you brave souls who dared be Americans when that meant speaking out for the soul of your nation, against a torrent tide of madness. It became the lot of the few to speak out, even when the greatest newspapers and news broadcasters were silent, and when our very Congress was spineless and complicit. You stood in small groups on street corners with signs. You wrote letters and you protested and you emailed, emailed, emailed and shared what you could find out. You suffered name-calling and abuse and many of you went to jail. Our founding fathers led a revolution with bravery, but they were a strong brotherhood and sisterhood of great personalities acting together, and sometimes—this time—it was just you, and just him, and just her on a street corner with a sign, and I want to say how proud I am of all of you, for the tide has turned and you have turned it.

And sure, we have a long way to go, and the suffering is only beginning, and the forces of fear are still in their ascendancy, though we now see their moral arc. We know now that a sleeping nation has awakened and our dear neighbors and our Congressmen and newsmen and who were so long asleep or so bent under their anchor desks in fear have begun to remember who they are and what their jobs are.

And who was it who held the torch while they were away but you, and you, and you—ye band of sisters and brothers?

Can we see forward to a time when the American government represents, all over the world, the best and happiest instincts of the American people? Can we see a time when we, each of us, can live in responsible balance with nature and all other people? Can we evolve to our better selves as a nation, whose people are at the reins of our own government and whose harsh past, harsh from its very beginning, can move into the light? What better thing have we got to do?

Indeed, we have waited for the last minute, for the glaciers of our beautiful old planet are melting and the people we have injured and oppressed are no longer impossibly far away. We have come to a century of come-uppance, and we can, I believe in my heart, come up to it. We have no choice, nor would we want any other choice but to do our honorable best in the broad world and here, at home.

And now we have our election coming. Well, we all have jobs to do in the next months. Many of you will work for candidates. I think you must do that, and spare the fighting among yourselves in favor of moving the message out to those who have given up on voting. We need those votes, friends, and they are not attracted by negative campaigning.

For myself, I intend to do one thing in this election. Let me tell you that, for many long years, I worked in a shoe factory here in Manchester. I know what it means to be a workingwoman. It is hard in this culture, for there are many demands placed upon you. There is little time for anything but for life's essentials.

But, in this election, voting has become one of life's essentials.

I want to help as many working women as possible by bringing them what they need to register to vote and to see that they have the time off to vote, the rides to the polls or the reminders they need to do this important thing for themselves, their retirement, their families, and for their America and its freedoms and its justice.

I love my little house in the woods of New Hampshire. I am comfortable there, next to a bright stream. But I will be happy to run an errand, and I will do it very soon. I will travel to work sites where women work, in order to bring them the time they need to register to vote. I will walk through many towns to do this, finding as many workplaces as I can, and I am going to buy a little red wagon for my voter supplies. I will be happy to be driven between towns so that I can cover the ground more quickly than when I walked the nation. My friends have helped me map it out.

I hope to be around for several more elections, but you never know. If this is my last, then my last wish is that America's women, who worked so hard amid great violence for the right to vote, might please take voting in this next election as their sacred duty. It is not particularly easy to travel at my age, but I hope they will take my little sacrifice as a nudge to inconvenience themselves, and to vote.

Our friends and neighbors are full of common sense, and that is what a democracy requires. If they have good information from awakened news people and from candidates who will please, God, spare us the platitudes and spend their millions on useful information so that a great nation might make an informed choice, then we have good reason to let our hearts fill with hope. We must all talk-up the election. We must all share information with our neighbors. We must speak in calm tones and respect the dignity of our opponents even when it is clear they are scoundrels, for the tone of our society is a part of the substance of our society.

We must encourage our free press as it sputters back to life. Not only must we demand and encourage good reporting, but we must take the best stories and copy them out and share them with our friends and neighbors—to double their effect. And we must encourage the news networks to get back in the business of exit polling during the election. Many of us are worried about the honesty of our elections. The networks pulled away from exit polling because they thought—or they say they thought—that they got it wrong in Florida. In fact they got it right. Exit polls do get it right and they are our best insurance now for an honest election.

And for ourselves more personally, we must vote and take our neighbors to vote and make calls from lists that we must make to see that this is a turnout like no other. And then our democracy will be safe enough to begin its larger awakening, and God help us to see that day, for the world and all nature awaits.

Finally, let me say that my hope is that we all vote so that our leaders will be expression of our highest civic values. You know, it is interesting that the United Nations headquarters is in our country. It is interesting because the United States is in a real sense a union of nations. Look around your community and you will see your fellow Americans who are Iraqis and Palestinians and Jews and Russians and French and Irish and Africans and South Americans and Europeans and Catholics and Mormons and Buddhists and Sikhs and Moslems and Baptists and Asians and Pacific Islanders and all the rest. This nation is a union of the world's people, and that is a grand thing to celebrate. Our president and our other leaders must be worthy of that America, and they must be men and women of peace and creativity and joy. Only with such leadership, where all our children are raised together with the best we can give them, where our adventures into the broad world are unselfish and full of light, can America prosper and survive this amazing time. What work we have to do, and how we do love it! Thank you, friends.

Save the World But Do Your Homework

Ms. Haddock speaking at Simpson College, in Iowa, September 25, 2003, to the assembled freshman class, for whom her first memoir was required reading.

Thank you. I want to sincerely thank those of you who really took time to read my story. I want to also thank those of you who, because of other serious commitments, at least skimmed the book. And, most of all, I want to thank those of you who quickly described the book to your roommates who would have liked to have had time to skim the book...

Let me talk for a few moments about our position as Americans.

We Americans are less than five percent of the world's population and we consume over 25 percent of the world's resources and produce well over 25% of the Earth-warming carbon dioxide. You and I, as Americans, simply consume too much, and quite a bit more than we produce ourselves. That is not an economic model that can be spread across the world, unless folks from some other planet will send us things to keep us going. Otherwise, all the world cannot consume more than it produces, can it?

So, there are two good ways we can go from here, in addition to an infinite number of bad ways.

The first good way is that we can respect the idea that life is lived differently in different parts of the Earth. We can live as we do in the U.S, although more sensibly; we can pare back our own consumption to make a better fit with our own resources, so that we are not in the business of exploiting other lands and propping up bad governments who will allow us to exploit those resources. I can actually imagine us doing this. I can imagine leadership in America that helps us become self-sufficient for our energy needs, for example—and I can imagine leadership that shows us the way to do this without trashing our atmosphere and our wildlife preserves and without tearing down more of our beautiful Appalachian mountains—blasting their tops off to get at the coal.

I can imagine leadership that leads us to once again make our own chairs to sit in and our own televisions to watch while sitting in our own chairs. After all, we will not be able to buy dirt-cheap goods from other nations when their workers are finally being paid fairly and their environments are being protected. So, if unfettered international trade means to raise wages and standards, as some claim, the incentives for such trade will fade away as wages rise abroad. Without the incentive of cheap prices from these nations, we will be back to making our own coffee tables and our oscillating fans—and what would be wrong with that, as we indeed need the jobs?

At that point, those foreign nations would have to rely on their own citizens to buy their own goods, and that is the decent position they were in before colonialism disrupted their natural economies.

A natural economy, indeed, is a good thing. It requires honest government to work fairly, which is the trick. But when it is in place, people provide for themselves, a middle class grows, and democracy has the firm ground it needs to flower, though it has not done so in many places.

Nations, even if they are mostly self-sufficient, will still trade commodities—one nation will have too much of this and will need some of that—tin and oil and steel and kiwi fruit and coffee and champagne. But, for the most part, labor—which is to say our lives—need not be one of those commodities. Labor can instead be expended to produce the goods, foods and services needed by one's own family, community and nation.

It is, after all, hardly sensible to transport a chair halfway around the world when it is so easy to make a chair near home by people who need the jobs and who have the wood and the cloth.

The second good way we can go is this: We can invent new ways of living that are indeed exportable, because they do not expend more resources per person than they produce. The world loves and despises our lifestyle. They do not respect the wastefulness of it, but they do like the freedom and glamour of it. They wear our jeans while they protest against us, and that should instruct us. Those jeans, and our music and much of our cultural content, represents the freedom of the individual to express their unique personality and potential. That, as an expression of our constitutional freedom, is America's chief contribution to the advance of civilization, and it is appreciated and embraced. The symbols of it may be denim jeans and cola drinks, but they are nevertheless important symbolic statements. The blue jeans worn under a burka and veil in a repressive culture are symbolic of individual resistance, individual defiance, the promise of individual freedom and the development of individual potential.

That joy of life, joy of fairness and freedom, joy of personal development and expression, is a fair thing for us to export, for we have an unlimited supply, and many other places in the world are hungry for it. If the 21st Century is to be another American Century as some would have it, let it be because we have the creative imagination to joyfully lead the world in ways that actually work for everyone, that sustain our world, that bring happiness and freedom.

We can no longer use our power to take from others to make easy lives for ourselves. That time has ended. The world got smaller on September 11th in many ways. While the terrorists use religion as their excuse for violence, the violence is really about poverty and the class warfare that our international ways of doing business—and the links to political corruption—have created in the world.

If we are capable of creatively leading the world, let us do so. If we are not, let us profit by make our own chairs and let others profit by making theirs.

Not long ago in America we celebrated the creative hand that made what we needed. When that respect for labor, including artistic labor, resulted in the rise of the unions, just after the turn of the 20th Century, America grew a mighty middle class and a generous standard of living. Labor mostly did that, not capital and not armies of occupation.

I will begin a new project next week to get working women to register to vote in greater numbers, and I shall begin in my own part of the world, in Boston and Cambridge, just down the road from my home in New Hampshire. I will begin my adventure where a tree once stood.

On Brattle Street, a couple of blocks from Harvard Square, there is a little bakery with a small yard in front of it. There used to stand a large chestnut tree in that yard. There also used to stand a blacksmith's shop and his family's home in that yard. A few steps farther up Brattle Street lived an old poet named Longfellow, who would walk past this yard and hear the clanging of the blacksmith, his old friend. He wrote the now classic poem that you may have heard many times, but I want you to listen to it now as an expression of respect for the labor of the local worker, unencumbered by the disease of debt and not priced-out of his own community. Sing along if you know it.

"Under a spreading chestnut-tree..." (She recited the poem.)

Thus at the flaming forge of life, indeed. I have included in my book some stories about my father, about how he loved his work in a furniture factory, how his muscles glistened as he hand-pulled the ropes of the great elevator, how he whistled home to us on his bicycle for lunch, how his employers respected him with decent treatment and decent pay. Many good things have happened since then to make the American workplace fairer for women and minorities, but, in the aggregate, it has become less fair to all. It exploits, now, rather than respects. There is no assurance, as indeed once there was, at least for the free people, that a life spent in loyal labor would earn not only respect but security for one's family. That is a great loss that we must repair, just as we must repair our relationship with nature and with our neighbors around the world.

Creative leadership at the political level is hard to come by today. Creative leadership may come from other areas— business, art, science—and that is fine. But creative political leadership needs to come now from your generation and from you.

So please have confidence in your creativity. Don't let the demands of the workplace or of academia dampen your zany spark for joyful living. Wear jeans under your burkas, even when the burkas are business clothes. Insist on seeing the world through your own new eyes, and bringing your surprise gift of the new to the crumbling institutions of those who now hold power only by force—that power should be held instead by those who earn it by creatively serving the needs of the people.

How shall we live? What kinds of dwellings and communities shall we live in? How shall we get around? What shall we eat and where and how will it be grown? These are among the old questions that need new answers, and soon. I hope you will have confidence in yourselves to remake the world while there is yet an opportunity to do so.

And I ask you to be a patriot and defend the Bill of Rights that make our nation a beacon of freedom in the world. You have a right to representation if you are arrested, and so does everybody else in America. You have a right to not be held without evidence and you have a right to have that evidence reviewed by a court, and so does everybody else in America. You have the right to read any book and not have the government peeking at what you are reading and thinking, and so does everybody else in America. That, very simply, is what America is. Our highest public officials swear when they take office to defend those rights against all enemies, foreign and domestic. You are seeing in your own time the gravest attack on those rights in the history of our nation. They are your rights and your freedoms and you had better get out in the streets if need be and defend them, for once they are gone they are hard to gain back.

Work to protect the best part of the American experiment: our legally enshrined freedoms. Once you have done that, dear ones, work to remake America's way of life so that it is in balance with nature and with the needs and dreams of the whole world.

And don't neglect your studies.

And a final few lines, if I may, from Edna St. Vincent Millay, from her famous poem, "First Fig," which may be useful for you on those late study nights:

> *My candle burns at both ends;*
> *It will not last the night;*
> *But ah, my foes, and oh, my friends*
> *It gives a lovely light!*

Back at Harvard

Ms. Haddock speaking at the John F. Kennedy Forum at Harvard's Kennedy School of Government, October 2, 2003. She began her campaign, Working Women Vote, with this speech in the school's atrium amphitheater. Students and professors watched from the seats around her and from the layered balconies above. Just before she began, David Gergen came out of his office like a squirrel, asked if there was any food with this event, and disappeared when told there was none. She considered the speech a letter to the Supreme Court, as the Harvard podium would give her words additional heft. McConnell, the California Democratic Party and others had sued to overturn the new McCain-Feingold law. The Supreme Court, soon after this speech, upheld the law, though, several years later, in Citizens United, they reversed themselves.

Thank you. It is a great honor to be here at Harvard's Kennedy School of Government. I thank you for inviting me and for coming this evening to hear me.

I have spoken to Harvard students before, though the circumstances were quite different. Young men—for they were all men—of the Harvard Business School would come to their lunch and dinner, and a young girl in a booth at the door would ask to see their meal cards. It was 1927. Several of the students would bring me books to read, as I seemed intent on learning things. Oswald Spengler's "Decline of the West," which had come out in 1922 and was a pessimistic prediction of the despotism and worldwide warfare to come, was still what everyone was reading and discussing. So I was constantly brought that book by young men, and I always said I was glad to finally have a copy to read.

The pay for my job was not much, but I saved it up and enrolled the next year at Emerson, after working the summer as a maid at a Nantucket inn. I had a head start at Emerson thanks to all the books the Harvard boys lent me when I worked here.

I am deeply honored to be speaking from the podium where last week a true hero of democracy spoke to you—Polish president Lech Walesa. I wish I could have been here for that, although I do know some of what he said: In speaking of the Polish shipyards in the 1970s and 80s, he said, "there are special places where you can feel the future."

Quite so! There are places and times when the future of the world seems hanging like a chad, waiting for one butterfly's wings to move the world this way or that. We are poised on such a moment, and I think most of you can feel it—can feel the future. The world is waiting to go this way or that, and our individual efforts in the next year are those butterfly wings. Our glaciers are melting; our democracies and our basic human rights are poised for advancement or destruction; our American economy and our role in the world—so many things—are now poised to go this way or that. It is almost too much to contemplate, too much to worry about. We can feel the future, though we don't yet know which future it will be.

So much of my own energy lately has been devoted to campaign finance reform. The bill that we finally got though Congress is now waiting for the Supreme Court's decision. Like so much else, it is poised on a delicate balance. It will probably come down to one vote, and that may be the vote of Justice O'Connor once again. We can only pray for a good outcome.

The McCain-Feingold bill that became the law and is now before the Supreme Court does chase corporate money out of our federal elections, which is a good but imperfect accomplishment— if the Court will let us keep it. The very high political price paid for that victory was a doubling of the limit of personal money that can be donated to a campaign, sending it to $2,000 per person, per election, with the primary and general election counted separately. That's a lot of money, and I suppose the most heartbreaking scenario would be if the Court struck down the prohibition on corporate money but left in the doubling of the personal money limit. We are praying for the Court's wisdom and lately that is a hard prayer.

The issue is this: Can we keep our democracy human-scaled, or is it to be a playing field only for financial giants? Have we, the people, lost our government? And if we have, what alternatives for action do we have that are worthy of our peaceful hearts?

If I were a lawyer, and if I were allowed to speak before that Court, I would have told them about so many people I met on my long walk who came to actual tears when they described their frustration at the loss of their America. "Beyond our control now," they said. "Bought right out from under us," they said. "All in the hands of fat cats and scoundrels"—that is what so many people said and do think, and they have much evidence to support their opinions.

The law that is now before the Supreme Court provides that corporations cannot finance federal candidates for office. It further provides that ads that look and smell like campaign ads, when run during a campaign, should be financed by individuals, not by corporations, and that those people should file disclosures like any other campaign committee.

No human being, acting individually or in a group, is deprived of speech by the new law. The law in fact allows the speech of the individual to again be heard. It is a modest patching-up of the old campaign laws, in that the first prohibition of corporate money in our elections was the good work of Republican Teddy Roosevelt.

Some of the Justices seem uninformed of the fact that American democracy is in crisis and that Congress has now acted only in response to that crisis, doing so quite modestly and begrudgingly. Indeed, listening to the Justices ask their questions during the oral presentations a few days ago, I pictured them with powdered wigs, monocles and snuff boxes—they might as well have been in the 18th Century and on another continent, as the "let them eat cake" comments were sadly numerous.

I don't think that a 93-year-old former shoe factory worker should know more about the situation than they do, but that was the sinking feeling that came over me as I listened to them. I wished that I could drag them by their frilly collars to the living rooms where real Americans shared with me their disgust for the—excuse me—whorehouse that Washington has become—tragically become, indeed, as so many of our sons and daughters have given life itself for our freedoms and, chief among them is our freedom to govern ourselves through the election of representatives who will represent us and not just the rich and not just the powerful, and who will be our champions against the corruptions of big banking, big medicine, big energy and all the rest.

If the new law's modest sandbags against a flood of corruption cannot be allowed by the Court, then we must rethink our country in fundamental ways, although that rethinking may be unsettling and dangerous. But here it is: The great masses cannot be left thinking that they are powerless under this system, or they will in their own way chose other systems. The people are the seat of power itself and they are not likely to stand by while the air they breathe and the water they drink and the milk of human kindness itself is poisoned by the greed of a powerful elite, and while their own ability to provide for themselves and their families and communities is eroded toward poverty and treadmill credit enslavement. No, the presumptions of the elite, unchecked by a government of the people, are spiraling toward a collapse, and if the Supreme Court Justices cannot stand apart from the elite long enough to see the emergency, then change will come in unregulated ways—or the ways of the demagogue—that must make us tremble.

While we work—and we must continue to work—to weaken the unfair influence of the rich and the powerful international elite in our elections, we must also look for ways to strengthen the ability of ordinary people to have a meaningful voice. I think we are seeing that in the Internet and its fundraising capacity. It is opening a new era in our politics, both in terms of communicating information and fundraising, and it looks a lot more like democracy than does the $2,000 a plate chicken dinner and the $200,000 corporate donation. I hope you all will give a little bit of money and other energy to your favorite candidates, and the Internet offers easy ways for you to do so. If we all give a little to the champions of our values, then a people-powered democracy—the only real kind of democracy—can have a fighting chance against the chicken eaters.

It is interesting that today's New York Times reports that China's president is calling for more democracy in China as an antidote to corruption. Large political systems have corruption. The opposite of corruption is democracy. People tend to not choose to be oppressed and exploited and starved when they have a voice in the matter. Look at the great tax giveaway to America's richest of the rich and please see it as a failure of representative democracy, which it is. See it as a profound crisis, which it is.

And to Sandra Day O'Connor, who gave us the Florida decision and all that came from it, here is your chance to square your account with heaven and history.

Now, isn't it too bad the public doesn't own the airwaves so we could really have some inexpensive campaigns? Wait—we do own our airwaves? We do issue cable franchises to our cities? Well, then, it is too bad that we don't act the proper part of the owner. Why should we pay through the nose for our own air during campaign season?

Because so many new forces are in play, I will not be overly discouraged if the imperfect campaign reform bill is rendered even more imperfect by our imperfect Supreme Court. I will not call them by the names I may be thinking. Indeed, if human-scaled politics is to prosper, it requires a civil tone, and we are surely in control of what we say, and it does take the cooperation of both sides to have or not have a shouting match. I do not mean that talking nicely will stop the rise of fascism, but I do mean that we can fight with the words and values of our higher civic sensibilities, even as we do battle.

The harsh divide between the political right and left, and

indeed between the political right and the old middle, is now becoming dangerous. Points of view, often fueled by misinformation, unthinking xenophobia and racism, are pushing us into a time of domestic as well as international confrontation. The far right now equates honorable dissent with treason and terrorism. The angry voices on talk radio and in the newspapers and websites do not fully understand what they do. They do not grasp what happens when civil temperaments and good humor and respected differences of opinion are eroded by the acid of insult, interruption and shout, and when, little by little, the lower potentials of human nature are let off their leashes and instances of violence begin to rise, as they have done at other times and places in the history of our species...

All of us must exert ourselves in the coming months. America and the world will be dramatically influenced by the coming election.

This is a special place; this is a special time in America when we can feel the future. It is frightening, but it is exciting. It is your future more than mine. I wish you luck, and I ask you to wish me luck and lend a hand where you can. Thank you and goodbye.

On the Road Again

Ms. Haddock's began her voter registration journey immediately after her Harvard speech. After brief stops at Yale and in New York City, she began work in Pennsylvania, beginning at the Crayola crayon town of Easton, then to Philadelphia and cross the state to Pittsburgh. Ms. Haddock's remarks to a chapter of Green Party members on the University of Pennsylvania's Kutztown campus, October 8, 2003:

Thank you. We live in interesting times. Arnold Schwarzenegger won the California governor's race last night. Lions are turning upon their tamers; billion-year-old glaciers are melting; Pentagon warlords are running for President as Democrats. Next, UFOs will be dropping chicken potpies on hapless vegetarians. Nothing makes sense anymore.

I was with Molly Ivins last week in Cambridge. She made a speech at a YMCA and then we went out for a drink. She said that, even after Bush annexed Iraq, oil prices in America are still so high that Texas wives who want to run over their husbands are now having to carpool.

So yes, general mayhem. It feels like we are in someone else's world. I feel disoriented, like the time on my big walk across the country that we stopped at a large restaurant for a Coke. It turned out to be a strip club. The Coke was fine, but I felt so overdressed.

In fact, I often feel overdressed for this world these days. But here we are, and we must live our lives and we must represent out values in the world, despite the sometimes shallow and false aspects of our surroundings.

I am on a trek now to register Americans to vote, especially working women and first-time voters. We the people have been playing with half our team; only half of us have been voting. I am going to try to do my small bit to bring more players off the bench and into the game, especially now that there is really something to vote for.

Many people have not been voting because they believe that there is no point. There is now a point. This time, no one will be saying that a few votes don't matter. No one will be saying that there is no difference between candidates. Not this time.

And for those of you who are worried that corporations friendly to the present administration are rigging the voting machines they manufacture, you must all insist that the news organizations get back into the business of exit polling as a check against crooked machines. The news organizations said they were getting out of the exit polling business because they got it wrong in Florida. In fact, they got it right in Florida and they must get back on the job if we are to have confidence in our elections— confidence that is critical to the very peace of our society in the years ahead. I was cheered to see that exit polling was a part of the coverage in California yesterday. Let's push for it every chance we get, and, long term, let's get back to hand-marked paper ballots so that everyone will have faith in our elections.

Now, let us think about the fresh voters we are bringing in—men and women, young and old. There are 64 million workingwomen in this country, most of whom are eligible to vote and only half of whom are registered. They have busy schedules and many demands upon their every hour. That is why I have decided to take voter registration to them –to as many as I can get to, and as many as my friends will help me get to. America's workingwomen are overworked and underpaid. They only have time for life's essentials. This time, voting is one of life's essentials and I mean to help them come off the bench and into the game.

Unmarried women, working and otherwise, are a group

of great importance in the coming election. Some 46% of American women over 18 are single, according to the census. In 2000, only 52% of them voted. By contrast, 68% of married women voted. The difference, I think, has to do with their harried schedules fending for themselves in a tough urban culture.

I hope we can make it easier for them to register and to vote, and I hope we can encourage them to examine the issues and the candidates to see where their own interests lie.

On the road, I will not suggest how people should vote, only that they should vote. They should study the issues and the candidates for themselves, and we will be all right if they get enough good information. I am not endorsing candidates because everyone is as capable as I am to decide. All I ask is that they consider the blood and sweat that have been spent on this government of the people, by the people, and God help us, for the people, and that each of us will understand that it is a great offense to those sacrifices if we do not do the one thing asked of us in return, which is to study the issues and to vote.

I hope you will ask your relatives and friends to be voter registrars in their workplaces and schools. Send them to me—I'm on the Internet—and I'll send them the forms and posters and supplies they need.

All of us must exert ourselves in the coming months. America and the world will be dramatically influenced by the coming election. This is a special place; this is a special time in America when we can feel the future. It is frightening, but it is exciting. It is your future more than mine. I wish you luck, and I ask you to wish me luck and lend a hand where you can.

Now, assuming we get Americans registered to vote, and assuming that we get them to the polls, whom shall they vote for? We are back to that old struggle of electability versus philosophical authenticity. I think it is true that Americans want to elect people who seem real, who come across as absolutely dedicated to their beliefs and unselfishly dedicated to those beliefs. That seems more important now than the beliefs themselves. In addition to being fully dedicated, candidates must have star quality, charisma. A Teddy Roosevelt would be just right. A Harry Truman would do well.

I don't want to say whom I think should be the Democratic nominee, as I don't want to confuse my message –I am sticking to the voter registration message.

But I will say this to you, as most of you are Green Party members: Many of us were, some months ago, worried that the Greens would put up a presidential candidate, and that doing so might split the vote. My friend Ronnie Dugger went to speak with Brother Ralph and ask him not to run. I will now disclose what happened: Brother Ralph refused to say yes or no. He has said that he may or may not run, depending on whom the Democrats nominate. And, of course, whom the Greens nominate—for Ralph doesn't decide entirely by himself.

If the Greens run a presidential candidate in 2004, that candidate may spilt the vote, even slightly, which could be enough to reelect the president.

Democracy is much at stake this time, and such an outcome will certainly damage your party's future. It is a moment in history, I believe, when you must make a tough strategic decision.

In the longer run, you must have a clear notion of how you will achieve victory as a party. Is your idea of victory that you will be as big as the Democratic Party? Bigger, perhaps? Do you have a time frame for this? How long will it take, and for how many years—ten, twenty, thirty—will America's political left be split by this rise of your party? What will happen to America's democracy and the world's environment during your rise to power?

If you cannot imagine success—a success that is responsible not only to the welfare of your party but also to the welfare of the nation and the world—then you should consider simply taking over the Democratic Party and turning it to your values. The doors of the Party are not locked. It is hard work, and you will not have the secure pleasure, as you now do, of hearing nothing but reassuring echoes from people who believe exactly as you do. But it may be the responsible fight, unless you indeed have a socially responsible plan for the rise of the Green Party that I haven't heard and can't imagine.

If this is a tough decision, I remind you that Arnold Schwarzenegger won the governorship of California last night and anything is possible in America.

But that is your business. It is my business, as an old Democrat, to also push hard for the environment and for justice issues. I have worked hard on nuclear issues and to get corporate money out of our political campaigns. You share those interests. All our interests may be the same: public financing of elections, secure elections, single-payer health care, sustainable development, alternative energy, pure and natural foods.

Because you and I share these values and these issues, I wish nothing for you but success. Do not marginalize yourselves. Take your rising energy and your expanding army and invade the most fertile valley. That valley is not the general electorate, but the Democratic Party. Get involved and stay organized as the Democratic Greens. Bend that party. Educate it. Rise within it and lead it during the critical 21st Century. Lead the party and the nation and the world away from colonialism and exploitation and irresponsible use of people and the planet. Lead it toward sustainability and health and justice and the empowerment of each person and the development of each person's full potential.

For better or worse, mostly worse, America has a two-party political system. Third parties are good things, because they move the other parties toward new issues and new positions. Third parties are bad things when their egos for their institutional interests overcome their interest in moving society toward their values.

The Greens have a great opportunity in 2004. It is to bow out. It is a hard opportunity.

There are millions of Americans who are suddenly ready for change. We mustn't present them with a broken home for their new involvement. I am constantly amazed at how widespread is the general sentiment for reform—for a better America.

When I was walking into Washington DC in 2000, we came down K Street—lobbyist row—to make a big noise below their windows. Jim Hightower had a megaphone and led us in chants. When we passed a statue he would jump up on its pedestal and make a great little speech. We had bagpipers and noisemakers. We had David Crosby and Paul Wellstone and a dozen or two other Members of Congress among our two thousand. I looked up and saw a window crank open. I was ready for a mean face or worse. Two young women appeared and they unfurled a banner: Go Granny Go!, it read.

Even where we least expect it, there is support, strength, friends, fellow human beings who are ready for a brighter world that better represents their dreams. Let us get our acts together and give them an army worth fighting in. It is the army of love and of light.

That is the party we share. Let us make organizations that represent our unity. Thank you.

Bulls in Democracy's China Shop

Ms. Haddock's October 20, 2003, remarks at Gettysburg College:

Thank you. I have begun traveling the towns of our nation and talking to the half of America, young and old, who usually do not vote. I am learning a great deal.

It is true that, three years ago, when I was 90, I walked from coast-to-coast to raise public awareness for needed campaign finance reform, parts of which passed Congress. What I am learning this time is that I am not as young as I used to be. I am a little older and the trail is a little harder, as each new year now ages me like three, but the Americans along the way are as kind and caring and as full of love for their country and each other as ever they have been. It is a great joy.

I am determined to make this trip and meet as many Americans as I can, and get to the bottom of the question, at least for my own satisfaction, of why so many people are not voting and what we might do to turn that around.

Many simply despair of politics. They are not much interested in voting for the lesser of evils, if that is to be their choice.

Many work so hard and long each day that they have no time left for registering or for voting, especially when they see only marginal differences from less than inspiring candidates in an election process that raises up the least promising candidates. Many young people know they should vote but do not get around to it, as if it were extra credit homework.

Many see politics as a dark world of self-interest and forever recycled baloney. They see the major parties not as great clubs for their participation, where they are welcome, but as special interest groups. "Only special interests vote," a fellow in a Bethlehem coffee shop said. The rusting hulk of the Bethlehem Steel works, now closed for four years, was just down the hill.

The new definition of "special interest group" seems to be any group of people who regularly participate in a political system that does not seem to ever move the people's interests forward. So the environmental groups are seen sitting right beside the mountain-removing coal companies and the belching chemical plants. All of them, in frustration or in villainy, keep saying the same things, and are so very predictable. They seem to be looking out only for their own points of view.

Many of our fellow citizens, though they do not vote, are worried about the state of our society, about the prospects for our children, about the health of our environment, about simple justice in the workplace and in society. They worry how they will be able to afford the future – the school costs, health costs, retirement, and last month's bills.

Politically, people are hungry and discouraged. They do not even remember, as I do, that there was a time when hard work came with the reward of security. People used to feel more in control, more able to provide for the future of their families. But that sense of control has been lost, and it is a loss of freedom, of living freely. For freedom is about having control and options.

So, despair sets in. They are unaware of the fact that they are suffering a kind of depression. But depression is often about giving up when a bright future no longer seems even possible. It is about assuming the negative, and that is what has happened in our civic lives: mass clinical depression. Not voting is but one of the many kinds of giving up that happens.

In this state of mind we are easily tempted to vote for any bull heading for the china shop of politics-as-usual, while actual leadership in a civilized democracy must be positive and creative, not negative.

And what about my point of view? —the citizen asks. What about my dignity? If you just talk past me with your slogans, you render me invisible and worthless. So why should I take time out of my day to go vote for you?

Isn't all this really about alienation? Isn't it about the monstrous loneliness we have inherited as so many of our natural communities have dissolved into formless urban tissue and harsh landscapes of strangers and strip malls and brutal careers? Isn't community what we long for, even when we rail against the policies that would build community? Don't we need to be more a part of it all, as owners somehow?

And behind our despair is still our dream of community, of mutual respect, of the beautiful community. I believe that it is all still there, waiting for leadership that is real. Our despair is great because our dream for our country and our community is great.

Until that day when the system measures up, many will not vote. By not participating, they believe that, at least, they do not allow themselves to be led by the nose through an empty exercise. That resistance is self-respect. They maintain their resistance, even though they know that some candidates indeed represent big trouble for their future. They know they should go vote, but cannot manage the stink of it.

But for many, it is the little things about voting that stop them: the no clear place to register, the no parking space near the county court house, the fear of looking stupid when they go to vote and don't know exactly how it is done. These little things would be worth overcoming if there were candidates worth a parking space, but there are none, they believe.

And how far away now seems that day, even if it was in a mythical past, when we Americans—free Americans anyway—had a sense of belonging, of ownership in our communities? How long since we interacted with each other and discussed the issues of our community and our nation as civic equals and as people responsible for our shared future?

The voter in a healthy democracy needs to be a kind of renaissance person of wide interests and wide knowledge, whose sense of responsibility falls as a gentle warmth over the region and the nation. We long to be that person: aware, respected, equal in power. We resist participating in a lesser way. We fall into private worlds where politics becomes alien to us. It is not a world for us, though we know it shapes the world in which we live and threatens us and our families.

I am haunted by the man in the coffee shop who said the only people who vote are the special interests. Much of this man's life in a steel town has been directed by political leaders who decided which industries would survive and which would wither. But he could not imagine having a real say in any of it. That is simple despair.

A young desk clerk, Christina, working late at a motel in Easton, said that she was considering registering for the first time, because the issues with children were not being addressed and she felt she had to do something about that. She is registered now, of course, because I always have the forms with me.

She is taking a leap of faith. She does not have candidates in front of her to believe in, but she knows the system needs something new, and she has decided to be it.

I think that she is on to something. What do you think? How do you energize a system? How do you make a revolution except by stepping over the line and changing the equilibrium of the status quo with your own presence?

In a way, she follows in the great footsteps of those who gave her gender the right to vote. They thought that, by taking their part in the battle of society's ideas, one vote at a time, they might make a difference, and they did.

One vote at a time, they liberated their sisters from the presumption of inferior status. Women still struggle for fair equality, but they are no longer presumed to be the pack animals of our society. They have great opportunities now to define their own lives on their own terms. Their participation changed their status and changed society in ways more profound than any candidate could achieve, and indeed, they achieved all that in spite of rarely having the right candidates to vote for.

It is a fact that the direction of society is set by whomever shows up to participate.

Politics will be different with Christina in it as a new voter and as someone who asks questions of candidates and who thereby changes how candidates and elected officials think. Politics will look better, field better candidates, deal with issues that it otherwise would neglect, and all of that will gently change the community and the nation. Each of us has exactly that effect on our entire society—we can scarcely imagine it. When we put ourselves in the fray, even that little bit, the effect is magnified to an astonishing degree.

We must somehow drag our fellow citizens, at least in their imaginations, down to the war memorials in the town plazas to imagine a conversation with those young people who gave up their lives for their country and its freedom. Imagine that they thought they were giving their lives for the idea that we are a self-governing people. Self-governance is the basis of our freedom—indeed we can easily understand that. Together, let us imagine that we owe these fine young people something. Do we not? Are we to change the system, influence the course of events, by our very presence in the system? Is their sacrifice worth our finding a parking space and registering to vote and returning to vote? Are we not obliged to walk into the room where self-governing people decide the fate of their land and people?

Will we not do this for our own futures and for the children's future and the future of nature itself?

If the system is not worthy of us, can we not make it more worthy by adding our love to it? Can we find the missing community, the missing honor, the missing leadership, the missing excellence in our system by adding what we ourselves might add to it, and do we not owe a debt of democracy to those who died for our freedom?

And so, will you register to vote, brothers and sisters? Here I come at my age and it is difficult to visit all these towns. But it is my honor to stand before my fellow citizens and implore them to take their places as equal members of our national community. And if anyone has been waiting for an invitation, I bring it to you now.

Let us invite Americans to be Americans and not just taxpayers, residents, occupants, consumers. Let us help our friends tap into the deepest rivers of life's meaning, for it can and should mean something special to be a citizen of one of the world's great democracies.

How to break the spell of despair? If the despair is about the loss of power, then the antidote is to empower. How do we do that?

Molly Ivins was recently visiting me in New Hampshire. On my back porch, she talked about the great concerns we now share regarding the direction of the government, including the assault on our civil liberties, the assault on the environment, the assault on sensible paths to peace, the assault on important social programs and all the rest. But she had us laughing.

She said that the Iraq war wasn't giving us any cheaper gasoline, and that gas prices in her Texas were so high that wives who want to run over their husbands are having to carpool. And Jim Hightower was on the porch with us, with more humor to keep us going.

We keep going in tough times with the fuel of love and humor, so don't be afraid to laugh at our common troubles or your own. And what happens when we laugh at our political opponents? They lose their power in that moment. We are suddenly equals or better. We have our power back, at least for that instant, and the encouragement lasts.

Music is another way we empower each other. That is why the great protest movements have had their great music. Music lifts our spirits, reminds us of our values, and empowers us to fight on. You know that in your own life, when the right song can cheer you up and get you moving. It is the same for the larger community, when it needs to get moving to overcome its problems. Pete Seeger wrote me a letter the other day, and he draws a little banjo next to his signature. He knows that it isn't enough to believe that this land is our land—we have to sing it out, to feel it rightly.

Humor and music may be all we have sometimes to drag ourselves and our fellow citizens out of the despair that we must not let ourselves succumb to.

What I am most sure about is that a revival of American democracy depends less on email and advertising than on our meetings in churches and living rooms and public parks again. Let these meetings be face-to-face, full of humor and music, and let the progressives who are desperate to revive our civic health be the organizers and inviters and hosts of these gatherings. Are we not the side of politics that believes in togetherness? Then we should have get-togethers all the time, and draw our circles wider and wider.

Many of today's activists were first awakened by William Greider's book, "Who Will Tell the People." I was reading through that wonderful book last night at Lou and Patricia Hammond's farmhouse in Gettysburg. Here is a passage:

"Strange as it may seem to an era governed by mass market politics, democracy begins in human conversation. The simplest, least threatening investment any citizen may make in democratic renewal is to begin talking with other people about these questions as if the answers mattered to them. Harmless talk around the kitchen table or in a church basement will not affect anyone but themselves, unless they decide it ought to. When the circle is enlarged to include others, they will be embarking on the fertile terrain of politics that now seems so barren." Unquote Mr. Greider.

Well, half of America needs waking up, inviting, empowering. I have heard of people in this town who are doing it. Virginia Schein is hosting a gathering in her home. Jake Schindel does so at the Ragged Edge. It is not too distant from the meetings that began our country. The kitchens, the spirited tables at the Green Dragon public house on Boston's North End. Americans are a positive and free-spirited people. They will always conspire to be free, to live in a land of justice.

People often talk about politics as a kind of warfare. The hills and meadows of Gettysburg are right outside these windows, this beautiful evening. These hills have seen enough of war. So lets talk about peace, instead. Politics is warfare unless you are sharing love instead of hate and arguments. People just want to be included, respected, listened-to and loved. Let us compete to be best at that, and the war is over.

So, for goodness sakes, register and vote and participate joyfully. Take your part in this great moment and in this adventure of the soul. Thank you.

After events in Pittsburgh she entered West Virginia. On November 4, 2003, the following report was emailed by Mr. Burke to Doris's friends and to those who had volunteered to register voters around the U.S.:

Dear Friends, we now have exactly a year before the election.

Doris is plying the hills and hollows of West Virginia. Yesterday she registered people to vote in historic Cabin Creek, where Mother Jones once railed against the inhumanity of the big corporate mines and raised an actual rebellion of miners—an uprising second only to the Civil War, in numbers.

At the top of that hollow, Doris yesterday paused atop Kayford Mountain, at Larry Gibson's cabin. During the last dozen years, the destruction wrought by mountaintop removal coal mining has turned Larry's once-idyllic landscape into a horror of blasting and flattened mountains and buried forests and streams. The surviving streams run black with toxic goo. Larry has refused to leave the mountain to make way for the destruction, despite being shot at, burned out and driven off the road. Great stones have fallen from the sky onto his family cemetery from the blasting. Doris prayed and cried with him in that place. From that shattered landscape, the coal flows down in seemingly endless freight trains and barges to the electric plants that spill toxins into the wind and into the water and even now the mother's milk of American women. It continues at such a pace—instead of being reduced by the introduction of alternative energies—because of political payoffs at the highest levels. The biggest local coal baron takes credit for spending the millions of dollars that brought West Virginia's electoral votes to Bush— the critical difference. He did it, and successfully, to protect mountaintop removal coal mining. So we stood there at ground zero of this new American era and feeling very full of emotion for the work.

The night before, very tired after a long day, she was nevertheless in a loud and rocking music club in Morgantown, packed with students from the University of West Virginia. They signed up individually and by group to help her table for new voters at Walmarts and other stores. She electrified the young people with a rap number that had them shouting along, with their fists waving to the refrain: "We have so many dreams / They run the gamut / But the only way up / Is to Vote, Dammit!" She then gave out "Vote Dammit!" lapel buttons and stacks of self-mailing voter registration forms.

Today she was on the Marshall University campus in Huntington, West Virginia. Her address to students is below. I hope you will pass it along to your friends and allied organizations. We need your personal participation. You will notice in the speech that she is purposefully projecting personal strength. That is what this election is all about. All the talk of war and danger has turned the electorate toward strength. Those candidates who express personal strength get the attention of voters. Those who do not, don't. We are learning that the strength factor even applies when it is a 93 year-old talking up registration and voting.

She was also tabling on campus, where people lined up to register and to get their "Vote Dammit!" buttons. This is something that you can do wherever you are, and we will be happy to send you the buttons and registration forms that are self-mailing and can be used in any state.

Let's Talk About You

Doris "Granny D" Haddock speaking at Marshall University, Huntington, West Virginia, Tuesday, November 4, 2003:

Thank you. I'm sure you expect to now hear something about my life, but I am here to talk about your own personal biography, not my own. So I will only briefly touch on my life.

I am 93. Three years ago I walked from California to Washington DC in order to gather up more support for the effort in Congress to get corporate money out of our federal political campaigns. The bill I was walking to support, the McCain-Feingold Campaign Finance Reform Bill, passed Congress, and not just from my efforts but many people's efforts. It now awaits action by the Supreme Court to see if it is Constitutional.

When I walked into small towns, the newspapers and televisions did their stories, and I used those moments to talk about how there is too much corrupt money in politics and how we must write our Congressmen to pass the McCain bill. It was a fairly effective thing to do, as the towns and cities piled up. Even large newspapers had me in to talk to their editorial boards, like the Dallas Morning News, and many papers, including that one, got on the campaign reform bandwagon. So one person can make a difference, even if a small difference, and a small difference is often the difference between victory and defeat.

It was hard walking across the deserts, as it was summer and very hot. I walked across 1,600 miles of deserts and the hills of Texas, and 3,200 miles in all.

When I got to the Appalachians it was snowing hard and I had to walk uphill in blizzards, and I do hate walking uphill, even without blizzards, but I had some volunteers with me and we made it, though it was very cold and hard. The harder it was, the better the news stories were, of course, and the more people learned about campaign finance reform. Sacrifice, you see, is an important part of political reform.

When I was in Cumberland, Maryland, my 90th birthday, it snowed so hard that I worried we could not go on, as the roadsides were piled high with snow from the snow plows. But miracles come to those who put their full hearts into important work. I discovered that there is an old canal, the C&O canal, that runs from Cumberland all the way into Washington, DC, and so I got my old skis and I skied along its bank for nearly 200 miles. That way I finally got to Washington. There were about 2,300 people there to greet me, including many Congressmen. We all walked together those last miles, making a racket down K Street, which is lobbyist row, to tell them their days were numbered—or so we hope.

Well, they are still there, but we clipped their ears back a bit with the McCain bill, and democracy is about keeping at it. So we will keep at it.

That is quite enough about me.

Let's talk about you.

You have come of age in extraordinary times. History is poised on a sharp edge, and you don't know how it will turn out. Will your America become a fearful land, less free than my old America? Will you tell your grandchildren that, when you were young, you could go into any library and read any book and never fear that the government was taking notes over your shoulder? Will you tell your grandchildren that, when you were young, you could walk into any music club or restaurant or bus and never even think of worrying about some act of terror?

Will you tell your grandchildren that you remember an America when the government was not all-powerful, that there was a time when you had a right to a lawyer, that you could not be held secretly in jail for years at a time or just disappear into the system? Will you tell your grandchildren that you remember an America when families owned small businesses and when America had a strong manufacturing sector, and when there was a strong middle class on account of these things? Will you amaze them with the information that old people used to be cared for with a system of social security? Will this seem amazing to your grandchildren, whose lives will be lived in fear and insecurity as underpaid service workers and regimented consumers of giant corporations?

266

Let's hope that your children's and grandchildren's world will be freer than yours today—safer, more prosperous, more beautiful in a more secure natural environment. But that can happen only one way: it will be the result of your having lived your life in a heroic-enough way so that your children and grandchildren find themselves in that better world.

We are in a time of trouble. The glaciers are melting; temperatures and weather patterns and harvests are changing, despite what the coal barons of West Virginia and their bought-and-paid-for politicians will tell you. Collapsing harvests are driving people into the cities of poorer nations, where they live miserably. Some 150,000 people die before their time each year now because of global warming. That number will of course grow to a great flood. We cannot fix it entirely, but we can certainly stop making it worse; we can halt the wasteful burning of fossil fuels.

West Virginia is such a beautiful state, but how will your grandchildren know it? In the coalfields of southern West Virginia and Kentucky, you are allowing the total destruction of the mountains and the filling in of the hollows with rubble. The explosive equivalent of one Hiroshima bomb is use against your mountains every eleven and a half days. Your grandchildren may ask why you allowed this—why you did not form human chains across the roads used by this monstrous corporate undertaking? Or your grandchildren may praise you for your courage in saving this beauty for them and for their children.

The environment of democracy is also under siege. The freedoms supposedly guaranteed by our Bill of Rights are under extreme pressure from those who would lead with force instead of creativity.

New, creative leaders must take the stage and be willing to look squarely at today's troubles and see past them to a better world. The creative leader sees possibilities unseen by others. But be sure the creative leaders you embrace lead from love and not fear; freedom and not cruelty and oppression. History has seen both kinds, rising from times of trouble.

And don't be afraid to be a leader, yourself. We can all do it on the issues of our passions. For example, I have asked many to help me, and I will now ask you to help me, too. I will ask you—I do ask you now—to sign up to help register people at our voter registration tables.

That's all leadership is. It's asking for help.

You will not be alone if you help me; hundreds of people and small organizations have signed up to help us, and we are enough to change history, in our way.

I am an old Democrat. I don't care if you are a young Democrat or a young Republican, or a Green or an independent or if you are an anarchist because you like to be so bad and you look so good in black.

I don't care what you believe, so long as it is a belief in the future and in a better world. For this life is about service to each other. It matters little what you do or how successful you are, or what your old sins or crimes or shortcomings might be. If you give your life to the service of others, that is love and it is redemptive and joyful and will make your life and your soul complete.

And I am saying that this is not an ordinary moment in the history of the planet. It is a glorious time of trouble, a time of change and challenge, and the forces of heaven look upon us now and say, well, what are you going to do, little ones? Do you, as Americans, have the courage of your Constitution? Are you prepared to help lead the world to happiness, or to ruin? And which of you will lead, and who will follow? And which of you will be but the furniture of this age, the hapless consumers, the glaze-eyed and hypnotized, and who will be awake and brave? Who will say, I am for love in the world?

Will you ask me to help you, to follow you? I will, you know. Just ask for my help.

For I happen to know your secret—that you are the center of the world, that your actions ripple out and change everything, that your life is not only important to the world, but critical to it. I believe in you and in the biography that you are beginning to write in the world. I am reading your book right now and it has a wonderful beginning.

And all I ask of you, so that we may be brothers and sisters in the work of our hearts, is that you will vote and help others to vote. That is the baseline, the beginning point of our citizenship as Americans.

We are blessed to be Americans. But this blessing came by way of blood and toil, and we must respect the sacrifices made for us and for our freedoms by finding our own voices, taking our own stands, and, damn it, by voting! Thank you!

The Morning Side of Monticello

Ms. Haddock's November 11, 2003 letter emailed to friends and supporters:

Dear Friends, I woke up this morning in Charlottesville and looked up the hill rising above me. It is a little hill, Monticello, the plantation home of Thomas Jefferson. The first light of the day was brilliantly reflecting in the windows of that clockwork little home atop the shining brow of that hill, where one of the chief architects of our freedoms once so brilliantly thought and wrote.

Mr. Jefferson is a good symbol for the complexity of the American experience: a slaveholder who wrote about the self-evident rights of people to be free. His courage at the crisis moment of our young nation, and his great mind and eloquence, certainly redeem him, at least a ways, in America's rearview mirror.

A moment of courage during a great time is often the thing that redeems us of our shortcomings. So it has been for so many of our friends and relatives in the great wars that have so fully tested their courage and made their faults fade in our estimation.

It is Veterans Day. It is a day for calling-up those old friends and family members who summoned all their courage to do the right thing as they saw it in difficult times.

I will call the surviving veterans in my family today. It is always so welcome a call. It adds meaning to lives otherwise compromised by the complexities and conflicts of industrial life. I hope you will make such a call today yourself, and will pass along this reminder to others.

I am on my voter registration trek. The old van is in the shop today, so we cannot move on to Richmond for a day or two. I will therefore do some voter registration tabling at the University of Virginia here. I am also rounding up volunteers who will help us table at the big stores next month, all over the country.

But for this morning I am looking at the glint of sunrise still flashing in the eyes of Jefferson's place. It is moving to see it still so alive and brilliant, as we all must be if our democracy is to move forward again.

As it is with this old van where I am writing, this is a time to make repairs to our democracy, and it's a day to thank those who have gotten us here. Sincerely, Doris

Note: In Asheville, Ms. Haddock met a young tattoo artist, Blue Broxton, who took on Doris as an art project. She painted the Working Women Vote van with images of women voting, the march of suffragettes, and Rosie the Riveter. The van was thence called Rosie, and sometimes Rocinante—in homage to Don Quixote's steed (and Mr. Steinbeck's camper truck). Blue learned to gather voter registration signatures and stayed with the trip for many months, all the way back to New Hampshire where she continued voter registration for the Kerry campaign and Doris.

Ms. Haddock used a small collection of stump speeches through the swing states. Here is a sample taken from a speech at the University of South Florida, billed as a voter registration rally and picnic:

Thank you. I hope you are not taking your studies here just for the purpose of becoming comfortably secure as somebody's wife, somebody's husband, somebody's employee, somebody's taxpayer. I hope you feel within your heart a spark of life that is far greater than any of that.

For here you are in a world, and at a time, where heroes are required. You may not quite see that. It may not impress you that the polar ice lost 44% of its thickness in the last 40 years or that there may be great dislocation of people, great famines, great epidemics as a result of the new weather.

You may not see exactly what I see when I say our democracy, our freedoms, are melting away, too, and that even a few years ago, when you were born, an American citizen had the right to a lawyer and an appearance before a judge, and all that is melting away in the shadow of the 9/11 attacks.

You may think that the inconveniences at the airport are unavoidable, when they are the direct result of a foreign policy that has favored our corporations at the expense of the American People's values of peace, world democracy, and economic fairness. You pay billions now to subsidize the primary and secondary effects of the unbridled greed of a new class of globalized robber barons, and heroes are required if we are to have the resources to care for each other, to educate our children, to provide for our health, to secure free and happy lives under our own healthy trees and under our own free and safe skies.

I am not exaggerating when I say that a heroic life is calling to you, and that you must rise to that call if you are to live in a good world. And this heroism begins with simple acts of faith such as voting.

Stopping at Peace River

From Florida, January 19, 2004, Ms. Haddock sent a message to her voter registration activists via email. It describes a stop in a Florida church where Ms. Haddock and Ms. Broxton arrived in church hats that were the proper style for the congregation. They were met with great applause. Mr. Burke introduced her, describing the physical sacrifice involved in her walk. Her letter:

On this occasion of Martin Luther King, Jr. Day I thought we should take a moment to reflect. It has been a busy few days, filled with Dr. King's spirit and memory. Yesterday morning our voter registration trek took us into the arms of Faith Pentecostal Church in Avon Park in central Florida. The music and energy were inspirational beyond my ability to describe. The Pentecostals, once called the Holy Rollers, know how to tap into the divinity and the sublime joy of the present moment. It is in the gospel singing and in every clap of the hand, as each instant is felt and celebrated. It is in the spontaneous dancing and expressions of profound connection—the melding of hundreds of lives into one caring and loving community.

Though we were of a different race and belief, the ministers welcomed us to the all African-American congregation and, with voices of awesome moral authority, they exhorted everyone to register to vote as a solemn obligation, and designated several women who would head it up.

The minority vote is the sleeping giant, not only in Florida, but in nearly every state. It is sleeping because people are full of despair. Pastor Brown told us that the people stopped voting when the politicians stopped caring about regular people, caring instead for their rich donors.

We spoke to the congregation of how Dr. King guides our work, how effort and sacrifice mark the road to meaningful social change. The ministers brought us all up to the front and brought down a blessing upon our trek, that it might be safe and successful.

After the service we headed west to St. Petersburg MLK Day Parade. Our van will be in the parade, gaily painted for the occasion by Ms. Broxton, our traveling artist. Our voter registration volunteers will be working the parade route, on both sides of our van. We will distribute 1,000 or more self-mailers.

We paused by Peace River along our way to St. Pete. Peace River is but a few miles from Troublesome Creek—a reminder that we always have a place to regain our composure and energy. Every day we meet people whose lives sparkle with curiosity and awareness and activism. We struggle together—all of us with beating hearts—for the responsible, joyful community: a place and a politics of human scale and responsible communities.

Sincerely, Doris

Don't Split the Left (Again)

Ms. Haddock's remarks at the annual Forest Council progressive gathering in the Shenandoah Valley, May 29, 2004:

Thank you very much. Last October, I began a journey to encourage people to register and to vote. My travels have taken me through most of the states east of the Mississippi, from Key West to Duluth. Along the way it has been my pleasure to see glimpses of the next America emerging from the pain and exploitation of the present toxic and unsustainable order—now wobbling toward its political fall.

Certainly, our president has done all he can to speed the demise of the old order and to lay bare the issues and the competing forces at work in the world. As he has undermined America's position in the world and America's security, he has also set the stage for the crash of the American economy—now stripped of proper regulation of its banks and more. We do not take joy in that, but we can look with hope to the new life that may come after.

We hope for the rise of the more human economy, long suppressed by the joyless self-colonization by corporations. For every hundred dollars now earned by the average American worker lucky enough to have a job, the top CEOs make $30,000. That's a 300-to-one wealth gap that has put the American dream in the deep freeze. It is a winter that must be made to thaw.

I had a glimpse of that new American spring the other evening in downtown Asheville. I was walking down the street when I came upon a small urban square called Pritchard Park. The sky was cool and starry. A new moon sat atop an old building across the square—it sat next to an old civil defense siren up there. In the square were about twenty drummers drumming—all kinds of drums making a great and pleasant rhythm for the town. Near the drummers were about a dozen young people playing hacky-sack—tossing around a little beanbag with their feet and knees. They were amazingly talented. There were about six younger children with hula-hoops, and some middle-age people dancing.

Asheville is a creative town. Its people are awake and alive. The arts are thriving in a natural economy of local produce, local music, local businesses. If you go to Starbucks, you will see progressive volunteers in front of the store, handing out free cups of fair-trade coffee to satisfy your coffee craving without your having to go inside and do business with that company. There is a joyfulness to the town and to life in such places. I have visited many such communities and seen the gardens, the home industries, the recycling ethic, the sense of social fairness that thrives in such places. These can be the opening points of the next America. It is so clear that neither major parties represent these people—you can almost understand their reluctance to participate and vote in the ethically corrupt system.

Before I left Asheville I stood on a street corner with a North Carolina soldier named Jimmy Massey, and with a group of citizens organized by Veterans for Peace. As they did in Detroit, the passing cars and trucks honked in approval for ending this war that is morally so over. Jimmy left the Marine Corps—the love of his life—because he would not participate in the continued slaughter of innocent civilians in Iraq. He had done that, and had enough of it. He is a big fellow with a great, honest and friendly face that makes the poignancy of what this government asked him to do all the more wrenching. Very simply, he is trying to be a good American and his commander in chief is not. He came back because he is morally strong enough to know that Americans must not become storm troopers for the oil companies and their captive politicians. He is part of an awakening.

Oh, how we Americans who are awake and alive are discouraged sometimes. How sad we are to not be of the bright nation that brings environmental sanity and health and nourishment, and the freedom and prosperity of self-sufficiency to the world. How tragic to know that, by losing control of our government, by losing control to the corporate interests that now control our government, we have unleashed such trouble in the world.

It hurts to know that we are exporting torture and

injustice and incredible environmental and cultural devastation. It hurts to know that the same forces are at work in our own country, tearing down our mountains for cheap coal that is not cheap at all if you count the cost of a lost environment. Those forces are also stealing our water from our farms and towns so that it can be sold back to us in bottles, because the rest of the water is too polluted to drink, turning our children into hypnotized consumers, controlled by orchestrated fears and nurtured ignorance.

But, as I say, this is the toppling regime, the garmentless king, if we will work to make it so. A new and green America can emerge.

In a town north of Detroit they are building a community radio station. It will operate outside the law, as Clear Channel has secured all the frequencies and will not provide any useful community news. Pirate broadcasting is not new, but in this instance the city council and the mayor are backing the station. It is an uprising of sorts.

My little van was parked on their street overnight. I expected to see a ticket in the morning. Instead, they had put hoods over the parking meter and left a note that I was welcome to park there as long as I liked. The mayor brought over some donuts and coffee. Isn't that the America we want and deserve?

Uprising is in the air: over 235 cities and towns have passed resolution defying Ashcroft's very un-American Patriot Act. The simple thing about our president is that you can easily tell what his new laws are about if you put the word "not" before their titles.

In another town closer to downtown Detroit, Highland Park, the old order is seen in its nakedness. Chrysler Corporation pulled out, taking millions in public money with them. The town was left in bankruptcy. The conservative former governor sent in a special manager to take over the town. She is a fan of privatization, and has hired, at huge salaries, her privatization pals. The elected city council now has no power and often must meet at a McDonalds because the little corporate dictator will not let them meet in city hall. She is arranging to sell the city's water utility to a giant international water company. They will not have to bid for the purchase, and they will not have to put any money down. So corporations have colonized Highland Park and destroyed democracy there.

Perhaps the community will decide to stop exporting its money and start building a natural economy—a post industrial, post-colonial economy. It begins with shopping only at locally owned businesses and starting up the gardens and markets that will nurture the growth of a new middle class. We must be like Gandhi in India, refusing to wear garments made in England from India's own cotton, when India can very well make its own garments.

I have walked and registered voters in the Jeffries Housing Project of Detroit and Cabrini Green in Chicago and in the streets of Highland Park, and I have met so many people ready for the new America. The prison culture is not working. People will not forever stand for it. "Live Free or Die!" is painted across the back of my camper. People everywhere seem to relate to it in their comments. They have had enough and are ready to render powerless the powerful and bring justice where there is now only unfairness and exploitation.

Certainly we can help a more natural economy to rise. We need not import chairs from halfway around the world if a woodworker in our own community is out of work. We do not need preserved or mutant foods from afar when we can have fresh and natural foods from the vacant lots of our neighborhoods. Our children need not to eat junk foods in school cafeterias when they have unused playgrounds that could grow a botany class and a good lunch—and this is happening, too. It is creative disengagement from the old order, and creative reengagement with each other and with the processes of life. But it needs boosting. It needs hard work to prosper.

I am not advocating a return to simpler times: indeed it is simpler to eat a Happy Meal at McDonalds than to have a community potluck feast. I am suggesting a return to real life in all its richness. And I am not suggesting that we build walls or forgo trade with other nations: Communities can trade their specialties with each other, as can regions and nations—but we need not go overboard with the concept; it is not rational to trade for what our own unemployed people can easily make here at home, and any savings we realize in trading with slave societies are soon lost as we lose our middle class and become a debt-burdened society ourselves.

While we build a new America from the rich soil of our own hearts and neighborhoods, if we only will, we must also work from the other end: We need local, state and national leadership that will help transform the American way of life to something closer to our national dream, and something closer to a sustainable vision of responsible life "unto the seventh generation." I don't look for many those leaders to be on our ballots just yet, but we will prepare the market for them by growing the progressive vote, and we will raise our young people to become those responsible leaders. The children in preschool today will rise up to save the earth, and they will do so in anger and in love.

But right now, in this year, the future goes both ways for America: toward a long dark night, or toward the opportunity for a new beginning. We owe it to the world to clean up our act; we owe it to ourselves to rid ourselves of the exploitive commercial, governmental and military institutions that do not protect and serve us, but instead endanger and harm us. It is a revolution of the heart, and I do see it welling up in many, many hearts.

We have work to do in the coming months. We have to help educate America's voters, for they will not get good information any other way. We must reproduce the best news clippings about what is going on in America and in the world, and get them handed out in every neighborhood and at every bus and subway station.

The second thing we must do is to get our friends and the people in our towns to register and vote. We must take responsibility for that in our neighborhoods and workplaces.

Third, we must deal with that part of ourselves that is the selfish progressive, capable of doing more harm than good in the coming months. We are the selfish progressives when we think it is all about us. We require the perfect candidate who reflects our views precisely. If we cannot have such a candidate, we may not vote, or we may vote for someone who cannot win, just to show our support for our precious opinions. This grandstanding is more important to us than the lives of all the people who will die and be exploited if a cruel leader is elected as a result.

The old joke is that the left forms its firing squad in a circle. The truth of that is in the selfish progressive's belief that politics is not for the practical advance of the common good, but is a showcase for personal sentiments. Progressive meetings, you may have noticed, tend to take forever, as all of us must fully expound our views on everything and how we came to our opinions. It is such a bore when other people speak, and so wonderfully enlightening when we finally get a few hours to speak ourselves. It is, in other words, a monumentally selfish exercise much of the time—an exercise in self-validation that would be better done in therapy.

Doing the right thing no matter how many people are hurt is always the wrong thing. It is a kind of intellectual fascism that, while nothing so bad as political fascism, is damaging nevertheless as a tyranny of the mind that does harm to others.

I hope the Nader candidacy is not again to become a meeting ground for such narcissism at the expense of other people's lives.

I know I have just lost many of you, but hear me out.

I am concerned about the future of the Green Party. My friends in the Greens tell me that they are building a party and that they must look to the long view. If they are right, here is the long view: ten to twenty years of party growth, during which the left vote will be split and the right wing will have the institutions of government all to themselves. Another ten to twenty years of equality between the Greens and the Dems, during which the right wing will have another era of unchallenged power. Then ten to twenty years when the Greens outpace the Dems, but the Dems are still a factor and the progressive vote is still split. So, say, thirty to sixty years before they can see some victories. Will there be anything like justice and liberty and nature left to work with by that time?

Do the Greens have a better scenario to meet the real and present danger to the planet? Here it is: let the Greens and progressives take over the Democratic Party, whose doors are unlocked and whose halls are unguarded. That can be done in two to four years. If the energies of the Green Party were transferred to a Green Caucus within the Democratic Party, real progress would be possible quickly.

It is time for the factions of the left to understand that, unless they have a practical strategy for early victory, they stand in the way of justice, of environmental protection, and of peace if they continue to split the left's vote. If they can actually win elections in some districts without the risk of a split, then that is a different matter, of course. And securing ranked choice voting will do much to allow people to vote Green without splitting the left. You should promote it, as I will. The Democratic Party itself, if it had half a brain, would do so, as well.

But if any fellow progressives are in the game only to hear themselves pontificate and wax eloquent about their wonderful values and their brilliant grasp of the issues—while others starve and die, I ask them to instead join Toastmasters where they can do no harm. Politics is not about posturing but about winning and then representing the interests of millions of people. When you take up the sword of politics, you play to win on behalf of your people, not to look pretty in your uniform. Americanism at its best is when we abandon the "we" of our beleaguered class or gender or suffering group in favor of the aspirational American "we," where our historic inequalities can together be righted as we work together.

That same narcissism that we of the left are particularly prone to, by the way, may be on display in the convention cities this summer. Millions of television viewers trying to decide whether or not to jump ship from the incumbent will look at the mess on the streets in Boston and New York and say, well, if I have to choose sides, I know I'm not on theirs.

The conventions are a time for massive action, but it had better be well organized and designed to convey real information respectfully to the American people, or it will be a selfish and damaging exercise in adult play at the expense of thousands of lives and the environment. I urge those non-delegates going to the conventions to carry thoughtful signs designed not to show only their anger, but the truth. I urge young people to consider the conventions not as an opportunity for mayhem and fun, but for service to their country and their world by using their creativity to open, not close, the hearts of the millions of Americans who will be watching. Let's look good out there. It is not in protesting alone that we find our power, but in creating change in the hearts and minds of millions of Americans.

We have the power to do this because the facts are on our side and because most Americans do care about the air, water, forests and mountains of their world, and most Americans do not side with corruption and exploitation and greed. But we can only enlarge our tent by attracting people into it through our earnestness and our ability to admirably represent truth and love.

So I come to you, a conference of the greenest of Greens, to make my suggestions among friends. You are a powerful group, and I have come to speak the truth as I see it to you.

We all know that this election is the most important election of our time, so far. It is a time indeed for our patriotism, our love and our strength of will. Our mountains depend on what we do. Our air and water. Our children and their children. The people of the world. Nature itself is, like no other time, in the balance. It is not a time for circular firing squads or childish, if satisfying, displays of anarchy. It is a time for the grand majority of Americans to be proud of each other for rising up at a time of crisis and doing the right thing.

And after the election, from the slums of Tampa to the sad towers of Cabrini Green, and from the co-ops of Asheville to Madison, Austin, Ann Arbor, Gainesville, and the ten thousand other American communities of people reawakening to life, we have a new America to nurture and an old America to begin putting away. Thank you.

I Walked—Now I'll Run

When the Democratic candidate for U.S. Senate from New Hampshire quit the race at the last moment (his campaign manager had absconded with campaign funds), it seemed that the incumbent senator, Judd Gregg, a Republican, would run unopposed. That was a problem for Democrats, as Gregg was a close friend of President Bush and was Bush's sparring partner in practices for the big debates. So, if not pinned down with a challenge in his home state, Gregg would be an effective national surrogate for the President in the coming campaign.

Gregg was rated as the nation's most popular senator in his home state. Therefore, though it was surely a losing proposition, Ms. Haddock, now 94, called the Democratic Party and offered herself as candidate. They accepted her offer.

In her campaign, she accepted no PAC money. Volunteers, including expert advisors on health, defense and the economy, arrived from Harvard and other universities and from D.C., to pitch tents in the woods across the stream from her forest home. That was the first campaign headquarters (it later moved to an historic mill in Peterborough).

Ms. Haddock, like so many people in her politically alive and sometimes politically brutal state, had hosted presidential candidates in her home and had connections with many activists and progressive organizations. They all brought their activism and connections into play to support Ms. Haddock's quixotic move. The Democratic Party, state and national, seemed almost embarrassed to have a 94 year-old candidate, and did not actively support her. Even the Democratic candidate for governor, John Lynch, was publically dismissive of her in his televised debate with the Republican. She was not invited to the Democratic National Convention, though, by tradition, she should have chaired or co-chaired the delegation, as the U.S. Senate *candidate.*

When New Hampshire's Democrat Secretary of State would not allow the use of "Granny D" as an additional identifier on the ballot, she had her middle name legally changed to that, forcing her more well-known name to appear. While she lost, as expected, she brought in a bit more than a third of the vote, twice what pundits had predicted. She carried Portsmouth and some other communities. More important, she did pin Gregg down, and her campaign recruited enough new voters, both old and young, to help swing New Hampshire into the blue for the presidential race. That was her main hope in running, which allowed her election night party to be a victory celebration.

Her televised debate with Sen. Gregg won her the audience poll. A high moment in that debate was when Gregg, whose flood of television ads featured him fly fishing in a stream, challenged her criticism of his environmental votes. "I have seen your television ads, Senator," she replied instantly, "and I hope you did not drink that water you were standing in..." She went on to knowledgably report on the toxicity of New Hampshire water, mostly from pollution coming from as far away as Ohio Valley coal plants, a crisis his votes in the Senate had not helped.

She used nearly every day of the campaign, which included walks across the state, to educate voters on the need for campaign finance reform and argue against a second term for President Bush.

The following is Ms. Haddock's formal announcement to run for the U.S. Senate, made in the lobby of the New Hampshire State House, Concord, Thursday, June 17, 2004; it was rated by the head of the political science department of a New Hampshire university as "the best announcement speech in American politics this year and perhaps any other."

Thank you. My name is Doris Haddock and I am a candidate for the U.S. Senate from New Hampshire. While I am happy to step forward in the absence of other Democrats, I certainly do not do so as a sacrificial lamb. I am running to win. I am a realist, of course, but I am not a defeatist.

For those who may be concerned about my age, let me say that I have outlived most of the things that can kill me, and am good for another election or two. Nevertheless, I make my pledge right now to stick to one term, and I have the biological ability to follow through with that pledge, while Mr. Gregg, who, two elections ago, made a pledge to not run for a third term, has neither the ripe age nor, it seems, the willpower to deliver on his promise.

For those who may doubt my capacity to serve, let me assure them that, while I may struggle for the right word from time to time, I can yet string my words together somewhat better than even our current president. And, while I need glasses for some reading, I can see clearly the difference between a necessary war and an unnecessary war, and the difference between a balanced budget and a deficit. Most importantly, I can read the Constitution and its Bill of Rights very easily and clearly, and, when elected, I will do what so many others in today's Washington have not had the decency to do, which is to abide by their oath to defend it.

I am running for the U.S. Senate against a good man, Judd Gregg, who has allowed himself to become an enabler of George Bush and his neocon scourge now afflicting our nation and the world. I, Doris Haddock, am running so that our voters might at the very least send Mr. Gregg a message that we expect our senators to represent common sense and the interests of our country and of our working people and children, even when to do so requires the courage to go against one's party.

And I am running to do a favor for my many Republican friends who are most uncomfortable with how far their once-venerable party has strayed—once a bastion of sensible federal spending and small business defense. I am the angry grandmother of the New Hampshire family, come off my porch to ask young Judd what in the world he is thinking when he supports Bush's military misadventures, supports the transfer of billions of our tax dollars to billionaires, and supports the shipping of our jobs overseas with tax breaks that actually encourage this tragic loss. New Hampshire has financial problems because the tax dollars we pay—and we pay plenty—are being wasted in Washington instead of returned to our people, our schools, and our real security needs. Mr. Gregg, I am not running to give you a scare; I am running to win, because I think almost anyone could do a better job representing our American values and our New Hampshire needs, and I am indeed almost anyone.

Mr. Gregg is a good and likeable fellow, rather like a charming but troubled son-in-law. We do like the fellow, but we shake our heads at what he has done to the precious treasure we have entrusted to him.

How might I, in the U.S. Senate, serve New Hampshire— my birthplace and always my home?

We the people need a peace loving government that protects us and our values by promoting peace and justice in the world. Terrorism is the twisted child of poverty and injustice, and we cannot buy our way or arm our way around that fact. We cannot support cruel dictators and expect otherwise. We must become energy independent so that we are free to pursue justice and not self-interest in the world's affairs. I will work for that. I applaud Mr. Gregg when he stands up for energy independence and for the environment, but I pledge to do more, and to move America toward responsible stewardship of our resources for our children's children, and for their children's children, which is the only true conservatism.

We the people need well-funded education for our children and the best health care for each other. School funding—a crisis not only in New Hampshire but in nearly every state—can be much relieved if we can get back more of the federal tax dollars we pay. And if Mr. Gregg would not enable the neocons to transfer so many billions to the billionaires, we could do so. If Mr. Gregg would work for more justice instead of more bombs, again we could do so, and pay for all the health care we need. I will vote to bring the resources back to the people who need them, who in fact provide them by their hard work and sufficient federal tax payments.

The largest con of the 20th and 21st Centuries is the globalization of the workforce. We need to encourage the localization, not globalization, of the economy—and thereby strengthen it and humanize it. Our political leaders have failed us monstrously in this matter, as more and more of our jobs, and more and more members our middle class, have been sold down the ocean. Mr. Gregg, though he is a fine looking man and a good New Hampshirite, should be ashamed of his role in this ongoing destruction of America's economic base—a loss to every family.

Look at our beautiful state—its waters, its air, its great forests and mountains—and, oh, its people! We do not need much to live well here. We need to be left alone in most matters. We need to join together in other matters, where joint action can create great resources for our children and each other. We of this Granite State are blessed with common sense and deep community. I should be most honored to represent these things of ours in Washington, and let them see what flint we are made of when they try to take away our peace, our justice and our common treasure.

But it is not enough to elect our representatives so that they might stop bad things from happening. They must have a vision for the future of their people. That should be what every campaign is about. It shall certainly be so with mine. Thank you.

The Five Nations

During her 2004 U.S. Senate campaign, Ms. Haddock spoke at a Fourth of July town picnic at the History Center of Portsmouth. Her remarks (after sharing a meal with a man dressed as Lincoln):

Thank you. I am honored to speak to you all today, on this special day of the American year.

We tend to think that our form of government began with Tom Jefferson and friends, but they were only extending a tradition of democracy that existed on this soil for centuries before they came.

When our founders—specifically, Constitutional Convention member John Rutledge of South Carolina and his Committee of Detail—were struggling with the form of the new U.S. Constitution, they carefully studied the constitution of the Iroquois League of Nations, taking it as their model. That great Native American constitution, which originated somewhere in the 14th to 16th Centuries, was well known to the early Anglo settlers, who wrote it down for the first time, just as the Native Americans recited it to them. In a moment, I shall read from it.

The animal symbol of the Five Nations of the Iroquois was the eagle, like ours, perched high with its eye looking out for any danger to the peace.

Another important symbol of the Five Nations was the cluster of five arrows. Look at our dollar bill and you will see our newer cluster of thirteen arrows in the iron grip of the eagle. The Iroquois Constitution says this: "As the five arrows are strongly bound, this shall symbolize the complete union of the nations. Thus are the Five Nations united completely and enfolded together, united into one head, one body and one mind. Therefore they shall labor, legislate and council together for the interest of future generations."

Well, that would be us. They, too, are our forefathers. And in times of trouble we should take their council.

They had wise laws. While the men had all the power in council, the women had the power to choose the men who would lead—a workable balance, for their day—more about the women's power in a moment.

The men and the women had their own, highly democratic council fires, where concerns could be voiced and presented for action to the nation.

They had quite an elegant disarmament policy, which went like this:

"We now uproot the tallest pine tree and into the cavity made thereby we cast all weapons of war. Into the depths of the earth, down into the deep under-earth currents of water flowing to unknown regions we cast all the weapons of strife. We bury them from sight and we plant again the tree. Thus shall the Great Peace be established."

They had two houses of legislative deliberation, plus an executive and judicial branch, more or less, and veto powers, impeachment, and a fair justice system that respected the dignity of every person. We should not admire that history as outsiders; we should embrace it proudly as a part of our own history, ever working to mend the historical divisions that might keep us from accepting its wisdom and humanity.

We would do well to install our new senators and representatives in the same way that we Americans did when we were the Five Nations. Here is a part of the ceremony, addressed to any new representative arriving at council:

"Your heart shall be filled with peace and good will and your mind filled with a yearning for the welfare of the people. With endless patience you shall carry out your duty, and your firmness shall be tempered with tenderness for your people. Neither anger nor fury shall find lodgment in your mind and all your words and actions shall be marked with calm deliberation. In all of your deliberations in Council, and in your efforts at law making, in all your official acts, self interest shall be cast into oblivion."

In all your official acts, self-interest shall be cast into oblivion.

There is the model we still hold in our hearts for our democracy, isn't it?

Here is how, in their constitution, the Iroquois instructed their leaders to begin their great meetings:

"Offer thanks to the earth where men dwell, to the streams of water, the pools, the springs and the lakes, to the corn and the fruits, to the medicinal herbs and trees, to the forest trees for their usefulness, to the animals that serve as food and give their pelts for clothing, to the great winds and the lesser winds, to the Thunderers, to the Sun, the mighty warrior, to the moon, to the messengers of the Creator who reveal His wishes, and to the Great Creator Who dwells in the heavens above, Who gives all the things useful to men, and Who is the source and the ruler of health and life."

There are many beautiful passages in this first American constitution. It lays down specific rituals to keep the peace: For example: "If any man or any nation outside the Five Nations shall obey the laws of the Great Peace and make known their disposition to the Lords of the Confederacy, they may trace the Roots to the Tree and if their minds are clean and they are obedient and promise to obey the wishes of the Confederate Council, they shall be welcomed..."

I like some of the specifics, rather reminiscent of the Old Testament. For example:

"When the Lords are assembled, the Council Fire shall be kindled, but not with chestnut wood."

We in New Hampshire might understand that, as chestnut wood sparks too much, and they wanted a peaceful meeting, without their robes catching fire.

If you want to know how the U.S. Constitution provides for a bicameral congress and the separation of powers, listen to this:

"In all cases the procedure must be as follows: when the Mohawk and Seneca Lords have unanimously agreed upon a question, they shall report their decision to the Cayuga and Oneida Lords who shall deliberate upon the question and report a unanimous decision to the Mohawk Lords. The Mohawk Lords will then report the standing of the case to the Firekeepers, who shall render a decision as they see fit in case of a disagreement by the two bodies, or confirm the decisions of the two bodies if they are identical. The Fire Keepers shall then report their decision to the Mohawk Lords who shall announce it to the open council. If through any misunderstanding or obstinacy on the part of the Fire Keepers, they render a decision at variance with that of the Two Sides, the Two Sides shall reconsider the matter and if their decisions are jointly the same as before they shall report to the Fire Keepers who are then compelled to confirm their joint decision."

So the Mohawk and Senecas were what we call the House; the Cayuga and Oneidas were what we call the Senate, and the Firekeepers were the conference committee or sometimes the Supreme Court, more or less.

As for fairness, listen to this:

"When the Council of the Five Nation Lords shall convene they shall appoint a speaker for the day. He shall be a Lord of either the Mohawk, Onondaga or Seneca Nation. The next day the Council shall appoint another speaker, but the first speaker may be reappointed if there is no objection, but a speaker's term shall not be regarded more than for the day."

They had a special take on women's rights:

"If any Confederate Lord neglects or refuses to attend the Confederate Council, the other Lords of the Nation of which he is a member shall require their War Chief to request the female sponsors of the Lord so guilty of defection to demand his attendance of the Council. If he refuses, the women holding the title shall immediately select another candidate for the title. No Lord shall be asked more than once to attend the Confederate Council. If at any time it shall be manifest that a Confederate Lord has not in mind the welfare of the people or disobeys the rules of this Great Law, the men or women of the Confederacy, or both jointly, shall come to the Council and upbraid the erring Lord through his War Chief.

"If the complaint of the people through the War Chief is not heeded the first time it shall be uttered again and then if no attention is given a third complaint and warning shall be given. When the Lord is deposed the women shall notify the Confederate Lords through their War Chief, and the Confederate Lords shall sanction the act. The women will then select another of their sons as a candidate and the Lords shall elect him. Then shall the chosen one be installed by the Installation Ceremony."

So, you see, the men were in charge only for so long as they behaved and served the people well and showed up for work. But if they are really troublesome, there is a remedy. Pay attention, Mitch McConnell:

"Should it happen that the Lords refuse to heed the third warning, then two courses are open: either the men may decide in their council to depose the Lords or to club them to death with war clubs."

Now, how did the Five Nations deal with housing, homelessness, the distribution of wealth? Quote:

"The soil of the earth from one end of the land to the other is the property of the people who inhabit it. The Great Creator has made us of the one blood and of the same soil he made us and as only different tongues constitute different nations he established different hunting grounds and territories and made boundary lines between them.

When any alien nation or individual is admitted into the Five Nations the admission shall be understood only to be a temporary one. Should the person or nation create loss, do wrong or cause suffering of any kind to endanger the peace of the Confederacy, the Confederate Lords shall order one of their war chiefs to reprimand him or them and if a similar offence is again committed the offending party or parties shall be expelled from the territory of the Five United Nations. When a member of an alien nation comes to the territory of the Five Nations and seeks refuge and permanent residence, the Lords of the Nation to which he comes shall extend hospitality and make him a member of the nation. Then shall he be accorded equal rights and privileges."

So, you see, America's first immigration policy was quite humane, as it should be.

Now, as in the Old Testament, there are some sections that are less than generous, but overall you can see that the American sprit we embrace, enjoy and celebrate is more Native American than European. Isn't that a remarkable fact, hidden so long by the shame of our genocide against them and our education system that neglects our own history?

They did go to war from time to time, but, unlike our modern arrangement, the people had a say. Listen to it:

"Whenever a specially important matter or a great emergency is presented before the Confederate Council and the nature of the matter affects the entire body of the Five Nations, threatening their utter ruin, then the Lords of the Confederacy must submit the matter to the decision of their people."

It is a long document, and I have only read a small part of it for you, so that you can get its flavor and wisdom. We are people in a land of free people—people who have served each other with dignity and sacrifice for many centuries, going back long before the European invasion. On this Fourth of July, let us thank our Native American forefathers for what they have given us. Thank You.

The Very Definition of the Mature Mind

Ms. Haddock's remarks at Alliance for Democracy Convention in Boston, Massachusetts, Simmons College, Wednesday, July 21, 2004:

Thank you. Well, Friends, here we are in a city that has known the struggle of free people against tyranny, their rise above personal self-interest, their rise during the occasions of human emergency to move forward with courage, with intelligence and a long view to the future of the people, and with great energy and a perfect concentration on victory. "We must all hang together or assuredly we shall all hang separately" is a phrase spoken in Philadelphia by a man of this city—a phrase that again has personal meaning to us.

We are not so far in time from 1776. My own life extends over 40% the way there.

There is a man working in my campaign office whose distant grandfather planned Revere's ride and roused him to it that fateful night. This descendant planned my trip here, in fact.

All of us have not so much come to this city, but come back to it, at least as the surviving spirits of our ancestors. Our forefathers and mothers, whether they were free or slave, elite or servant, newcomer or native, whether they fought for human freedom at Lexington or Omaha Beach, or at a segregated lunch counter, have given us something to defend, and we now have our moment to take our part in the continuing joyful struggle that is America in its ongoing revolution against oppression and unfairness and cruelty. We rise up as the human spirit defends itself. We rise up to defend each other. It is in our genes.

So we are in Boston again—our noble and rebellious blood mixed through the generations, but still easy to come to a boil at any danger to our independence. And we are here together as civic friends, true friends, and, as history may record, as Americans who care nothing for safety nor comfort when truth, love and the Constitution are at stake.

What sacrifices are we willing to make? This morning I will speak of several necessary sacrifices. For some of you these will be easy or no sacrifice at all. For others, they will be hard but necessary.

I come this morning to talk about John Kerry and the coming demonstrations during the two conventions.

Four years ago I looked at the poison of big business support for the major candidates and I advised my friends to vote their hearts, to let the chips fall where they might, on the theory that, even if their third party candidate lost, they would be building a constituency for such candidates in the future.

I was very wrong to suggest that party building was more important than the risks of a Bush presidency. While none of us knew how bad it would be, those of us who spoke out on the issue had an obligation to do our homework—to know more about the hidden agendas of the candidates.

I still believe we must vote our hearts, but we must inform our hearts.

I have done my homework. In fact, we have had our homework done for us, for we know who Bush is and what he represents. We know the danger of another Bush term. We know the danger of splitting our vote.

I am for Kerry. My heart is completely dedicated to this victory.

If that is hard for some people, let me ask them to think about it this way. Imagine you knew John Kerry since the Vietnam War days. Maybe you were a fellow soldier or a nurse or a friend back home. Over the years, you have stayed in touch, exchanged long phone calls and birthday cards and kidded him about marrying well. You've ridden on the back of his motorcycle and shouted for him to slow down.

We forgive all sorts of things of our friends, so, when you argued with him about his vote on a big issue close to your heart, you were angry, but you knew him well enough to be willing to stick with your friendship.

And you might defend him even in his absence, say at a dinner party. John Kerry is bad on the environment? No way, you would defend. He has one of the best environmental voting records in Congress. As president, you assure them, he would be addressing the critical issues of our day, such as global climate change and the myriad issues that connect with that crisis.

Further, you might assert that his political skills would mean that his strong position on the environment would enable him to move an agenda forward, while, in contrast, a president like Ralph Nader might rail against Congress like an Old Testament prophet, but get nothing through. Yes, you would assure any doubter, though you have problems with some of John's votes, he would be better for the environment and better in the necessary political work ahead than Nader or anyone you can think of.

And you might say the same for John Kerry regarding health care and civil liberties and justice issues, and on, and on.

Now, our problem in America today is that not enough of us have been on the back of his motorcycle and on the receiving end of his personal friendship and loyalty.

But in this American crisis, he is indeed our best friend, and we had better be his, and do everything we can for this friend. Will I be among those who put pressure on him to take bold steps after his election? Indeed, inside or outside the Senate, I will, and I will be protected in those protests and in those walks and in those utterances by the document we will have saved so that it might continue to save us: The U.S. Constitution. That will not be as true if Bush is again president.

Can we hang together long enough to protect our freedom? Some people will continue to say that, yes, four more years of Bush would be a disaster for the entire earth, its people and its environment, but they just don't have it in them to vote for John Kerry for one reason or another. I do not see Mr. Kerry as the lesser of two evils, but some people do. For them, I say that the very definition of the mature mind, the responsible mind, is not only being able to sometimes accept the less attractive choice, but to embrace it with all your energy.

The haughty progressive who is set on casting a vanity vote, a vote to validate their own wonderful perfection on the issues, a vote that may split the left, is the least progressive person you know, for they are willing to risk another Bush administration, which makes them party to the future killing of innocents abroad and the imprisonment of innocents at home.

Politics is not pure, and pretending that it can be does great harm. You must get the soil of real politics under one's manicured fingernails to practice democracy. It is about winning so that people can be protected and served. It is not a showcase for your brilliant opinions.

Such people simply need to grow up emotionally, and become real men and real women who will fight for justice and for their fellow human beings and for nature itself on the battleground at hand, not the ideal battleground of their musings. Vote-splitters get in the way, take up space, and hinder those who will make the hundred leaps of faith necessary to be engaged in the real world and do battle in the war between the forces of dark and light, between fear and love.

John Kerry has a long record of supporting women's and minority' rights, and of opposing discrimination based on sexual orientation. He has worked to boost fuel standards, worked to limit pollution, worked to boost alternative energy, worked to stop drilling in the Arctic Preserve, worked to protect public schools and the social security program, worked to oppose the flood of guns in our society, worked to oppose tax windfalls to the wealthy, worked against Star Wars funding, worked to provide resources to the poor. The list of what he has done is a long one, and the list of the things you might argue with him about is a short one. His vote on the Iraq War was terrible.

Two centuries ago, there were probably Americans who didn't quite like part of the Declaration of Independence or who did think George Washington was just the right man to lead the Continental Army, or who thought there should be a few more articles to the Bill of Rights before they would sign on. Those foot-draggers are not even footnotes now.

So, buck up. Get real. This is a time for action, and our man is John Kerry.

We ask our favorite leaders, as I will ask Dennis Kucinich, to serve with all their hearts, too, when the flags and banners of the Democratic Convention come down in this city next week.

With good men like him, I shall be voting my heart, my whole heart or damn near enough of it, when I vote for John Kerry.

I think all Democrats who can, should vote early by mailed ballots, so there will be a paper record of their votes. You may have suspicions about the voting machines, but I assure you that the Secretaries of State and the town and county clerks of this nation take their jobs very seriously and our paper ballots in their hands will be our best defense against any secretly rigged or otherwise malfunctioning or sabotaged machines——and the Bush Administration can please stop talking about putting off the election.

If we vote in advance, we will be free to volunteer on the Get Out the Vote projects in the swing areas.

Now, let me say a word about one other thing we must do, which may be a sacrifice for some people and time off for good behavior for others.

Many, many Americans will decide which side they are on as they watch the national conventions on television and as they read and hear about the events.

They will look at the pretty politicians and delegates, and they will look at the people on the street. They will identify with one group or another.

Every rowdy, rude, pushy person in a demonstration, whether in Boston or New York, creates a vote for George Bush. Every clash with the police is another swarm of votes for Bush, and therefore clashes will be provoked.

Should we demonstrate? Yes. We should demonstrate respectfully.

In New York, we should have signs that speak the truth respectfully. We should look like and sound like people someone would want to know, not people someone would want to run from.

Some people will think they have a right to express their anger and their creativity and they are right. But, is their need to express themselves a higher value to them than saving our Constitution or the environment of the earth or the lives of thousands of people?

This is a moment when people on our side are going to be fully tested for unselfishness and maturity.

If they want to move history, they have to persuade their fellow citizens. Ranting and raving will not help, and will in fact do harm. If you want to persuade your fellow citizens to follow you, you must speak and act and even dress the part of a thoughtful, respectable citizen.

You may say, "That's not who I am, Granny. I have to tell it like it is."

Yes, I hear you. It is the sound of children playing while people are dying. We are a little spoiled in this country, and we do not take seriously enough our responsible role in the world. Angry demonstrations have their place. The WTO demonstrations in Seattle, for example, got the world's attention and opened a conversation. The same demonstration outside a nominating convention would be as counterproductive as the 1968 Chicago convention demonstrations that brought us Nixon.

Our individual actions as citizens, even as non-voting age young people, have important effects in the world. People live and die, the environment thrives or dies, people are tortured or tutored, according to how we vote, and how we influence the votes of our fellow citizens. Understanding that, we also understand that demonstrations at election time must be more Gandhi and less tantrum.

In this moment, we must shed our policy differences and personal or group feelings of injustice or victimization or disrespected identities and act as one people, one voice, one voting block. After the election we can resume the hard work of fighting out our differences and moving our own issues forward. But for now, we stand as one for democracy, one for justice, one for liberty, one for a peaceful and sustainable future, one for the Constitution, and one for John Kerry.

In Faneuil Hall

Though Ms. Haddock was the New Hampshire Democratic Party's U.S. Senate candidate, the party failed to invite her to the Democratic National Convention in Boston. Her candidacy was never mentioned from the podium, nor was she—one of the finest orators of the new century—invited to speak. She therefore crashed the sessions and the parties, obtaining credentials from friends, speaking at side events, and gaining press that was well received at home. She also met political consultant Joe Trippi, the former campaign chairman of the Howard Dean campaign, at a bar near the convention hall. They hit it off, and Mr. Trippi made himself available on the phone and occasionally in person during her campaign.

Ms. Haddock speaking in Faneuil Hall, Boston, Tuesday, July 27, 2004 during the Democratic National Convention:

Thank you. Feel this place under you and around you. Know where you are. All the world knows the story of how the Americans became a free people, how they declared their independence, how they devised a constitution that is still an engine of fairness, of improvement, of justice and freedom. But the story seems remote sometimes. So feel this place under you. Know where you are. Remember who we are.

This room, these walls, echoed the words of Sam Adams as he stood in this place and reminded Americans who they were and what they must do. In this very room we Americans heard George Washington and Daniel Webster shape the new Republic.

In this room William Lloyd Garrison helped define an American value system that could no longer admit of human slavery, and he defined nonviolent resistance in a way that was persuasive with Ruskin in England and Tolstoy in Russia and Gandhi in South Africa and India, and from Gandhi back to Martin Luther King in America—from this room.

And here spoke Susan B. Anthony to move our engine of equality forward again.

And here spoke John Kennedy and so many other

Americans who loved freedom and justice and who pushed us to be a better people, moving ever along and up the Freedom Trail.

Feel this place. Remember who you are and why you are here, and understand that all of them and all of us are of one mind and sometimes are of one place. We are in this room. And perhaps those who have come before us are in this room yet, to see their work continue and be the real spirits of our inspiration.

Feel this neighborhood around you: The street corner of the Boston Massacre is but a few steps behind me; The Tea Party was but a few steps behind you. Revere's house, the Old North Church, are but across the way, still there, still living containers for our aspirations and our shared courage. Remember who we are and how we rise up when our liberty is threatened!

We are not a people to be trifled with, Mr. President. We are not to be trifled with, ye corporations who press down upon us like a plague of King Georges, turning our middle class into greeters and our lives into credit card indentures!

We shall have our lives in freedom and we shall have our democracy as it was given us, made better by our own sacrifices.

We are here. Our revolution needs defending in this moment. We are come back to our room where we devise strategies and double our courage. We are in this room. We breathe its air. We hear its soft assent.

So. What is our plan? What shall we do?

We are having an election. As some will distrust the machinery of our voting, let us use mailed ballots—all of us who can.

Let us do nothing until the election except work on our campaigns and prepare people to vote.

After the election, let us repair our old ship of democracy with some new sails and masts, starting with the public funding of our elections and thereby the removal of special interest campaign donations. Maine and Arizona already have good programs, as you may know. Arizona's is under attack by a repeal put on the ballot by right wing interests. We must help Arizona keep its clean elections system. I will certainly go there.

In this state, Speaker Finneran cannot stand forever in the way of an improved democracy. Get him unelected, and revive clean elections here. I know this is in the works.

And it is in the works in Iowa, and in West Virginia, and in Kentucky, North Carolina, Florida, Oregon and many other states. I have been there and seen the work, and these efforts merit your support.

And with or without the clean elections reform, we must

end the double-dip pillage of public resources by broadcasters and cable systems, that get their airwaves and franchises from the public for a song, then charge their highest rates for election commercials. We need to require broadcasters to apply their lowest contract rates to election commercials, less fifty percent. This will reduce the leverage of fat cat donors.

Doing democracy ourselves is what it is all about. The Bill of Rights Defense Committees, now successful in over 300 towns and cities, are a model for us in moving many reforms that, in combination, will renew our revolution and return our politics to the human scale, where our freedoms and our futures can be protected.

We must work for other improvements, too, such as ranked-choice voting, where you can rank your favorite candidates and not risk splitting the vote.

And beyond the mechanics of campaigns and voting, we must understand that a nation can be free only so far as it is educated. Failing schools go hand in hand with the rise of oligarchy and worse. Underfunding of education is a conscious suppression of the citizens, and we must stop it and replace it with K-through-university funding for all who will choose it.

There are many things we can and must do.

If the president is defeated in November, this work will be easier. And the defense of our tax wealth and our environment and our Bill of Rights will be easier. If he is not defeated, our work will be harder, but we will do it anyway.

For, in this place, we remember who we are. We are the people of an imperfect union, the ordinary people of a great Republic still in the making, and, in that, we are no ordinary people at all. And it matters not if we arrived in the Ice Age or yesterday.

Indeed, if you are new to America, know that three-quarters of the freedom fighters of 1776 were born across the sea. Remember what America is: it is you the newcomer, as this is your place now. You have a voice here among equals. Know that you have a new duty to participate. The great word, by which we live and survive, is participation, because, as is said, democracy is not something we have, but something we do.

This is our place. This is our time to be in this room. And when we are gone, when we have all passed through this life, others will come to this room after us and remember what we did in our time for the American Republic. Thank you.

Reorganize the Democratic Party

Very early in the 2004 campaign, Ms. Haddock worried that the followers of Dennis Kucinich and the followers of Governor Howard Dean might not come together to work for the eventual nominee. She urged both men to begin planning for a merger of their supporters. She, in fact, hitchhiked in Florida to meet up with Mayor Kucinich at one point, urging him on the matter. He agreed to try (as did Mr. Trippi). When the Boston Democratic Convention was finally underway, Ms. Haddock spoke at a large meeting of the resulting Progressive Alliance; Thursday, July 29, 2004:

Thank you. There are so many things that I do not have to say to the people in this room. I do not have to go on and on about the danger our democracy faces right now. I do not have to lay out the case for the Bill of Rights or the environment or fair trade or world peace. I do not have to reason with you as to the case against torture or dictatorship. I do not have to speak to you about how we must not split our vote this year. I don't like preaching to the faithful, so let me tell you something you may not have thought about.

Our present emergency is upon us because our civic society has been dumbed-down by pared-down newsrooms, pared-down radio and television news, by dumbed-down schools, and by a corporate-run economic rat race that keeps people so busy trying to make ends meet that they have neither time nor energy left for the civic affairs of their town or nation.

You certainly know all this, and we celebrate the rise of independent media and the use of books and films to fill-in some of the gaps. But the gaps are awesome, and democracy cannot long survive when the people are not well informed with the truth, well interested, and well supplied with time and resources enough to participate.

But there is another thing that has been pared and

dumbed-down over the past two or three generations, and that is the art of politics itself.

If the politics of a century ago can be likened to a banquet, the politics of today is like a fast food burger.

I am going to try to sell you on the idea of a richer politics, so let me tell you what it used to be like. Everybody used to be involved. You went to your Elks Club or your Women's Club, but you went to your party meetings, too. You worked your neighborhoods. You talked up your issues and candidates. It was a fairly constant thing, not just during the election season. Why? Because democracy is a lifestyle, not a fringe benefit of paying your taxes. Self-governance is a lot of work, but it's where you make your best friends and have your deepest satisfactions, after your family.

Just before I declared for the U.S. Senate last month, I was on a 23,000-mile road trip to register voters. There were many housing projects and low-income neighborhoods where the people had seen nobody dropping by to talk politics since the last election—or ever. The Democrats may come around, we were told, every few years to ask for their votes, but they weren't there to listen to their problems or to help them craft political solutions. These people were of the opinion that, if the Democrats won or lost, their own lives wouldn't change much.

That is stripped-down politics. That is downright exploitive politics, when you come around begging for votes for your concerns, but you don't give a crouton in return. Oh yes, if your man or woman is elected, things will be better for everybody. But that is the top layer of the cake, but it does not trickle down, and in fact there is hardly any cake for the poor to eat. We have to put things right by being involved all year long, every year, and in every neighborhood that needs political help. That is movement building—not just stumping for candidates.

You will go to your home tonight, or to your hotel room, and you will turn on all the lights and have a nice hot shower, and watch television and not even think about the electrical power that makes it all happen. If you follow the electrical wires far enough away you will find West Virginia and Kentucky communities that are being ravaged without mercy by big coal companies, protected by corrupt politicians. The coal companies cut off the tops off whole mountain ranges, dump the rubble in their once-Eden-like valleys, and leave the mess to the people there. Every time it rains now, their homes flood. Giant pools of toxic sludge are everywhere, and when their dams break, toxins spill for miles. One recent spill in Inez, Kentucky, released more goo than the Exxon-Valdez, but this is probably the first you've ever heard of it.

Now, if you are worried if West Virginia and Kentucky go to the Republicans, you might first ask yourself this: Where the hell were you when they so needed your help? Where were you when residents of Cabrini Green in Chicago, or the slums of Ft. Myers or Miami or New Orleans or Los Angeles needed your organizing help and your voice added to theirs? They love their children as you love yours, and they only want decent lives. Do you think politics is just about raising money for candidates? Politics is about creatively serving the needs of your people, and the election is just the report card for how you are doing and how many people you have helped and how many people are following your leadership because you are always there for them.

So don't let this new progressive alliance be another can of Betty Crocker icing for a cake that isn't there. Organize not just to win elections but to deserve to win elections.

If we can help people in distressed situations solve their problems, they will be there to speak out on the larger issues that concern many of the people in this room. But few people will speak up about global warming until they have a warm house for their own children. Building a national constituency for change requires that we first work together to solve a wide range of personal issues for people.

The new meet-ups that have become possible and popular this year are a powerful force for change, but only when they go further than being just a gathering of like-minded citizens; They must become organizing units for bringing in people who are not yet like-minded. They must become organizing units for people who will do more than sit around and share their feelings about politics; they must be platoons that go out and get real politics done, and that means helping people.

This is an amazing moment in all of our lives, and in the life of our great nation. Never has our democracy been so challenged, and never have so many patriots of every age risen up to take their part in its defense. In the last two years, never have I been less proud of my government or more proud of its people, including the whole lot of you in this room. Thank you.

America's Road Less Traveled

Ms. Haddock speaking on Robert Frost's Farm in Derry, New Hampshire, Friday, August 20, 2004. It was a stop in her walking tour of New Hampshire during her U.S. Senate run. Robert Frost had been one of her husband's teachers.

Thank you. Robert Frost is connected to that strong spiritual and ethical river that flows through Whitman and Hawthorne, Melville, Cather, Dickinson, Clemens, Wilder, Muir, Douglas, Foster, Gershwin, Joplin, Sousa, and the almost countless others who were charmed and inspired by the musical words of our Founding Fathers and of our great and eloquent Native American leaders.

And from these voices onward, up to our own time and through the eloquence of Bernstein, Cohen, Copland, Ellington, Martin Luther King, Jr., Capra, Ginsburg, Pete Seeger, Ansel Adams and so many others of the modern era's great minds and writers, an idea for who we are and who we want to be as Americans has been shaped in our hearts.

We want to be a just and honorable people, trustees of a beautiful land and gardeners of a great democracy. We want to be a fiercely free people—good providers to each other and good neighbors to our townsmen and to the other people of the world.

This American spirit is an aspiration that defines not only who we are to ourselves, but to the rest of the world in how they want to think of us. It is what they love about us, and they do.

And despite all our hard times, our wars, our depressions, our genocides, our suppressions and oppressions, our experience with slavery itself, we still stand at the edge of woods dark and deep with our future ahead of us and this dream still in our hearts. We still are perched at Half Dome Rock and along the grasses of the Hudson and the forests of the misty Olympic Peninsula and in the mud of the Mississippi at Hannibal. It is still a most beautiful country filled with most wonderful people. And we are still young.

Yet we have come to a new time. We and our natural world are poised now at a parting of the road. One path leads where powerful nations have gone before. It is the road of silver and blood—the short, noisy road of empire. The other is a path no great nation has taken before. The only way we can take this less traveled road is to blow off the ashes from the still living fire of our American Revolution—where the people naturally rise against great and oppressive forces, and reassert the human heart, human freedom and our highest values as a people. Am I romanticizing the American Revolution? Well, I like to do that sometimes.

The only way we can steer our ship of state along this new and unmarked path is if we have the wheel in our own hands, and that is what we are doing here today and in ten-thousand ways across our country, where patriots meet and plan against the new King George of a runaway government, hijacked by powerful economic interests who care nothing for all the things we care for.

It is a revolution, though we look always for the peaceful way, as peace has more power by far when used rightly.

So, Mr. Frost, here we are, your countrymen come to your porch. You would not believe, Sir, what the powerful interests of this nation have done to your woods, your streams, your mountains, your people and their sons and daughters.

Would you walk with me, Mr. Frost? For we are walking toward the democracy you helped dream for us. We are looking to pick it up, wherever it was laid down.

By the end of this new century, America will be a different place, depending on which road we take in this moment, in this coming election.

I could conjure up a fearful world for your imagining, where any who wish to speak out must do so in a barbed wire enclosure, and where the police organize to beat up any of our children who stand up for justice and peace in the world—but that is already here, of course, as we saw in Boston and Miami and shall see in New York.

In Miami, fine children came to stand peaceably for justice in the world—to argue for fair trade for the people of the world instead of exploitive trade. These young men and women—and I know some of them and how fine they are—were obeying the police. They tried to leave the area but were cut off and gassed and shot with wooden bullets that blinded and scarred some of them. They were rounded up into trucks, their belongings and identification were taken from them and left fluttering in the street so that they could not get out of jail or get home. This shame is upon the City of Miami, but it is on our society, too, as it moves toward a police state of repression of our civil liberties.

That is the way it is now. And people, because they speak out peacefully, are visited by the federal police and told to watch what they say. This is what America has come to and is coming to in the shadow of dark leadership that cares nothing for the rights and values that so many Americans died for.

I could conjure up an old grandmother who goes into the

U.S. Capitol rotunda and recites from the Declaration of Independence, to urge the senators to free themselves from the special interests that bind them. I can imagine this old woman being handcuffed and arrested and jailed. I can imagine her coming back another time to read from the Bill of Rights itself, and again being shackled and jailed. But this time is already here, and this happened to me.

I can imagine people being held without recourse to lawyers or courts, endlessly in solitary confinement. This is here. I can imagine our country attacking a poor nation that never threatened us but had the bad luck to have one of the world's great oil reserves under its sands. This is real.

And so what is left to imagine down a dozen years or a half-century down this road? A ruined landscape? A broken spirit among the people? A fearful compliance in the machinery of death and not life? Other nations have gone that way. They ended poorly. Their people suffered.

Our safety as a nation is not something the current leaders of the American government seem to care anything about, or they would not be swatting hornets' nests in every corner of the violent world. They would bring calm and justice and prosperity to the world, for those are our only guarantees of security, and we have the power to bring those things to the world. These leaders care only to sell the guns and the Hum-Vees and the oil and the jet fighters and the airport bomb detectors and the insurance policies and the million products and services of a fear-based, waste-based, destruction-based, death-based economy.

If we want peace, we are not going to get it from this president or the Yes Men in Congress who vote with him at every turn. If we want our pursuit of happiness back, we will have to say enough to these career politicians who have sold us down the river and we must take on these offices ourselves, sending the lobbyists and their money away for a long time. There is, you know, a bribery bill that would put most of them in jail if it were enforced, and I shall look into that as a Senator, if a miracle happens.

You see what harsh news we bring to your porch, Mr. Frost.

But we see the path you told us about, too.

We see the one less traveled by great nations. I can imagine the end of this century quite differently. I imagine the great Appalachian Mountains in all their beauty, the coal operators long gone and the people again making a thousand good uses of the bounty of nature. I can imagine great arrays of solar cells and all the newer energy technology, harvesting the energy we need here at home from the natural processes of nature. I can imagine a people who look to their children as the nation's greatest resource, and they nurture them with an imaginative and engaging education and a perfection of health care.

I can imagine a nation where the freedom and creativity of the people bloom in a daily display of great joy and abundance. I can imagine a political environment where there is still the great moving balancing act between the rights of the individual and the rights of the group. I can see the day when government has become much smaller, more the town hall, because great scale is no longer needed to keep check on monstrously over-scaled corporations that once terrorized the people, and no giant machinery is needed to protect us from the mayhem we incite in the world. In this vision of the future, it is the small business, the creative enterprise, the family-sized group that drives the economy so efficiently and profitably, and in balance with the natural surroundings. We will learn to do all that in this century, at least to some serious extent, or we will die.

We must choose life, choose leaders who will begin us up that path, and who will reject any allegiance to the economic special interests that now drive politics.

The people are so tired of this corrupt and dying system. But we are a special people in the world, and the world knows it very well. They look to us now to shake off this misdirection, this mis-leadership, this long nightmare. So, let us do the thing that no great and powerful nation has done before: Let us take that less traveled path where might can be used as a force for justice and good in the world. Let us understand that the course of history is in our hands.

And let us breathe this air of Mr. Frost's great America— our America. This is our life. Let no one take our America or our joy from us. Let us be neither its wage slaves nor its credit indentures. With our own small but many hands upon the great wheel, we will better steer with love this great ship of ours. Thank you.

U.S. Senate Campaign Speeches

Senate Campaign Stump Speech No. 1:

In several locations around New Hampshire during her walking 2004 U.S. Senate campaign, Ms. Haddock made these and similar remarks to civic groups and other gatherings:

Thank you. When someone runs for high elective office, that person owes the voters an explanation of how he or she will make decisions—not simply that this issue or that position is favored, but a deeper explanation of political and personal philosophy behind those decisions and positions, so that the voter will be able to choose not simply among advertised gift baskets of positions and slogans, but among leaders.

I would like to describe, as briefly as possible, the four corner posts of my political philosophy that would, if miraculously I am elected, guide my decisions and my service to New Hampshire in the U.S. Senate.

The first is my strong belief in the necessary human scale of democracy. I believe that anyone who has served his or her community and who enjoys the respect of that community ought to be able to run for office without having to raise obscene amounts of money from people and organizations who will expect much in return, and who do not even reside in the candidate's state or district.

If such transactions are not exactly the selling of a politician, they are certainly the selling of access, and that is the sale of stolen goods—the access belongs to the proper constituents. If an official is constantly running to fundraisers and constantly meeting with major donors and their lobbyists, then that access time is not being spent with the constituents who are thereby unrepresented. Taxation without representation is as bad today as it was in the months and years before the American Revolution.

Therefore, you will see me take no PAC money or other special interest money, left, right or middle, as it interferes between elected official and citizen. It gets in the way of impartial decision making, and it physically gets in the way, by taking up a senator's calendar, while the needs of New Hampshire citizens wait and wait.

My belief in the human scale of democracy also makes me a great believer in civic education in our schools, local decision making wherever it is possible, and a high vigilance in the defense of our individual liberty and free speech. The attacks made in the last few years against our Bill of Rights are more frightening to me than any threat from outside our country. Our Constitution and its Bill of Rights define who we are. On the other side of the coin, I have never been more proud of my fellow Americans than when they have stood up, passing hundreds of town, city, county and even state resolutions to stand by the Bill of Rights and call the Patriot Act for what it is: a misnamed treachery against all that our soldiers have died over two centuries and all that our citizens have worked for and suffered for.

In my long walk across America to do my part in promoting the passage of the McCain-Feingold Bipartisan Campaign Finance Reform Act, I met thousands of people all along my way who felt they were no longer represented. They felt alienated from their own democracy. Returning the human scale of democracy must be something all of us work for and, when necessary, suffer for and even go to jail for. The American Revolution was about the refusal of ordinary people to be oppressed by powerful forces. It is a revolution that never ends and it goes on in this year, this month, today. The cold winds of oppression never stop blowing, and it is our struggle to always stand against them as fellow patriots, armed with our Constitution and our intention to be free people who have control over our own lives and our own pursuits of happiness.

Now, all that will tell you how I will vote on bills about special interests and campaign laws and the proper enforcement of bribery laws. But it will not tell you much else. So let me say that I am a believer in the politics of "what works."

By that I mean that I am a practical person from practical New England. If you tell me that you are pro-life, I will say that you will want to help put programs in place that advance your goal. You will be interested to know that the teen abortion rate in most European countries is about one-eighth of ours. You will join me in asking, "what are they doing that we should be doing?" What they are doing, in fact, is worlds apart from what we are doing. I am for life, and I therefore am willing to learn from those who are successful.

Success, as you will learn in this instance, has nothing to do with restricting a woman's reproductive rights. It has to do with public health education, public health services, and a more humane and appreciative attitude toward our young people and their lives. If someone is truly pro-life, they will want to join me in looking at what works. If, on the other hand, a pro-life attitude is actually a cover for something else, perhaps for a philosophy that believes all proper authority flows from God to the president to the nearest male, then you are not really pro-life at all, but a simple authority addict, and you should get a therapist.

So I can get into arguments when people say that they are for something, but will not use the practical arena of politics to do something effective about the problem. They sometimes are happy to make it worse and let people suffer, so that their invisible lines of authority are not given interference.

The fact is, many people who have allowed themselves to become voices for great restrictions of freedom and great defeats of public policies that help people and promote life and decent living are victims themselves of a great loss of personal power that has happened to them because powerful economic forces have unraveled our middle class, our Main Street family businesses and our sense of control over our own lives and the fortunes of our families. The people who have been caught up in the angry victimhood sold by the billionaires who finance the far right have in fact been robbed of their love of country.

The power that people lost with the loss of the middle class was masterfully misdirected against government, rather than against the perpetrators of that theft. And by demonizing our own self-government, the robber barons are able to steal even more, because the government's ability to regulate them is neutered.

The anger from that loss of power has not only been misdirected, it has been brilliantly manipulated to set us against each other—people of other races, other income groups, other genders. Divide and conquer. We have been turned against ourselves to prevent us from taking the power back from those who really made off with it. And so, even the former hardware store owner now working at Walmart thinks his enemy is the man of another race, or the environmentalist, or the woman who speaks up for her rights, when his real enemy is signing his paycheck and shipping any remaining middle class jobs overseas.

I am a practical person. I want to see what works and use it. I will not use my religion or my fears or my old grudges as my marching orders in the political arena of problem solving. We are, of course, personally guided by our own religions, but in politics we must also to be guided by the simple ethics of the Golden Rule and a pragmatic intention to serve each other, making accommodations as necessary so that things might work well for as many people as possible. Ideologies can get in the way of Golden Rule; indeed, we should not regulate other people and their families in ways we would not want for ourselves—for our sons and our daughters.

In matters of national security and terrorism, I will of course support those who work tirelessly to avert violence here and abroad. But I will also want to know what will work to end this conflict. What are the conditions behind this conflict that need to be resolved? That is the question that can lead to real security. Certainly a foreign policy less aimed at securing oil and less intent on propping up dictators, and a foreign policy more dedicated to alleviate injustice and poverty can be among the policies that work better to secure our safety. If it works toward the solution of a critical problem and if we can afford it, I am for it, and don't cloud the issue with Biblical prophecies and the angers and horrors generated by the problem itself.

What works best when it comes to health care for our people? Clearly, everyone in a civilized society needs access to health care. Finding the right program will be easier for senators and representatives who do not take money from the pharmaceutical and health insurance companies involved. Finding "what works" is easier when you are not on the dole from half the players.

I have talked about some of my guiding beliefs: that democracy needs to work at the human scale, so we all have access and representation; I have talked about the politics of "what works," meaning that I will look to real solutions that are working elsewhere, not to political ideologies.

Finally, let me talk about the role of government itself.

Americans tend to dislike overlarge and over-powerful government, but we don't much like overlarge and over-powerful corporations, either. I think it may be wise to bring them both down in scale, like a kind of disarmament program. I think government should be "us," not "them." I think it is the New England Town Hall, the New Hampshire House, the school board. When it becomes something other than us it gives the sociopaths in our midst a good opening to want to tear down and underfund and privatize all government programs, no matter how important and worthwhile. In many respects, a big nation needs a big government.

But any messiness of government at the federal level works to the advantage of politicians. A very large part of their daily work involves untangling red tape for their constituents. The more difficult the red tape, the more worthy a politicians looks for reelection I would rather make government work better for its citizens than let it be a big tangle for politicians to deal with, one constituent at a time.

If I don't help achieve that as a senator, then I won't have done much to change Washington. I think we send our elected representatives there to make a difference. They shouldn't be just untangling red tape; they should bee spending their time on the larger issues of our future, and this includes making college as free as high school, because today's college is the economic equivalent of yesterday's high school.

Who among our representatives now has the time and energy and vision to look at the credit disaster now threatening our middle class? Isn't our middle class worth saving? What can we do to get people out from under this problem? Is that not a useful purpose for our treasury? Do we only use it for bombs, when real homeland security involved the economic health and stability of our people? Believe me, as a senator from New Hampshire, I shall certainly do what I can about this disaster, and I won't have to look over my shoulder at any donors from the banks or credit card or mortgage companies, because I won't have them as my donors. My only donors are the real people, and that will be enough.

So now you have an idea of how I would come to make decisions on your behalf, and not on behalf of the special interests. I hope my thinking is close enough to your own that you will consider voting for me. In any case, I thank you for your time this afternoon. The fact that you are curious and giving your time is the best argument I can think of to make the case that democracy is strong in America and we will get though any troubles that come our way. Thank you.

Senate Campaign Stump Speech No. 2:

Thank you. So many of you have been encouraging me in my new project, and I thank you for your volunteer help and your connections and, yes, your donations—which are coming in much faster than I expected.

There are many people who are doubtful that a 94 year-old woman can get from here to the U.S. Senate, and they are right. But there are reasons for my run.

We live in amazing times—times that history will record as a great moment of peril for our democracy. One of the more amazing facts of this moment is that we are, all of us, stepping up to do what we can, even those of us who might rather be enjoying some time off.

I am now running for the things I have walked miles for: a

decent government that represents the values, the needs, and the highest aspirations of our people—a government where the people do participate, and, through their cooperative action as a local, state and national community, become that government. In this, we send our neighbors and, yes, our grandmothers to Congress, because the professional politicians have just not worked out. Democracy cannot be hired out. There is too much power involved, and it corrupts absolutely if we, the common people, do not manage it ourselves with a humble spirit and a willingness to cast our own self-interest into oblivion.

That phrase comes from the constitution of the Five Nations of the Iroquois, which was used as a model for our present Constitution. In swearing in leaders to the great democratic council, they were sworn-in as follows:

"Your heart shall be filled with peace and good will and your mind filled with a yearning for the welfare of the people. With endless patience you shall carry out your duty and your firmness shall be tempered with tenderness for your people. Neither anger nor fury shall find lodgment in your mind, and all your words and actions shall be marked with calm deliberation. In all of your deliberations, in your efforts at law making, in all your official acts, self interest shall be cast into oblivion."

Friends, we cannot afford a "we the people" and a "them the government." We must do this democracy ourselves.

So, a vote for me is a vote against special interests, but let me talk about just one of those things I am for: I am for real security for our nation and its people.

Some politicians of our acquaintance seem to think the question is, "How can we defend ourselves in an increasingly hostile world?" But the better question is, "Why is the world becoming a more dangerous place for us?" That is the question that can lead us toward real security. Though it is a long road, the very act of beginning brings great rewards. Beginning such a journey is what authentic political leadership is about, and I am not afraid of long journeys.

The world is now too small, too full of people, too full of powerful, pocket-size weapons for us to think we can have a safe world if it is not characterized, in every far corner, by justice, productivity, the nurturing of every person's potential, and a responsible balance between personal freedom and personal responsibility.

What does that mean in terms of how and where we, as a nation and as families, get our energy and our food? What does it require of us in adapting our urban forms, our lifestyles and our commercial systems?

If our choice is between a strip-searched, fortress America and, on the other hand, the beautiful world we long for, what is keeping us from making the beautiful choice? Is it the distortions of the political system? The special interests? The selfish posturing of people who call themselves leaders, but who, in fact, only take up valuable space at a critical time for us?

Well, we thank them for trying their best under the constraints of a corrupt system, but we the people are going to have to do this ourselves, because our children, our schools, our health care, our position in the world and our hearts need better representation.

It comes down to this: if you want something done right today, you have to run for Congress yourself, or at least send your grandmother or a good neighbor. That's is what we have come to.

As for my opponent, I think he is a fine man and he votes the right way as often as his big donors will allow him to do so.

He is a good friend—schoolmate, actually—of the President, and is an effective surrogate for the President on the campaign trail. I am therefore hoping to keep him pinned down in New Hampshire—he would otherwise be running unopposed, you know. That, alone, is worth this trouble. And of even greater importance, we are using my campaign to register new voters, young and old, throughout New Hampshire. We can help tip the balance in New Hampshire for Mr. Kerry.

So, there are good reasons to run, and we know what we are doing.

Thank you for listening and please vote, however you feel about these things.

Senate Campaign Stump Speech No. 3

My candidacy for the U.S. Senate is curious to some, as I am 94 and am a newcomer to campaigning for office. It is a curious thing, but these are curious times and my age is the least of it.

When our country was founded at a time of great challenge and courage, young people and old stepped up to take action, and there age accounted for nothing. My age accounts for nothing, for this is not about me. Millions of Americans are waking up to a crisis in our land. They struggle together to save their towns, their jobs, their freedoms, and to save the America that we hold as our aspirational goal.

I have met many people who are well informed about the issues of the day. They listen to Public Radio and in-depth news shows; they read newspapers and websites on the issues. That is all good and necessary, but information is wasted if it does not inform action. We don't need the world's best-informed reclining nudes and couch potatoes. We need people who get up, get dressed, and get in the ring as candidates and volunteers, letter writers, meeting attendees, phone callers, door knockers, and who are not shy about speaking the truth as they understand it. I am seeing more and more people who are doing exactly that, and I hope you are one of them, or will now join them. It is joyful work, despite the dark issues that motivate us to take action.

My candidacy is but one small wave in this rising sea of action. So look not at me with any more curiosity than you might look at an old man struggling off to war in an ancient time, or a young man or woman with no choice but to make the defense. It is an old story on our planet, and it is never about this person or that, but about the long struggle of people to preserve their dreams and their freedoms together.

So if I awaken your curiosity, turn your curious mind next to the great changes that swirl me, and so many others, into action. That is the story; it is not about me; it is more about you than me; it is about the people who will live in this nation for many years; who expect to move freely in this land; who will raise children here; who will drink from its streams and breathe its air; who will speak their minds as free men and women. Or not—or not, because they lost their freedom.

Our situation is this: Large economic interests have combined against the interests of ordinary people, and have used their almost unlimited supplies of money to distort and take over the political system. Our continuing American Revolution, which is the rise of individuals against oppressive forces, is in danger as never before.

As they often do, these powerful economic forces, corporate forces, have operated like puppet masters through the cultural extremists of the far right.

Our political life is our civic life, not our religious life. Politics is supposed to be about finding practical solutions that work for the good of the people.

Some of our neighbors profess a belief in the sanctity of life, but they are in danger of seeming insincere, because the sanctity of life, if honestly considered, has to be about more than being against abortion. It must include being for the feeding and educating of children and assuring that they have proper homes supported by well-paid jobs. It must include strong support for helping immigrants escape conditions elsewhere that endanger the lives of their innocent children. But I am probably not describing the preferred policies of these neighbors. So what is wrong with the picture? The puzzle pieces only fit if you will assume that their stance against abortion has nothing to do with the sanctity of life, but instead is a cover for the idolatry of male power, which is what it is. For in their embrace of war and their resistance to saving the very earth, they show themselves: they are only about and all about authoritarian power and its hallmarks: cruelty, force, division and death.

They are against the things that would actually reduce unwanted pregnancies and the need for abortions; they are against the things that would help young urban men and women find their ways to colleges instead of prisons; they are against the medical research that would cure a hundred diseases and save millions of lives; they are against the personal freedoms that define life itself. They are supported in their campaign against life, against things that work, against human values, by the corporations that prosper by selling hospital beds, medicines, graves, artificial limbs, new prisons, police equipment and bombs.

Those on the far right who say they are for life are pawns in a monstrous game of manipulation that redirects all their personal anxieties about their own lives and their own powerlessness toward a sociopathy that hurts us all, and hurts and kills people around the world for the benefit of a few billionaires who evidently do not give a hoot about the lives of their own grandchildren on this planet.

But who are we—we the rising sea of discontent—and what power do we have?

We have the great majority of consumer dollars to spend this way and not that way. We have the great majority of votes to elect this candidate and not that. We have the ability, with millions of small contributions, to fund the candidates who will represent reason and human values. In short, we have all the power and we must use it.

My campaign is nothing special in this coming reversal of political power. It is just that I am an early riser about not taking PAC money and relying on small donations, and you see me a little sooner than the rest. But, as someone with a chronic bad back who has enjoyed acupuncture, I am prepared for arrows in my back that come to pioneers, because I know that other—and far better—candidates will soon be out there and coming your way, and nothing will stop this movement toward real representation of our needs and values.

It is the continuation of the American Revolution, which is

our everlasting energy and courage to put the needs and freedom of individuals over the oppressive powers of a powerful elite who would take our wealth and our power and our freedom if we sleep late and let them. Well, we will not, will we? Thank you.

Senate Campaign Stump Speech No. 4 (fragment):

I am an old conservative from the Granite State, the Live Free or Die state of our New Hampshire. By conservative I of course mean that we value self-reliant lives in caring communities, and that we are thoughtful and responsible in providing for our future—and for the futures of our grandchildren and their children. We see a future where our families live in balance with the natural beauty of our land, and in responsible accord with the world. We see our families supported by their own businesses and by responsible, local businesses; we see our children well-educated; we see them enjoying long, healthy lives—a return on the investment we have all made as taxpayers in the development of medical miracles.

This is not a liberal vision of the future: nothing is for free and we pay for it all with taxes not wasted on wars and subsidies to oil companies and the like. It is not a big-government vision of the future, as much of the existing bigness is a response to corporate power that is overlarge and should be cut into pieces. When that happens, we can afford to cut the size of our government, too.

Those who waste our public resources are not representing our traditional and conservative values. Those who rush to war, wasting the lives of our youth and our reputation in the world—and damaging our real security—are not from the granite cliffs and hardwood forests of any America we know. Those who divert our common treasure in order to provide tax windfalls to billionaires and who encourage and reward companies who escape their fair share of taxes by moving their front offices overseas or, indeed, who move their jobs—our jobs—to faraway lands, are not representing us in any way.

The American values that compelled me to step forward when I walked across the U.S. for campaign reform now compel me to step forward to fight an incumbent who no longer represents the woods and the granite and the people of his birth. I remember those values, and most Americans remember and feel those values. How could I stay at home and watch it happen when no one else would run against him to represent the people?

Senate Campaign Stump Speech No. 5

Made in several retirement communities during her on-site voter registration effort:

Thank you very much. Candidates come and go, and all of them have their issues and their strongly-held this and that. You have heard them. Well, I am not the usual candidate, in that I am coming at this project very late in life; I am not building a career but ending a long, productive life. But, indeed, I am not through with my life, any more than you should be through with yours. I think we can all say this: What an honor and privilege it has been to have lived in America as an American. What grace is ours, thanks to the work and courage of so many. We have lived charmed lives, compared to the lives of the people of many other lands and times.

Though our great experiment of a nation has never been even close to perfect in its application of justice and equality, we are driven by an aspirational dream, and that dream has always, in the end, moved us forward to more justice and more equality.

The rising arc of our story, however, requires that we be a free and self-governing people, so that the innate good in the human heart, which I surely believe in, drives our historical progress.

We are experiencing what may be a little downturn in the chart of our story, or what may be more than that: the beginning of a descending arc, if we let it.

From time to time I have been informed that I may not live forever. But, I do not want to contribute myself to the thin topsoil of New Hampshire until I have done what I can do, as one person might, to push things forward and upward. You may feel the same, and you can do the same, if you will register or reregister to vote.

It is a question of whether this is still our country, our government, our democracy, or whether, as our founding fathers warned us, we have come to a time when economic forces have combined against the interests of the people to such an extent that they have taken over the institutions of government and set a course for their own enrichment at the expense of democracy and justice.

I think we have come to that crisis, and in times of crisis you may see young people and old on the battle lines because everyone must do what they can. Well, I have seen the Americans we are in the peace marches. I have seen the strollers and walkers and canes, as young parents and teens and students and workers and elders take their stand for their country's highest values and their dreams for their people.

I am here because the people we thought we sent to Washington to represent us are in fact representing the forces that oppose our interests and our values. These representatives send a bit of bread and a few circuses our way so we might think they are representing us, but in fact they are spinning us in manufactured fear so that they might have more power over us, and they are selling off our good jobs and our global environment and—and this is the part I most cannot bear—trashing our Bill of Rights that represents every star and strip of our flag and every drop of blood spilt honorably and courageously under it.

So I am your unlikely and improbable candidate for the U.S. Senate. If I win, I will serve you and our Constitution. I will hold the fort and do what I can in the Senate while others prepare to run and be elected and come help turn things around.

If this is the common people organizing against the forces of oppression, then it is the renewal of our American Revolution, and that is fine.

This is our time to act. We have but a few weeks to make a great difference. I hope you will help me and some of the candidates who have come here to meet you. I am behind Kerry, if you want to know. But remember that the U.S. Senate and thereby the Supreme Court in the balance, not just the White House.

And I ask for your vote in my Senate run. I have no strings to the special interests, and I will do the right things for our country, as a New Englander knows how to do from birth. Thank you.

Election Night

Ms. Haddock's U.S. Senate campaign headquarters was a grand brick mill building in Peterborough, with a waterfall showing outside the windows—all by the light of a rising three-quarter waning moon. Her remarks, at 1 a.m., November 3, 2004:

Thank you. What we have done over the past four months has been a labor of love for our country, its democracy, and its people. There are many Americans who are awake to the fact that representative government is slipping away from us. This campaign was an opportunity to expand that awareness, and to awaken people to the idea that our democracy can be a beautiful thing. It can be the engine of our highest values and of our dreams for each other in our long climb to a better world.

My effort to run without special interest funds is the high trail to a better future. My townspeople here tonight and my friends all over New Hampshire and America, encouraged my every step.

We have proven that one person and her friends can have an impact on the present corruption. We have gotten a ways up the mountain, and we will set up a camp here so that others may take the next steps in the next election, using small donations instead of large. It is no picnic to run a race without special interest donations. But those who will make the climb, regardless of their party affiliation, merit our support.

I invite Senator Gregg, whom I now congratulate on his victory, to join this reform.

So we have come a ways up the mountain. Tonight we will see where the base camp will be for the next assault by the next climber, supported by regular citizens making small donations.

I am not finished walking on Democracy Road. This campaign, thanks to all of you, was a wonderful opportunity to connect and to change hearts and to bring more people into that great feeling of participation in the greatest work of our lives. And the work of our lives, and all its love and friendship, is still growing within us.

This is a night for New Hampshire, which has gone into the blue again on the presidential vote, where it belongs. This campaign—all of you—helped with that, bringing in thousands of new voters.

Friends are waiting to see what our next work will be. We will have good nights and bad, but we will never be discouraged, for it is the walk itself that we love. Thank you.

The Boston Post Town Cane

Many New Hampshire towns keep a tradition begun by the Boston Post newspaper in 1909 to honor the town's oldest citizen with a gold-knobbed cane (see it in the frontispiece of this book). In March of 2005, that honor fell to Doris Haddock, of Dublin, New Hampshire. Her remarks on the occasion:

Thank you. I know there has been some trepidation in the hearts of my more conservative townspeople that awarding this historic Boston Post Cane to me might just encourage me to misuse the honor as an opportunity to promote some crazy notion such as the idea that democracy ought not be for sale or that wars should not be started with false reasons. I will refrain from all such eccentric political ideas on this day, or at least for this hour.

I therefore pledge to never use this cane to ride any U.S. Senator out of town, even if he or she continues to accept floods of special interest money and continues to represent only their rich donors. I hereby swear to use another stick for that.

I pledge to never use this cane to make a stomping noise in any lobby or other place where my now reduced voice might be insufficient to peacefully redress my grievances; nor shall I place a flag upon this good and historic stick, which has long been passed down, elder to elder in this town, or in any way nail a sign, affix a pitchfork prong or wrap a torch wick upon it, even when truth and fairness demand that a noble stick be found.

And, truly, of the many things I love about my town and my neighbors, the thing I love most is how I have been treated with gracious love, even by those who have not been politically swayed by my irrefutable screeching. I respect your opinions and you respect mine, and that is the essence of Americanism and is indeed the bond that joins us as neighbors and friends.

I thank you for this honor, given, as it is, against your better judgment. I do love you all and thank you very much from my heart.

Making the Party More of a Party

Ms. Haddock's voter registration trek through the swing states in 2003-4 led her to believe that the Democratic Party was uninterested or incompetent at creating and serving communities, thereby losing election after election. She was also impressed by the organizing power of the joyful activist Pete Seeger, who had become a friend, and by the New York City activist Bill Talen, who poses as Reverend Billy to promote a joyful kind of anti-consumer resistance with his frequently arrested Stop Shopping Choir. At her speeches in the shadow of the Democratic Convention in Boston, she laid out a new vision for the Party, as she later repeated in this essay, sent to friends and supporters in early 2005:

Dear Friends, we Americans admire the pro-democracy activists whose courage opened much of the world to freedom in the final decades of the 20th Century.

We remember and honor the poet revolutionary Vaclav Havel of Czechoslovakia, where Charter 77 rendered the flowers and songs of a "Velvet Revolution" that proved more powerful than the guns of oppression. We remember the shipyard hero of democracy, Lech Walesa, of Poland. We remember those who stood nonviolently—most of them nonviolently—in Russia, in Yugoslavia, in Tiananmen Square, in East and West Germany. It was their fearless living that ended the Cold War, not Reagan's saber rattling.

When people stand united with certain courage against oppression they often win.

To say we are oppressed in America sounds remarkably like the whining of spoiled children. We live such privileged lives, compared to many in the world—it is true. We have our cars and our homes or apartments, most of us, and our television shows and our clean cities and glittering stores and theaters and a thousand kinds of systems and conveniences and communication devices and all the rest that seem to work and serve us with well-maintained reliability.

Our homes are now filled with the cheap products of slavish societies, and our streets are safe because those who dare move against their systems are locked away—even their forced prison labor can serve us, too. But we are free and happy, we think. We are Americans. We need no Velvet Revolution, for our lives are sufficient; they are velvet couches, made in China, affordable to us because the best part of the price is paid by others, by the exploited worker overseas, by the unemployed fellow in our own town, and by his children who pay in a thousand ways.

So, we have it made. Yes, it is a problem that we Americans use a third of the world's resources and that we often get the cheap resources we desire by destroying democracies around the world and installing dictators to whom we can dictate.

But everyday injustices must flow somewhere. Indeed, they gather into great rivers that flow through capitals and pentagons, where the selfish energies combine and become the bombs and machine-gun rattles of our bloody agents in the world. Our vote every four years is a weak ceremony of little importance compared to how we live our personal lives, which empowers either good or evil in the world.

And I think it is a fact that no man or woman is truly free whose life is built upon the suffering of others. Slavery enslaves the master and the slave. And so we take off our shoes at the airport and are too dumbed-down to think why, and we send our children to factory schools that are the abattoirs of their tender imaginations and grand potentials, and we are too hypnotized to think much of it. We bow our heads to our bosses without clear minds to mourn for our human dignity—for we dare not miss a paycheck or else the credit card and mortgage bales on our backs will come crushing down on us, and that is all that matters, we have been programmed to believe, not think.

Can you afford freedom? Are you free to make big changes in your life, or do you have too many obligations to others? Financial entanglements have come to define human relationships, so that the elite may prosper.

Was it not ever so? Did not the frontier farmers and the townspeople feel the constraints of their position, their obligations to family, church, community? They did so. I remember this life. It was imperfect, but it was different from today: people chose their oppressions and built lives. They were pawns in their own schemes and social hierarchies, and they were fodder in the wars of the elites, but there was a sense of freedom that is missing now.

Today's oppressions have organized themselves in inhuman ways that work against our interests and against the interests of society itself. It is evidenced in so many new ways, from unnecessary wars built upon great lies, to election frauds and the dismantling of social programs by the device of other great lies, and the creation of permanent war so that power over us may be extended forever in ways small and grave. Our shoes are to come off at the airport, our children are to be shot and blown up, and our debt is to be the great burden that keeps the bales upon our backs and all of us in our places. There is, in other words, a permanently vicious aspect to life today that was only an occasional visitor to us before, when the wars came, when the union contract expired. The boot of greedy oppression is now always at our necks, it seems. And, like medical companies who own Congress or oil companies who own White Houses, it seem to have become the nature of the beast, widely understood and generally, if grudgingly, accepted.

But the pursuit of happiness? There it is, a phrase central to the world's idea of America. If some people in this country could erase those words from our Declaration, they would do so—and replace them with something more religious or otherwise authoritarian and demanding of obedience and obeisance, instead of the nurturing of our human potential.

But the words remain there on that parchment, with fading ink but indelibly upon our hearts and imaginations.

A happy uprising is due to defend our dignity, and it must not be the whining of spoiled children but the song of freedom of brave men and women who are prepared to let the bales upon their backs fall and mix with the old tea in the harbor.

There is a cycle to human history that the historian Arnold Toynbee identified, and let me tell you or remind you about it: He said that a creative minority of people rise during times of great trouble or insecurity to show the people a new way forward. The new way forward is not always peaceful, as in the case, for example, of the opening of the American frontier, which was genocide, but it does create a new way of survival and prosperity for those following the creative leaders.

Over time, however, as Mr. Toynbee says, changes bring other changes, and the creative minority cannot keep pace. The people need a new way forward, but the entrenched leaders have no new ideas. The old leaders then retain power by force, by law, by prisons, by economic indenture and by wars. This is the end phase, after which a new creative minority rises with a new way forward.

The difficult condition of the working class in this country and around the world is now propelling the search for new creative leadership. It expresses itself in anger on the political right and disgust on the left. We are at a time, exactly now, when terrible leaders or wonderful leaders will arise and be embraced.

One of the ways to tell one from the other is that the terrible leader will rise by dividing people and demonizing people, and making empty promises to attract followers. The good leader will rise by bringing people closer together as a larger community. The good leader will also attract followers; not with promises, but with real acts of successful progress that serve the interests and needs of the people, and therefore ought to be expanded onto the larger stage so that more will be served and helped to live prosperously and happily.

This wonderful phrase, the pursuit of happiness, is the always-rising red magma of our collective political souls—the energy source for all our elections and uprisings including this next one.

The next one? Let it call not for our selfish enjoyment of other people's labors, but for the freedom to live meaningful lives in a land of justice, where our democracy is our tool to better the Earth as a happy human outpost in the cold universe; a warm reprieve from the heartless and fatal logic of time and space, and a reflection here and now of God's love or for brotherhood. Indeed, brotherhood is another word for democracy.

Our only real future success can come from the promotion and spreading of a lifestyle that we model with lives of joy and justice and sustainable common sense.

We need to turn the tide: War breeds consumer materialism—the Civil War brought the Gilded Age; the First World War brought the Roaring Twenties; The Second World War brought on the material binge we now maintain with ad-hoc wars as necessary. Wars destroy all other values, leaving only materialism. Can the process work backward? Can we bring peace by living in more sensible and beautiful ways? Yes, for the future is always being forged in the present. Lives of joy, if we create them, will bear joyous fruit.

Serving each other is the joy of life. It does us no good to rise up every four years and comb through housing projects and poor neighborhoods, begging for votes, when we were needed there all along—needed to bring joy and education to the children, resources to parents, tools for self-representation and community progress.

In the current push in the Democratic Party for a new national chairman, the debate centers on how to better reach more people with our political message, when our elections are but report cards for how we have served our communities all along. The work of a successful party or movement depends on how well it organizes people every day for the improvement of free and joyful living, for the power to shape their futures and care for their children, for the power to extend their higher values into the world and thus serve their dreams of brotherhood, justice and the peace that comes naturally from that. This peace needs no armies or preemptive slaughters; no torture chambers nor even the taking off of shoes at airports.

If a party or a movement is to be successful, it must become the place where people go for personal help, like the union hall or the old Grange hall—a joyful place in every neighborhood where people help people.

Let us string lights in the trees and bring out tables of food. Let us purchase the things we need from the workers here who need the work. Let us invite the musicians and the artists and the academics to do their part. Let us do, in short, what we would do if the present order fell to feathers with all its mortgages and credit cards. It will do just that if we so elect.

Look at me: I am still alive, and I am looking at you, and you are alive. This is our world as much as anyone's. We who are old enough to see both edges of life can understand that we have a choice between fear and joy, and between victimization and service. All elections and other indications to the contrary, happy days are here again when we but say they are and make them so. We do not turn our hearts away from injustice or suffering, indeed we mend them as best we can with our joyful engagement and our courageous non-cooperation with the forces of fear and death. And no one can take away our joy, for even our suffering for justice and brotherhood is joyful.

This is our Velvet Revolution, American style. We resist what we must and what we can, but our victory is not in defense, but in a cultural offensive made irresistible by the power of love and courage, pulling our people together, and our own lives together, over time.

We have tried this before in America. Things got in our way: drugs, wars, fears. We became parents. We became distracted. It is now time to get it right. Thank you.

You Are the Master

Ms. Haddock spoke on a campaign finance reform panel at Yale on April 14, 2005, and later to a group of undergraduates at a master's tea on campus. Her remarks at both venues:

First, the clean elections panel:

Thank you very much. I have come here not to teach, but to learn. So after this brief hello, I will sit and hear what people have to say. It is only my job to remind you what you already know, which is that money has too much influence in our politics.

Some several centuries ago we began this democratic republic with the idea that there are good, well-read, thoughtful people among us who, if we got them to sit together as representatives of our various communities, might wisely chart the future of the nation and agree on its necessary laws, taxes and defenses.

But big money has petrified many members of Congress. The constant drip of money has turned them to salt or marble, depending on their party. They no longer can move in ways that serve their constituents.

It is rather the case that big money players now push around these stone statues as they please on a chessboard that no longer resembles a map of the United States.

The point of the game now is to "starve the beast" of government. The very wealthy and corporations want this accomplished because government is our common instrument of community action, and therefor their natural enemy. Government is our tool by which we defend our own interests, our own freedoms, and by which we promote a rational and humane presence in the world. It is under attack because the international business elite and the fundamentalist authoritarians on the far right are, by all evidence, set against our freedom and our interests. Oh, the far right want to protect one right: the right to own weapons that would be of no use whatsoever in a true revolution against an evil government, which is their little-boy fantasy, but are quite useful in dividing and conquering ourselves.

Now, how do we respond to this challenge? Certainly by reforming the existing campaign finance reform system, which currently allows special interest players to buy our representatives away from us. The public financing of election campaigns—a fundamental reform—returns ownership of the representatives to the people. Even where that reform passes into law, it requires a constant battle to preserve it because big money never sleeps.

And beyond the money of campaigns, there is the money paid to lobbyists. The special interest lobbies now spend billions. The nonpartisan Center for Public Integrity reports that, last year, interest groups spent more than $3 billion to influence the federal government. Total spending by lobbyists from 1998 through mid-2004 was $13 billion. Verizon Communications Inc., General Electric and Edison Electric Institute each laid out more than $100 million over the same period. Since 1998, Lockheed Martin Corp. spent roughly $89 million on lobbying and received $94 billion in government contracts. If you wonder why the U.S. is selling F-16s to Pakistan, upsetting our relations with India, it's because the makers of those airplanes are, more than you would like to think, running our government. That particular defense contractor and several others were the lobbying behind the purchase of electronic voting machines that may have given Mr. Bush the White House last year. The exit polling numbers were off by an average of five and a half percent in Mr. Bush's favor wherever those machines were used. If you think I am making this up, I am not, though neither am I certain of it. We do need, however to be certain of our elections.

Reforms are possible and necessary, and they won't happen without your energy. This is, after all, your nation, your world, and you should take responsibility for making it run well. If you give up on it, you are the servant. If you keep working to improve it, you are the master. Thank you.

How Power is Taken

Ms. Haddock's remarks the same day at Yale's Silliman College:

Thank you very much. I want to thank you for your invitation—this is such an honor and joy. In the last several years I have traveled far and wide across America. I have seen so much and met so many interesting people. As a child I had great dreams of adventure and love, but real life has surpassed my dreams.

I have walked through small towns and great cities—deserts, farms and mountains—feeling under my own feet the expanse of America and seeing with my own heart the wonder of its people.

I met Jamie, who feeds the alligators near Orlando—I helped her register to vote. She has in her heart a plan to protect the animals of Africa and the world. I met Winnie, whose life is dedicated to democracy in St. Petersburg, and I met Al, who is dedicated to Winnie. In Tallahassee I met Susie and Dan, who hold up democracy there, and so many others.

I have traveled under the necklace-festooned trees of New Orleans, where I bartended for an evening and met young people and old whose eyes and hearts are open to life, and who have made their lives a happy struggle for love, freedom and democracy. We celebrated all of it from a balcony in the French Quarter—we Republicans and Democrats, we Greens, Libertarians and we others.

I have walked Missouri and Oregon and many other places, and marched over my own hills, always beside people who are awake and walking in beauty, though they worry for their nation.

For it is a challenge, always, to defend wisdom and love, especially in times when fearful superstitions, parading in the false costumes of faith and honor, come burning our books and scattering the mileposts of our past in order to drag us back to the darker ages before the moment when brotherhood and the Enlightenment hatched their great partnership called Democracy in America. Our freedom stands upon that yet living but threatened pact.

I have walked and preached in defense of the human scale of things, for democracy requires its main streets and its barber shops; its hometown newspapers and its crusty editors; its small business owners and a great, overflowing wealth of jobs and schools and the surpluses of time and wealth so that we might have a community. There is no wholesale version of democracy that works. There is no corporate substitute that is not enslavement.

The institutions and conditions that we require to be a free people are under siege as never before. If we let it go, what will happen? Will we become a nation that allows torture and secret prisons?

Do not say it is already so—I know. And yet no leader is held accountable.

Imagine that the minority party's leaders are attacked with anthrax in their Senate offices, and that their votes then jump to the military march. Yet no one is arrested.

Do not say it has already happened—I know.

And that the most basic of our rights, which is to speak freely, to have our day in court and a lawyer if arrested, are no more in America? What treason is this against the same Constitution our leaders swore to defend?

Can we imagine a day when our elections are no longer honest, when exit polls show great deflections, as they did in Eastern Europe where we screamed and demanded new elections, but in this nation the press hardly takes note and the election goes unchallenged, uninvestigated, despite the best evidence?

Do not say it is already so—I know.

And if you think I would not be complaining if my candidate won, then you know nothing about me, for we are not talking about politics, but about our freedom. And it seems that our freedom now depends on paper ballots and the smashing of the infernal voting machines with our sticks and sledges—if that is what is necessary to preserve our freedom.

The lobbying that pushed these electronic voting machines through Congress was paid for by defense contractors— more rightly called offense contractors—who make F-16s and such. Why indeed would they care? Well, we know. Even India now knows.

My speech has taken a dark turn, but it will soon brighten.

But these are, indeed, serious times, worth mentioning on great occasions.

Do you think that an old woman might enter the U.S. Capitol building and read aloud from the Declaration of Independence without being arrested? I have been in jail for that crime, and again jailed for going back and reading from our Bill of Rights.

We have come to such a time as that.

Without your courage, we will become a nation that sends thousands more of its young people to die for multinational profits, and its elders off to poverty—you see it happening.

You see the unraveling of community, of brotherhood, and of rational government.

Without your bright eyes and your comradeship, the whipping stocks and fiery stakes of bigotry will again appear in our midst, and no one's life, no one's beliefs, no one's children, no one's body will be safe or their own. It is not about politics, but freedom.

Many of you are awake and know these things. America requires all of your clear-thinking courage now.

There is hope, and we must always look for it. For instance, the legislature of the great Republican State of Montana has just passed a fiery bill denouncing the Patriot Act as anti-American, as have four other states and 372 cities and towns. It is proof that the American Revolution is a living thing. Further, a growing number of senators on both sides of the aisle in Congress worry that dismantling Social Security might not be a good idea, or that torturing people and keeping them in secret prisons for life might not quite fit the document they agreed to uphold.

What all these troubling issues have in common is that they are rooted in the sociopathic belief that government should not be an expression of community, that community should be reserved for church and nowhere else, and they are rooted in the anti-American belief that proper governance does not derive from the consent of the governed, but from the Almighty, for mad power always assembles high priests to anoint its authority.

It is not about politics—it is far beyond that—it is about freedom and the preservation of America.

I know I am speaking at a conservative institution. I am speaking about the conservation of our freedom, and about mustering the courage to defend freedom and to not follow along the road to its destruction, behind leaders who have traded old addictions for the new addiction of power.

But let me put these challenges aside and get down to the rocks of what I most need to say.

I should like to pass on my old flashlight to any of you who will take it, to help get you through dark times—a torch to help you see in confusing times. For the big things are the same in public life as it is in our personal lives.

How do you see, when in the dark, the difference between demagoguery and proper leadership? Or between friendship and mutual exploitation? Or between a good idea and a bad one?

Let me explain.

In my travels I have met many great leaders, and there is no difference between a good leader and a good friend, or a good parent. And some of the best leaders I met only think of themselves as a mother or a father or a volunteer, when in fact they are quite the same as the best of the world's political and spiritual leaders. They all do the same one thing that marks them well:

Imagine, if you will, that you own the world. It's yours. You can make this thing happen, or that, and it pleases you when all of it works happily.

Now imagine that, through some accident, you lost your memory and no longer understand that it is your world, that you have the power to make it run properly, and that you have the responsibility to be its proper owner.

Now, you have a very good friend. This friend comes around to remind you whom you are—to remind you that you own the world and have great powers to create happiness for yourself and others. This friend reminds you that you have the power to be whatever you choose to be, and do whatever you choose to do.

Well, my friends, I have discovered that we each have extraordinary power to change the world and to create happiness for others and—through helping others—for ourselves as well.

And some people are so evolved and beautiful and so full of love that they take great efforts to remind us who we are. They empower us with our own power. They enthuse us with our own spirit, our own love of life.

Here is how you know if you are truly being a friend to someone and if they are being a friend to you; here is how to know if a public leader is a good leader, or not: it is this: is this friend, this leader, filling people's minds with the leader's own ideas, trying to prop them up with the leader's own energy? Or—and here is the difference—waking them up to the fact that they are quite brilliant already—that they have come into this Earth with their own genius and power?

Is there a reminding and a building up, or a humiliation and a tearing down? For the tearing down is how power is taken, and there is much power to take, and when it is taken it is concentrated in ways that do us all great harm.

After being in the presence of this friend or leader, is one left with ones' own energy, enthusiasm and fearlessness brought forward, or with depression and feelings of powerlessness and fear? Are we taken over with their energy and ideas, which are usually identifiable by the fact that they fly the flags of social division and unnecessary authority?

That is the only question you need in order to sort out your real friends and your real leaders from those who would exploit you—who, like pack rats, steal your golden power and leave in its place fear and hate.

And in this same fashion you can see how to be a good friend and a good parent and a good leader. It is all about empowerment, encouragement and trusting in the fact that each of us is a genius in our way, and trusting in the deep meaningfulness of life, and trusting in the great love that breezes away fear.

This spirit is naturally cooperative and positive; it naturally gathers us together and does not build walls and prisons between us.

It raises up our children to the glory of the future; it brings each person to his and her highest potential and greatest freedom. It helps and not hinders all of us in making the great contribution to life that we have come here to make.

And you will not see real friendship nor real leadership ever embrace bigotry and you will not see it misuse religion as a weapon of suppression and control instead of its proper use, which is a personal road to wisdom. And wisdom is always characterized by tolerance and generosity and joy, is it not?

I have met so many people in the last few years who know all this. You know all this, and I am just here to remind you, as a friend.

We are all at risk of being distracted from our purpose on this Earth. We have come into the world at a great time, and life in this moment is dramatic and full of danger and glory.

I know so many people who have risen to the occasion of this life. They fly the flag of love's vermillion, never standing aside, even when the forces against them are mounted and armed.

If our hearts and souls live forever, then there is no real danger—only the danger of a wasted opportunity to be truly alive, to have stood for something in this life. There are so many things to stand for, and the greatest of these is love.

Your friends and family will need you to remind them of their own power and genius. For each person you know is a genius at that thing they came into this world to do. We are here to remind our friends of that.

And we are here to remind ourselves of that. There is nothing we cannot do if we are free people. And what we do should be worth a life. Thank you all.

Hampshire College

Ms. Haddock's commencement address at Hampshire College, May 21, 2005:

Thanks to the staff and members of faculty and to President Prince, and to all of you graduates who chose me to be your speaker. I hope my message will be up to the occasion.

I am sure there have been times in your years here at Hampshire when you doubted you would ever see this day. But you kept going, one step at a time, and here you are. Sometimes all you can do in life, in the harder moments, is to put one foot in front of the other. You will always come to some new victory, despite your darkest worries and despair.

We, all of us, sincerely congratulate you.

Today will stay in your memory as a reminder that you have the power to shape your own life. That is not small change in your pocket; it is a great and golden treasure.

For it is the loss of faith in our personal power that drives the woes of the world.

When I was a child growing up in New Hampshire, my father worked in a furniture warehouse. It was modest work, but he gave it all his honest muscle, and, with what he earned, he knew he would be able to build a house and provide for his wife and five children, which he did beautifully. He felt in control of the future, and that gave him the emotional freedom to be a good citizen and a good neighbor.

When we feel insecure in our power to take care of our families and direct the future of our own lives, we fall into a kind of social mental illness that encourages us to distrust and then hate other people and work against their interests.

Radical religious leaders—unlike the wiser men and women of their faiths—promote that hatred when they make people feel powerless.

When people are made to feel powerless, either by religious despot or political preacher, they feel despair, even if they disguise the anxiety and pain of that powerlessness as piety or as patriotism—or both.

The current effort by zealots to pass laws against the interests of gay people is a good example of all this. We have had gay members of our society for as long as there are human records, but that does not stop some people from thinking it is suddenly new and dangerous and in need of suppressing. They do so partly out of sheer ignorance, of course, but their motivations are grounded in fear of their own powerlessness. The coming and going of anti-gay politics is a simple and accurate barometer of how much power is being stolen from the people by political leaders and their business partners.

In the Germany of the 1930s, when politicians began to pass measures harmful to minority groups, most especially the Jews, but also gays and many others, the average German was struggling to survive in a depression that came on the heels of the First World War.

It was not enough to be a hard worker in a furniture warehouse or anywhere else. Monetary inflation reached such an extreme in Germany that people literally carried cash around in bushel baskets to pay for their groceries—if they had cash at all. How could parents feel that they were in control of their children's futures and happiness? They could not. And, for the master politicians, it was an easy trick to redirect that insecurity and anger away from the leaders, who were indeed the guilty parties, and toward sacrificial victims.

That is what is happening in the United States today. It continues in ways that gives people great fear for their own futures. Our safety nets and our Bill of Rights are being cut from under us, for the financial benefit of a few.

If the great majority of Americans are feeling insecure and fearful of the future—of their children's futures—what might the master politicians do to redirect that fear? Well, you have seen it misdirected into piety and false patriotism.

You have seen it with your own eyes. People take their anger out with ballot measures against their gay neighbors. They defund our poverty programs and public schools. They intrude on the privacy of people in their most personal decisions of life and death, depriving them of their power over their own lives and bodies. They applaud the attack of other countries based on false evidence and they allow the mistreatment of their men, women and children of those countries with mass killings, torture, and a shedding of the Geneva Convention.

They meekly allow the anthrax attack on the minority leaders of our Congress so that those leaders will step to a more military march, and they accept the fact that this attack, made with the most traceable of chemicals, has produced no arrests.

They accept that, in the last election, electronic voting machines gave a five percent deflection from exit polls, all in the same political direction, and they accept the fact that this horror is not even reported by the media.

I am not, on this grand occasion, talking about partisan politics; I am talking about our very freedom.

Our freedom comes first from our belief in it. We have the ability to shape our futures. We are in charge of our communities and our nation. We bear responsibility for what happens here. The moment we lose faith in these core beliefs, we are no longer a free people.

I ask you to hold this day in your memory, to remind yourself that you have the power to make a difference in your own life and in the world.

I have to struggle for every breath now, but the air is still free, and you have come into your maturity at a moment when we, you elders, say to you, well, here is a great nation for you! Here is the land of the free, but, by God, it had better be the land of the brave if you would keep it. You had better be the patriots you now require.

But do not act from anger; the defense of freedom and fairness comes best from a loving and tolerant heart.

Accept no leaders who would lead you with fear or anger—who are forever dividing and punishing the people instead of uniting, encouraging and empowering them. Great leaders lead from a better vision of a possible future. Great leaders—and you must include yourself in this—lead themselves, their families, friends, communities, nations and their world from the great, golden idea that people should be free and should in every way be encouraged to fulfill their highest potentials and live life responsibly, as they choose. Great leadership comes from love, and great societies come from confident, mass empowerment.

Throughout your lives, your best friends will be the people who remind you that you are in some way a genius, that you have great gifts to give other people and the world, that you have the power to be happy and to help others be happy. Stick to those friends, and give that service to them in return. Apply the same rule to your political leaders. Do they make you feel your power as part of a great community? If so, support them. If, instead, they make you want to hide in a shelter, vote them out, work hard against them as a moral cause. We Americans—and this is a hard fact—always get the leaders who represent the moral landscape of our time, so we must be energetic parts of that landscape.

Not long ago I read from the Declaration of Independence in the Capitol Rotunda in Washington. I was arrested and jailed for doing so. That was quite a violation of my free speech rights under the Constitution, so I went back and read from the Bill of Rights. That landed me in jail, too.

Because I had spoken out as a free person, I felt freer in that jail than I often feel in the open air. I am not finished with being a free American, whatever happy costs await me.

I do not know what is in store for you. But I know that courage is freedom, and freedom is joy. Be fully who you are, letting the world get used to you—it will. Find a loving community of friends who support your ever-flowering growth, which is a lifetime proposition. And take seriously your role as an American. Understand what it means to be an American. It means to take responsibility for mature self-governance.

In a world where the polar ice is melting and atmosphere ozone levels are thinning daily, and in a world where the divide between the very wealthy and the literally starving is growing rapidly, where one American child in five goes to bed hungry. We must take our responsible and loving place at the table of power.

Our old revolution against oppression and unfairness is never concluded. It is a joyful revolution, if you will put yourself fearlessly into it, keeping always an open mind and a tolerant heart, for those are the true flags of justice and freedom. Let those lofty banners signify your life now and onward to the last day of your long, happy, meaningful and love-filled life. Thank you.

Ms. Haddock was thereafter mobbed by the cheering graduates.

Why Facts Don't Matter to Our Opposition

The following speech was made by Ms. Haddock to a Quaker political action committee at Orchard House, home of the Alcotts, in Concord, Massachusetts on October 6, 2005:

Thank you. On my walk across the nation several years ago, I had the honor of speaking from a pulpit where Dr. King once preached. How I felt the power of his words and his love somehow still echoing in that great room! More recently, on the anniversary of his death in Memphis, I had the honor of speaking from the balcony where he took his last breath.

You, of course, understand how his politics of nonviolence was informed by the sacrifices of Gandhi, and how Gandhi's nonviolence was informed by Tolstoy and Ruskin, who in turn were inspired by the American Quakers, working for the abolition of slavery. The great Quaker voice was William Lloyd Garrison, who spoke to this very group so many years ago—as did Emerson and William James and Julia Ward Howe and other voices for justice who spoke to you in dark times. And so, in the long shadow of these people, I humbly raise my voice today.

We meet in a time when two great and growing divisions are separating us as Americans: rich versus poor, and left versus right. I would like to speak to the second of these, as its resolution would help solve the other.

The political issues that divide the American people are great issues with severe consequences for the moral life of the nation and the fate of the planet. These are issues equal to the issues that divided us in 1860, and we should fear that.

In some ways the conflict of the Civil War was never resolved, but rather accommodated, in the same way that smoldering coals under ashes are but a fire asked to bide its time. The sparks now swirl up fresh. The heat and danger we feel is the old conflict between those who believe that authority comes from above—from an Old Testament God, delivered through husbands, presidents, preachers, ayatollahs and plantation overseers to people arranged in layers according to their assigned worth. It is a conflict between those authoritarians and those others who instead believe that all men are created equal and that the authority to govern issues forth from them, upward to their government—our common vessel of community—and not downward. This is the divide of 1860 and also of our own time.

Our differences are not locked into different economies of different regions, as was the case in 1860. Our differences are with our neighbors, our friends, our family members. We try now to argue this out peaceably across fences and dinner tables instead of across a bloodied continent, as before. But it is getting difficult to do so.

Today's conflict it is not only about the enduring unfairness between races, but also now a kind of involuntary servitude—one of the mind. It is the hardest kind to deal with, as the victims do not want to be emancipated. But they must be, if the suffering of this nation and of the world is to end.

Let us consider the self-repression of the political right. And in this argument, I am talking to some of my own friends and hoping they will open their minds to a new thought from me, for I offer it in good faith and friendship.

Where authority and power are believed to flow down from heaven to the White House and ayatollahs and husbands, then the free and joyful living of people stands in the way and can be quite the enemy of that organization chart. If you will remember the free spirit of those flower children who grew up in the 1960s, for example, you will also remember the harsh attitude that attended to their joys from the more traditional, often more rural, elements of our society, ending in gunfire at Kent State.

Those political leaders who rose from this time, who lived in this more open and free way—less constrained by the rules of authority—were especially vilified by the clan of authority. You need only to think of the harsh treatment given to the Clintons, who were of this generation and climate, to know the truth of this. And it fits the international pattern, of course, that the woman, Ms. Clinton, would be singled out for the cruelest stones.

What attracted such hatred? It was their freedom, their sense of equality, and their joys.

And here it is: Those living under the clan of authority are not given the privilege—the natural right—of living their own lives. They do as they are told, say and think what they are told.

Smothered is their curiosity and their healthy skepticism, and also their imagination, joy, freedom, and lust for life itself. When they see others actually living lives, they react with anger, as if someone had cut to the front of a line that, for them, never moves.

What is the proof of this theory? Those enthrall to authority, cowering under it, lose sight of their own lives. They will venerate above all else the symbol of the yet unruined potential of life: the curled-up unborn. The authority clan will have the image of an unborn baby as its flag, and they will claim to honor and defend innocent life, but that will be a great lie to themselves. For they will not be the ones to demand DNA testing of all prisoners on death row; they will not be the ones to demand health insurance for all children, or better nutrition in all schools, or peaceful alternatives to international conflicts. They will be the ones to rail against providing aid, for the authority clan parades itself as pro-life while it is a cult of death. Having died themselves, strangled by authority and fear, they cannot wish happy lives for others—they cling only to that magic symbol of what might have been. They relate to the unborn baby selfishly; it is themselves: unborn, still hoping for a life that remains unlived.

I am not talking about true political conservatives. People who follow leaders like Goldwater, Forbes, Will and Buckley do believe, in the great mainstream of American thought, that government is the council fire of community. They just want it not to be all consuming. But the people we are dealing with today, who are so far to the right of traditional conservatives that it is unfair to call them that at all, do not believe that our government is our council fire of community. They would replace it with a church, a strict family, and, as they have shown so many times in history, even with a dictatorship that derives from imagined divine or kingly powers, and with a reign of brutal authority that sanctions criminal aggressions on other nations, torture, and the suspension of civil liberties, the rule of law and the primacy of truth. How many times have we seen this happen abroad, and how many times have we wondered if we would have the courage and the character to stand against it, if it happened here?

I think every man and woman of us wants to be a patriot of this great nation. How sad to miss your cue when the alarm bell rings! How horrible to be enslaved to the wrong way of thinking at such a time of national crisis! We owe it to our friends and neighbors to awaken them if we can, so they might stand with us.

I will propose a mental experiment to see if we can find some breadcrumbs to lead our friends out of this dangerous maze.

Imagine that your friend is very much pro-life and pro-war and doesn't see the conflict. I think you might notice that this friend of yours lives a slipcover-protected life and has not even allowed herself the freedoms of a good fantasy life. Let's repair that.

Let me suggest that we take her to a good arts district, rent her a studio apartment full of art supplies above a good sidewalk café, find her a lover and come back in ninety days to see if her politics has changed. As she lives a real life, as she explores her own potential, as she meets a rainbow of good people, she will learn to let others live and enjoy their lives, too. She will want to help the young woman artist next door who gets into trouble. She will begin to be amused and impressed, instead of angered and depressed, by the joyful, free-living people of this beautiful Earth.

When people begin to really live their lives, the black and white certainties do not turn to shades of gray, but to the million-jeweled hews of the morning. That sparkle is the reality of life revealed. Life is about living, and about helping other real people get through this world with a minimum of pain and a maximum of human dignity. We simply can't do that with authoritarian politics and its deadly abstractions instead of real people. We can only do that with our love and our freedom to think for ourselves and act individually and as a community.

And that was the example of Jesus, wasn't it? Did He not challenge the organized church of His day, challenge its authority, and overturn its rules that had hardened into cruelties and corruptions? Did He not show us how we might act instead from the love and charity of our own hearts, and, in this rebellion, did He not say, follow Me? Are we not then, like Him, to think for ourselves? Is so grand a thing as the human mind meant to be wasted? Our founders were deeply spiritual and also deeply secular—a well-balanced condition of the mature mind that eludes today's political fundamentalists. Our founders respected human freedom and the urge toward greater equality. Over the centuries we have tried to make this nation a better expression of their intent, so that there would be no second-class citizens, no arbitrary authority that limited our life, liberty or pursuit of happiness. And the better angels of that Revolution do perch yet on our shoulders as we oppose the clan of authority, that cult of death, whose cloak of human oppression has cast its shadow over our children's future.

What must we do? We must bring the light of consciousness to people who are enslaved by the darkness. We must show them—make them see—the clear links between the Taliban and the American fundamentalists. It is about power, male power, and subservience.

The desperate attitude of the far right toward not only the unborn baby but even brain-dead people on life support reveals something about their true religion: they have little of it. There is nothing in their action that reveals a belief that life is eternal, that there is no death except as a doorway to something better. Their brand of Christianity simply does not relate to the teachings of Christ.

The worst of the hate-mongers who misuse the Bible to make million-dollar church incomes and push a political agenda of male domination and hate are easy to spot, for they cherry-pick Bible passages to suit their purposes. They disregard any turning of cheeks; they disregard the fact that Jesus never mentioned the homosexuality that they so fear. They seem not to fear that, as very rich men, they themselves might have a hard time driving their Hummers through the eye of the needle into heaven. They claim that every word of the Bible must be followed, but if they really believed that they would have stoned themselves to death years ago, as they are as sexually frisky and full of covetous looks as anybody else. They forgive themselves freely, of course.

They refuse a young girl an abortion for the same reason they would refuse her birth control: because in either case she would be exercising power and control over her own future—and such power and control is reserved for male authorities, below whom she is to cower and serve and reproduce. It is all about that, and we have to start saying so, so that the far right will no longer have women marching in its toxic ranks—at least the awakened ones.

If I ran the Democratic Party I would lay it all out in expensive advertising campaigns. I would have the sociologists and the psychologists talking about the tricks of mental slavery that are being used to trick decent Christians and other people into following un-Christian leaders and policies. As with any kind of mental counseling, progress depends on the spread of consciousness—of self-awareness. I would let more and more people come to understand the nature of the lies that surround them and defraud them. I believe they really are for life and for liberty, but they must be given better information, better moral and emotional guidance and support.

It is not easy. Imagine walking down a street in my Peterborough. You run across a retired couple and start talking politics. You somehow get on the subject of abortion.

"Listen," you say, "the Europeans have a very small percentage of the abortions we do in the United States. They have cut the number of abortions by providing better sex education, providing more contraception, and accepting a more open and honest attitude about the sexual lives of their young people. If your concern is to reduce abortions, surely you must become an advocate of these programs that actually do the trick!"

But the couple disagrees. They tell you "it isn't about doing what works in Europe and what might work here, it is about doing the right thing for the right reason, and following the word of God."

Well, that was a real conversation I had in Peterborough, though I'm sure they must have been visitors.

If you wonder why the other side of the political aisle seems so resistant to the facts, it is because they are not interested in what works, what is pragmatic; they are interested in obedience to authority. It is nothing less than mental bondage to the cult of authority. This is of course unworkable in the civic arena, where pragmatism is the belief system we must share as our common ground. The only way to break through that problem is if our few national voices of authority will please give these authority-dependent people permission to think freshly about our important issues.

There is another way out of this dark maze, and that way is leadership. Better leaders can make great differences in the life of a society, but we cannot elect them if we do not change from electoral organizing to social organizing.

When I went on a 23,000-mile voter registration journey before the last election, I walked through many housing projects and low-income neighborhoods where no one from the outside had dropped by to talk politics since the last election. The Democrats only come around, I was told, every few years to ask for their votes, if even that, but they weren't there to listen to their problems, to help them craft political solutions, and to stand behind them and amplify their voices. These people were of the opinion that, if the Democrats won or lost, their own lives wouldn't really change much. These are millions of wasted Democratic votes. Millions.

It is simply exploitive politics to come around begging for votes without giving so much as a crouton in return. We have to be involved all year long, every year, and in every neighborhood that needs political help. That is movement building—not just stumping for votes.

The residents of Cabrini Green in Chicago, and the people of the slums of Ft. Myers, Miami, St. Louis and New Orleans told me they needed our organizing help and our voices added to theirs—for they love their children too and want decent lives. Many of the streets I walked in New Orleans were later strewn with the drowned poor, as if America had progressed no further than the days of the Titanic, when those traveling life in steerage are never offered the lifeboats. So much criticism has fallen on the president for the flooding disaster in New Orleans, but the Democrats have had a long century to make life better and they have not done so. The New Deal and other programs, offered at a distance, are helpful but no match for a party meetinghouse in every neighborhood to raise the political competency and expectations of the area.

In all these places, I gave out information and forms to help people who had been in prison to get their voting rights back. They had no idea. The Democratic Party never bothered.

So politics is not just about raising money for candidates. It is not about trying to motivate people to register and to vote, if you have not motivated them to do so with your service to them. Politics is about creatively serving the needs of your people, and the election is just the report card on how you are doing and how many people you have helped and how many people know that their lives are changing because of what you are doing, in and out of office. They are following your leadership because you actually acted like a leader—you were there for them and they will follow you en masse to the voting booths.

We do get the government we merit or deserve, you see, and the crowd standing behind us in critical times is the crowd we have served through the years. They will also be there for the other issues that they otherwise might not work for. People will not speak up about the warm climate, I assure you, until they first have a warm bed for their own children. If you have helped them with that, they will follow you into new issues because they trust you and you have given them the extra time and resources to become involved. They are no longer living desperately, because of you.

So here are my two thoughts. We must help people see the mental traps that they are victim to, and we must do this by telling it like we see it, by asking them to see that the pro-life but pro-war movement is really a cult of death, that fundamental Christianity represents the opposite of Christ's teachings, that authoritarian control and elite profiteering are the strings of the far right's puppet show.

Let us indeed believe that all people are equal, but let us not assume that all political opinions are equal, for some are toxic and sociopathic and require our loving intervention. Let us intervene. Let us stand up in church gatherings; let us confront our friends; let us use the tools of mass communication to awaken people to the lies that bind them.

And let us return to real politics in the neighborhoods—especially those neighborhoods where we are most needed. As it stands now, people who do not receive the support they need from an ever-receding community are turning to the very megachurches that have been politically killing those needed government services. This is a dangerous tailspin that we can only arrest with a political return to the neighborhoods. Let us demand of our party leaders that we move from electoral to social organizing, so that there is more rock and less hot air under our candidates as we move into the future.

We also must drain the swamps of anger that fuel the far right. The true reason for that anger is a loss of power that has come with the rape of the middle class by big-box oligarchs and overlarge corporations, though a ventriloquist trick has been used to make it look like big government and the very liberals fighting for the people are the villains. We can only fix that by expanding the middle class and, in a million ways, giving people more power over their own futures. A candidate who promised to prevent banks or insurance companies from answering their telephones with computers would win any election. There must be so many ways to return a sense of power and respect to people, and all that will improve the tenor of our politics.

These are big projects. Do we have enough energy remaining for this sort of thing?

What is it to our souls when we have to just keep slugging through dark places? Why, after all that has happened in America, from stolen elections to the destruction of our necessary institutions of mutual help, are you activists still at it? Why, after seeing our country become the international symbol of irresponsible conduct, of torture, of political imprisonment, of destruction to the global ecosystem, are your spirits not smeared across the plaza under the treads of these tanks?

Are your hearts perhaps stronger and your souls deeper than you imagined? Yes, this is what you came here to do. There is no greater gift than to be given a life of meaning. There is no greater heroism than to bravely represent love in a dark time of fear and danger.

We are resolved to help each other. We are resolved to represent love in the world and to follow our national dream.

So look at the situation wisely and know that a good ending is not to be found under the paper moon of child's brief play. Accept and celebrate the fact that we are deeply engaged in a long, hard drama of global meaning. We welcome the fight. We welcome it, and, by George Washington, we are up to it. Thank you.

Just Take Over the Party

Ms. Haddock's remarks at a reform group's meeting in Des Moines, October 16, 2005:

Thank you very much. I greatly admire the stands that Iowa Citizens Action Network and Iowa Citizens for Community Improvement have taken on the central issues of our time, defending people-based democracy, economic and ecological balance, the defense of the human scale against the monstrous scale of overlarge institutions, and the necessary work of caring for one another with the food, housing and medical care that any civilized people worthy of that title must naturally and generously extend to one another.

Some thirteen years ago you guided through your legislature a bill that would have provided partial public funding for candidates who agreed to limit their fundraising and spending. The governor vetoed that bill, unfortunately. You were ahead of your time in suggesting the reform, and I hope the time will come for you to revisit it.

As you look at the serious issues that our governments need to address, such as health coverage and environmental protection, you must agree that large corporate interests must be tamed. It must be done while there is yet some ice at the North Pole and yet some sparkle to your drinking water and some sense of brotherhood in the availability of medical care. How are we to get the greedy interests out of the way?

I would suggest that you not lose faith in the idea of a clean elections law passed by your legislature and signed by your governor. It may not happen in the coming session, but the strength of organizations such as yours is that you can afford to take a long view of such battles. Create a model bill and start pushing it. Add up the cost to Iowans that has accrued since the veto of the bill 13 years ago—the cost in terms of campaign contributions that went to expensive campaigns instead of to

Iowa's real needs, and add up the cost of corporate welfare paid by the taxpayers so that the elected officials could pay their debts to their campaign donors. Keep tabs of that terrible number if it is possible to do so in some fashion that is honest and will be seen as legitimate by the public and the press.

That would be one thing to do, if it makes sense for your situation. I would suggest another as well:

At the beginning of the 20th Century, American voters— men at that time, of course—tended to be very involved in their political parties. They were very nearly social clubs. Great volunteer energies were expended there.

After World War II, and especially after the Vietnam War and Watergate, much of that energy was redirected into reform organizations. Parties still had there great and energetic volunteers, but not in the way that they had enjoyed before.

I want you to imagine that there are people in every Iowa political party who are very much dedicated to good government issues, such as campaign finance reform. Imagine that the party's candidates must deal with the fact that these vocal volunteers expect candidates to advocate for such reforms. That, friends, is where things can happen.

So, we must not divorce ourselves from power by placing all our reform energies into good government organizations. These organizations must be staging grounds and support groups and legislation development institutes for activists who agree to be fully engaged inside the political parties. If anyone is to take over our parties, why not the good government crowd? Why not people who believe in ecological sustainability and social responsibility? Why not people committed to getting dirty money out of the system?

I think civic action organizations like yours can make great progress on your issues by coordinating and encouraging action within the parties. I am sure a great deal of that happens as a matter of course, but it might be possible to organize it in newly energetic ways, rather than accidentally, and I think it would be worth considering.

I am not suggesting that anyone become involved in a party in which they are not in full agreement. Don't send out subversives. But provide good bills and good cheerleading to party volunteers who want to achieve significant reforms from your menu. In this way, it doesn't matter that you do not have popular initiative powers in your constitution: you will have found the great river that flows from your hearts to the civic and economic life of your people.

Reform organizations can be where activists from every party meet on common ground to share ideas, strategies and energies. Politics, by the way, should be fun and should be a good social opportunity to meet interesting people, and we must not introvert ourselves into specialized groups at the expense of this great and enjoyable give-and-take between neighbors and new friends.

The fact is, if we want to succeed in preserving natural life on Earth, and succeed in achieving a new and meaningful kind of brotherhood in this life, then we need the power to engage our dreams with the real world. Today, that power runs through the parties to the state houses and to Congress. It is our power—it rightfully belongs to the people. And just as in our own homes, we cannot clean house by standing outdoors.

Many people have died or have given their children and lovers to the defense of our position as a self-governing people. We must not hide away and wring our hands when our best and highest values are being destroyed before our eyes by a government captive to selfish interests. We must go into the fight where the fight is, and take our part. We are tougher than they are, because we have heart and soul and a view to the great issues. That is the source of our power.

Thank you very much and for the honor of being with you here.

Regarding Our Immigrants

In Bedford, New Hampshire, on June 9, 2007, Ms. Haddock spoke to attendees at a "Democracy Fest:"

Thank you. It is normally expected that, when given an opportunity to speak, I will talk about campaign finance reform and sometimes about the public financing of campaigns as a way of cutting the threads of the big-money puppet show in Washington and in the states.

But today I would like to talk about unauthorized immigration.

Of course, unauthorized immigration has nothing to do with the big money corruption of our political system. It is just a matter of people in distressed countries trying their best to find their way to better opportunities for their families.

It seems to be a big issue with our Republican candidates,

as they are well known to be the law and order party. That, after all, is why they are demanding that Scooter Libby pay the full price for his perjuries and obstructions of justice.

They are the law and order party, with the normal exceptions of the Geneva Convention and the U.S. Constitution, especially its Bill of Rights. But we know what they mean: When they say they are for law and order, they are talking mostly about keeping down the uppity poor folk. They are certainly not talking about the big corporations, hotel companies, agribusiness giants, retailers who employ millions of unauthorized immigrants but who make up for that sin with large campaign donations.

But I do not come to talk about corrupting campaign donations and the need for public campaign financing. I come to talk of unauthorized immigration and a little about corn and something about tortillas. I call it "unauthorized" immigration, not illegal, because I don't want to use words that confuse Republicans.

In saying that the Republican candidates are more interested in the immigration issue, I do not mean to imply that it is less important for any of us.

If you will look around the check-out lines at the grocery stores you will notice the widening measurements of our fellow citizens—some can hardly get through the aisles any more. We can certainly see for ourselves the problem of having too much cheap labor around to do all our yard work and housework. By my calculations, the roughly three billion pounds of extra weight now being carried on the hips of working-age American citizens is roughly equivalent to the combined weight of the unauthorized immigrants now in our communities. The math is clear and persuasive. Cheap labor is bad for every body.

But why are so many people risking their lives to come into our country now? When did this big rush begin?

It began when Mr. Clinton approved NAFTA—the North American Free Trade Agreement—and when he militarized our southern border at the same time. Prior to these combined actions, families crossed the border very commonly, especially during harvest seasons. After harvest, they would go home to Mexico or Central America because that's where they lived with their families in quite happy communities.

When the border was militarized, it became too risky to go back and forth. So they stayed.

Why did Mr. Clinton militarize the border? He did so because NAFTA was about to pull the rug out from under Mexico's small family farms. We flooded Mexico with cheap corn—exports that we subsidize to the tune of some $25 billion dollars a year by Congress to a handful of agribusiness giants.

Of course, I am not here to tell you why Congress does that, and what might be done to stop it. But they do it, and Mexican family farmers cannot compete. In the years since NAFTA was signed, half of Mexico's, and many of Central America's, small farms have failed. The only kind of farming that can now compete in Mexico is big agribusiness, which does not employ many people.

Tortillas in Mexico now contain two-thirds imported corn, and they are three times as expensive at retail level than before NAFTA. The people have less money, and the cost of food is rising. We have done that. Our precious Senators and Congressmen and their corporate cronies have done that raw and cruel exploitation in our names.

The result of undermining Mexican farms, as Clinton expected, was a rising flood of poor people moving from rural areas into Mexico's big cities, which have become so poor and overcrowded that all one can do is dream of going north across the border. Gang life has flourished as a result.

Now, if any Democratic candidates for President would like to show a little courage and intelligence, let them address the real cause of our flood of unauthorized immigrants. Will Ms. Clinton or Mr. Obama or Mr. Edwards or any of the other candidates face down the agri-gangsters that are behind this problem? Probably they will not, so long as Iowa has an early presidential primary.

Let me say that I am not ranting about these new Americans. When Mexico owned Texas and everything west of Texas, and when Mexico cut off migration across their borders, Europeans kept coming—crossing illegally in search of opportunities for their families. When Mexico got upset by this, we concocted false reasons for a war, and we illegally took those lands. So let's not stand on any moral high ground.

The people coming across the border today, with the usual exceptions, are family people with an incredible work ethic. Personally, I welcome them. I congratulate them for their courage and their dedication to their families. I want them to stay and become citizens, or, if some prefer, to return to their homeland at a time when there is international justice and a decent chance for their survival and prosperity at home.

I regret what the political corruption of our system has done to their farms and their communities back home—and I am not even mentioning the death squads we set loose in Central

America when those countries dared elect anti-American governments, and how that violence still defines the area. It is the fault of corrupt leaders of both American parties. We must speak this truth, even to candidates we otherwise admire.

So, candidates Clinton, Edwards, Obama and the rest: Do you understand the reasons why immigration numbers are growing? Are you smart enough to understand the situation? Are you brave enough to do something—to even say something about it? Or is the truth too big for you?

I ask you all to be good citizens and good Democrats. And that means to ask the toughest questions so that the interests of the people of our nation and of the world will be served. Isn't that what we're here for?

And do you see why I do not need to harp on campaign finance reform to cut the strings of the puppet show in Washington that allows these cruelties to continue? I didn't have to say a word about that, because you understand it. You understand what must be done. Thank you.

Citizens United's Floodgate

In January of 2010 Ms. Haddock sent a letter to her friends and supporters regarding the Supreme Court's—in Citizens United—gutting of key provisions of the Bipartisan Campaign Reform Act:

Dear Friends, ten years ago I walked from California to Washington, D.C. to help gather support for campaign finance reform. I used the novelty of my age (I was only 90 then), to garner attention to the fact that our democracy, for which so many people have given their lives, is being subverted to the needs of wealthy interests, and that we must do something about it. I talked to thousands of people and gave hundreds of speeches and interviews, and, in every section of the nation, I was deeply moved by how heartsick Americans are by the current state of our politics.

Well, we got some reform bills passed, but things seem even worse now. Our good government reform groups are trying to staunch the flow of special-interest money into our political campaigns, but they are mostly whistling in a wind that has become a gale force of corrupting cash. Conditions are so bad that people now assume that nothing useful can pass Congress due to the vote-buying power of powerful financial interests. The health care reform debacle is but the most recent example.

The Supreme Court, representing a radical fringe that does not share the despair of the grand majority of Americans, has today made things considerably worse by undoing the modest reforms I walked for and went to jail for, and that tens of thousands of other Americans fought very hard to see enacted. So now, thanks to this Court, corporations can fund their candidates without limits and they can run mudslinging campaigns against everyone else, right up to and including election day.

The Supreme Court now opens the floodgates to usher in a new tsunami of corporate and billionaire money into politics. If we are to retain our democracy, we must go a new direction until a more reasonable Supreme Court is in place. I would propose a one-two punch of the following nature:

A few states have adopted programs where candidates who agree to not accept special-interest donations receive advertising funds from their state. The programs work, and I would guess that they save their states more money than they cost, because they reduce the corruption of campaign donor payoffs—payoffs in the form of legislated subsidies and tax policies. Moving these reforms in the states has been very slow and difficult, but we must keep at it.

But we also need a new approach—something of a roundhouse punch. I would like to propose a flanking move that will help such reforms move faster: We need to dramatically expand the definition of what constitutes an illegal conflict of interest in politics.

If your brother-in-law has a road paving company, it is clear that you, as an elected official, must not vote to give him a contract, as you have a conflict of interest. Do you have any less of an ethical conflict if you are voting for that contract not because he is a brother-in-law, but because he is a major donor to your campaign? Should you ethically vote on health issues if health companies fund such a large chunk of your campaign that you are dependent on them? The success of your campaign, after all, determines your future career and personal financial condition. You do have a conflict.

Let us say, through the enactment of new laws, that a politician can no longer take any action, or arrange any action by another official, if the action, in the opinion of that legislative body's civil service ethics officer, would cause special gain to a major donor of that official's campaign. The details of such a program will be daunting, but we need to figure them out and get them into law.

Remarkably, many better corporations have an ethical review process to prevent their executives from making political contributions to officials who decide issues critical to that corporation. Should corporations have a higher standard than the United States Congress? And many state governments have tighter standards, too. Should not Congress be the flagship of our ethical standards? Where is the leadership to make this happen, now that Citizens United has created the helpful vacuum?

This kind of reform should also be pushed in the 14 states where citizens have full power to place proposed statutes on the ballot and enact them into law. About 70% of voters would go for a ballot measure to "toughen our conflict of interest laws," I estimate.

In the scramble that would follow, there would be a mad dash for public campaign financing programs on the model of Maine, Arizona, and Connecticut.

I urge the large reform organizations to consider this strategy. They have never listened to me in the past, but they also have not gotten the job done and need to come alive or now get out of the way.

And to the Supreme Court majority, you force us to defend our democracy—a democracy of people and not corporations—by going in breathtaking new directions.

Last Delivered Speech

Ms. Haddock was honored on January 24, 2010, her 100th birthday, in the chambers of New Hampshire's governor. Several hundred attended. Her thank you remarks were her last delivered speech:

Thank you all so very, very much. That you would take time from your busy lives to be here is a great gift to me, and I thank you for it. People have been asking me how I feel about the recent decision by the Supreme Court to strike down some of the campaign finance reforms that I walked for and have been working on for a dozen or so years.

When I was a young woman, my husband and I were having dinner at the Dundee home of a friend, Max Foster, when a young couple rushed through the door breathless to say that they had accidentally burned down the guest cabin down by the river. Max stood up from his meal. He set his napkin down. He smiled at the young couple and he said:

"That's wonderful. We have wanted to build something special down there on the river, and this will give us a chance to do that without feeling guilty about getting rid of that drafty old thing."

Well, I guess the Supreme Court has burned down our little cabin, but, truth be told, it was pretty drafty anyway. We had not really solved the problem of too much money in politics, and now we have an opportunity to start clean and build a system of reforms that really will do the trick.

Thank you all, very much indeed for coming here, for the cake, my little crown, and for absolutely everything.

The Swamp to Drain is Anger (undelivered)

Her last prepared speech went undelivered. It was meant for the September 11, 2010 Fighting Bob (La Follette) Fest in Wisconsin, an annual gathering of national reformers. Her death intervening, Ms. Haddock was able to attend in spirit only.

Thank you very much. Nations, more than their boundaries or resources or wealth, are a mental condition. A nation may be open and positive, hard working and fully confident of its future. It may send great white fleets around the world and humans into space. A nation may also be angry, self-destructive and cruel.

We are individuals and we are parts of a whole. The whole can be as troubled or as ecstatic and positive as its individuals. You all know this very well, and you know that, at the present time, America is angry and divided and mentally disturbed. Many of its citizens are turning away from obvious truths and embracing angry and dangerous fantasies.

If someone you know flies off the handle in an uncharacteristic way and will not listen to the clear facts, perhaps his dear wife will take you aside and explain that there is a major problem in the family to account for the outburst. It's hard to settle arguments and put away anger when we are desperately anxious about our future and our family. That sort of anxiety is driving America's politics today. Where does it come from? Anger and blindness to the facts are the children of powerlessness—powerlessness over one's own and one's family's future.

That anxiety is manipulated by self-interested grandmasters. In the 1950s, as great corporations began to wash away the family businesses of Main Street and as the new interstate highways destroyed the economics of a million small towns, the anger of those middle class families should have been directed against those corporations and the political officials in league with them. Instead, the anger was purposely and methodically redirected against a nearly phantom Communist threat inside America, against the civil rights of blacks, and against any expansion of government into worker protection, environmental protection and consumer protection. Because the anxiety was misdirected, it was not brought to bear on the proper cause of the anxiety, and so the anxiety only grew.

Corporations and the very wealthiest people began to finance the election campaigns of their foot soldiers in Congress.

They financed talk radio and propaganda cable television. In 1987, they destroyed the Fairness Doctrine in broadcast news programs. We now see millions of people whose anxiety has been hijacked and redirected against their own best interests.

In the Reagan years, all the stops were taken off things like hostile corporate takeovers and the rise of new monopolies, so that even the most ethical companies were forced to ship their jobs overseas and shutter their plants in American towns and cities to avoid hostile takeovers. This was all very profitable for the wealthiest elite. You might wonder why these people have allowed things to go so far that the Earth of their grandchildren is now endangered—perhaps fatally, and the answer is that they do not care about their children or grandchildren, so long as they themselves can buy the longest yachts at the Monaco yacht show. How embarrassing it must be if their checkbooks are unable to do so—perhaps as embarrassing as it is for a single mother whose bankcard is declined at the grocery store.

From those yachts are sent instructions that control what Fox News watchers and talk radio listeners will be upset about tomorrow. These abused and misinformed people will be used to stop all real progress toward real solutions, and the mass anxiety of the people will grow even greater, even as their homes are taken from them and their foods are poisoned and the climate warms to boiling for their grandchildren.

All this opinion engineering needs ready enemies, and so it is the Mexican immigrants or the Arabs or Muslims or any other Other will have the honor of being scapegoats and diversions. We could, after all, stop illegal immigration by improving economic conditions in Latin America, and we could end Arab anger by moving our economy from oil to solar, but those are big business considerations for proper discussion in the yachts off Monaco, not in our pretend Congress. The yachts off Monaco are sending no sons and daughters to the oil wars—at least no sons and daughters that they really care about.

So the anger of anxiety grows. Guns and ammunition now flow into our communities in semi-trucks for gun shows. The politics polarizes to the extent that some have no moral or patriotic objection to sabotaging the economy if it will mean more votes in the next election. And facts as plain as day—as plain as a birth certificate—will be insulted and burned in the streets.

Some years ago a dam gave way in Buffalo Creek in West Virginia, sending billions of gallons of toxic coal sludge down into a valley, where it destroyed towns and killed many people. That lake of sludge grew over the years behind that insufficient dam as corrupt inspectors signed reports and mines lied and continued to send sludge higher and higher. You can think of American anger in the same way, rising from the lies and failures to represent and the destruction of the middle class and its businesses and the loss of power that people sense over their own futures. When the dam goes, democracy will be hard to pull alive from the sludge. It will be very difficult. We will do it, of course, but it will be very difficult and people will have died.

If I were the President of the United States looking at all this, what would I do now?

I would do a great deal.

I would use administrative powers to do as much as I could to return a sense of personal power to people. Every notch will help defuse anger. I would require federally insured banks to have human beings answer their phones, and have local human beings assigned to personally help every customer, with full authority to make most decisions regarding those accounts.

I would find out in which other industries federal leverage might permit similar returns to the human scale, so that people had more daily moments when they did not feel so powerless against the machinery of modern life.

As the President, I would look at the companies that sell things to the federal government. I would give a purchasing preference to those companies that dumped their computerized, outsourced telephone systems and other systems of human contact in favor of a more human-scaled operation.

I would give a thousand preferences to small businesses. I would even subsidize small businesses directly, maybe funded by a heavy wealth tax on billionaires. I would order the agencies of government to buy American products when possible, even at a premium, and especially from smaller businesses.

Without turning my back on the environment or on worker rights and safety, I would start a campaign against the kinds of red tape that inhibit the creation of Main Street businesses and small-scale manufacturers. The object of these moves would be simple: to give more people a sense of control over their own lives and futures.

I expect a roomful of citizens could come up with a thousand things that make them feel disempowered and that might be changed. Little empowerments can build toward more meaningful power. People ultimately need to believe, and correctly so, that their daily efforts will bear the harvest they have earned.

We need to get rid of the anger created by all kinds of

financial debt borne by young people and old. When we owned the banks after the 2008 crash, we should have ripped up the loans. Why the hell didn't we? We still need to do it, because the stresses become anger and the anger is eating up our country.

And little things add up: All the fine print in contracts— you shouldn't have to sign a ten-page contract to listen to a song or share a family photo. All those little things are insulting to us, and they add up. Maybe we will need to take our shoes off at the airport for a while yet, but we shouldn't have to bow so low to every company that tells us to.

Stores ought to look for shoplifters and stop them, but devices that scan and beep at the doorways, and clerks who stop you at the door before leaving to examine your basket and your receipt are making an accusation that you are probably a thief, and Americans should not be accusing each other of such things without probable cause. It is dehumanizing. Our dignity demands a presumption of innocence not only in the courts but in our daily lives.

These little things that eat away at our dignity ultimately make us angry and alienated. So end those practices. Put consumer and government pressure to bear to make companies comply with a new golden rule of personal treatment in America. When people are treated with an expectation of honor, they tend to respond. The few that do not are not worth worrying about.

We need to do something about our middle and high schools, which are factories of alienation and stress. Let's do that first. We don't need Congress for that.

And when we do have a Congress that again represents the people, we need to return to the states the authority to limit interest rates that can be charged on loans and credit cards. States once had that power, and rates were generally limited to not much over ten-percent; but then the interstate banking lobby purchased Congress and we are all now paying for their yachts as a result. Let's make this a states' rights issue and confuse the far right.

The United States of America has an interest in the development of small, family-run local and regional businesses. Those businesses are good for the economy, good for communities, good for families, good for personal empowerment, and good for democracy. When we have a real Congress again, lets create a corporate tax system that discourages businesses from growing larger than they need to be. A computer company or an automobile company or an aircraft company may need to be large, but there is no reason for general merchandise stores to be overlarge. There is no reason for insurance companies or media companies to be overlarge. Returning the economy to a more local and more human scale is important and necessary for our political, cultural and ecological health.

While we are at it, we should get rid of corporate-run prisons. What is a greater insult to an American than to be locked up by a corporation? Anyone in that circumstance ought to have a right to resist. It insults all of us. If we fail to act on these matters, the sense of personal disempowerment will grow, and also its anger and its violence.

Returning a more human scale to our economy would also create quite a few jobs and quite a few new businesses. If a U.S. president would take up an aggressive campaign to return human scale and its personal power to Americans, I don't think he or she would find too many opponents, except in the yachts off Monaco. They would of course instruct Fox News to rail against this return to the Stone Age. But the anger that fuels their toxic enterprise and others like it would dissipate, and we might soon have a governable country again.

The idea of a social safety net, while constantly attacked by the wealthy elite and their followers, provide important ways to reduce the kinds of anxiety that otherwise disrupt society and democracy. If parents know their children will be able to attend college without debt, that they themselves will have a secure old age, and that the only time people will sleep outdoors in America is when they are camping, then they will be better neighbors, better parents, better spouses, better and more productive workers, and better Americans.

If there is one thing that would guarantee any President's election or re-election, it is this final suggestion: A President could administratively modify the procurement code of the federal government so that companies that do not lobby the federal government in any way except in open hearings are eligible for federal contracts worth over a million dollars. Otherwise, they aren't eligible.

This political disempowerment of corporations would result in a grand re-empowerment of average citizens, who then would stand a chance being heard by their elected representatives.

With every notch—and that would be a big one—anger subsides, racism subsides, we step away from the precipice now before us, and we move toward a much better America.

These are ideas someone might package and promote. A joining of left and right might be possible regarding elements of this package. A president or presidential candidate might even listen.

Frankly, I don't think we have much time to waste. Anger is what is in our way, and it comes from the disempowerment of us all, and from the alienation that results from disempowerment.

Thank you very much, and God bless the memory of Bob La Follette.

Doris Haddock's Eulogy

Ms. Haddock's March 14, 2010 funeral eulogy was given at the Dublin Community Church by Dennis M. Burke:

Thousands of news services, from Peterborough to Bangkok, from personal diaries to the New York Times, have reported these last few days on the life and death of Doris Haddock. In her life, she did not cure a disease or end a war. She did not write ten symphonies or do whatever normally occasions such notice. So what did she do? It is worth thinking about in this moment.

If people no longer spoke aloud, or if they no longer looked at things with their own eyes or through their own thoughts, if they let others do those things for them, then they would take it as unusual if one among them suddenly spoke up and dared see the world independently, describing without filter or permission the vivid colors and true conditions of the world.

It is difficult to understand why a lady from New Hampshire who did little more than take morning walks—though she sometimes did so without coming back for several years—should be so lionized in death, unless we also consider what has become of the world around her that made her exceptional by comparison. She is seen as exceptional perhaps because the rest of us have become a little too reticent, a little too slow moving in response to these times of high challenge.

A thousand people have told me that, when they reach her age, they want to be like Granny D. I have always agreed with them, but we have had it a little wrong. We must not wait until we are 90 or 100; we have to be, even today, a little more like Granny D. Our challenges will not wait for us to age.

Walking down long highways, I remember that sometimes she would want to look at the small things killed beside the road that others could not bear to look at. She was a great artist in fibers and colors, even in how she dressed. No one had more love for a good hat. She would see rich beauty in places where some would never dare look. She seems to have turned off her hearing aids for the lecture when the rest of us were told we must not look here or there, and told how some things must be presumed beautiful or ugly, true or false. She simply and always wanted to see for herself.

Too often, we are told what to think, even about ourselves. We are encouraged to trivialize our lives; to participate in our own reduction to mere consumers of products, passive witnesses to history.

She wanted to see for herself what she might become, what she might be capable of doing that was helpful to the people she loved, who were honestly everyone. She could see no defects in others without measuring them against her own shortcomings. Her anger was real and righteous, but it was about things and actions—it never lodged in her heart for long against people, even those whose actions she most opposed.

Because she could see our present democracy clearly, and because she could remember in properly punctuated detail the conditions of this self-governing country in her youth, this young lady of Lake Winnipesauke, this product of New England's town halls, this elder resident of the lanes where Thornton Wilder wrote "Our Town," this friend of ours who will be more durable to history than any Old Man of the Mountain, was the truer granite measure of where we have been going as a people and where we must go, one step at a time, into the American future.

The important thing Doris Haddock would have you remember was that she was no more special than you, and that you have the identical power and the responsibility to make a difference in the community and the world.

She received tens of thousands of messages from people who told her they had decided that, if a woman her age, of bent back, of emphysema and arthritis, could step forth to be a player on life's stage to make a contribution, then so could they, and so would they.

And so they did. Those people live all over the world. We can never know what good that legion of people has done and will continue to do. Have they cured diseases, ended wars, written symphonies? Remarkably yes, they do important work now all over the world, and they live their lives, by their own accounts, with more satisfaction and meaning because of what they learned by watching our Granny D. And politically, if you care to trace the origins of the present progressive energies, you will find at its root a bare handful of people, including Granny D.

Her youthful energy lives on through those she touched, just as the youthful energy of the people who raised her and taught her many years ago continued on through her. You could hear the voice of Jesse Eldridge Southwick of Emerson College of

Oratory in Doris's every word, and see, in Doris's constant energy, the creative joy of her Laconia High School teacher, Grammy Swain. If Doris was partial to the poetry of Robert Frost, it was because she knew him. He was her husband's freshman English teacher at Amherst. If you ever heard her recite "Stopping by Woods on a Snowy Evening," as I did on a desert road, you may as well have been in Frost's presence. All of those people lived on past their own lifetimes through her.

She was an extension also of those much younger than her, who are with us today. She was an expression of Jim and Libby Haddock's supportive love and many sacrifices, enabling her to become what she became. Her grandchildren and great grandchildren were her inspiration to keep working for a better world for them. She was an extension of the love and learning of her study group, led by Bonnie Riley and a remarkable circle of friends.

Beyond their warm living rooms, Doris traveled on a river of their love and energy.

If there were ever a list in marble of the names of the people in her personal world who supported and propelled her, who, in turn, were inspired and loved by her, it would extend three thousand and two hundred miles across America, and then across the seas.

Doris was always a little confounded by her late-life fame. She deeply believed that she was merely fortunate enough to find herself in a good play with a good cast. The old drama student never wanted to be more than a very supportive player, so that the leaders of our democracy might better move us toward the honest, just and kindly democracy ever just ahead, a vision that she kept as close to her thoughts as that old feather in her hat.

She would have us remember that our country is Our Town, that we each have the power and the responsibility to make a difference while we are alive, knowing that what we set in motion today will make a difference long after we are gone. Far more important than the old bodies we find ourselves patching up and hitching along, we are each also an idea and a vision of the world. We give the rising gift or dark weight of that vision to each person we deeply know. And that idea, that vision, is like the manuscript that grows from an old typewriter that will soon rust away to earth, leaving but the living manuscript. The Idea of us is the real us. The Idea is the living thing that survives because it lives on in our friends, survives in their hearts to help them better interpret and shape the world.

So, at the next turn of history and of opportunity, will we

not wonder what Granny D would have said, would have thought? It is a part of us now, a measuring tool, something new in us that thinks like her. That is Doris alive and still walking with us.

Finally, she would want us to remember to keep working at things and to take walks every day if possible; to send thank you notes; to keep asking for and expecting honorable changes; to stay strong.

After the recent Supreme Court decision that did damage to the bill she walked for, she asked me if I thought she might walk across the country again. I told her that she might only be able to do five miles or less a day. She had last month been in Arizona working on a book and doing three miles a morning. She calculated how long it would take her to get to Washington at three to five miles per, and decided she needed a quicker way to fix the Supreme Court decision.

Well, now it is up to us, of course, and we won't let her or our country down.

Thank you Doris. You didn't fear death very much—you told me so. You needn't have feared it at all.

Made in the USA
Monee, IL
07 May 2020